Where They Purr

INSPIRATIONAL INTERIORS AND
THE CATS WHO CALL THEM HOME

PAUL BARBERA

WITH QUEENIE CHAN

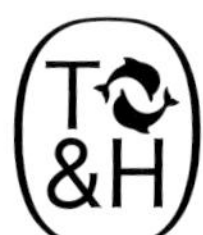

Introduction

'Is it a book about interiors or a book about cats?' That is the question I was often asked during the making of this book. The short answer is: both. It all depends on what you want to see.

Where They Purr began as a side project. The idea emerged while I was working on another book, *Where They Create*. As an interiors and lifestyle photographer, I travel a lot and meet many interesting people. *Where They Create* was inspired by my fascination with artists and their studios. I wanted to show creators in a raw, spontaneous way that celebrated their personalities and studios, as well as the processes behind their work.

One day, I was shooting Swiss artist Olaf Breuning in the New York City loft where he lived and worked, when I spotted his two regal British shorthairs lounging on a table. The cats instantly made the place feel more intimate, yet they possessed an air of entitlement – inhabiting the space as if they owned it. Within this human realm, the cats seemed like living, breathing deities; earthly yet mystical. I felt compelled to immortalise their elusive energy with my camera before the moment was gone. From that time on, I have continued to explore and document the intriguing and indefinable quality that cats bring to a home.

This book brings together two fabulous worlds: interiors and cats. However, capturing the enigmatic souls who occupy these beautiful homes poses many challenges. Firstly, how does one win over a cat in less than a day? Some cats are friendly right off the bat, but most are skittish around new people. One strategy I've developed is to ensure I always have a camera in my hand when I meet a cat for the first time – their curiosity about the strange object usually overcomes their fear and they will give me a sniff. Sometimes they may even allow a little pat. At this point, I turn away and start talking with their owner, pretending to forget the cat even exists. This method – which hinges on the fact that cats simultaneously love receiving attention and being ignored – usually succeeds in piquing the cat's interest. When I am ready to start shooting, I move slowly and calmly, to establish trust, and build from there.

Sometimes a cat will follow me around at a shoot, sometimes not. If they do, I generally just tweak their position if needed. If they don't, I may have to move the cat to a different room or even a different floor, which can be rather tricky. On one particular occasion, I had to carry a large cat (plus-size, you might say) up three flights of stairs. It was like carrying a sack of potatoes, but one with very sharp claws and the potential to wig out if I made any sudden movements.

While shooting for this book, I soon learnt that what is best for interiors is not always best for cats: I use only natural light, I mostly shoot handheld rather than on a tripod, and I try to avoid the need for extensive retouching – I find this gives my work a more authentic feel. But a black cat running around a dark home on an overcast day presents a particular photographic challenge, so I relied on my twenty-five years of experience – and three cameras on hand, each with different settings – to prepare for any eventuality.

At some point in every shoot, the cat will lose interest and won't want to play ball. Patience is critical in this game – I once had to wait more than two hours for a cat to re-emerge from under the bed! While I wait, tapping into the well of calm, I must also remain alert and ready to spring into action, as a cat can go from a state of tranquil repose to Olympic high jumper at a moment's notice. Perhaps unsurprisingly, the end of a shoot is often dictated not by me or a lack of daylight, but by the cat withdrawing because they've had enough.

Although I have been photographing cats for years, I have never done so with such purpose as during the making of this book. I am so grateful to all the people who granted me access to their beautiful homes and beloved feline companions. The resulting images, shared here, make all the scratches and days of editing worthwhile.

PAUL BARBERA

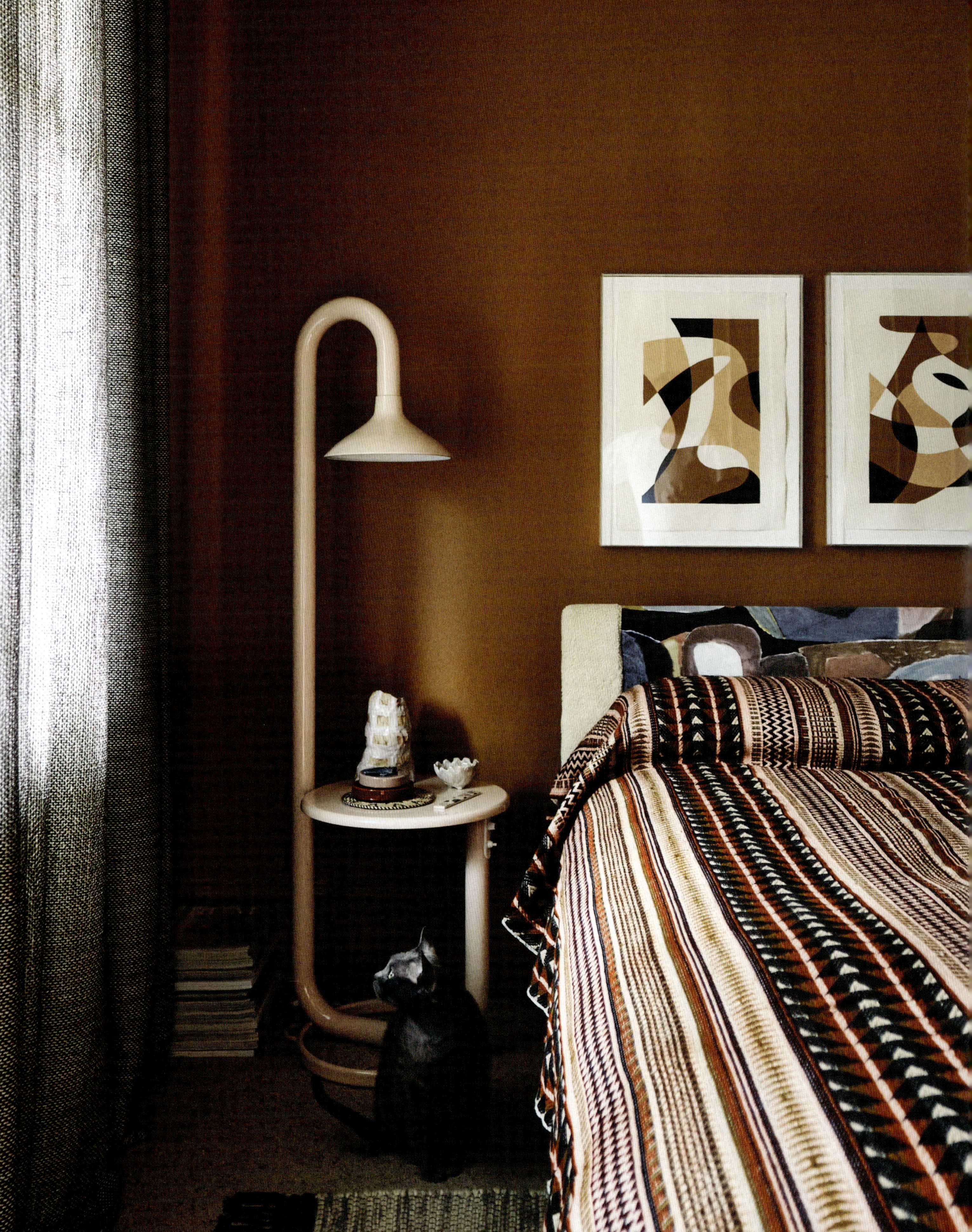

ELLIE

INTERIOR CURATION: SARAH SHINNERS / SIMONE HAAG

Ellie was adopted from a rescue shelter in Noosa, Queensland, as a tiny kitten. Her exact breed is unknown, but she's possibly part-Russian blue, part-Siamese. Her owners were told she was a boy and so they named her Rigby. However, at their first visit to the vet, their suspicions were confirmed: 'he' was actually a 'she'. It seemed obvious that her new name would be Eleanor – after Eleanor Rigby. She is now nine years old and lives in a cosy rental property in chilly inner-city Melbourne, but she remains a true Queenslander at heart – she's always chasing the sun and will bask in any bit of warmth she can find.

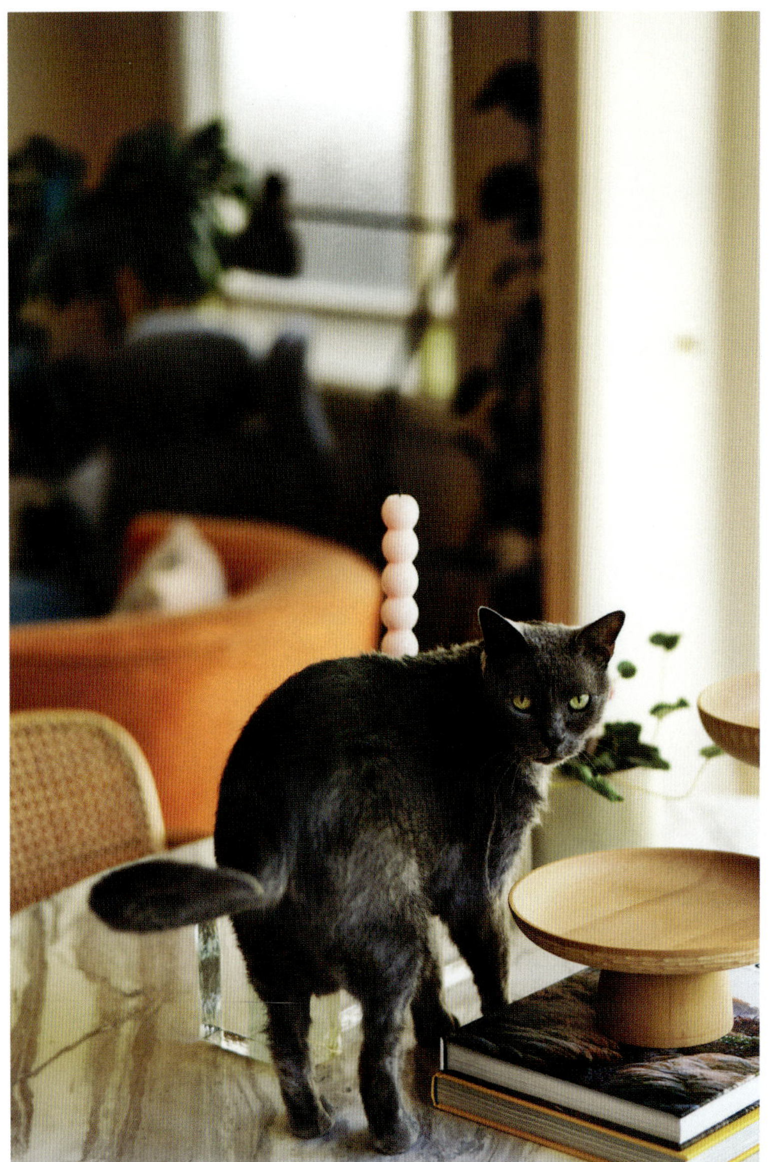

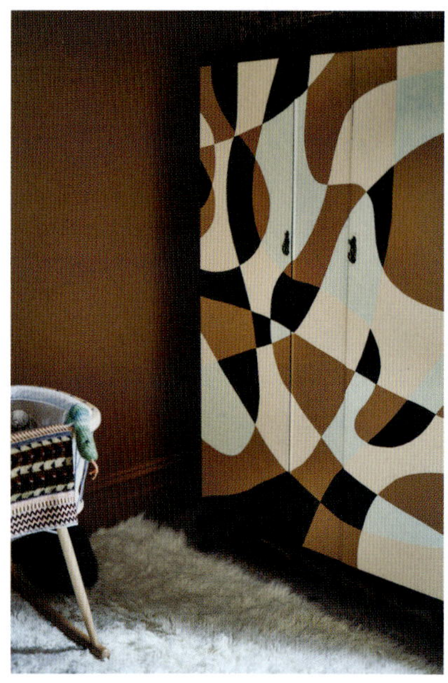

This beloved rental home showcases the power of interior decoration. Working with the existing architecture and fixtures, and introducing only furniture, art and objects, the occupants have managed to create a retreat that represents their own style.

Interior curation: Sarah Shinners / Simone Haag

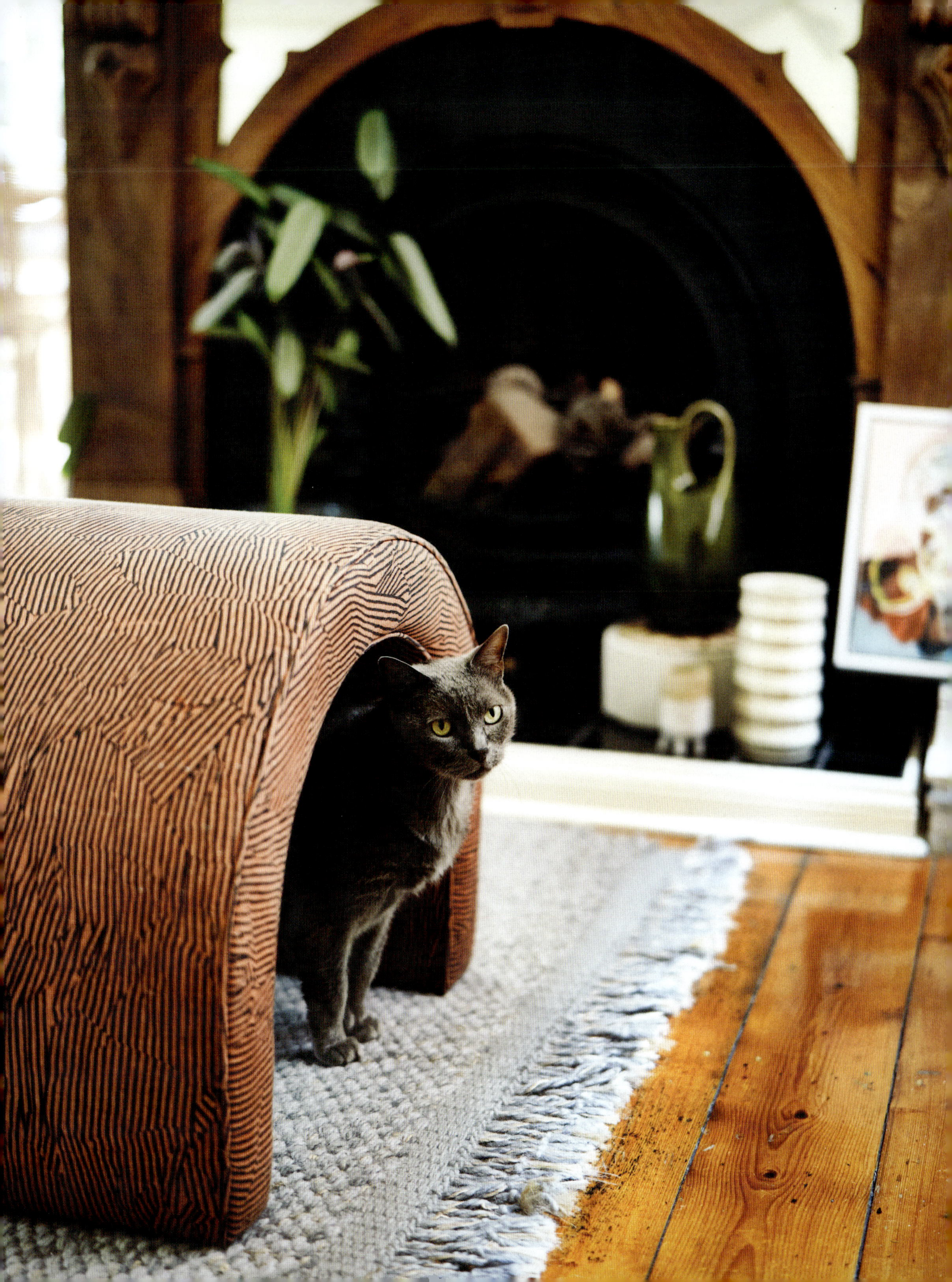

Ellie's daily routine is based entirely on sun location. In the afternoon, she heads upstairs to her favourite floating shelf in the living-room window.

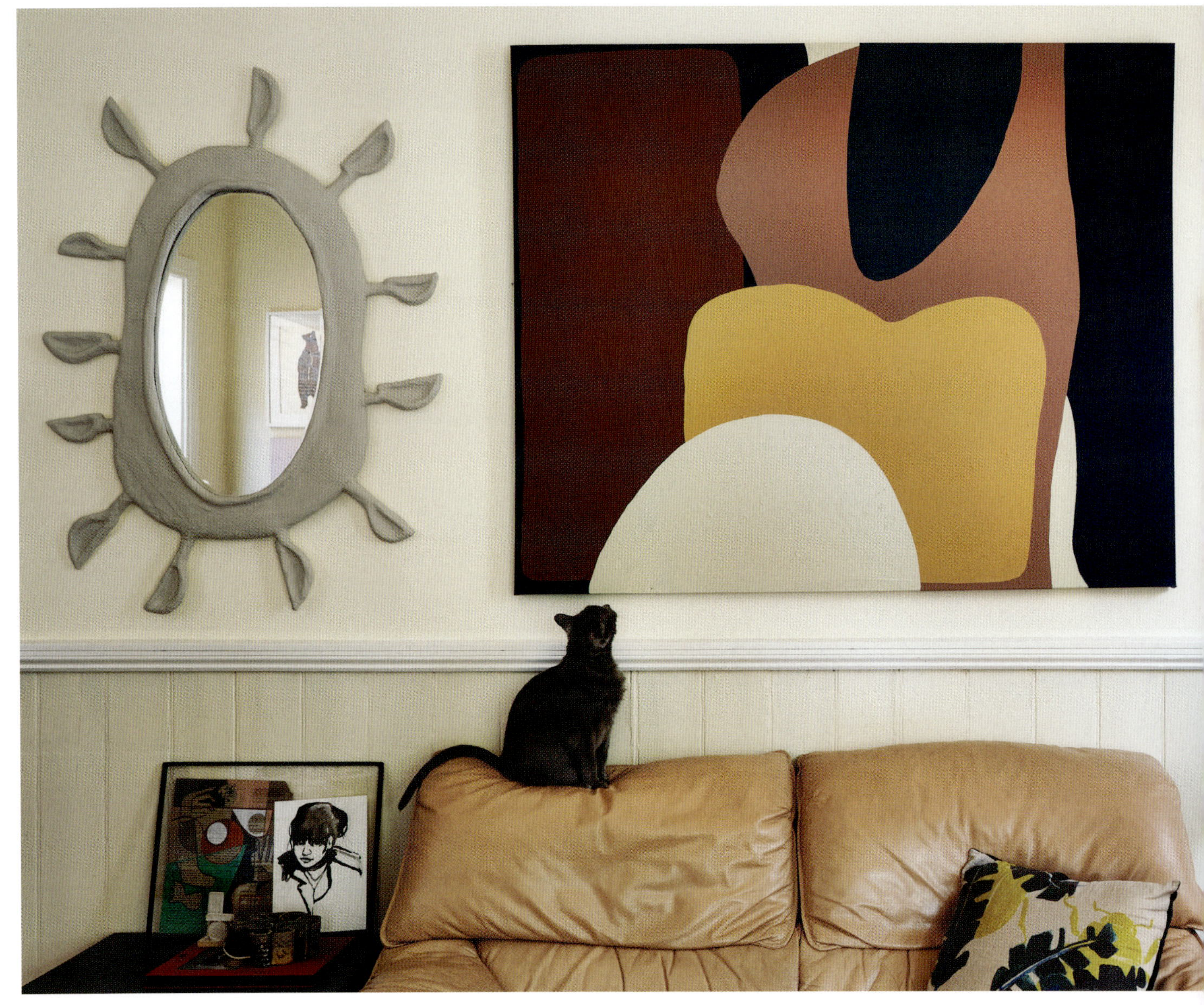

Interior curation: Sarah Shinners / Simone Haag

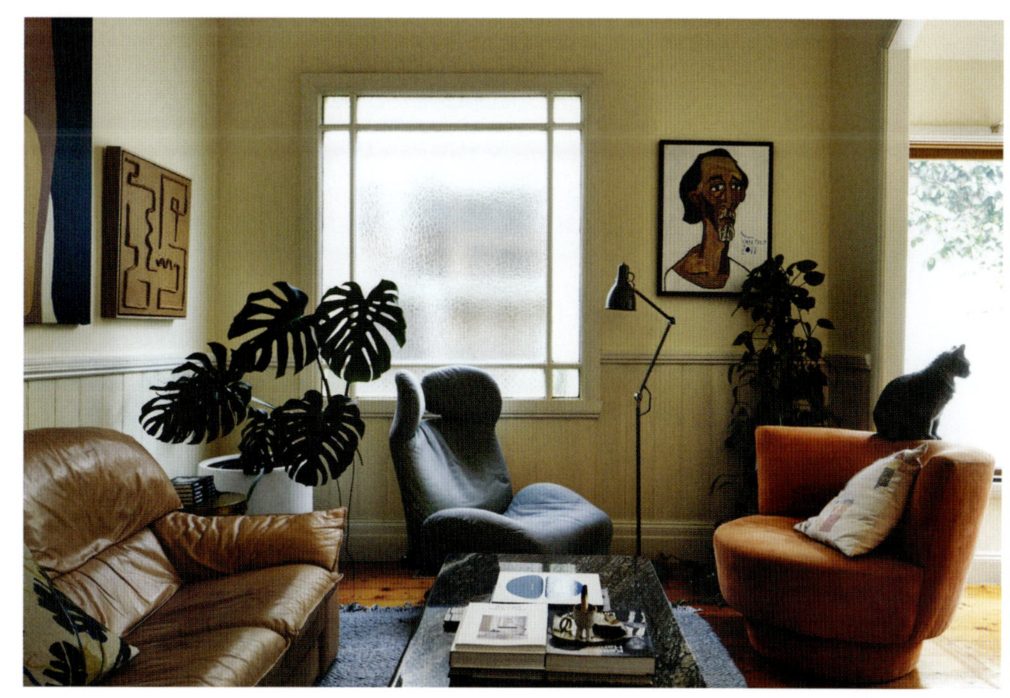

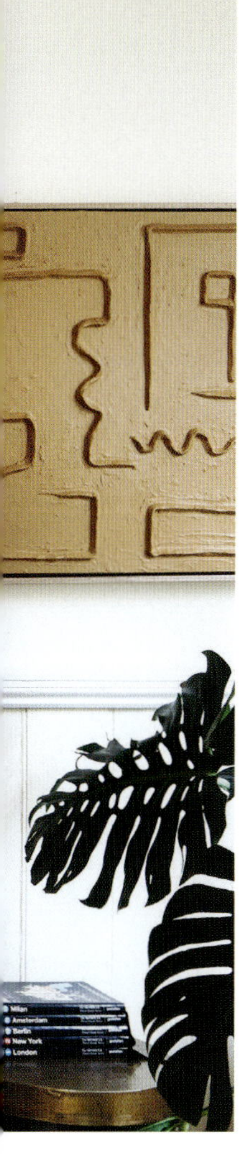
Milan
Amsterdam
Berlin
New York
London

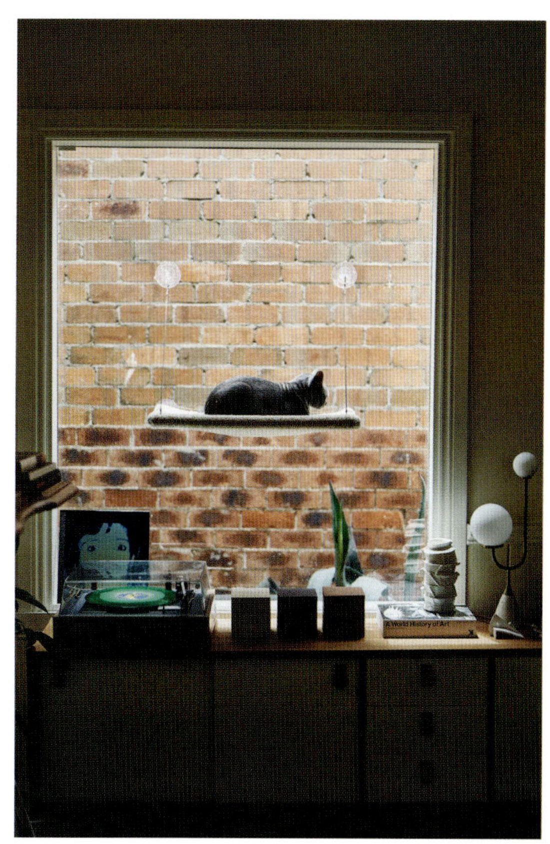
A World History of Art

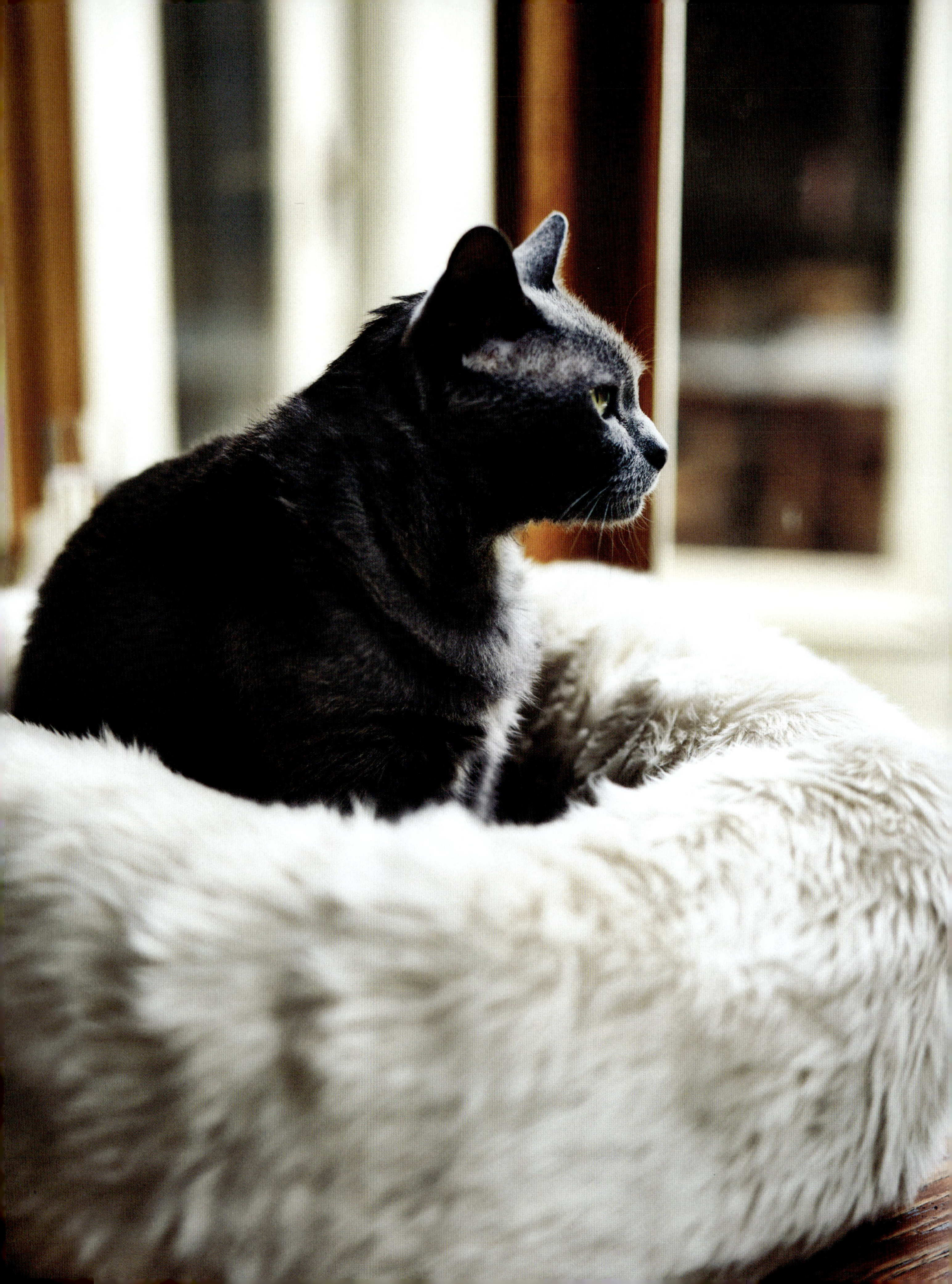

Q&A

DIVA OR DEVOTED FRIEND?
Both. It depends on the moment – but perhaps that's true of all cats.

EXTROVERT OR INTROVERT?
Introvert.

LAP CAT OR NOT?
Lap cat when it's cold – for a select few only.

OLD SOUL OR KITTEN AT HEART?
Definitely kitten at heart. She still has crazy moments now and then.

EXPLORER OR HOMEBODY?
Homebody. She's an inside cat – to keep her (and the neighbourhood birds) safe.

LAZY OR ACTIVE?
Mostly lazy – but her toys seem to move around quite a bit during the night, so there must be some nocturnal activity!

DOGS – FRIEND OR FOE?
Foe. She's only ever met one dog and she wasn't a fan. However, her owners love dogs, so maybe one day she'll have to learn to get along with them.

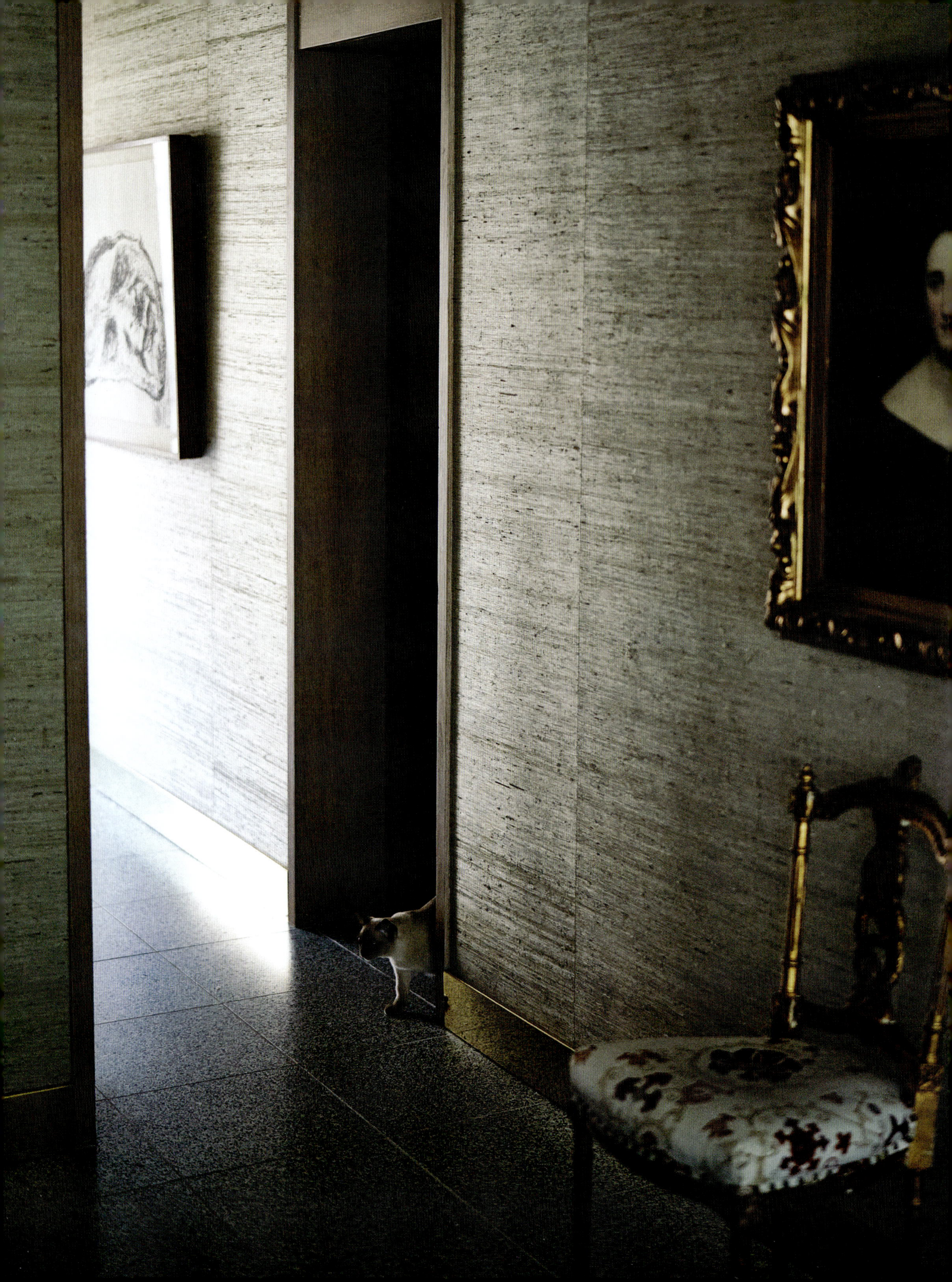

PUD

ARCHITECT: B.E ARCHITECTURE

Pud lives with a couple and is very much the third member of the family. He is very sociable and can usually be found anywhere his humans happen to be. Pud is easy to live with and is perfectly at home in the couple's intimate Melbourne apartment, but he also regularly travels with them to Hobart, where they have a spacious home with a garden. Pud is only seven months old but very self-assured. He is quite vocal, though luckily he's not as loud as some Burmese. He has certain routines he likes to stick to, including sleeping in his own room each night – he is not the kind of cat who crawls over his owners in the night or wakes them up at 5 am when he decides it's time for breakfast.

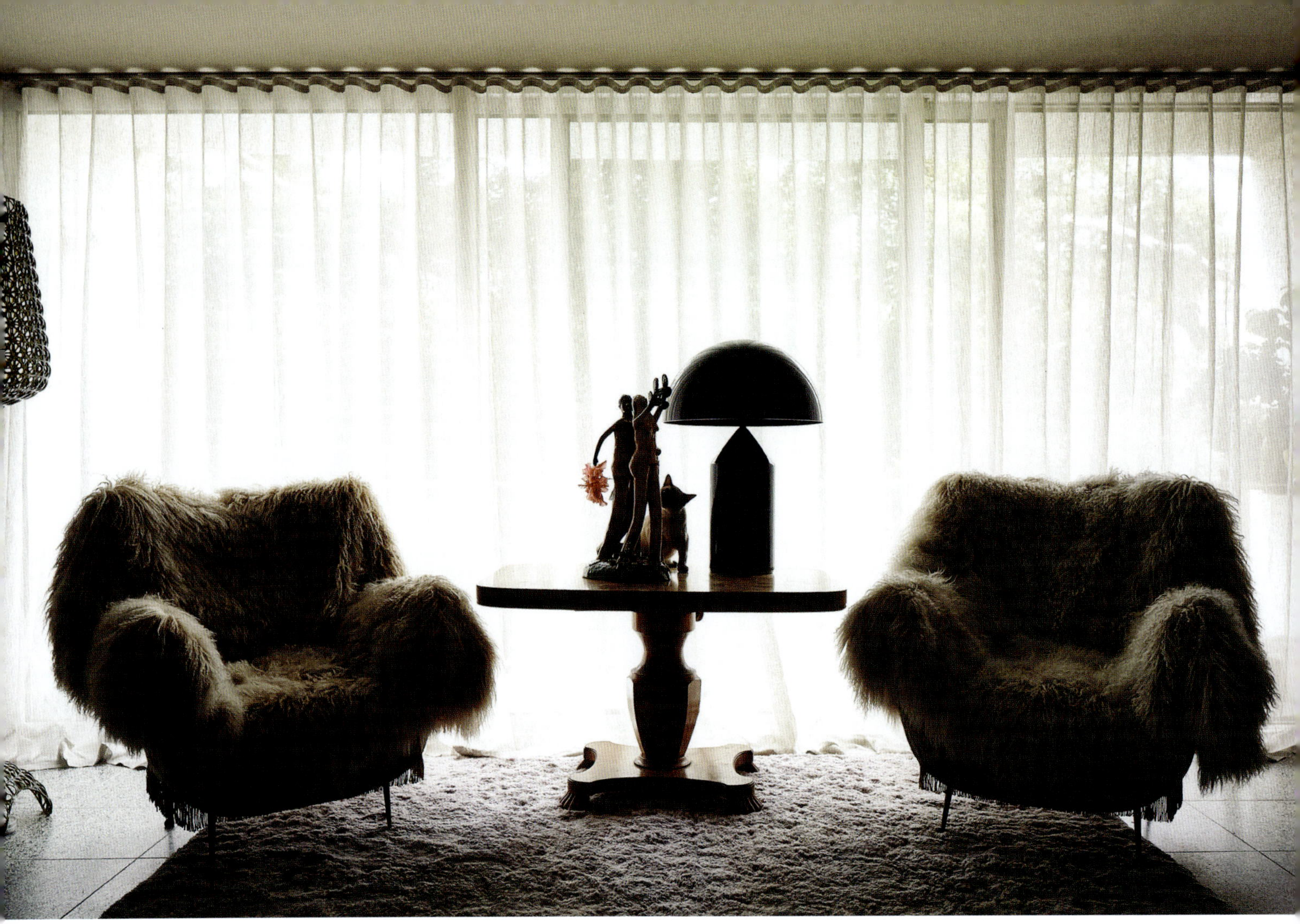

Pud's apartment is part of a 1960s modernist building set amid a leafy backdrop in the Melbourne suburb of Toorak. His home is like a nurturing cocoon and is the product of his owners' professional lives: one is an architect, the other an interior designer.

Architect: B.E Architecture

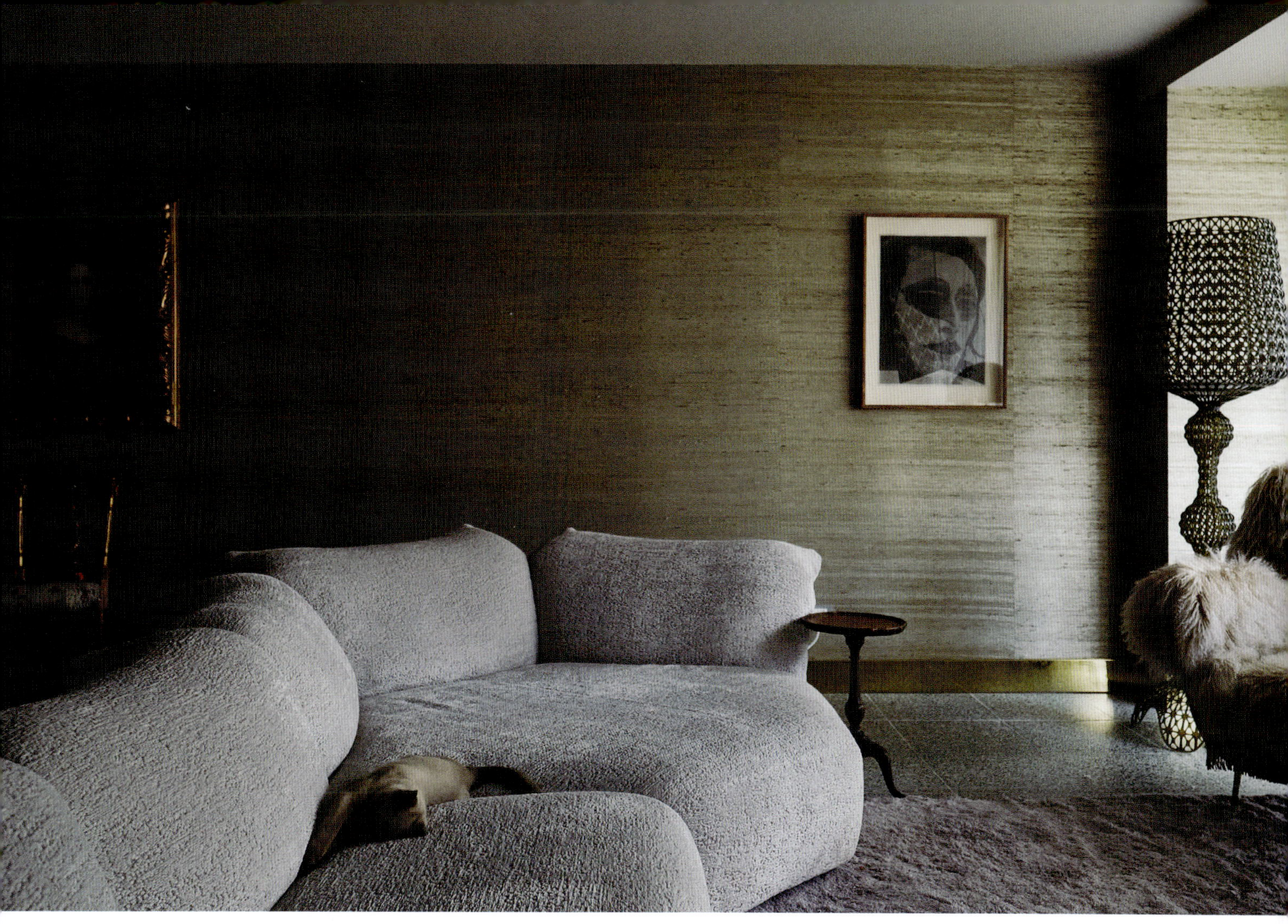

The apartment was completely rebuilt from its structural shell. Today, it feels like a villa in Venice, with its terrazzo floors and wheat-coloured grasscloth wallpaper.

While generally well behaved, Pud does have a penchant for climbing into lampshades, of which the apartment has many. His owners believe it is a display of mischievousness rather than curiosity.

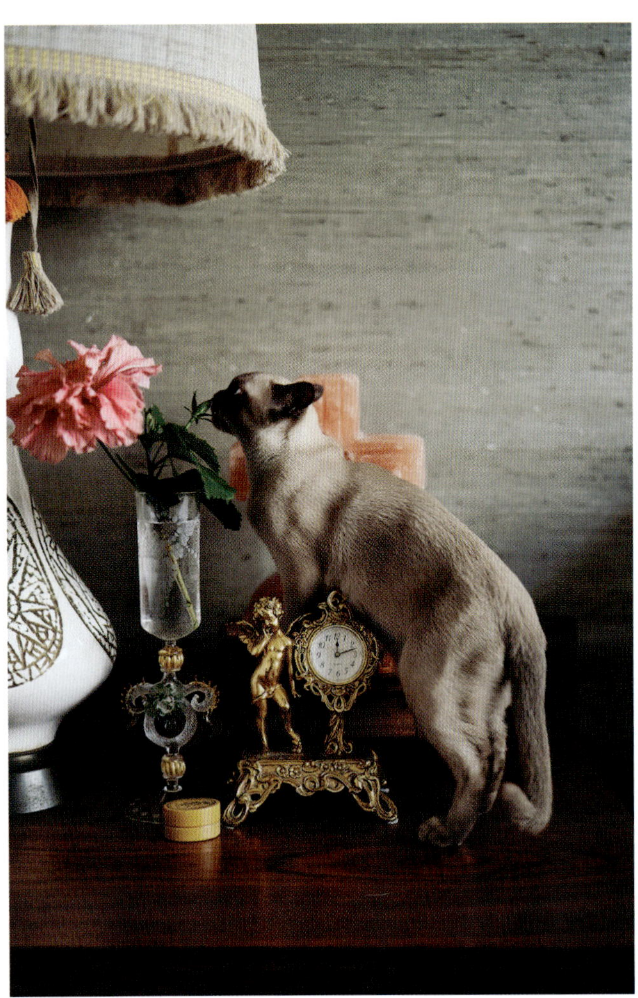

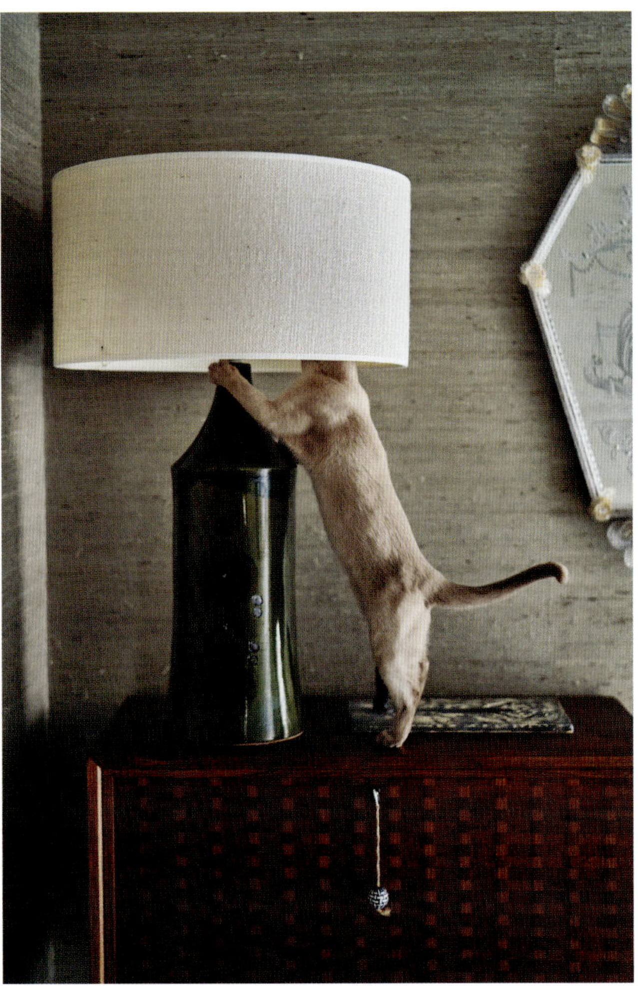

Architect: B.E Architecture

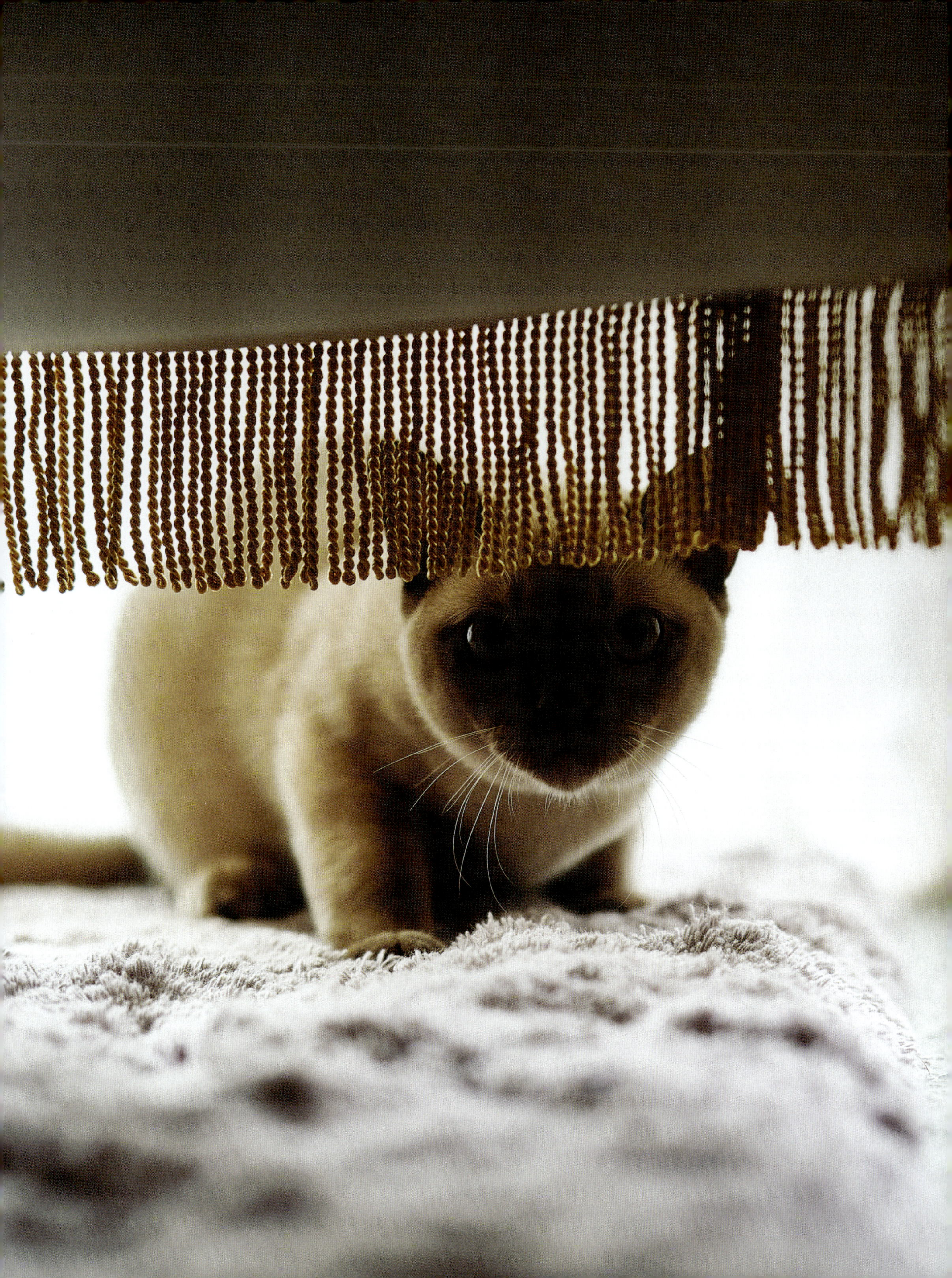

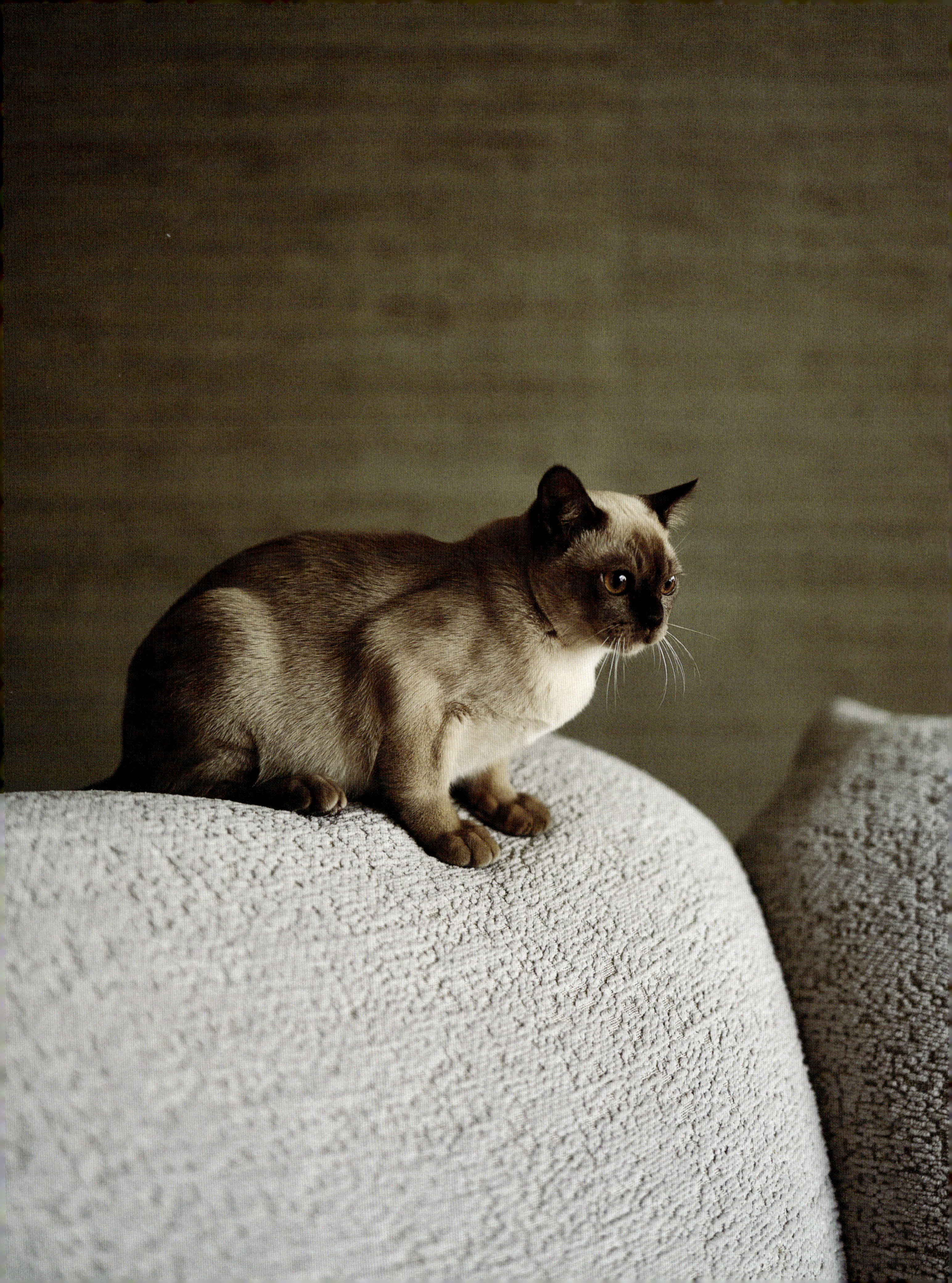

Q&A

DIVA OR DEVOTED FRIEND?

Diva.

EXTROVERT OR INTROVERT?

Extrovert.

LAP CAT OR NOT?

Not. There are moments when he likes to be close, but Pud prefers to perch nearby and keep an eye on things rather than sit on a lap and be stroked.

OLD SOUL OR KITTEN AT HEART?

Old soul.

EXPLORER OR HOMEBODY?

Explorer.

LAZY OR ACTIVE?

Active.

DOGS – FRIEND OR FOE?

Pud is a very curious cat and not overly fearful – he's more fascinated by dogs than scared of them. However, he has not had much contact with them ...

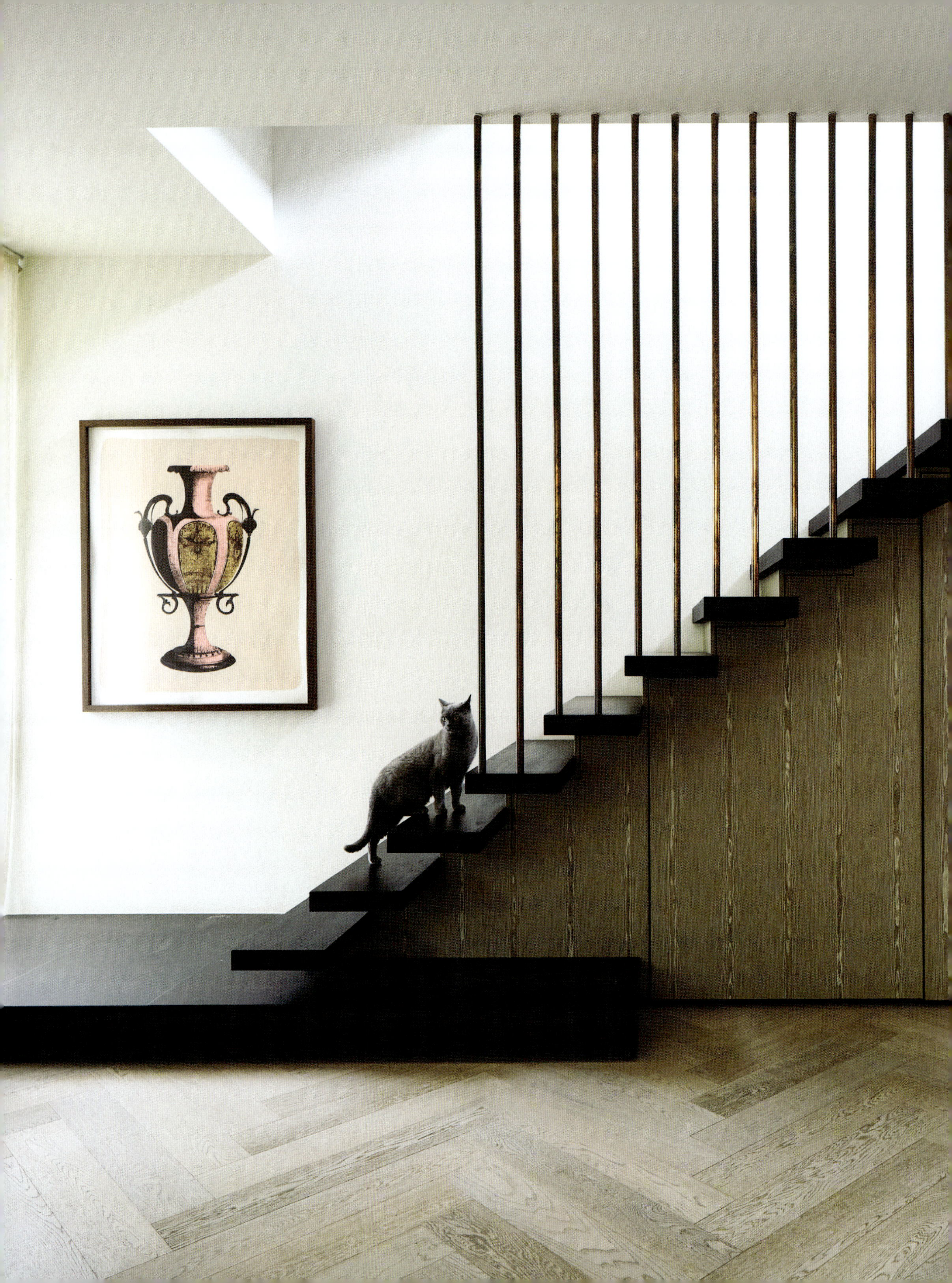

DIEGO

ARCHITECT: DOMINIC PICCOLO / PICCOLO ARCHITECTURE

Diego is named after the Mexican artist Diego Rivera. Had he been a girl, she would have been named Frida, after the artist's renowned wife, Frida Kahlo. A five-year-old British shorthair, he lives with a family that leads a pretty busy lifestyle, so it's a good thing he is assuredly independent – this is a cat who is far from needy. All Diego requires from his humans is a scratch under the chin, or on top of his head, first thing in the morning and a companion to sleep with at night. Other than that, he prefers his own company. Indeed, he is a master of stealth and has been known to break into a bag of biscuits or loaf of bread left momentarily unattended.

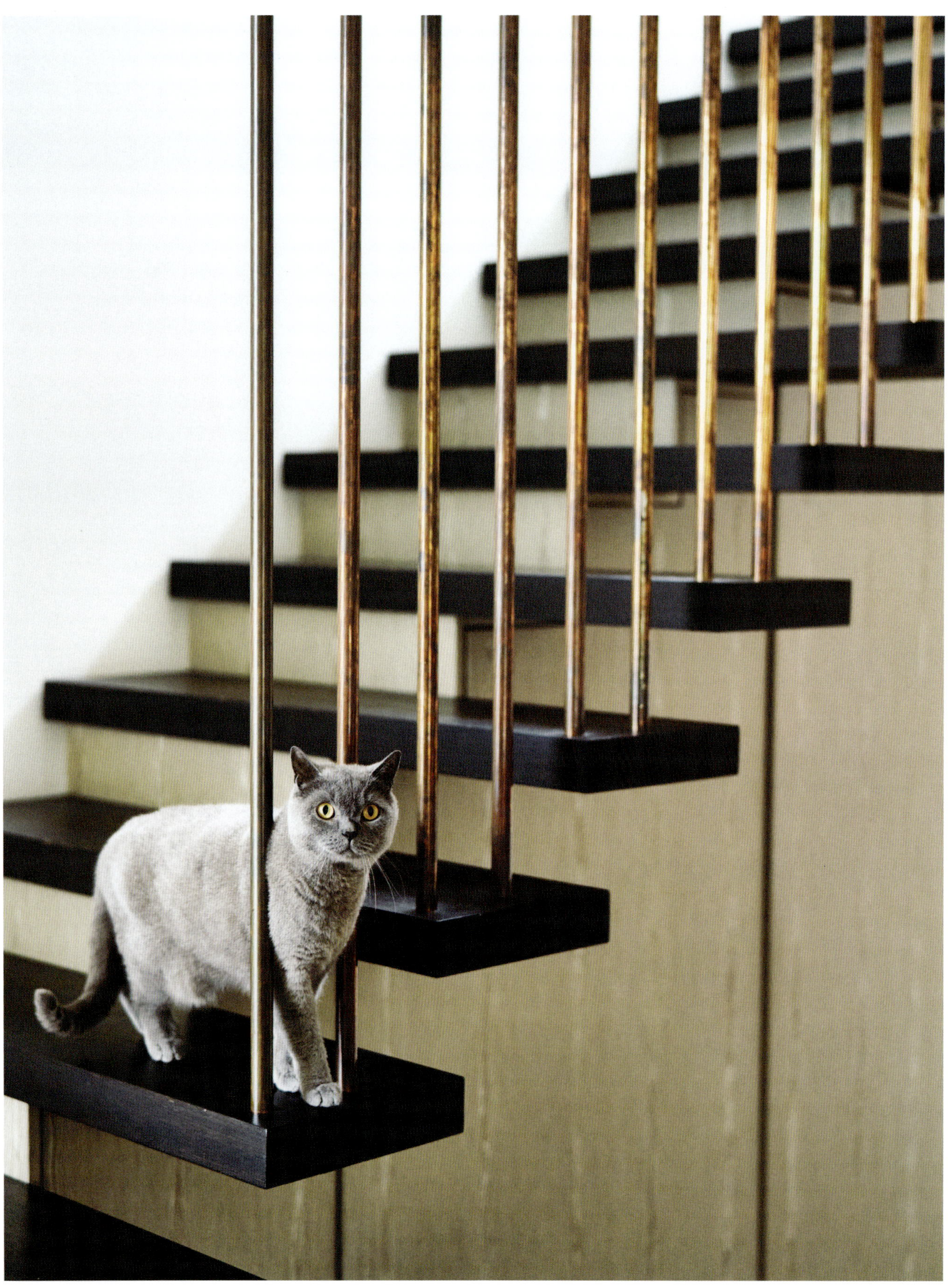

Architect: Dominic Piccolo / Piccolo Architecture

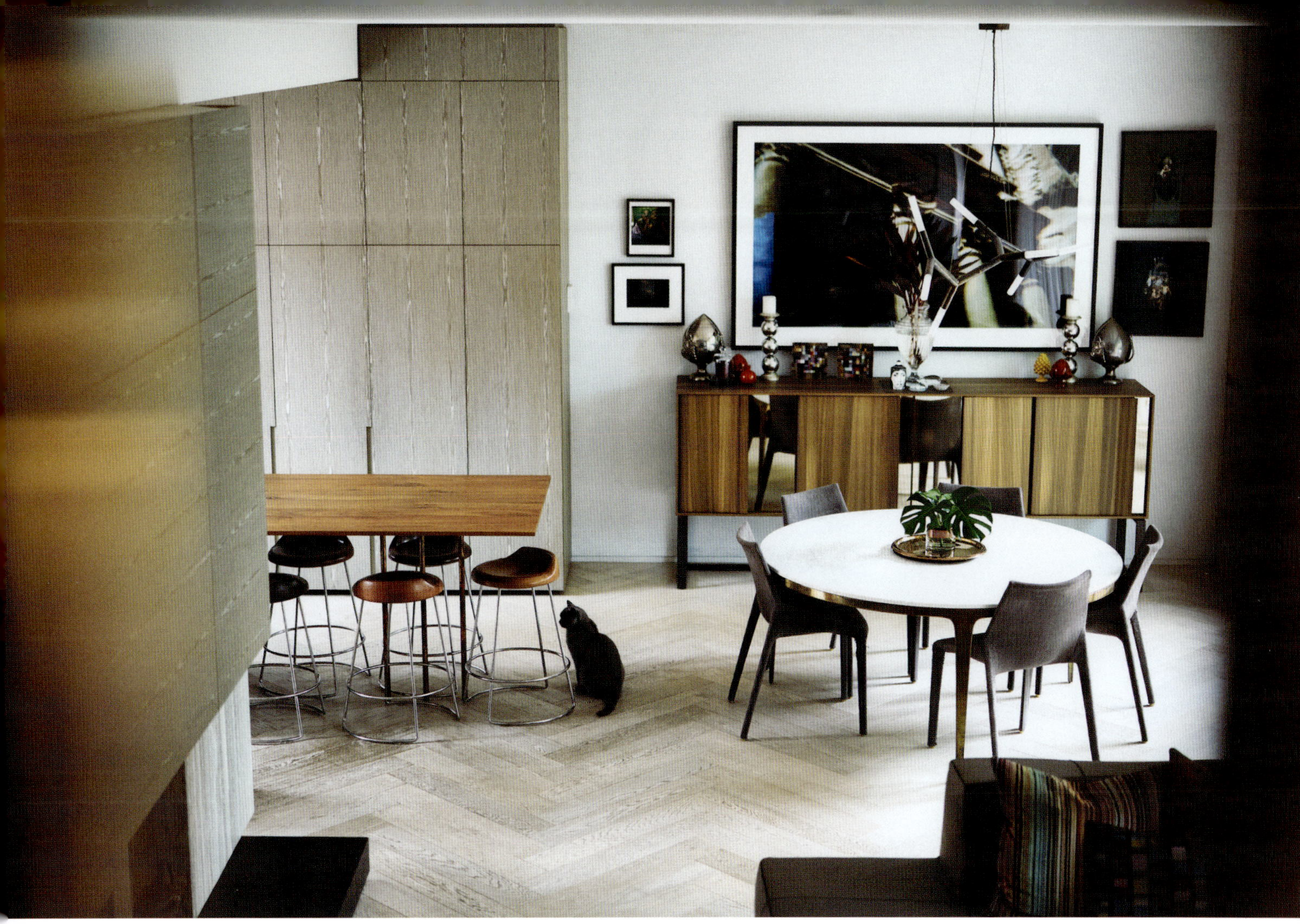

Diego's home is modern and comfortable. The land on which the house is built belonged to the family's father, and it was his intention to build two residences – one for each of his daughters and their families. Sadly, he passed away before he was able to do so. For his children, fulfilling his wish became a labour of love.

Diego's favourite spots to sit are all the places he shouldn't be: on the Italian dining-room chairs, the designer couch or the cashmere blanket in the bedroom – any luxurious surface he can find.

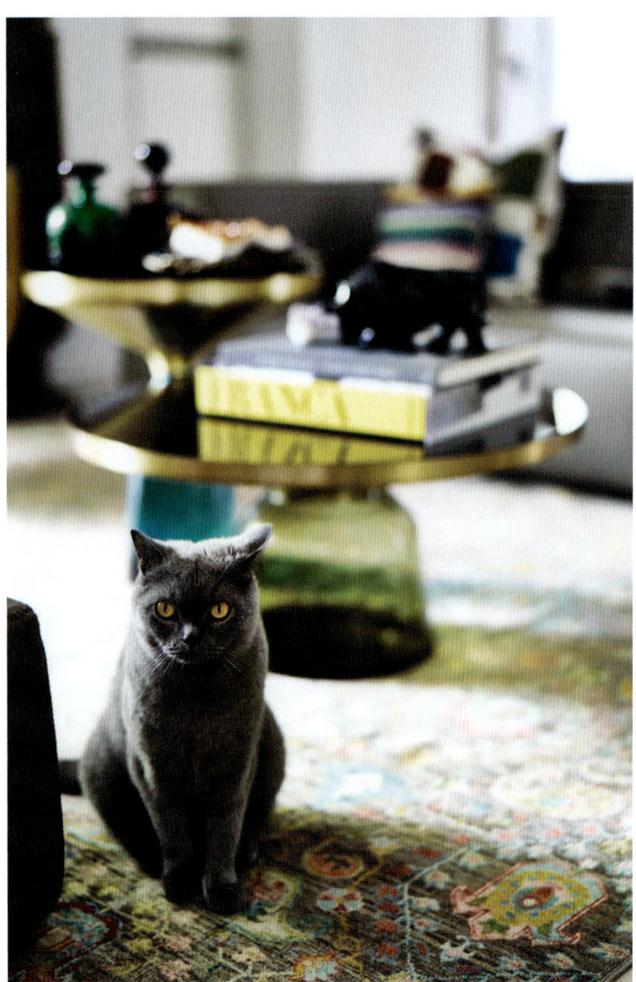

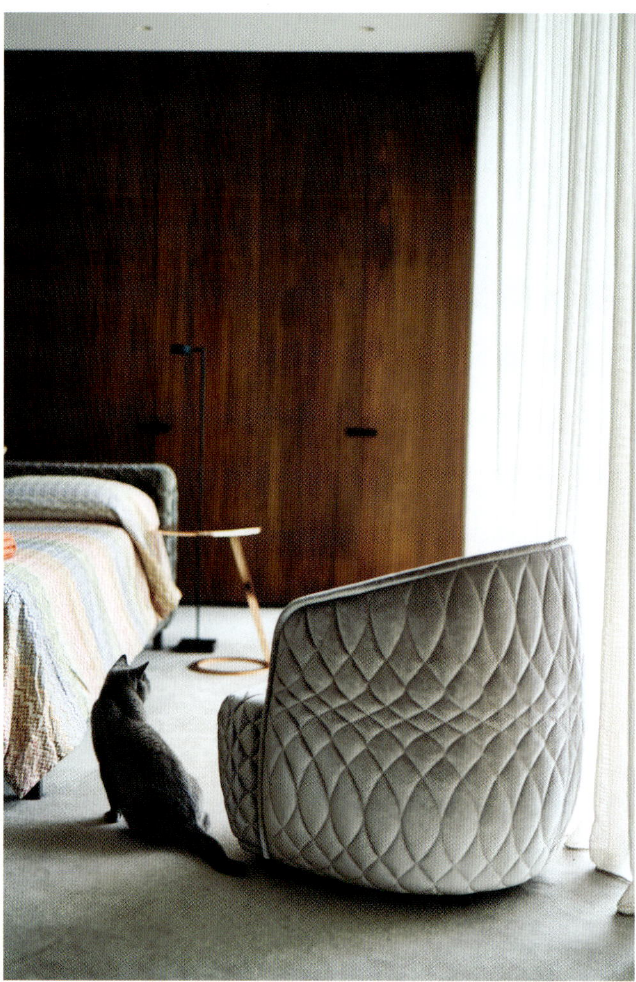

Architect: Dominic Piccolo / Piccolo Architecture

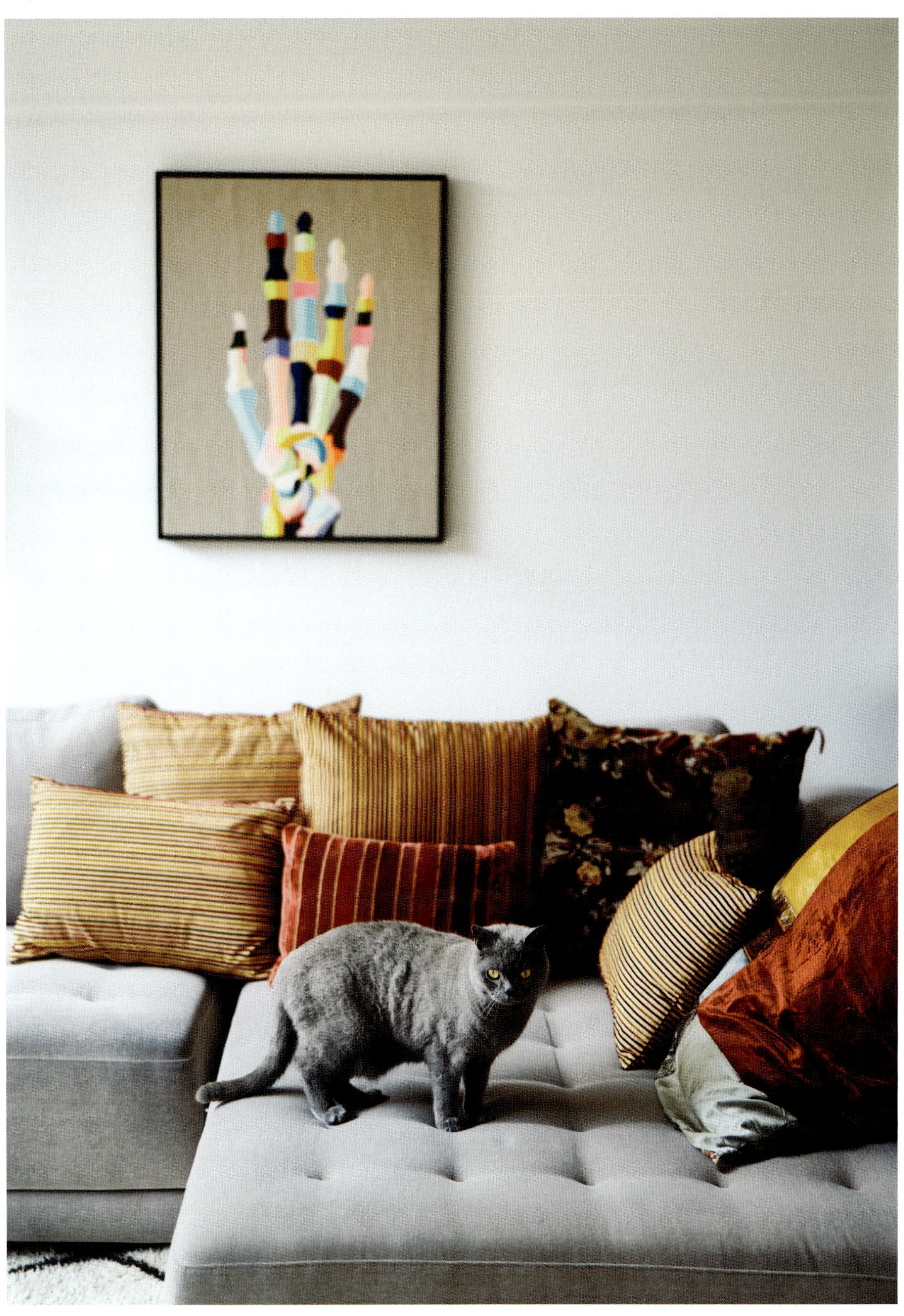

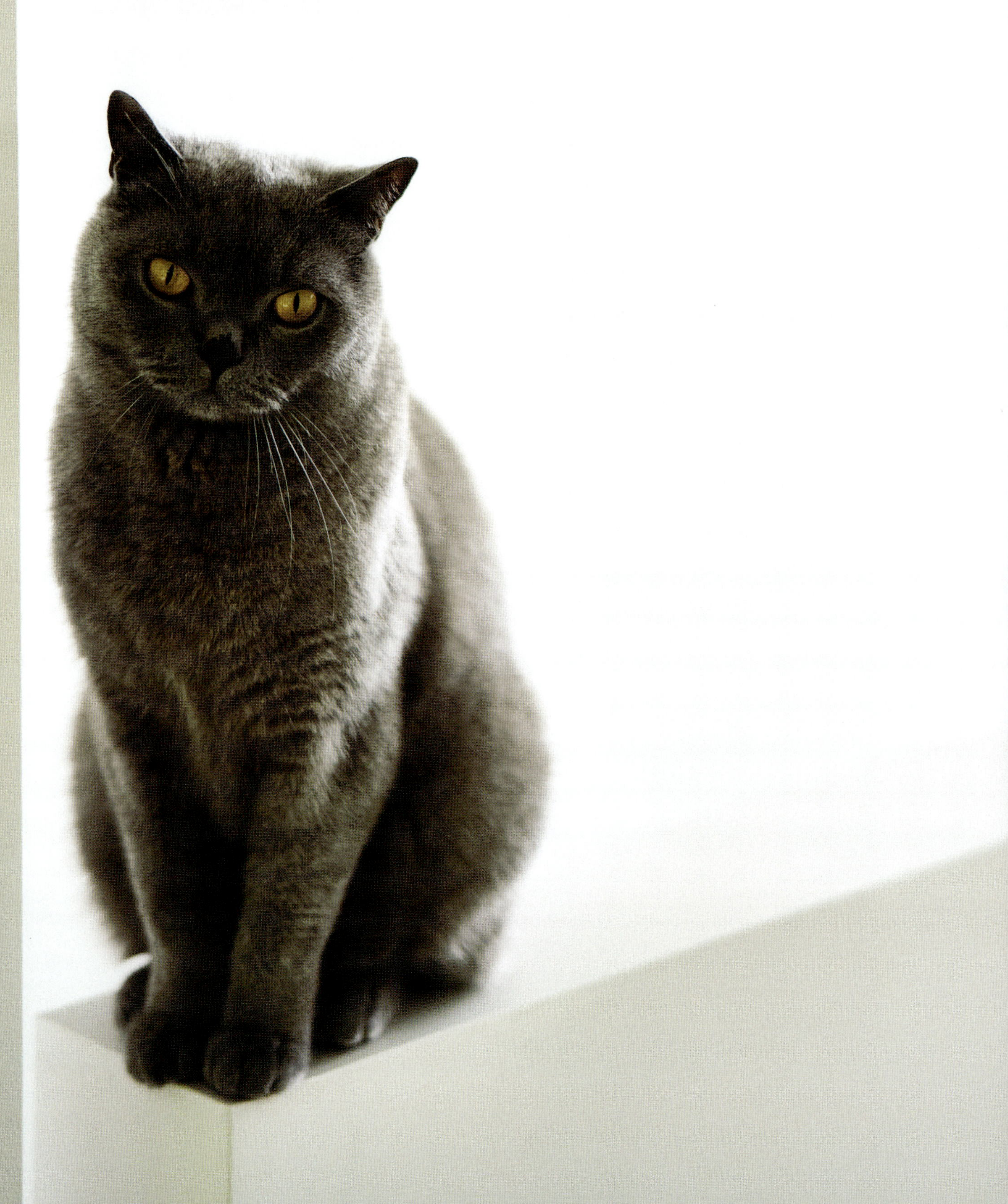

Q&A

DIVA OR DEVOTED FRIEND?
Diva.

EXTROVERT OR INTROVERT?
Introvert.

LAP CAT OR NOT?
Only when he feels like it!

OLD SOUL OR KITTEN AT HEART?
Old soul.

EXPLORER OR HOMEBODY?
A bit of both. He is pretty much a homebody when the family is in their city pad, but when he goes with them to their beach house, he is definitely an explorer.

LAZY OR ACTIVE?
Lazy.

DOGS – FRIEND OR FOE?
Foe: he is scared to death of them.

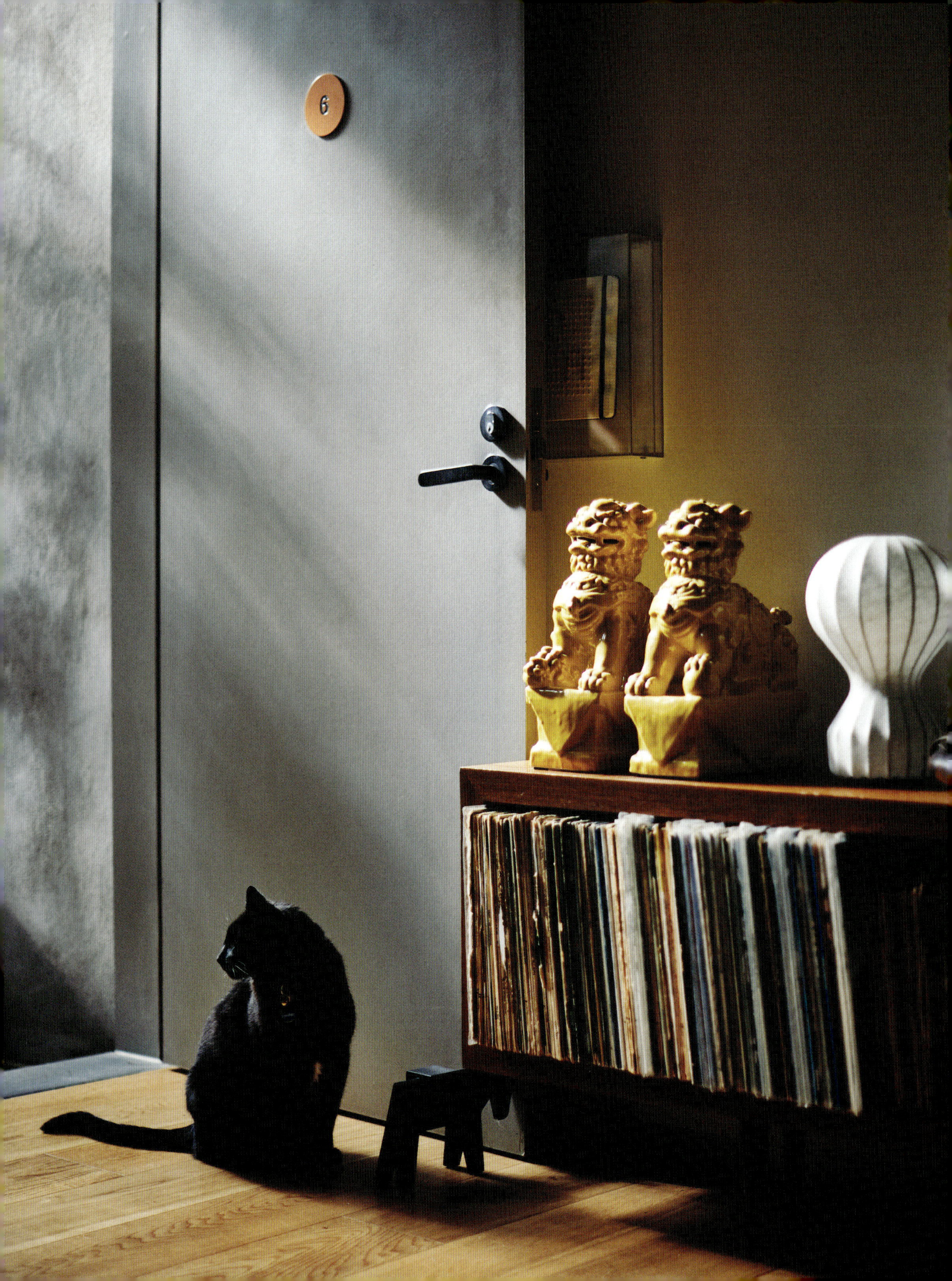
6

PANTHER

DESIGNER: KATHIE HALL / HALL STUDIO

Panther was just a kitten when he was spotted by his family in a Facebook post. A black Burmese, he displayed character and charm from the get-go. Now eight years old, Panther is still very sociable and loves to entertain. He lovingly welcomes the family when they arrive home, adores having guests over, and goes out of his way to greet the neighbours in the laneway.

Panther's owners have created a warm, rich home within a modest, modern apartment.

The courtyard garden, packed to bursting with greenery, provides a great space for entertaining.

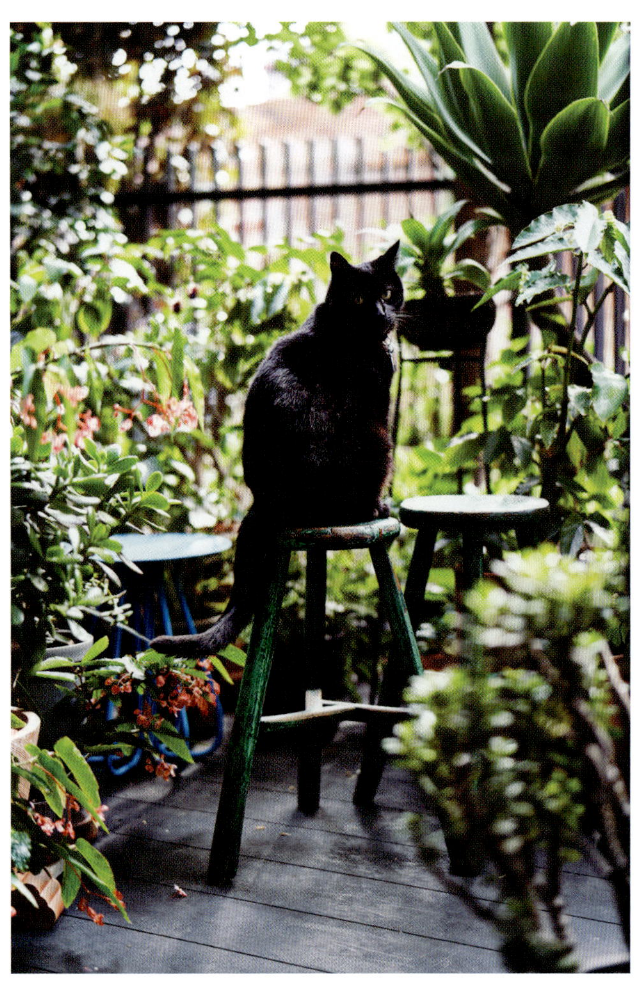

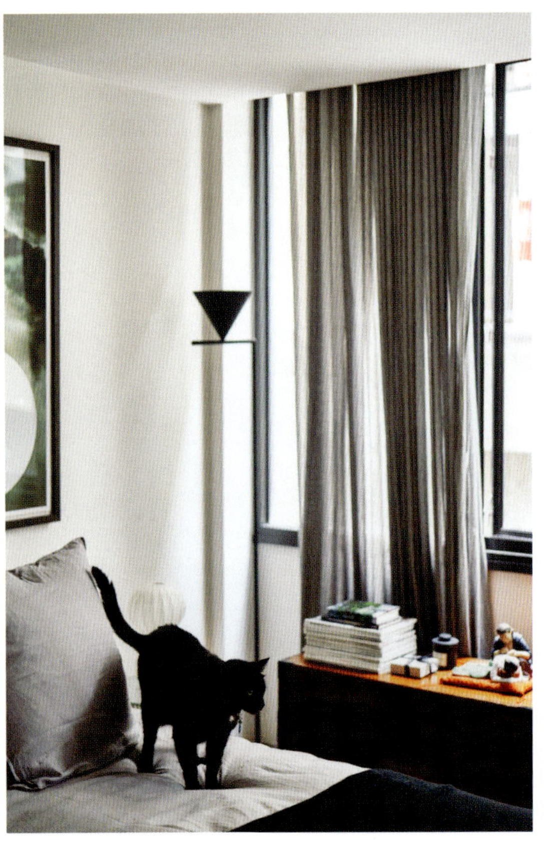

Designer: Kathie Hall / Hall Studio

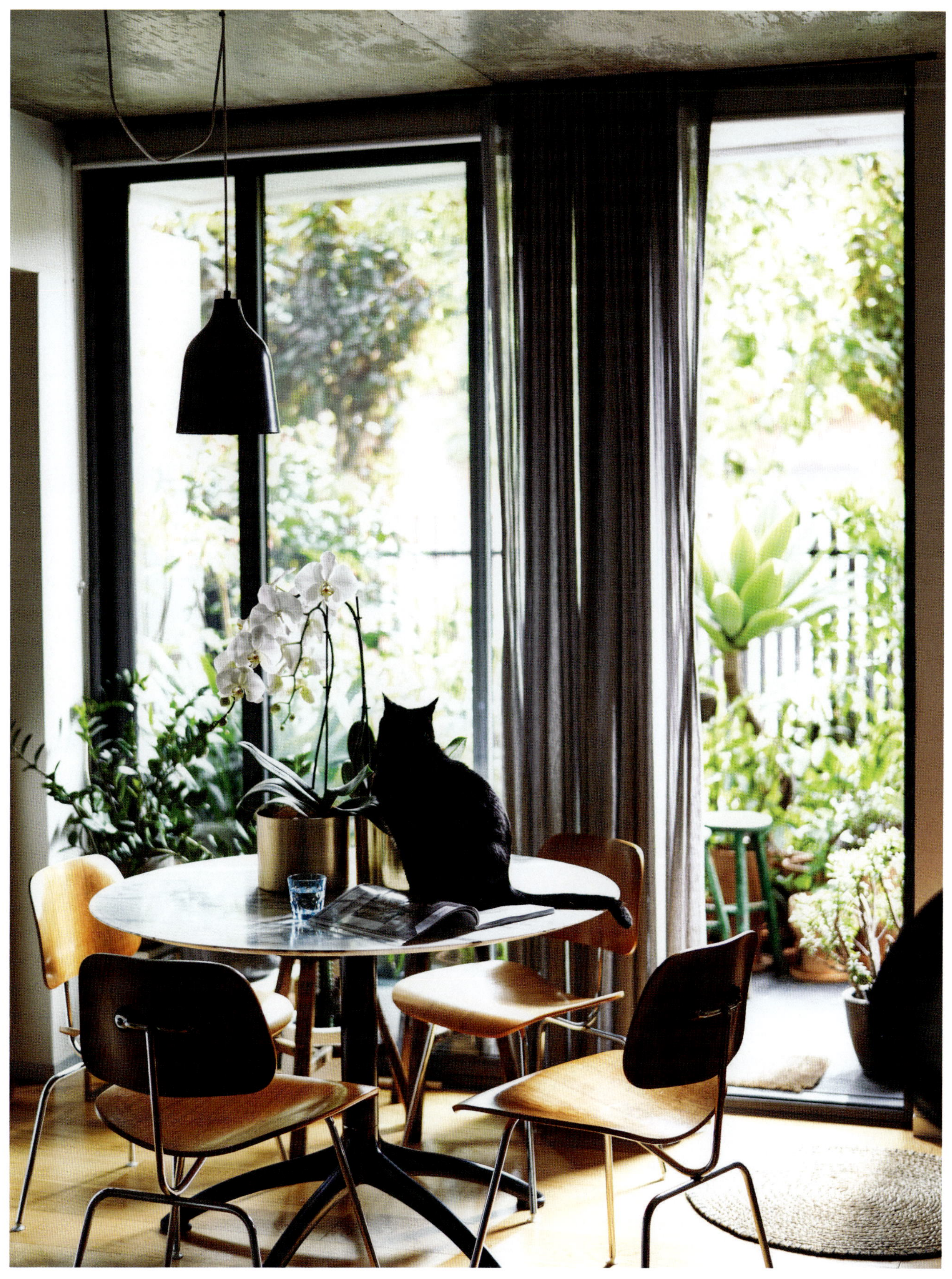

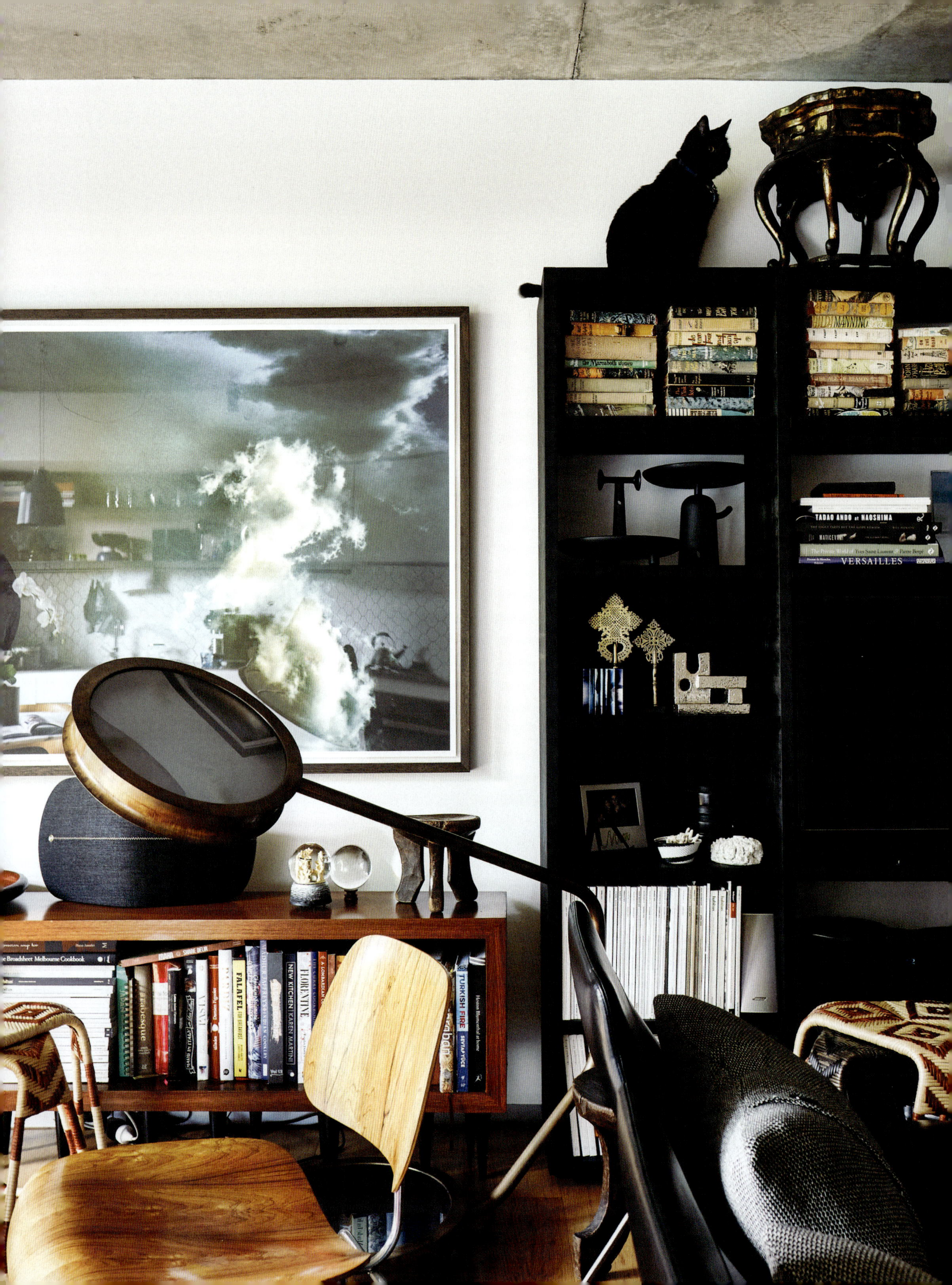
TADAO ANDO at NAOSHIMA
The Private World of Yves Saint Laurent & Pierre Bergé
VERSAILLES
THE AGE OF REASON
The Broadsheet Melbourne Cookbook
FALAFEL
FLORENTINE
NEW KITCHEN
KAREN MARTINI
TURKISH FIRE

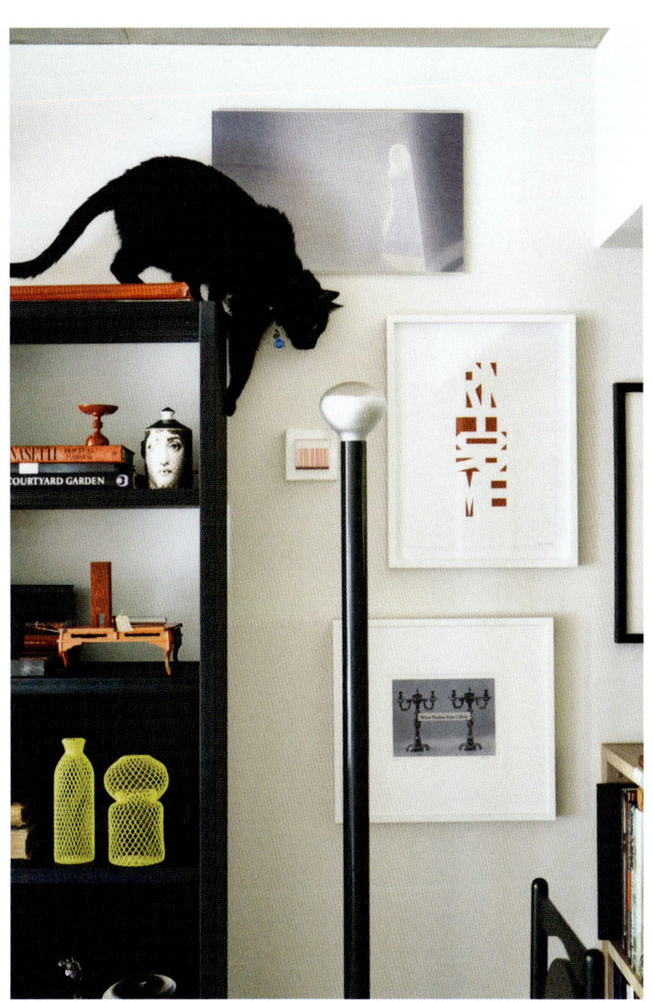

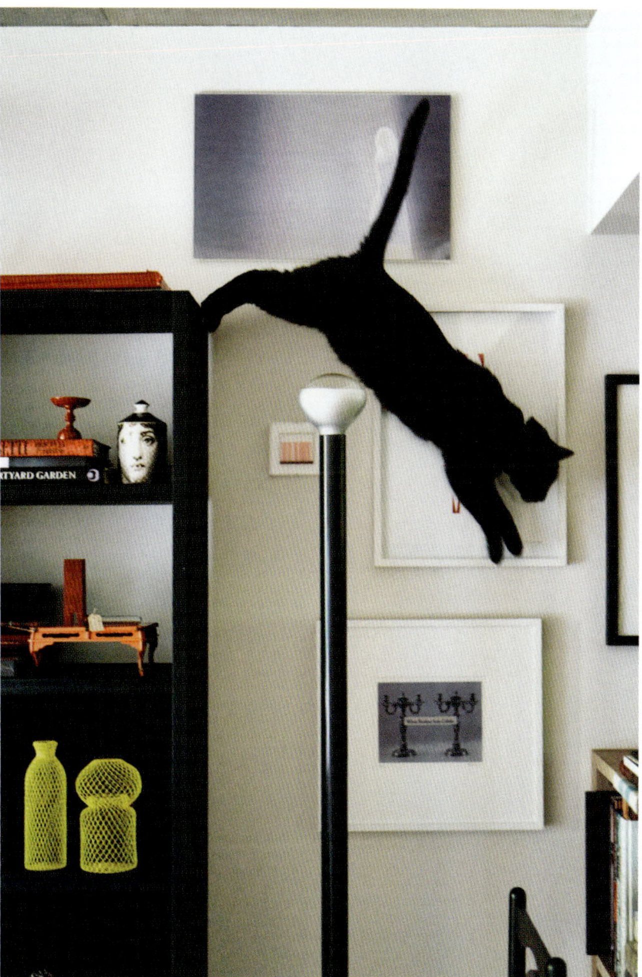

Panther loves to sit on the top of the Porro modular system, so he can survey his domain. Although there are many precious objects displayed on the shelves, he is yet to cause any breakages during his parkour practice.

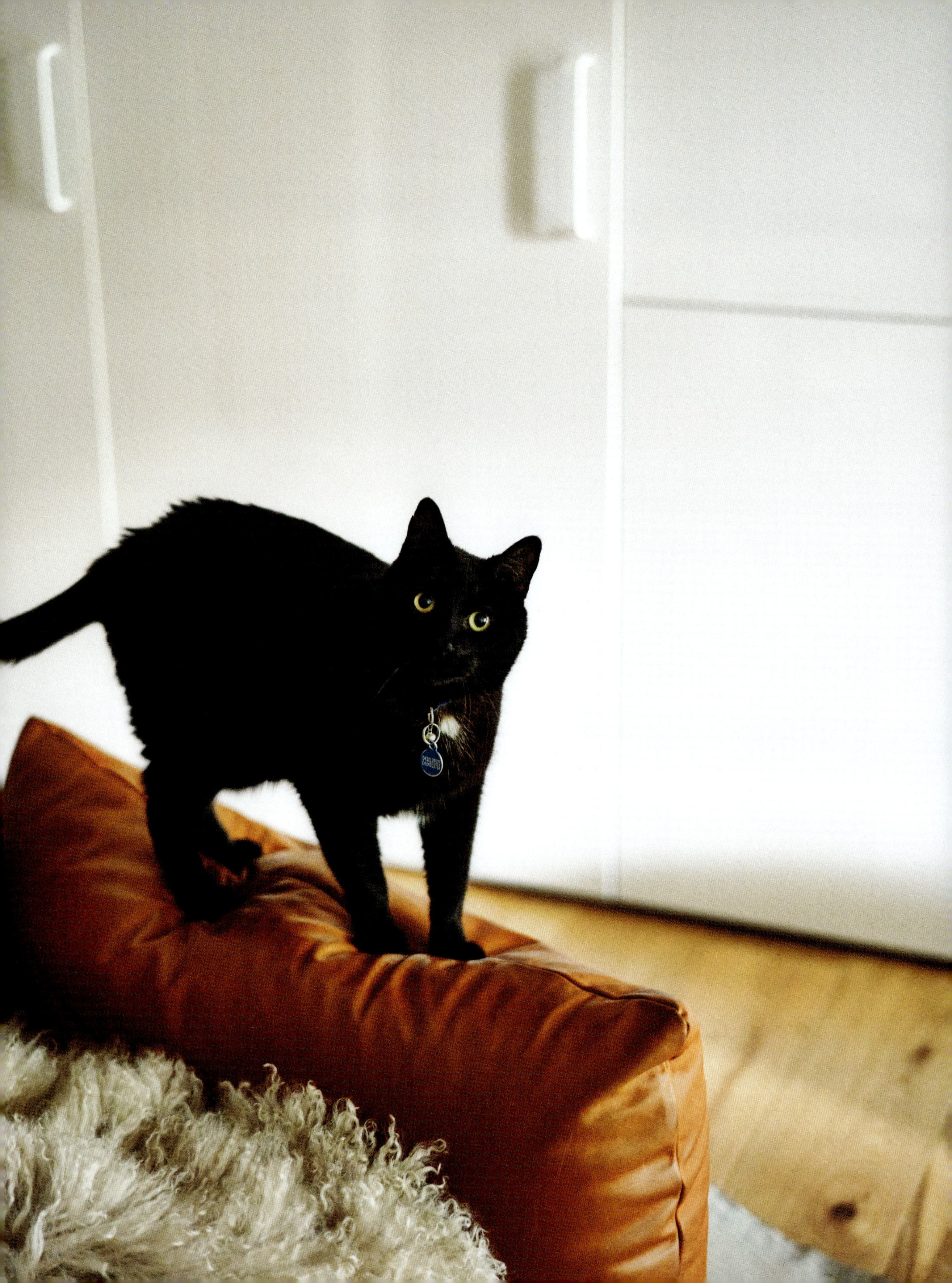

Q&A

DIVA OR DEVOTED FRIEND?

Devoted friend.

EXTROVERT OR INTROVERT?

Extrovert. He loves to be the centre of attention at any party, even the neighbour's.

LAP CAT OR NOT?

Definitely lap cat, but only on his terms.

OLD SOUL OR KITTEN AT HEART?

Old soul.

EXPLORER OR HOMEBODY?

Explorer – he loves other people's homes!

LAZY OR ACTIVE?

Typically lazy, but he has been known to leap up to the first-floor balcony, so he has a sporty side.

DOGS – FRIEND OR FOE?

Sadly, Panther's canine best friend recently passed away. He is now looking for another dog/best friend to fill the gap.

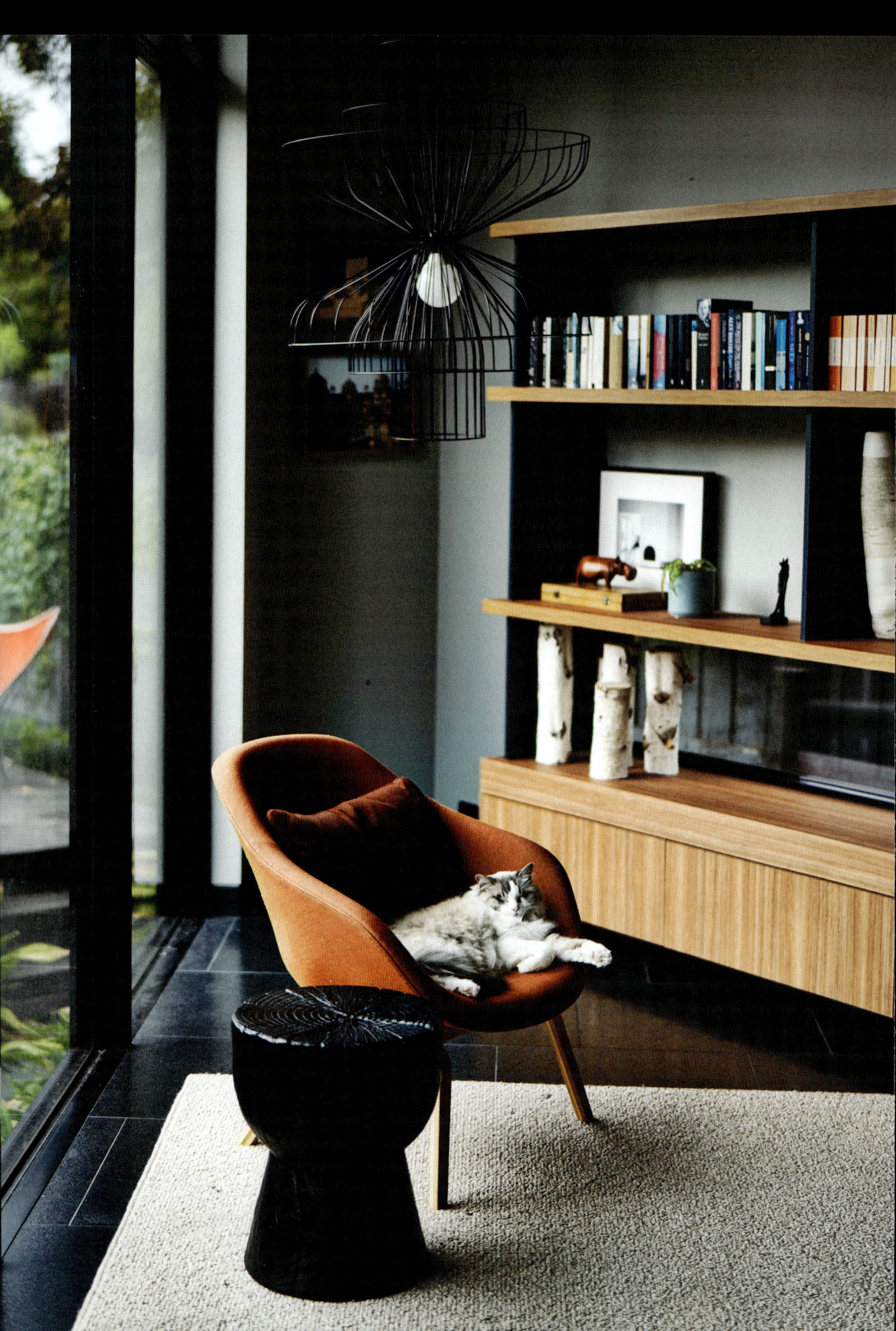

HUMPHREY

ARCHITECTS: RICHARD FLEMING AND ANJA DE SPA / MOLECULE STUDIO

Now ten years of age, Humphrey joined his owners as a tiny kitten, just a couple of months after they were married. The couple were looking for a playful, affectionate cat, and a close friend recommended getting a ragdoll. Humphrey's family has grown over the years, and, true to his breed, he is very tolerant of the children and happy when they play with him – his favourite game is 'fetch'. He also loves to stretch out his ample body to full length for a tummy scratch. The family's home has enclosed spaces outside so that Humphrey can roam ... but not too far.

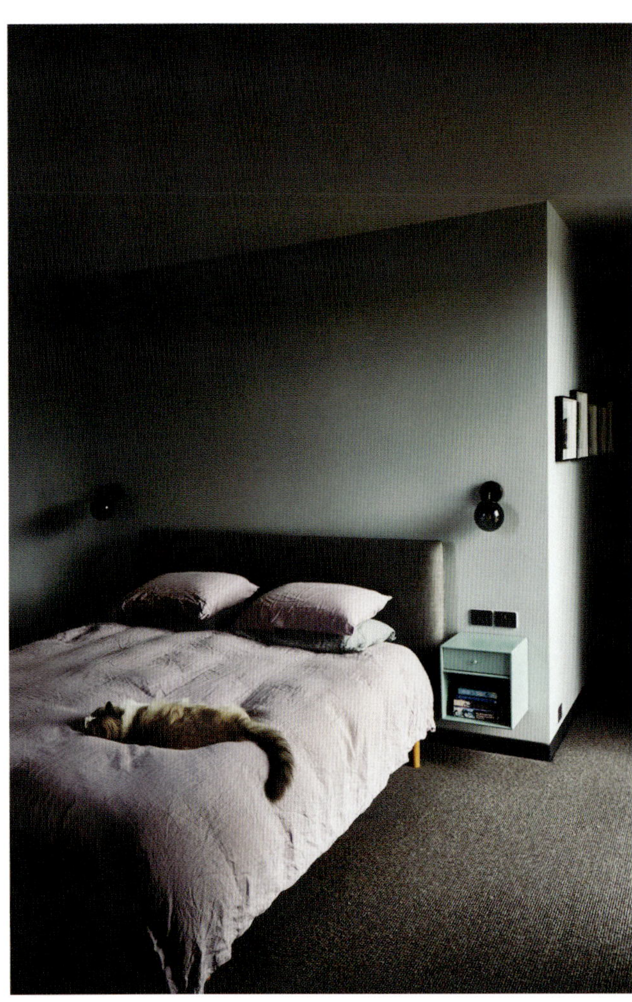

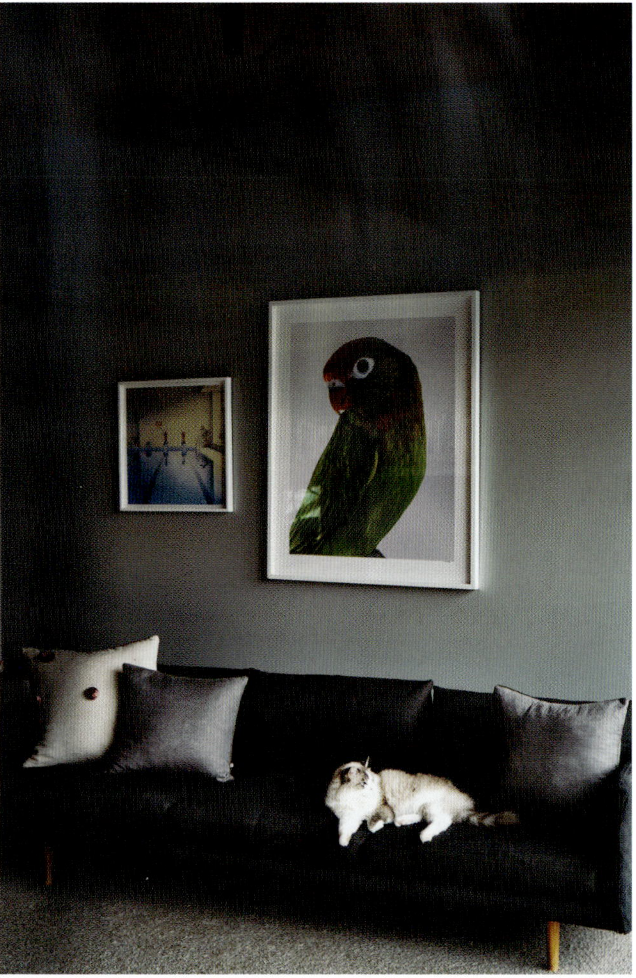

Architects: Richard Fleming and Anja de Spa / Molecule Studio

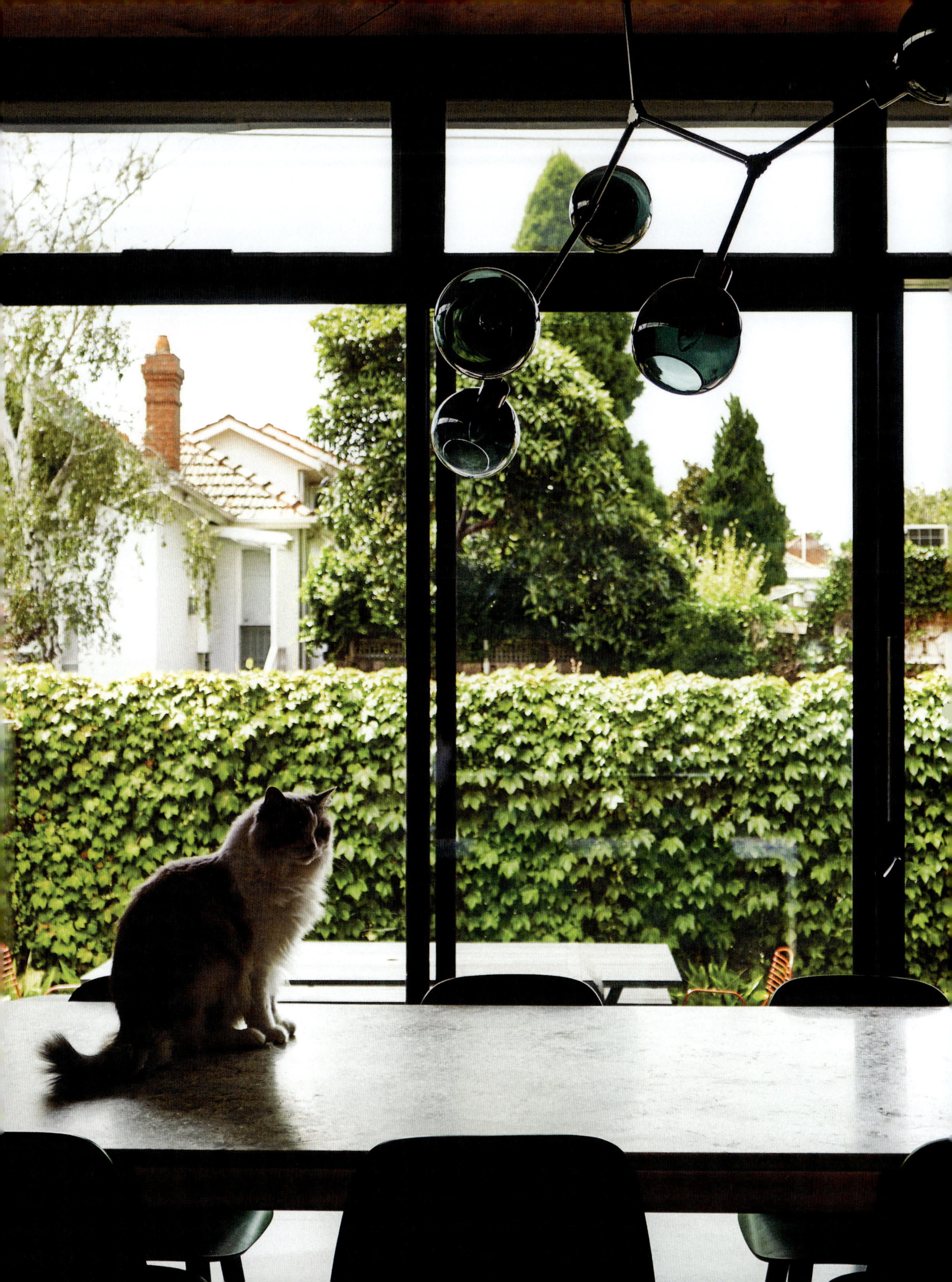

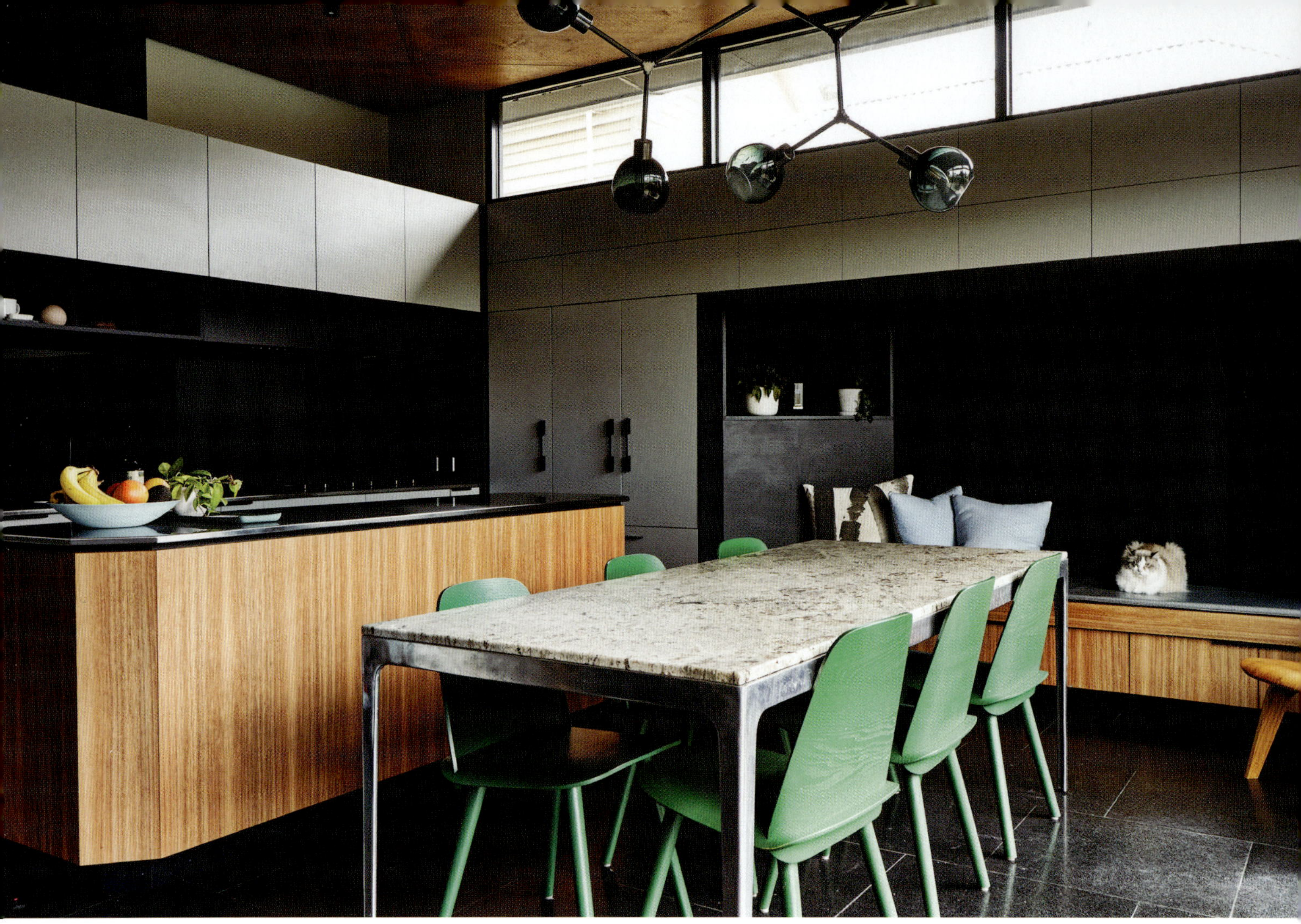

The home was built to accommodate a family with three young children, so hard-wearing and easy-to-clean surfaces were a must. These have been sensitively balanced with warm timber finishes and tonal paint colours to ensure the space retains a comfortable and welcoming atmosphere.

Architects: Richard Fleming and Anja de Spa / Molecule Studio

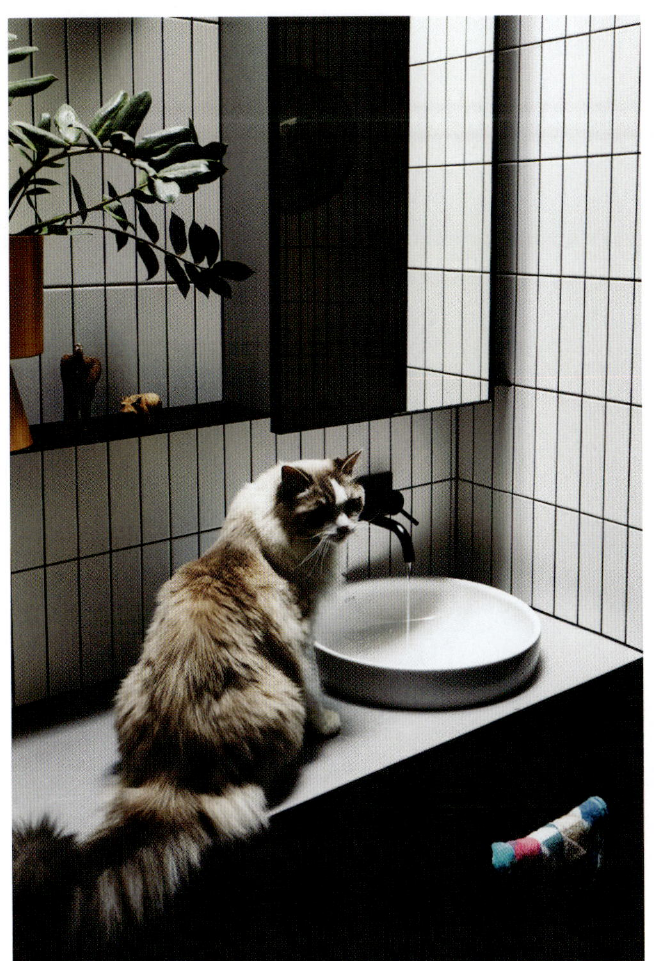

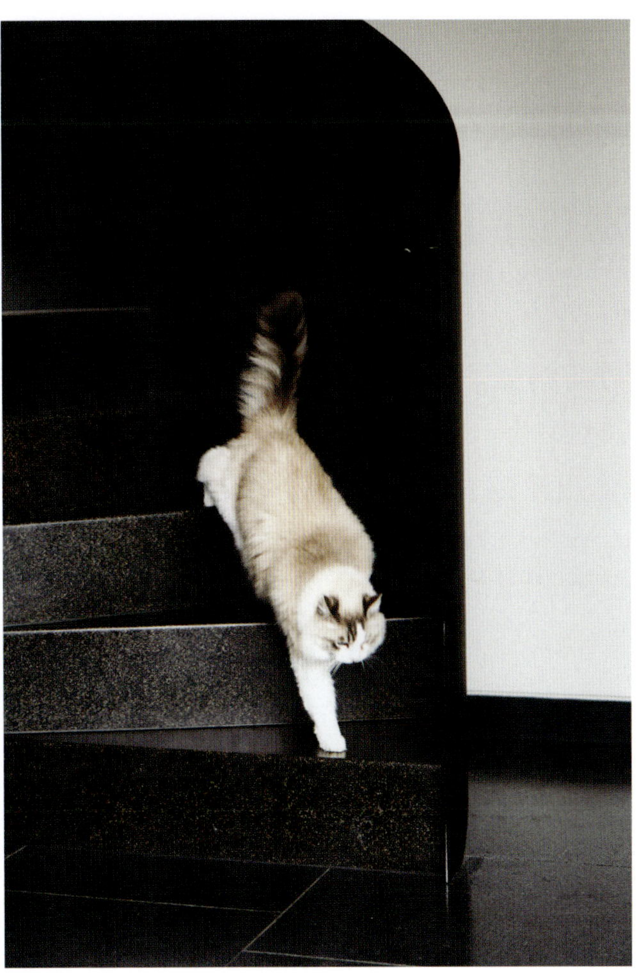

One of the unique elements in the home is the spiral staircase within a double-height plywood-clad void. It provides a lovely transition zone between the energetic living areas downstairs and the intimate sleeping spaces upstairs.

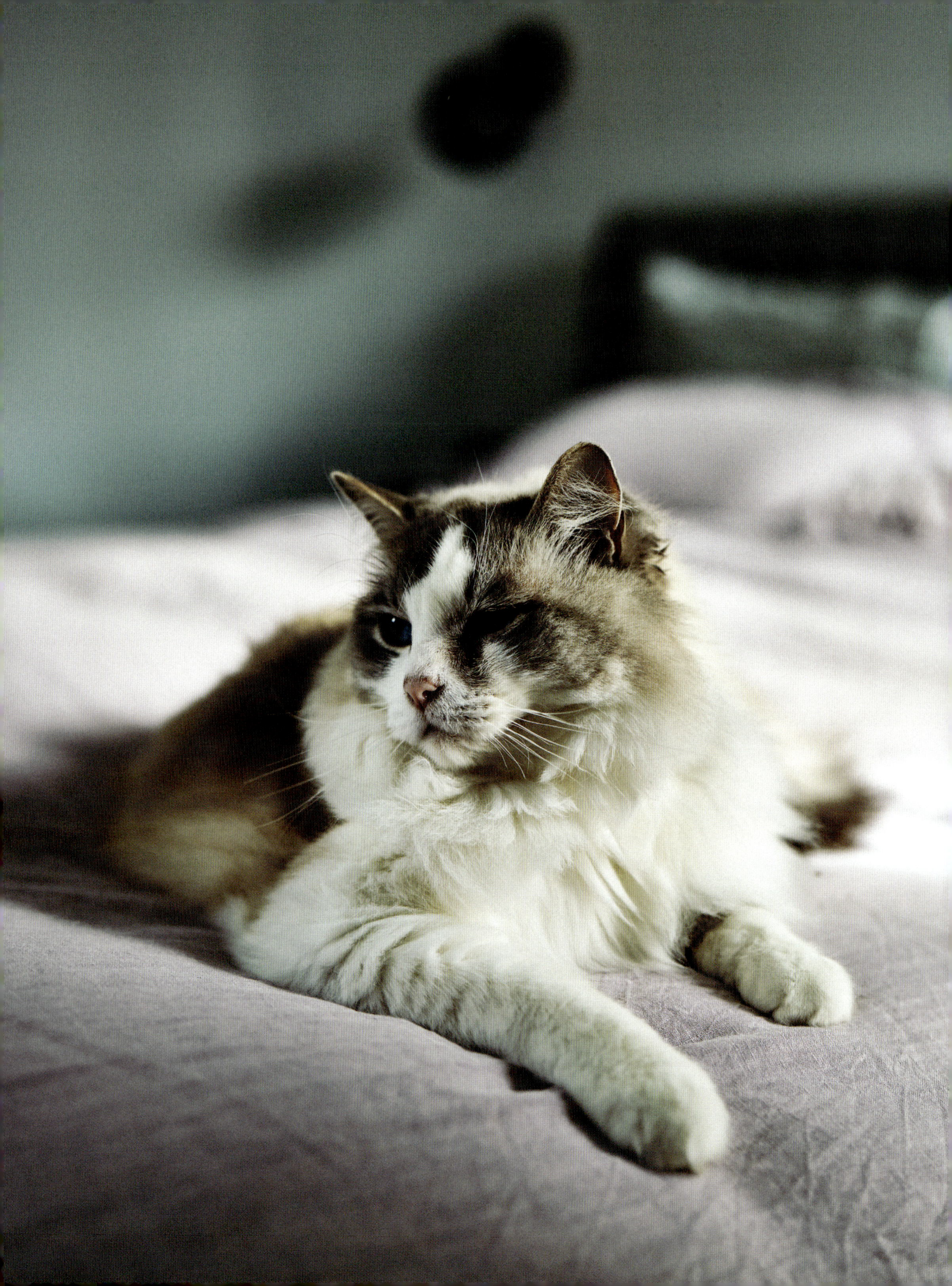

Q&A

DIVA OR DEVOTED FRIEND?
Devoted friend.

EXTROVERT OR INTROVERT?
Introvert. Though he enjoys playtime with the kids.

LAP CAT OR NOT?
Not. Unless the kids make him.

OLD SOUL OR KITTEN AT HEART?
Old soul.

EXPLORER OR HOMEBODY?
Homebody.

LAZY OR ACTIVE?
Lazy mostly, but with bursts of activity when it's time to play fetch.

DOGS – FRIEND OR FOE?
Friend.

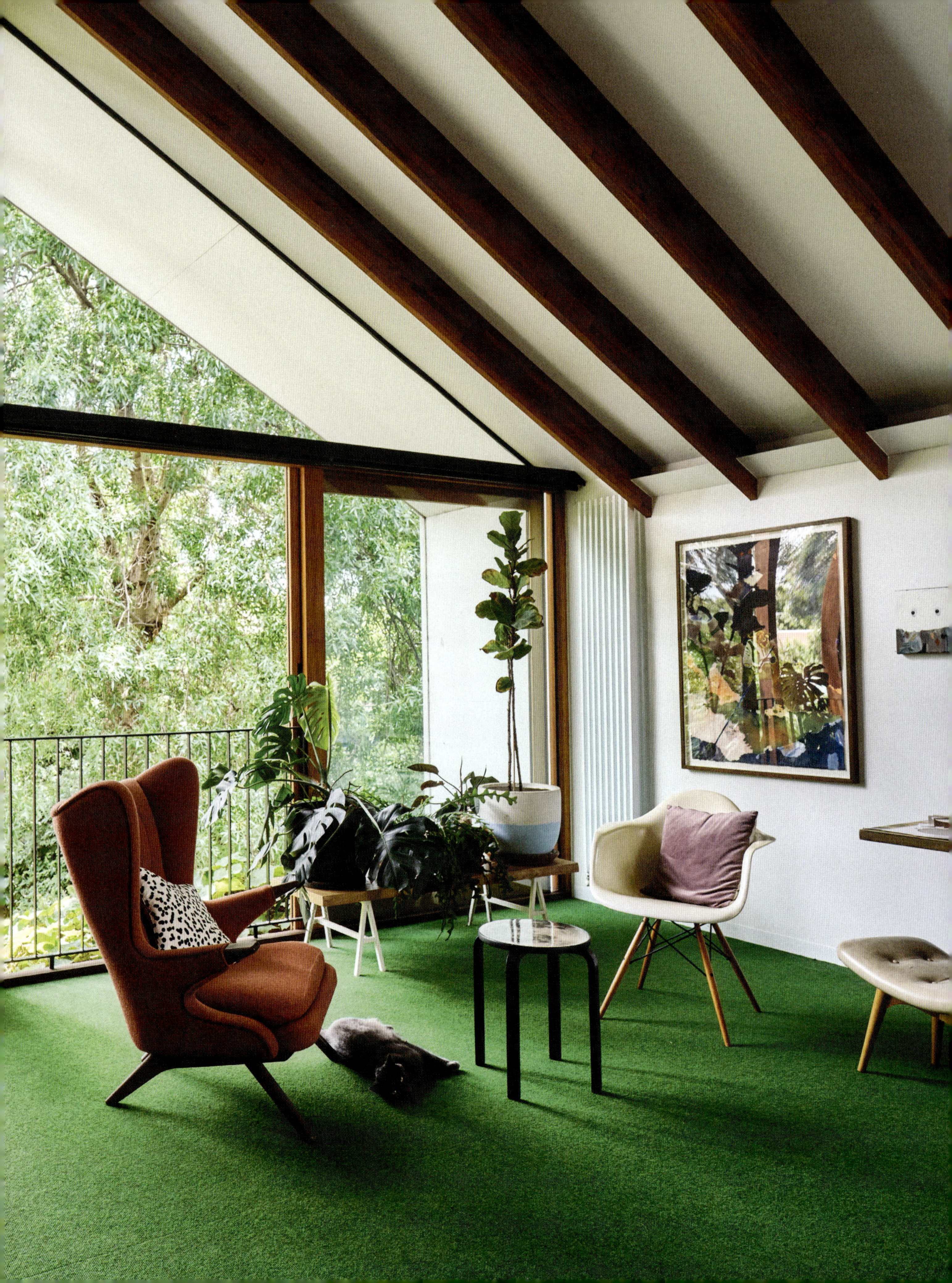

MALCOLM, AKA MOOGI

ARCHITECT: SIMON KNOTT / BKK ARCHITECTS

As soon as this family saw Malcolm, aka Moogi, sitting quietly in the corner at the adoption centre, they knew he was the rescue cat for them. And it was as if Moogi knew they would see him, without him having to do anything special to get their attention. Moogi is four years old and (possibly) part-Russian blue. His relaxed and unfussy manner has proved indispensable for living with this bustling family of four. He is perfectly happy to be stuffed into a kid's bed every night, and unlike many felines, he doesn't mind going along on family holidays. Moogi manages to snatch moments of peace amid the chaos, curling up on the home's heated floors or in a warm patch of sun.

Moogi lives with a creative family – an architect, an artist and their two children. The home features artisanal touches like a Danish woodfired interior brick wall, black porcelain floor tiles, and kitchen wall tiles hand-glazed by the artist.

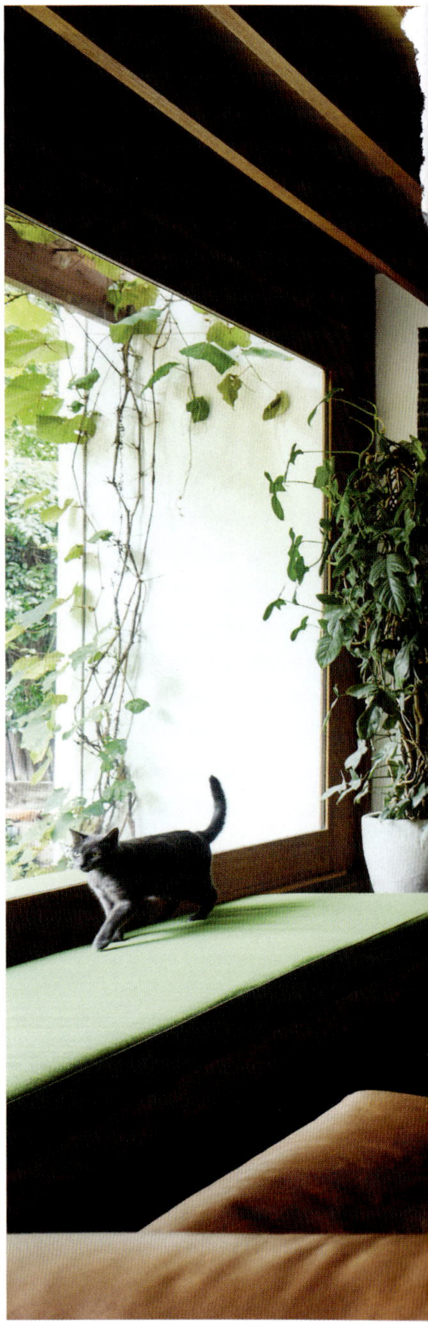

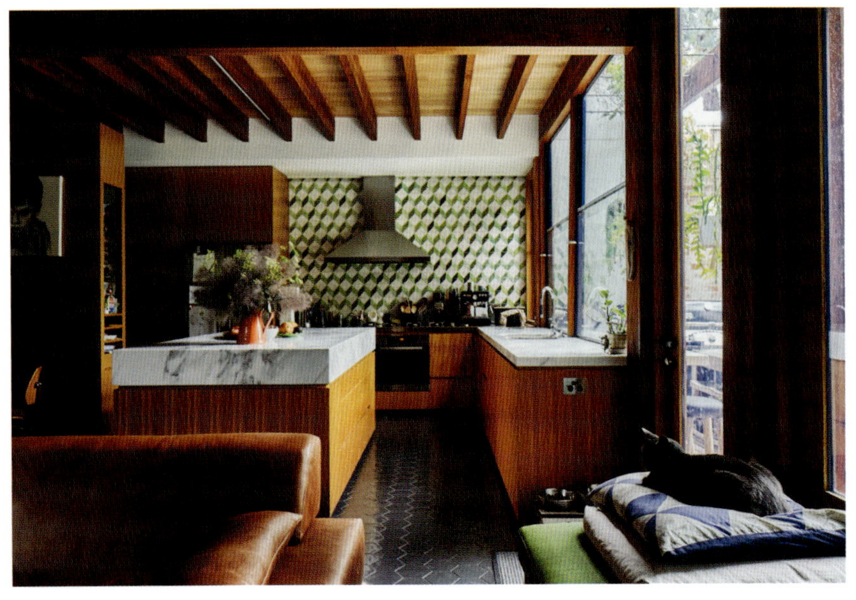

Architect: Simon Knott / BKK Architects

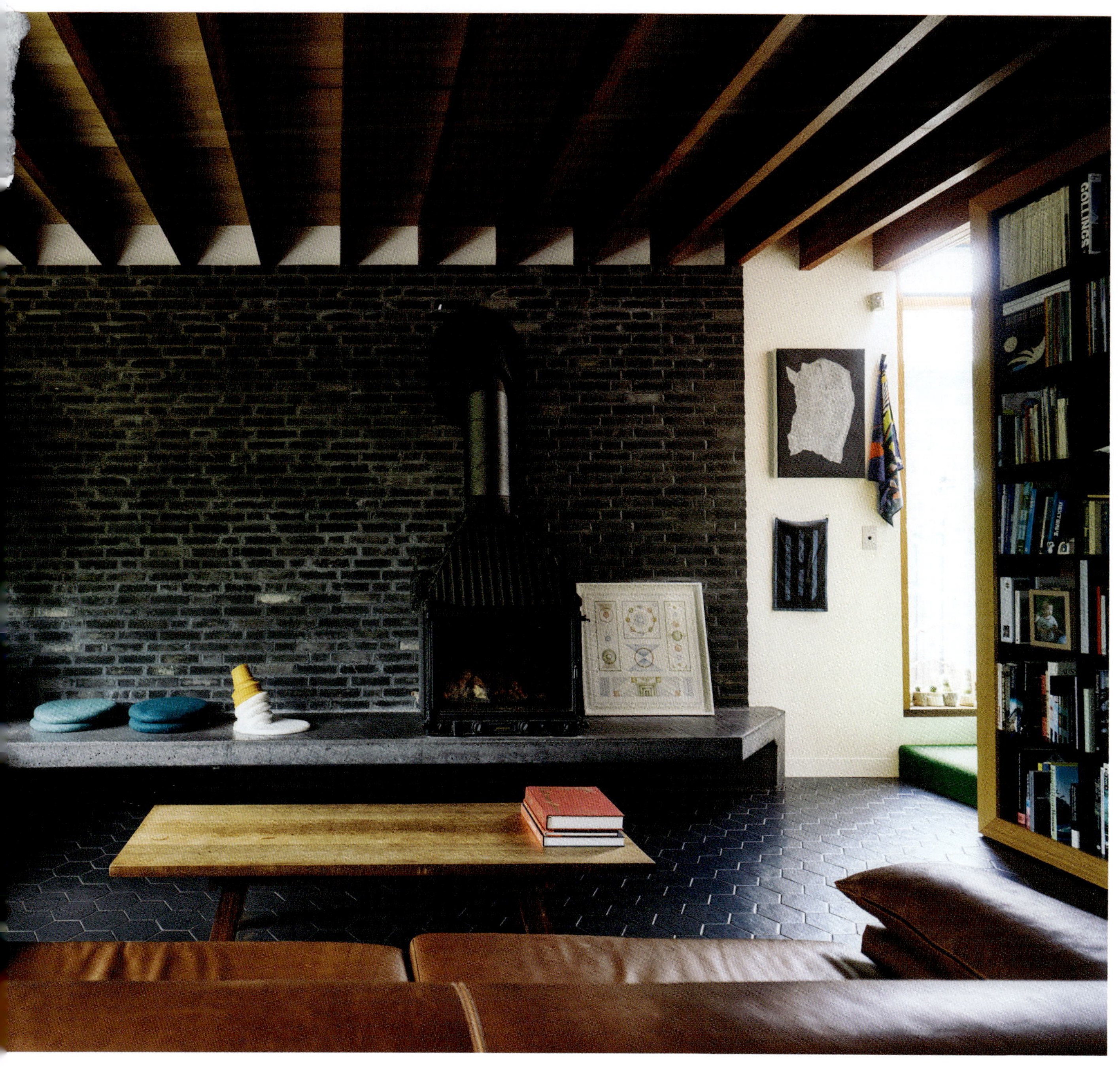
GOLLINGS

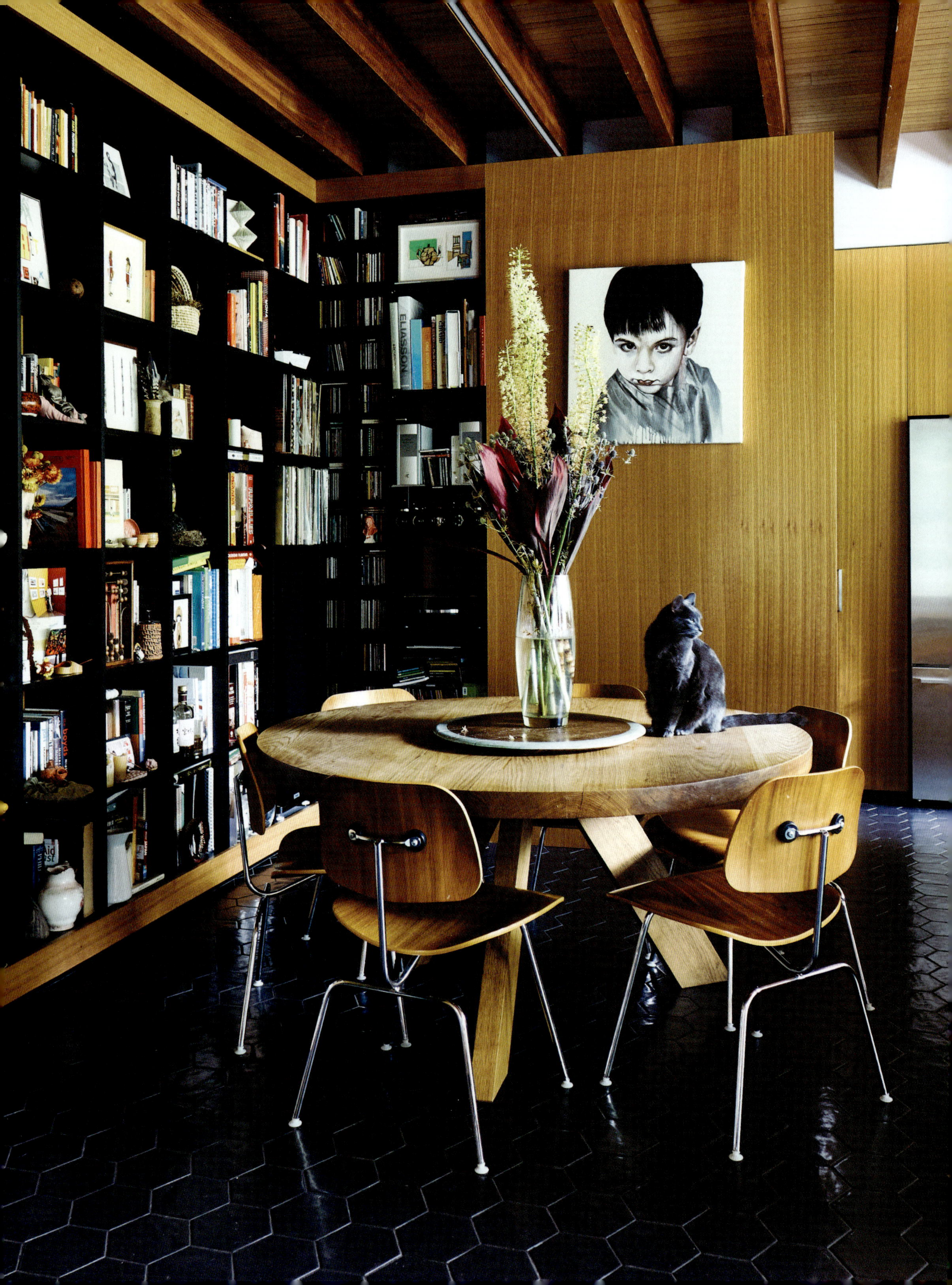
ELIASSON

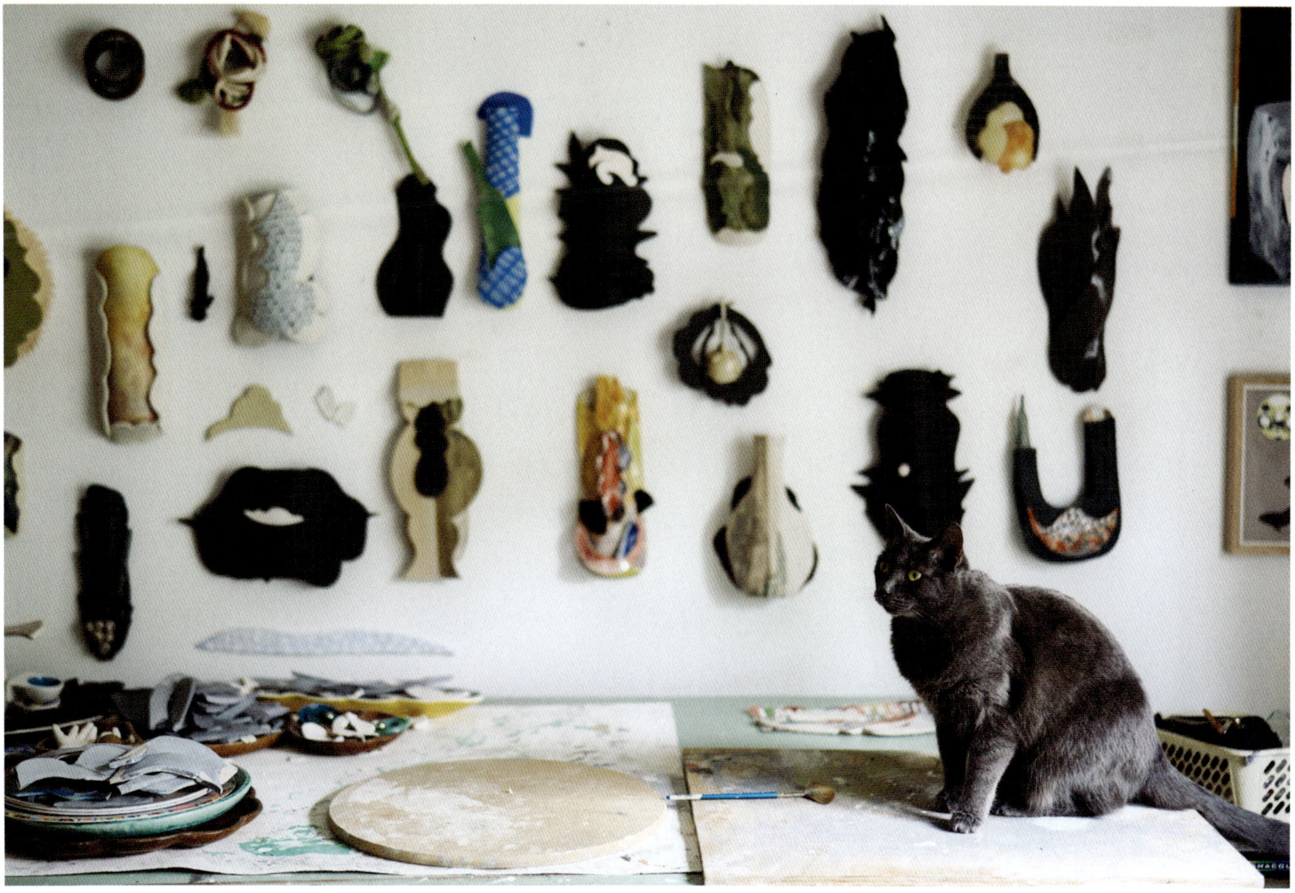

The front of the house – a Californian bungalow built a hundred years ago – includes the original floorboards, leadlight windows and cornices. The artist's studio is here, at the heart of the home. Sometimes she catches Moogi drinking the painting water.

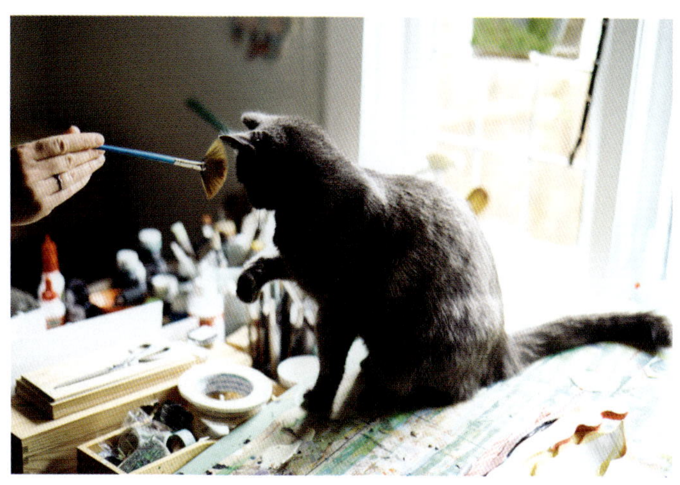

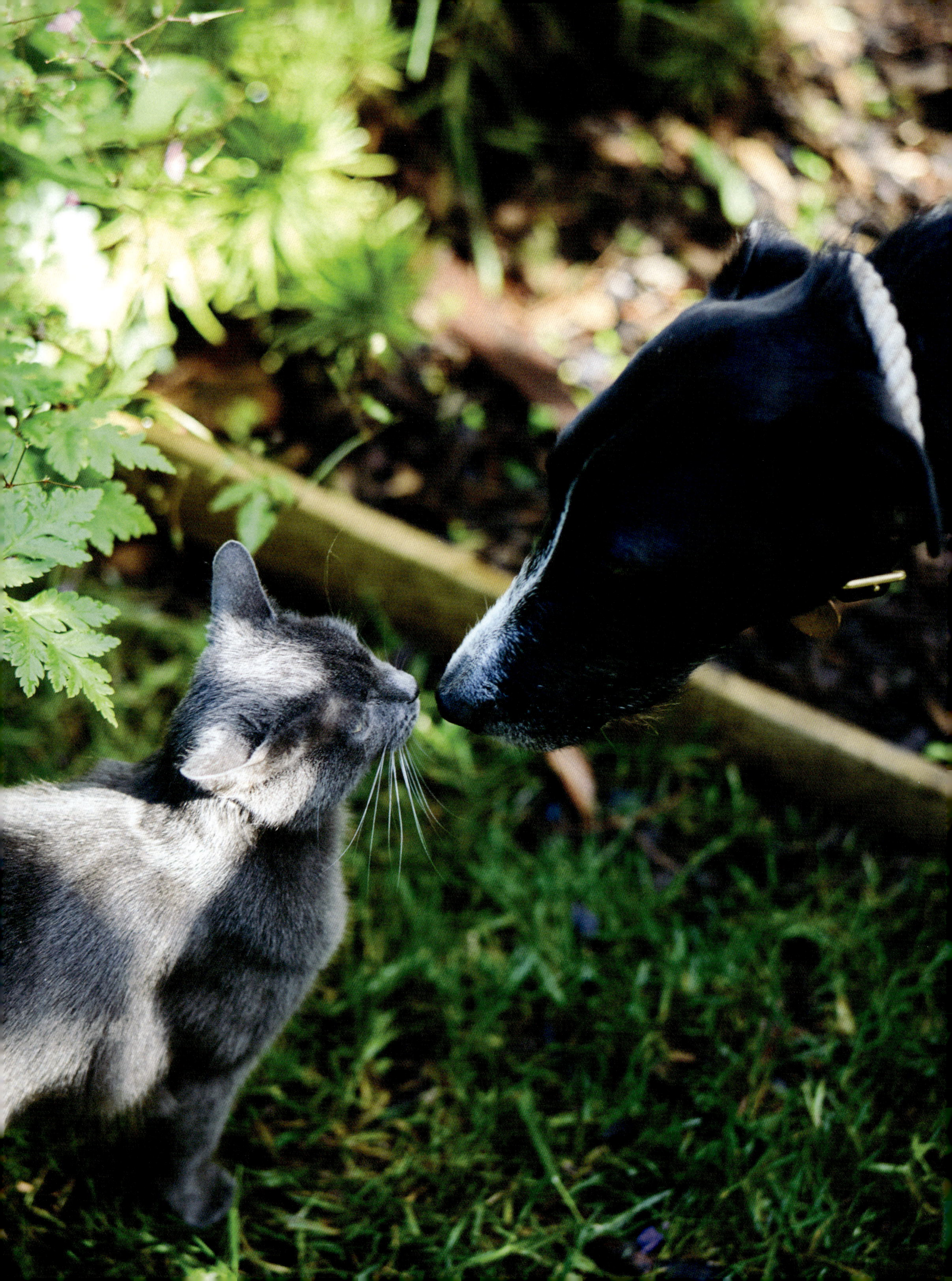

Q&A

DIVA OR DEVOTED FRIEND?

Devoted friend.

EXTROVERT OR INTROVERT?

Extrovert.

LAP CAT OR NOT?

Sometimes – more like a bedfellow.

OLD SOUL OR KITTEN AT HEART?

Kitten at heart.

EXPLORER OR HOMEBODY?

A bit of both, but it is doubtful he has ever killed anything ... maybe a mouse, or a lizard or two.

LAZY OR ACTIVE?

Closer to the lazier end of the scale.

DOGS – FRIEND OR FOE?

Best friends with the family's rescue dog, Wally. Moogi is the boss: a few swipes to Wally's nose sorted that out very quickly. Nowadays, the two are very comfortable with each other – every now and then you can catch them sharing the outdoor beanbag in the sun or rubbing up against each other affectionately around dinnertime. They have a very sweet friendship.

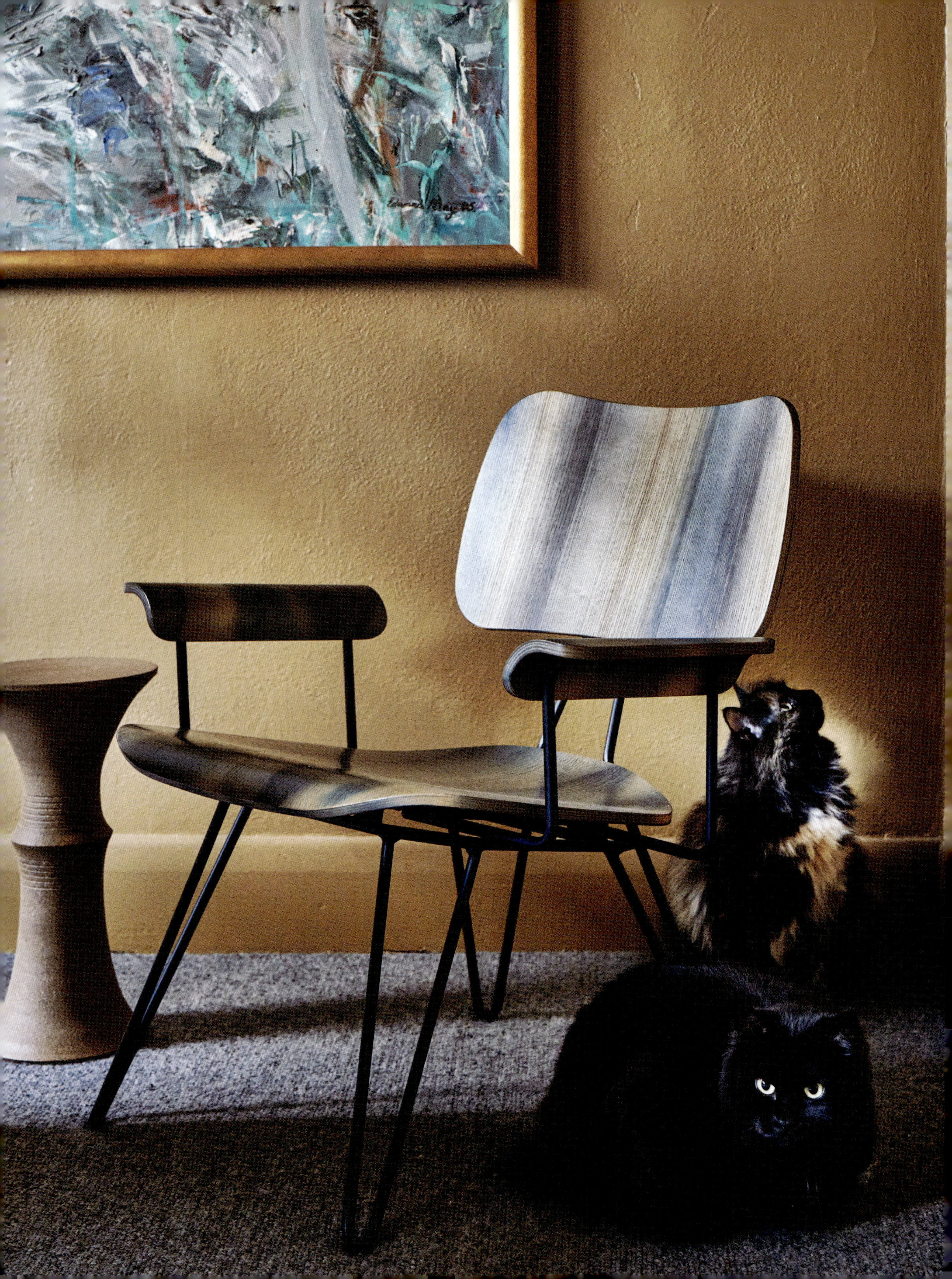

KOBE AND KUMI

DESIGNER: ADRIANA HANNA

Kobe and Kumi are six-year-old sisters: an apt gift for the family's twin daughters. Initially, one of the twins saw the cats as an unwelcome addition to the household, because she was terrified by the immense responsibility of owning a pet. However, this feeling was quickly overtaken by unconditional love. In many ways, the cats are a true representation of the twins – their constant fighting, for example. Such kitty-capers can be very amusing to observe, but they are certainly not encouraged. In the evenings, when the family returns home from school and work, Kobe and Kumi make for great companions, often choosing to accompany their humans wherever they may be in the house.

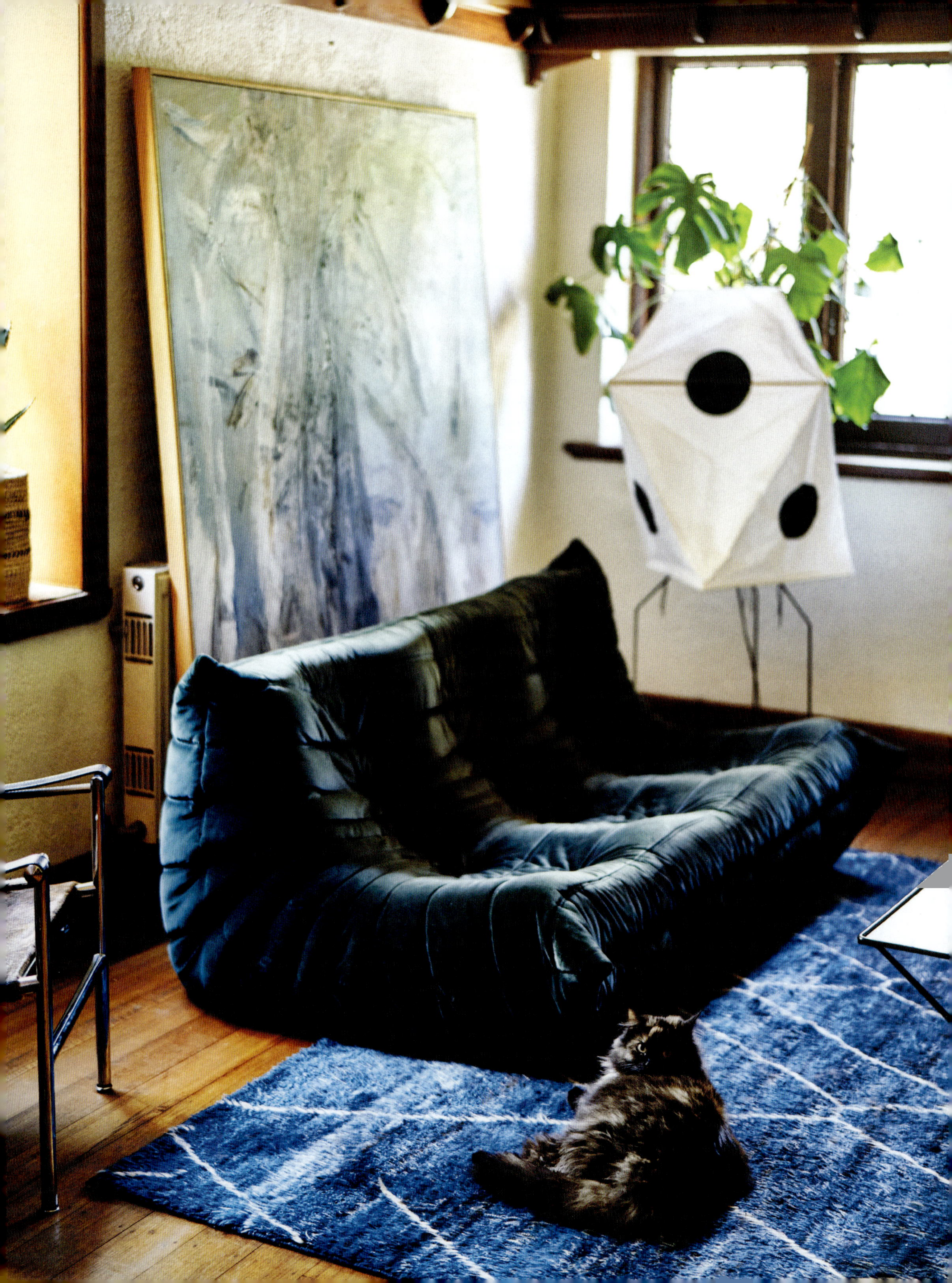

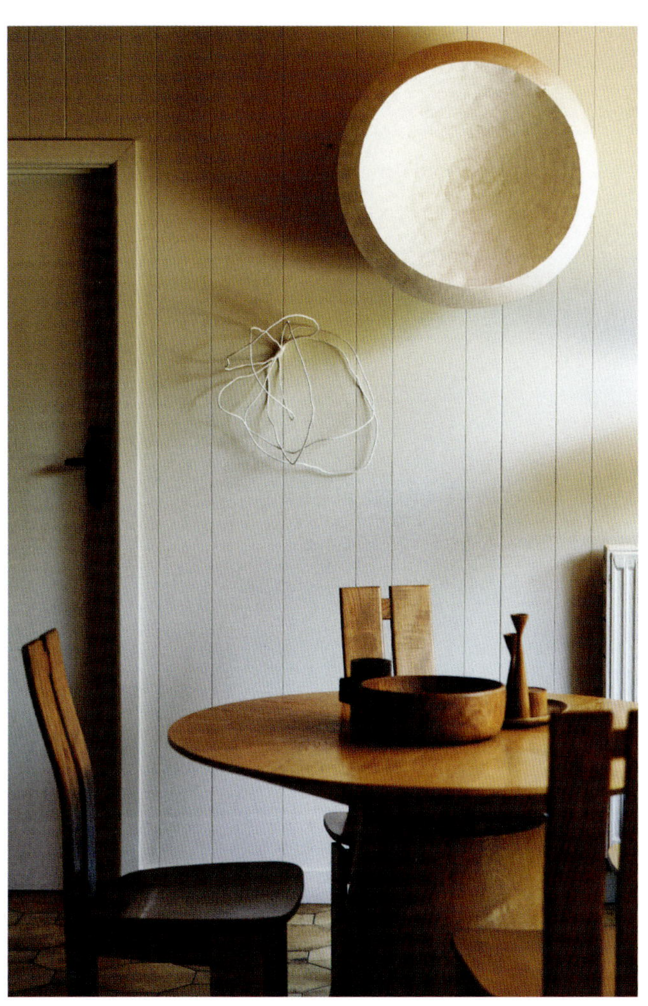

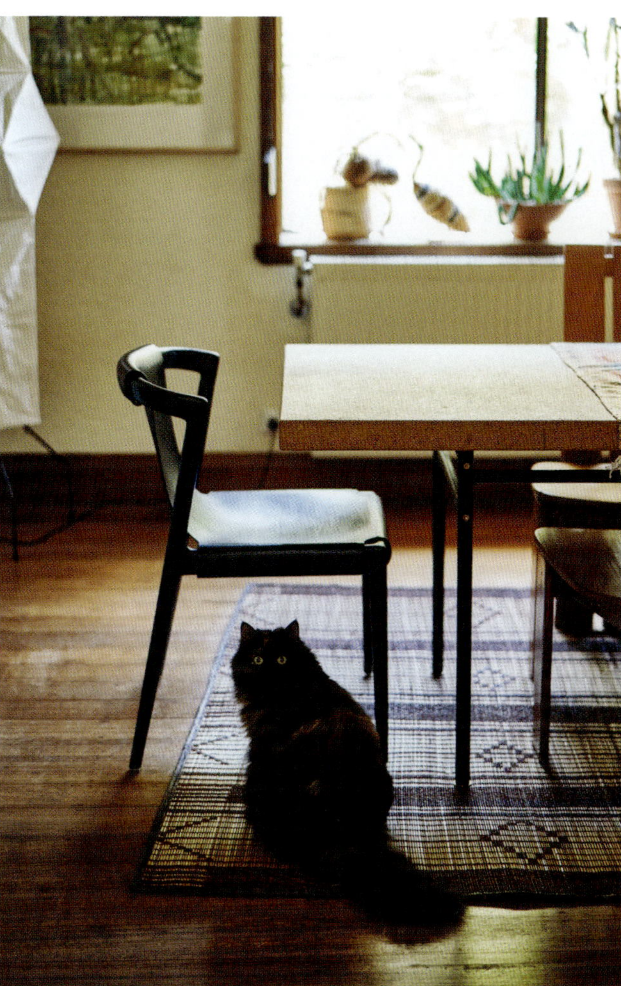

The home belongs to an architect and it serves as a visual diary of her admiration for both local and international 20th-century design. She delights in her collection's perpetuity, knowing that one day the pieces will be passed on so that others may enjoy them as much as her family has.

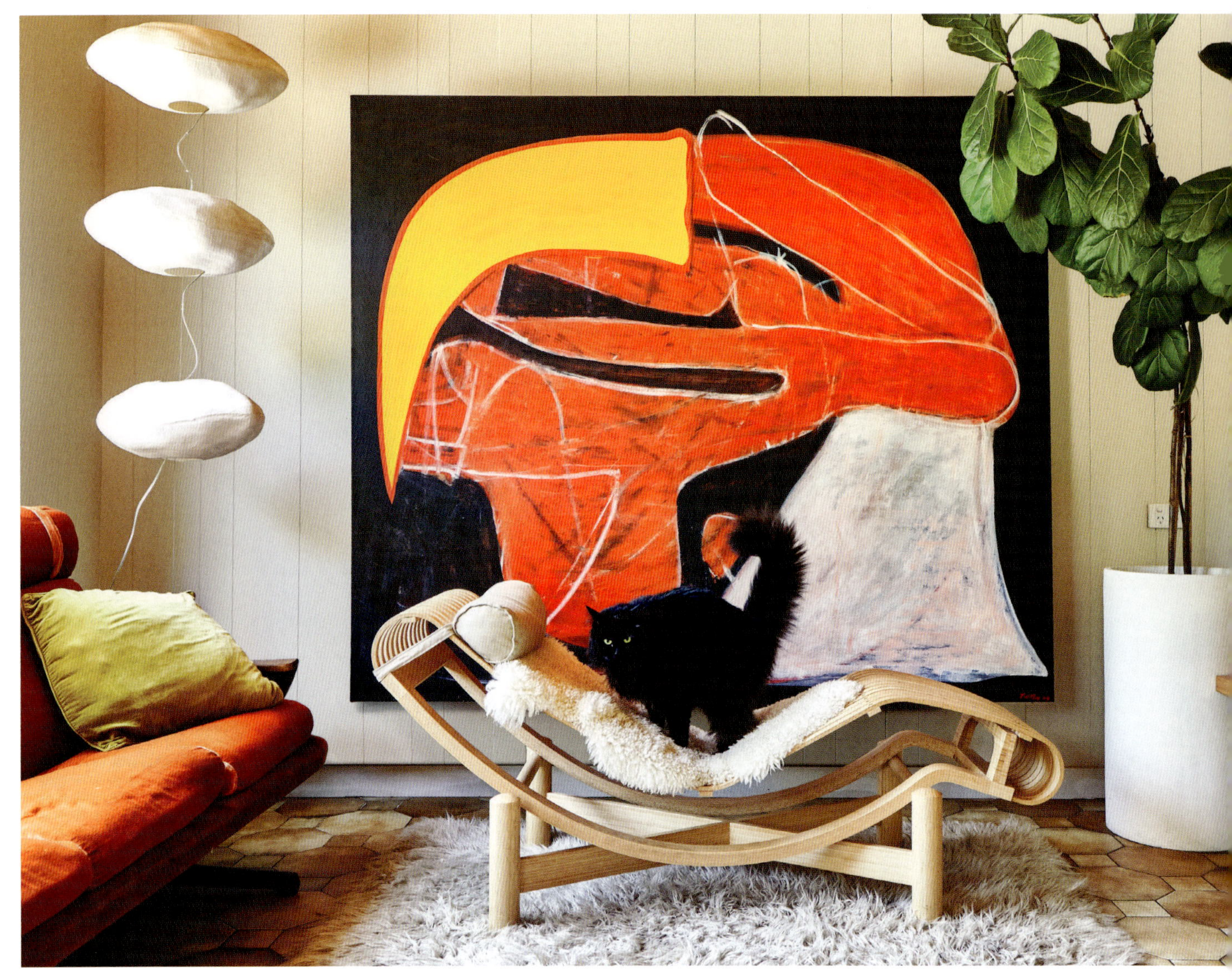

Astute use of colour and texture is prevalent throughout the home and it evokes a visceral and emotional response. Each room takes on a different palette or concept, informed by its function: the bedroom is dark and enigmatic, while the main living space is light and vibrant.

Designer: Adriana Hanna

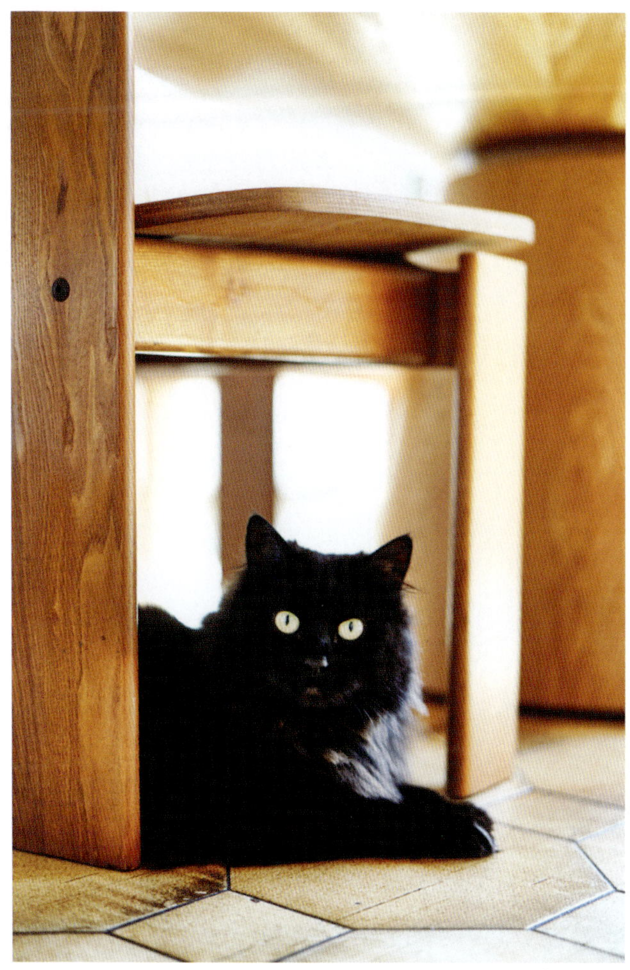

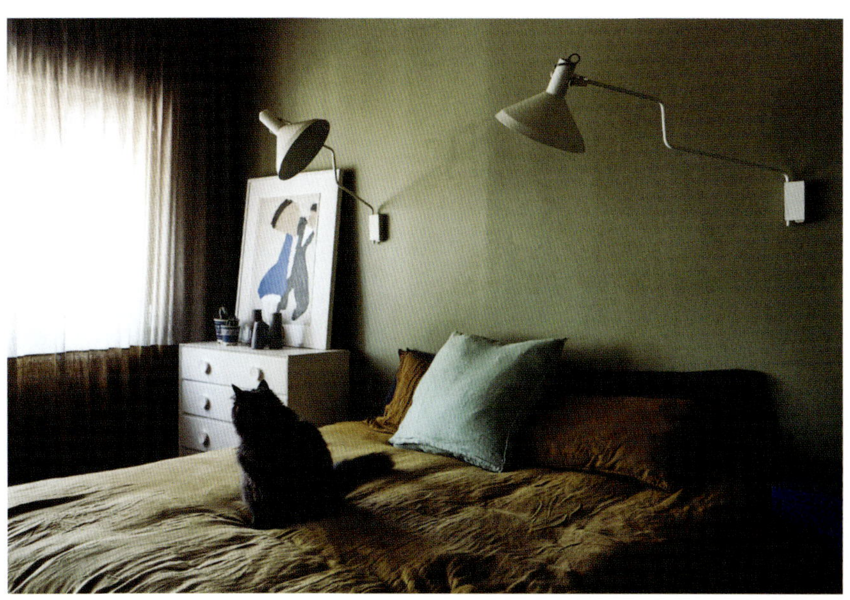

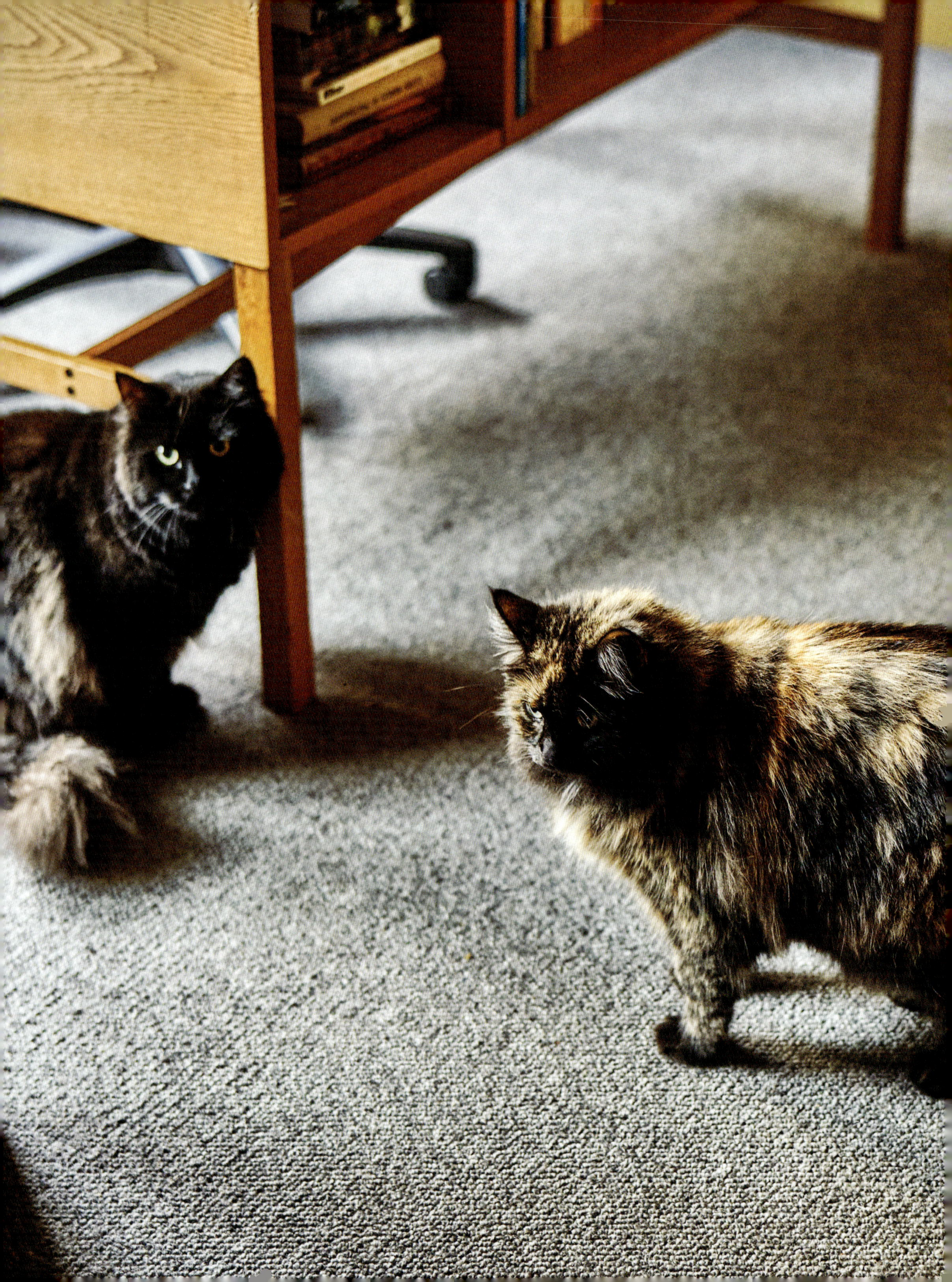

Q&A

DIVAS OR DEVOTED FRIENDS?
Extremely loyal, yet selective about their affections.

EXTROVERTS OR INTROVERTS?
Not entirely sociable and incredibly aloof. However, they never refuse a cuddle.

LAP CATS OR NOT?
Never on the lap, but always close by.

OLD SOULS OR KITTENS AT HEART?
Definitely old souls.

EXPLORERS OR HOMEBODIES?
Homebodies. When they're not cleverly hidden or camouflaged somewhere within the house, the pair can be found in the yard – more often than not up a tree or sleeping on a bluestone boulder – but never far away.

LAZY OR ACTIVE?
Lazy little ladies!

DOGS – FRIEND OR FOE?
Foe. The house is surrounded on three sides by neighbours with dogs – perhaps that's what keeps the cats close to home. They occasionally taunt the dogs by sitting in clear view, high up in a tree or on the fence.

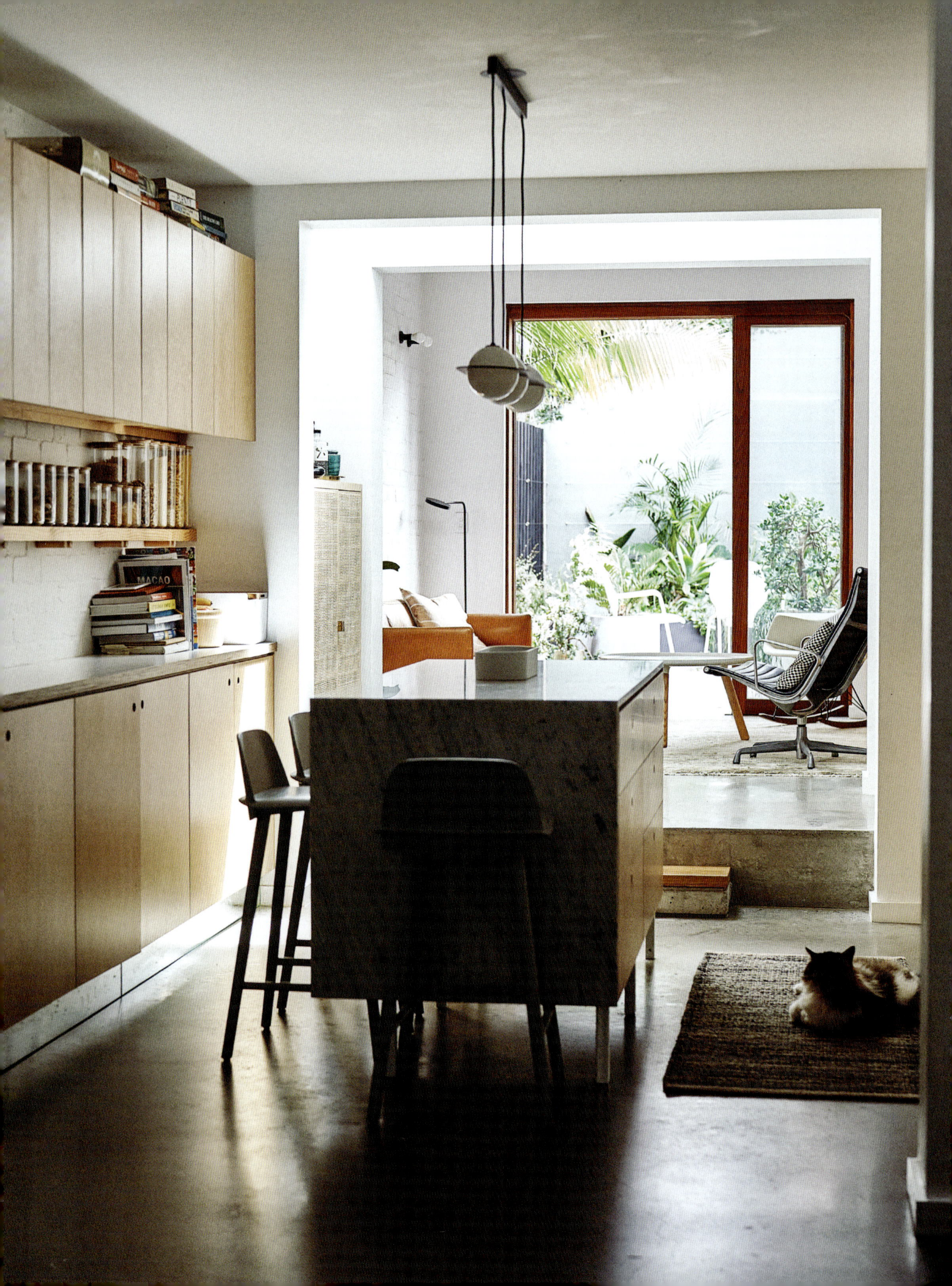
MACAO

REUBEN

ARCHITECT: HANNAH TRIBE / TRIBE STUDIO ARCHITECTS

Despite his enormous size, Reuben is a bit of a scaredy-cat and doesn't venture past the perimeter of his home. His owners adopted him as a kitten ten years ago through a pet rescue program – they were newly engaged and wanted to start their family with a fur baby. Reuben's breed is unknown, but there might be some Maine Coon in the mix, considering his size. He's quite food-oriented and can be vocal with his demands for biscuits. But he earns his keep as the home's resident cockroach killer and mouse deterrent.

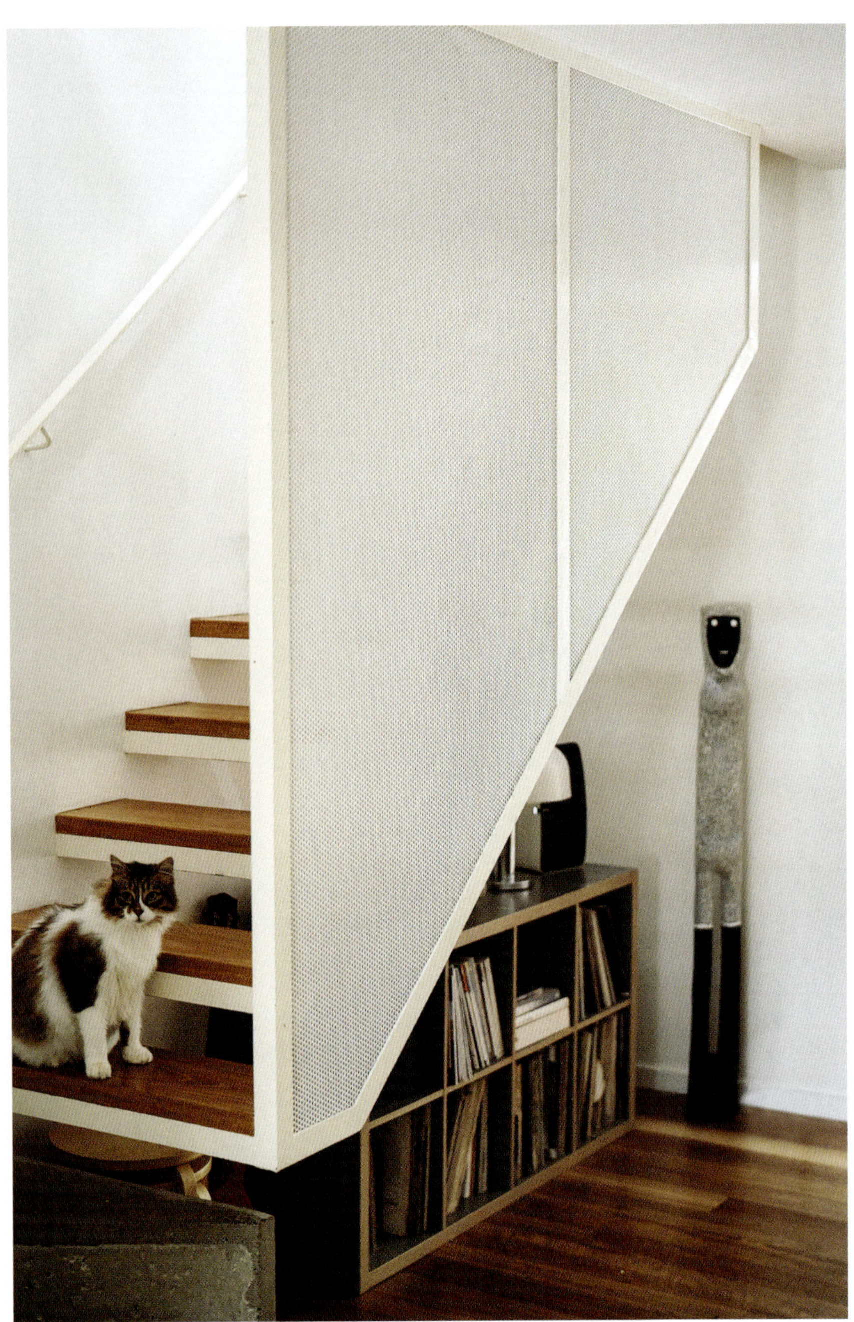

Reuben's home occupies a relatively small area, but every inch of space is utilised thanks to the architect's clever design. The terrace house is located in the inner city but feels a million miles away.

Architect: Hannah Tribe / Tribe Studio Architects

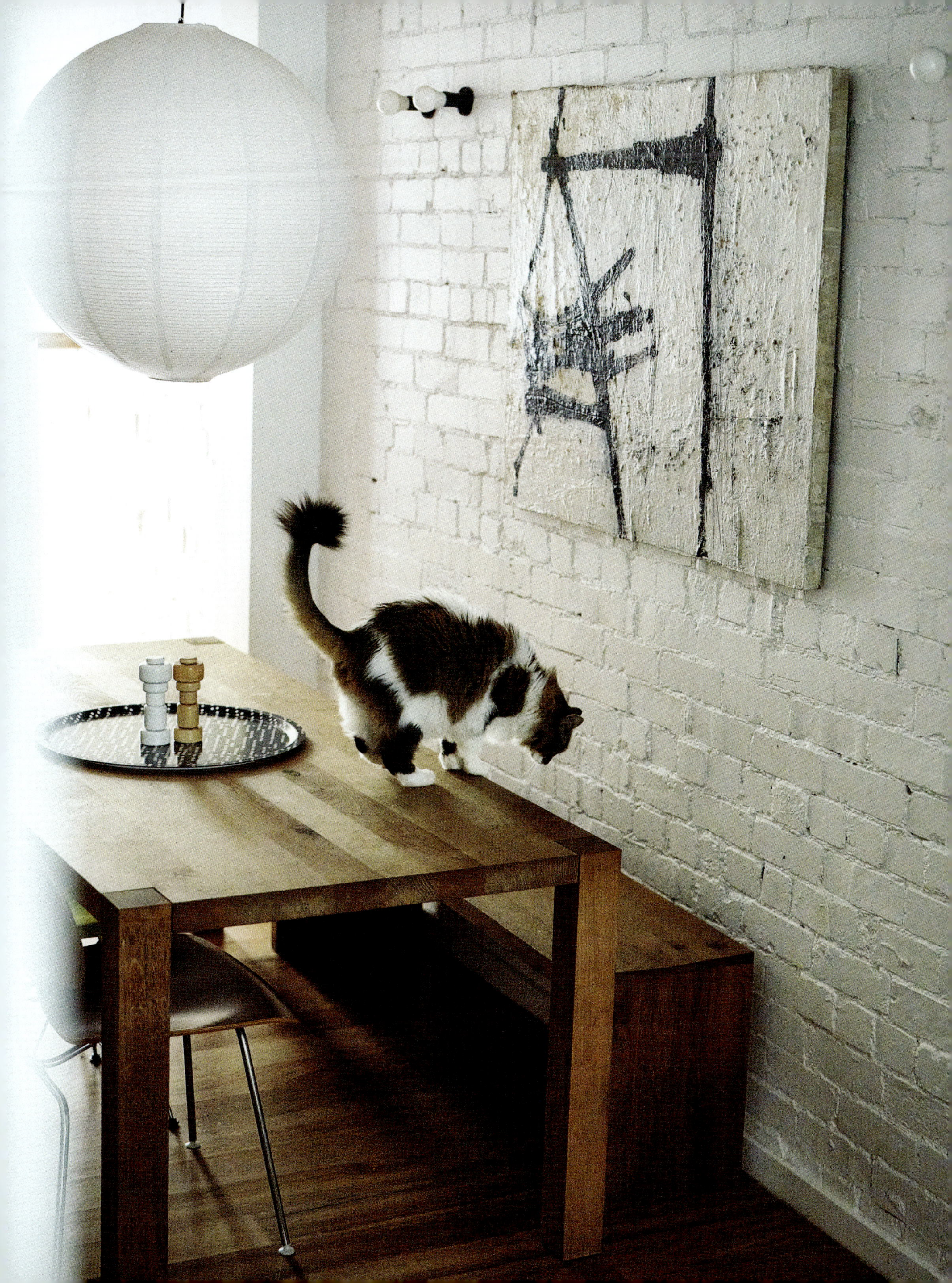

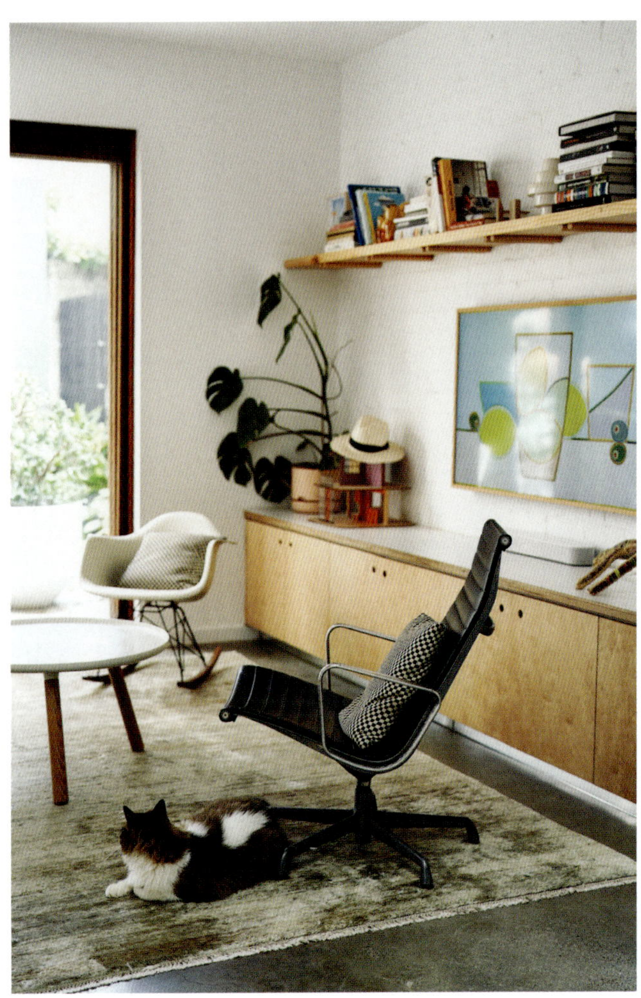

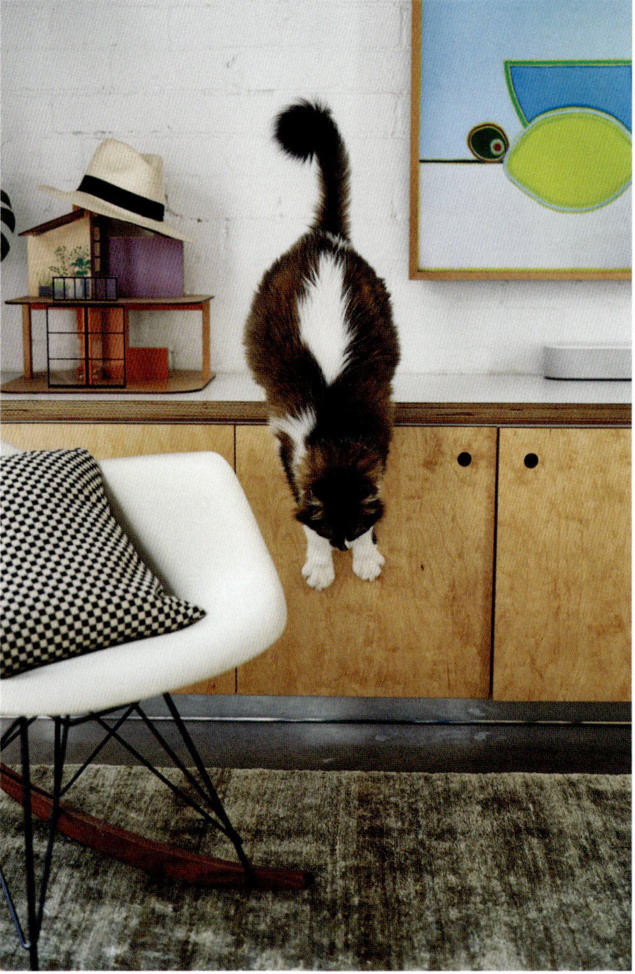

The home includes playful accents that reference Japan, and a healthy dose of Scandinavian and mid-century-style furnishings.

Architect: Hannah Tribe / Tribe Studio Architects

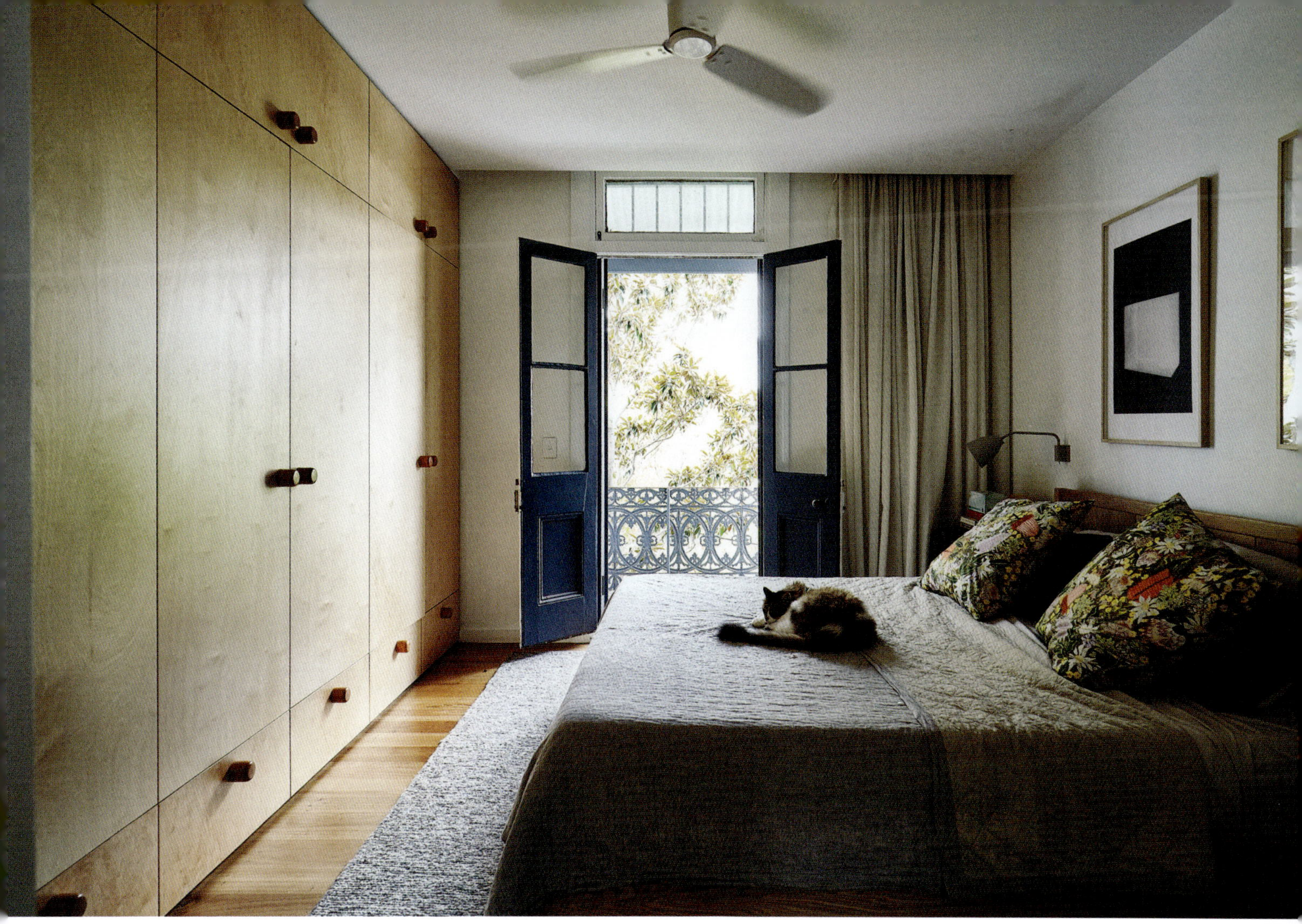

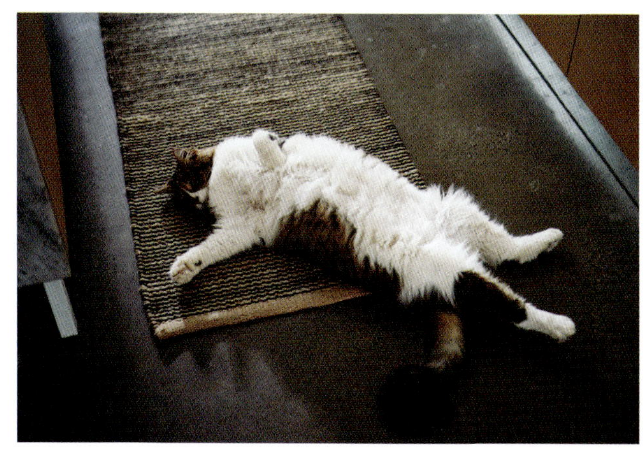

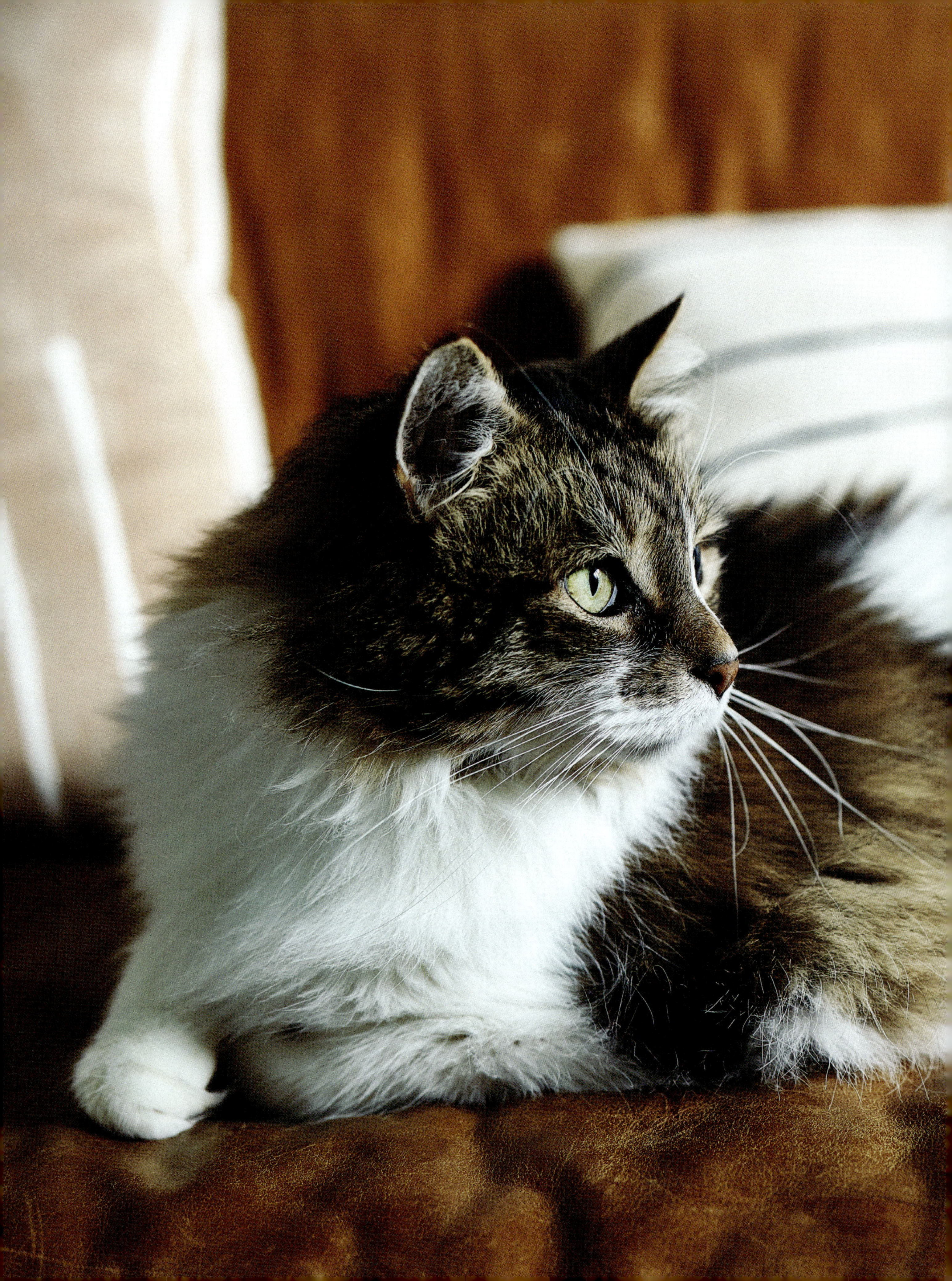

Q&A

DIVA OR DEVOTED FRIEND?

A little from column A and a little from column B. He is very demanding (and vocal) when he wants attention, food or affection, but is always available whenever his owner needs a cuddle. And he comes when he's called – like a dog!

EXTROVERT OR INTROVERT?

Total extrovert, but getting to be more of a retiring type in his old age.

LAP CAT OR NOT?

Lap, chest, head, face, legs – he is not fussy about the body part, as long as he can sit on it.

OLD SOUL OR KITTEN AT HEART?

He was the floppiest, funniest kitten, but age has changed him. He's becoming a bit more of a cranky old man now.

EXPLORER OR HOMEBODY?

Total homebody.

LAZY OR ACTIVE?

So lazy!

DOGS – FRIEND OR FOE?

Not a huge fan. However, he is very good pals with the family of possums that live in the backyard. He sits out there with them for hours.

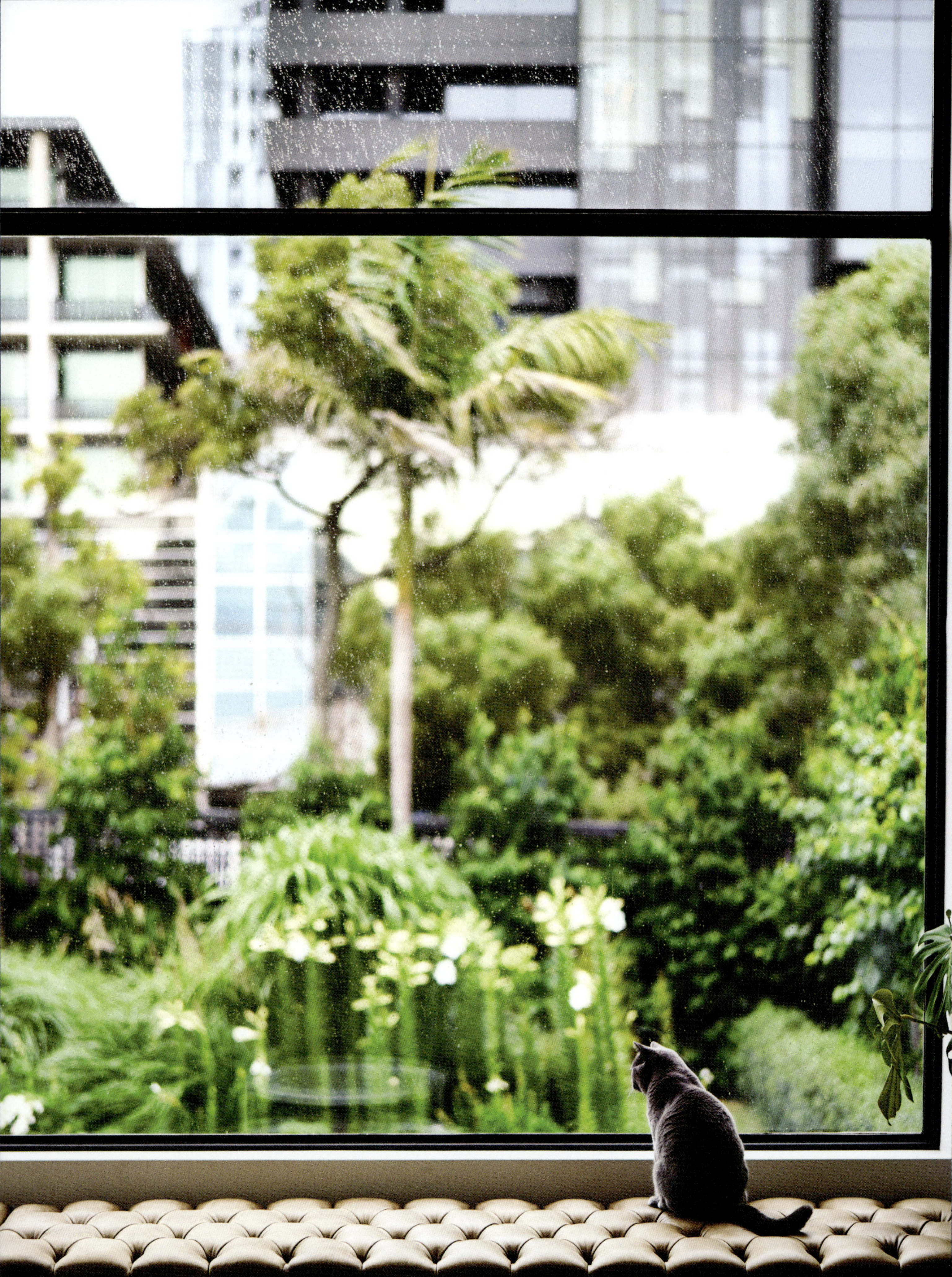

WINSTON FLUFFYBUM

ARCHITECTS: KATHRYN ROBSON AND CHRIS RAK / ROBSON RAK ARCHITECTS

Winston Fluffybum is a constant warm companion who brightens the days of the large family he lives with. A twelve-month-old blue British shorthair, he is super low-maintenance, sleeping around twenty hours per day. Perhaps it is this somnolence that makes Winston so exceedingly tolerant – even allowing the family's three children to pick him up and carry him around like a baby. He doesn't appear to hold such humiliations against them, though, as he generally chooses to sleep snuggled up with one of the kids at night. He seems to prefer them when they are asleep!

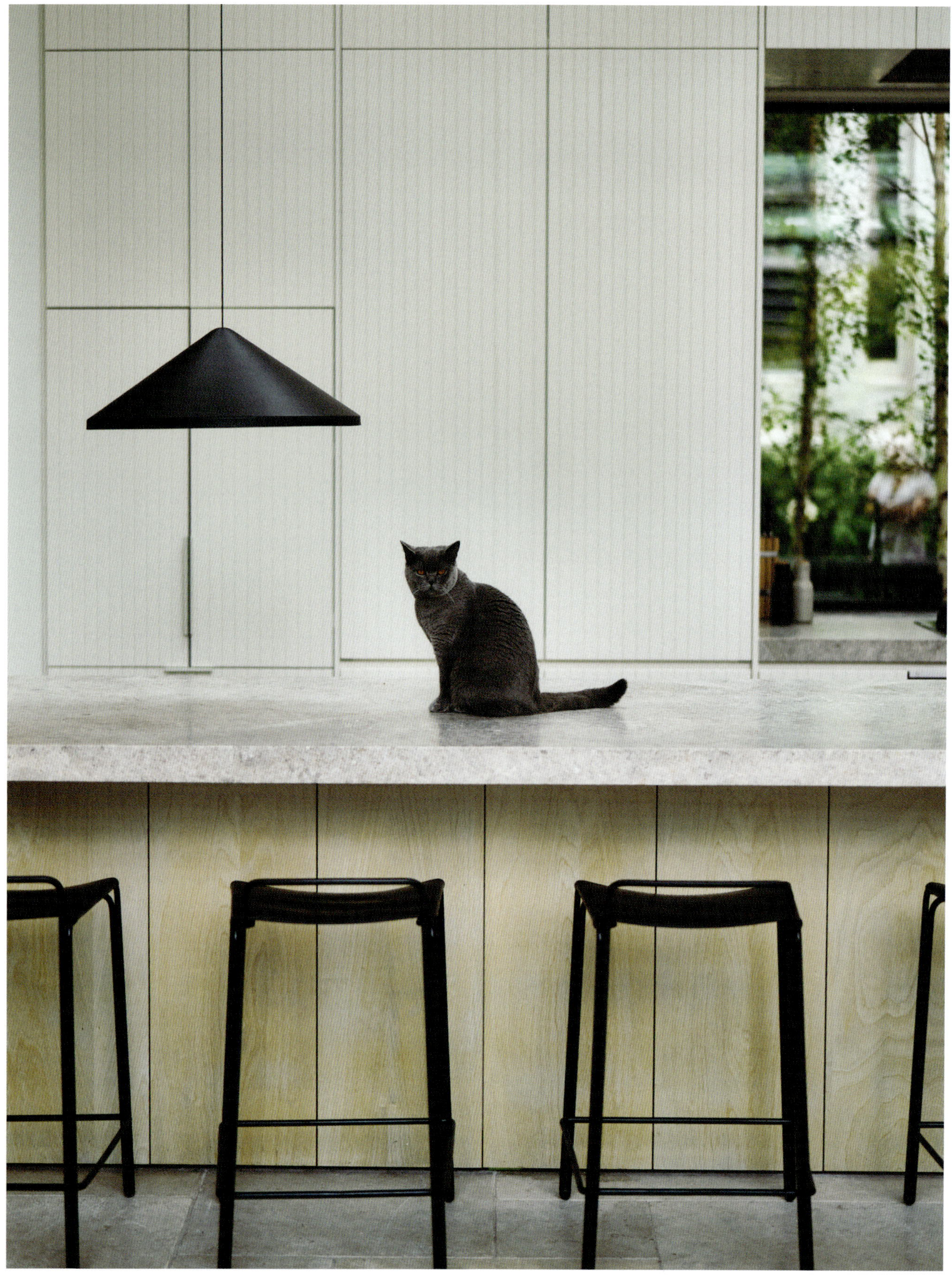

Architects: Kathryn Robson and Chris Rak / Robson Rak Architects

Winston lives in a late 19th-century Italianate residence with a modern renovation at the rear. It's a warm and generous home with lots of separate yet functional spaces to accommodate a growing family.

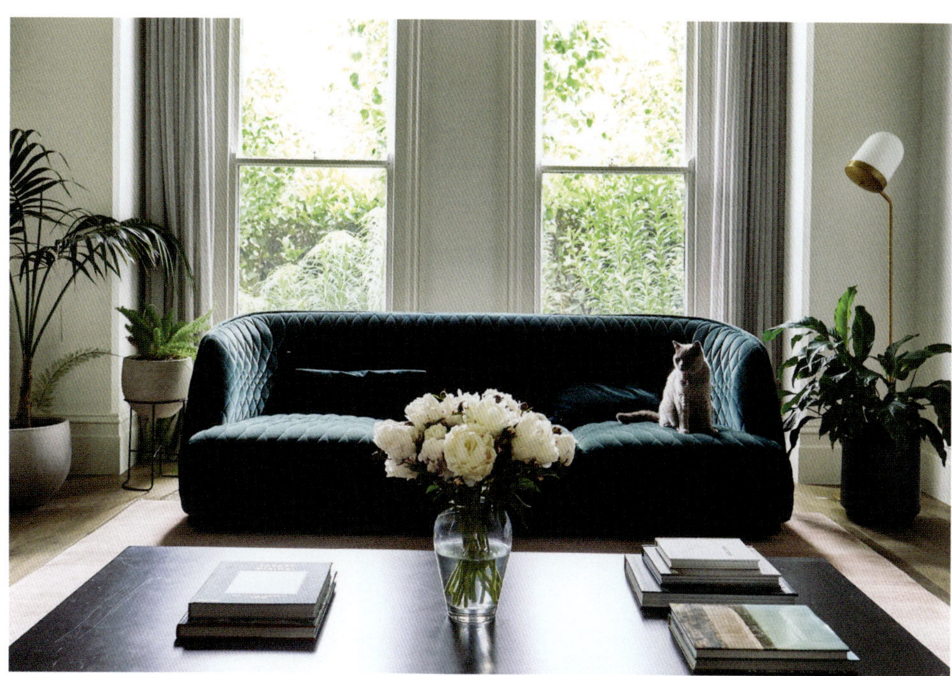

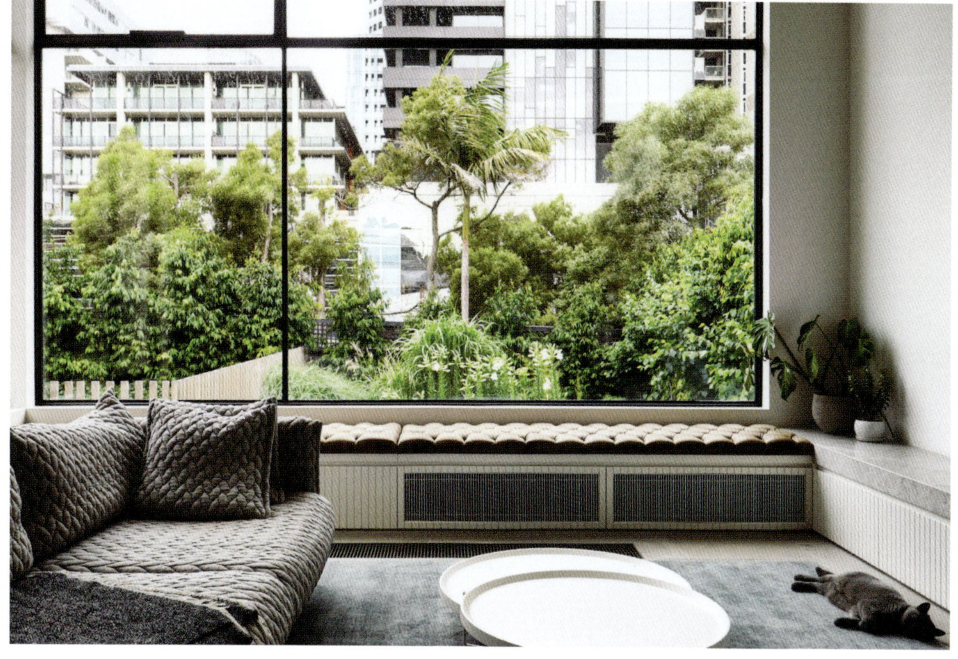

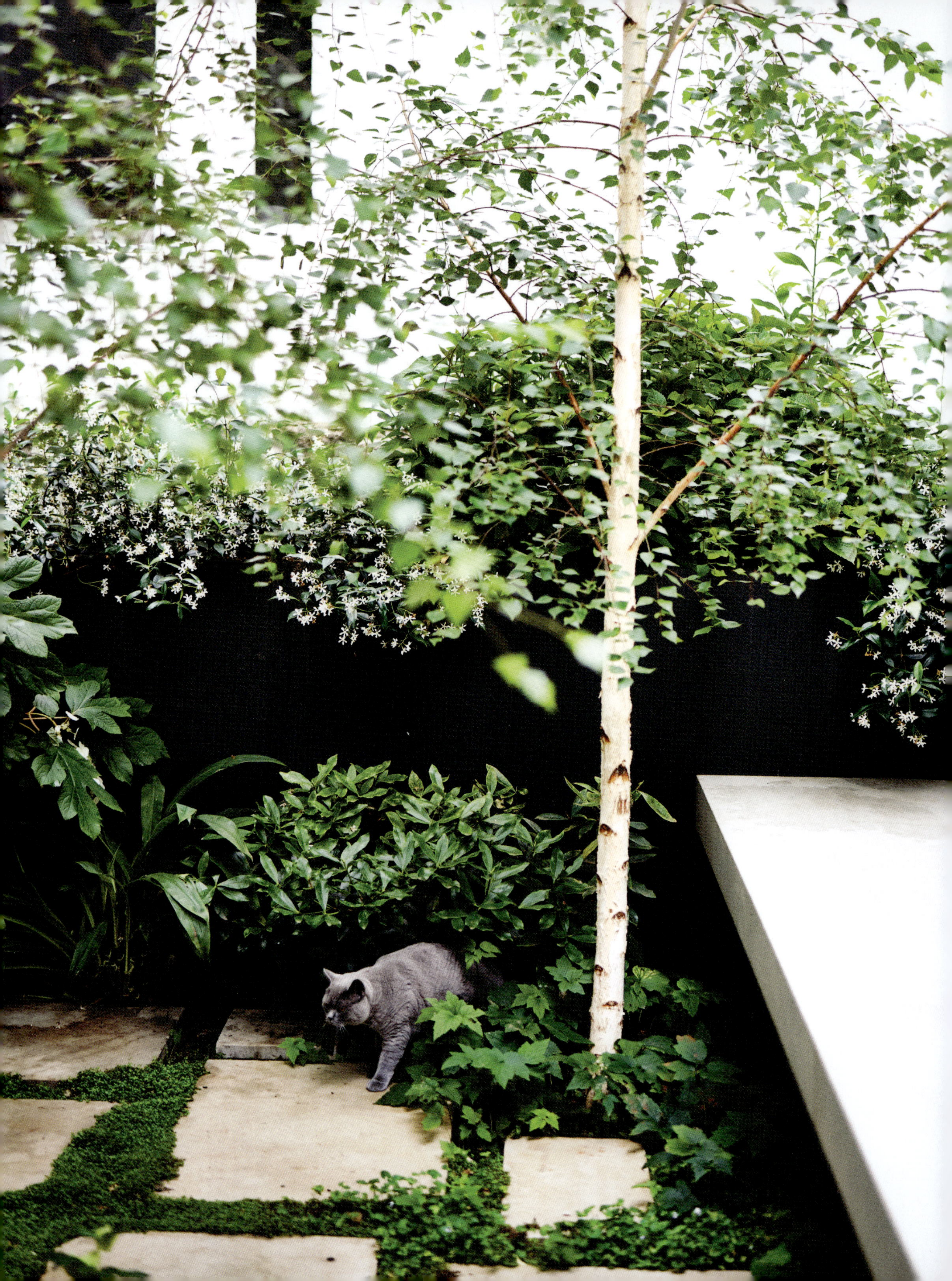

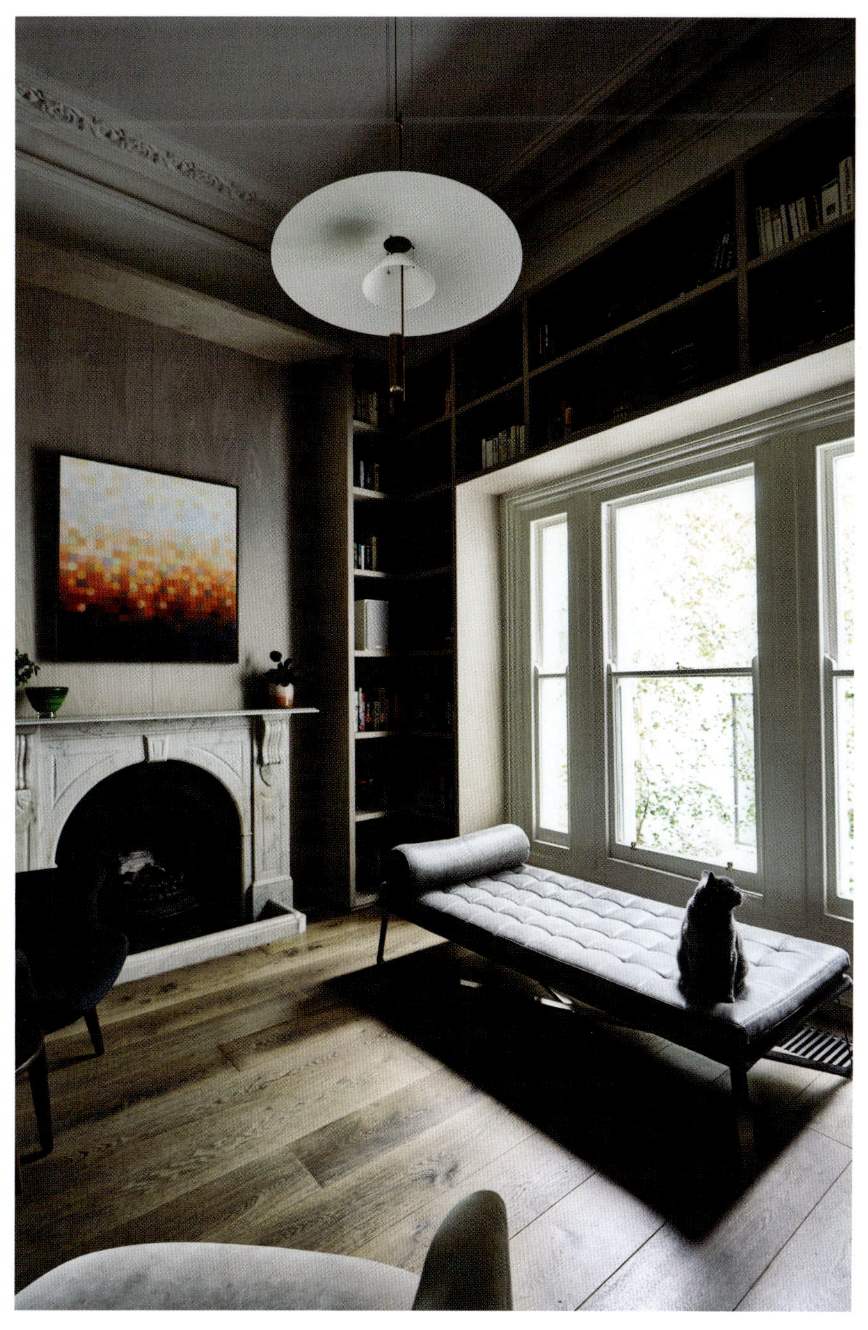

The family didn't have a need for the home's original formal dining room, so they transformed the space into a library. It's one of the most tranquil rooms in the house and is a beautiful place to relax with a book.

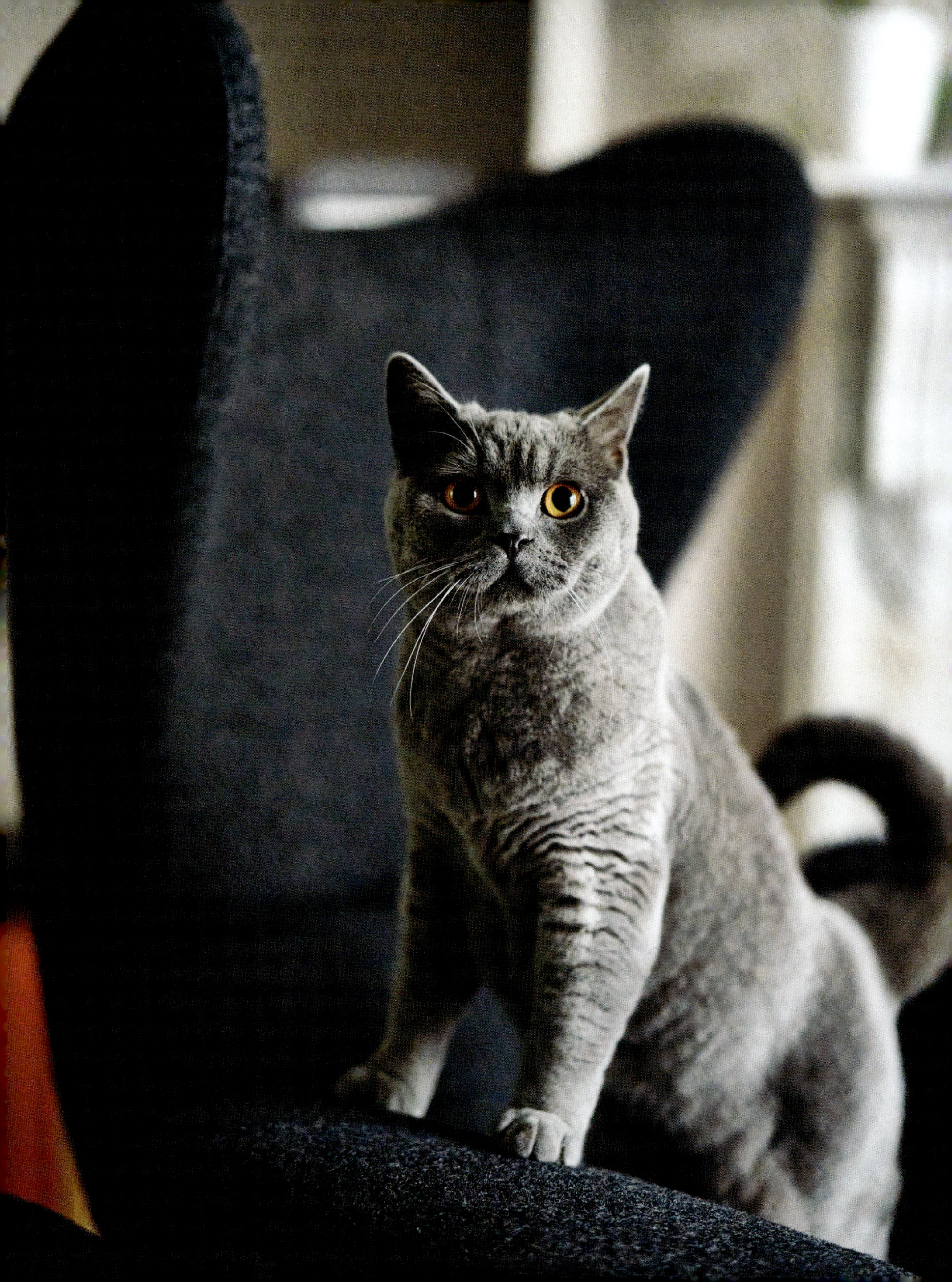

Q&A

DIVA OR DEVOTED FRIEND?

Elements of both. He maintains a sense of independence, but likes someone to be around to supervise it.

EXTROVERT OR INTROVERT?

He is quietly self-assured rather than extrovert or introvert.

LAP CAT OR NOT?

Not. While he must always be near his humans, he maintains a strict 'no cuddling' policy.

OLD SOUL OR KITTEN AT HEART?

Kitten at heart and everywhere else too.

EXPLORER OR HOMEBODY?

Winston likes to think of himself as an explorer and hunter – although his most triumphant catch to date is a blowfly.

LAZY OR ACTIVE?

Both. He snoozes the majority of the time, but when he's awake he plays vigorously. He loves to play fetch with a screwed-up ball of paper, so he is the ideal cat for a family that actually wanted a dog.

DOGS – FRIEND OR FOE?

He lives a rather sheltered existence and has never met one.

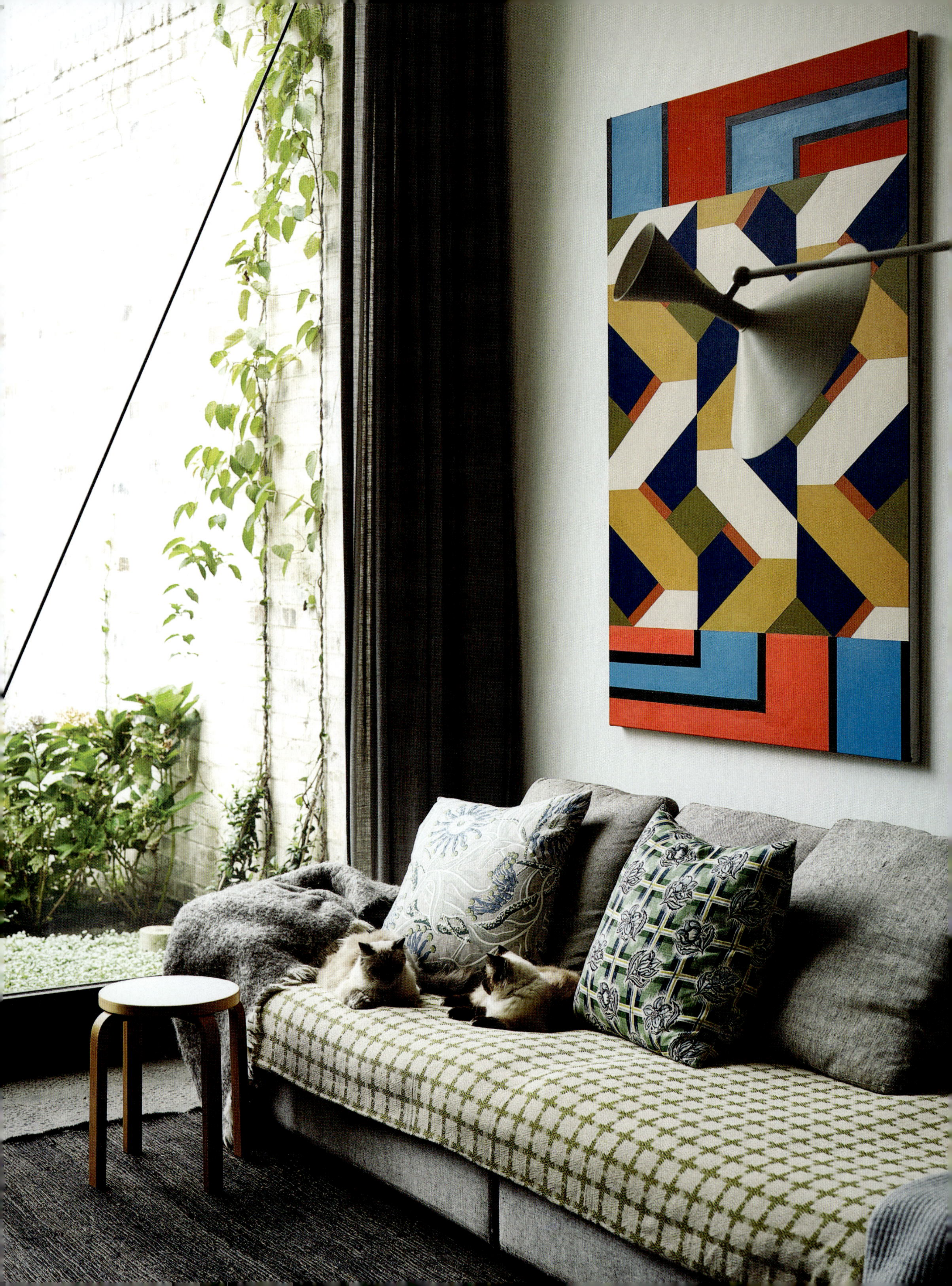

WOLFGANG, MINNIE AND ZAZA

ARCHITECT: EMMA REES-RAAIJMAKERS / ATELIER DAU

Wolfgang, Minnie and Zaza complement the madness of their chaotic family. In addition to the three cats, there are five humans living in the household, plus Alfred the miniature dachshund. The family's front door is always open, as visitors are frequently popping in and out. Despite the open-door policy, the cats remain happily housebound. Guests love the cats because they're so inquisitive and friendly. Zaza, a timid six-year-old calico rescue cat, has been around the longest. When the family decided to get a feline companion for her, their intention was to adopt one ragdoll kitten – but when they saw Wolfgang and Minnie, they realised they couldn't leave either of them behind. All three cats (even Zaza in her own eccentric way) are welcoming and engaging, and there's never a dull moment when they are around.

The trio's heritage-listed terrace home had only two bedrooms and a half-finished bathroom when their family moved in. The house was in a dilapidated state but retained some of the original detailing, including ornate ceilings, windows with coloured glass, and kauri floorboards.

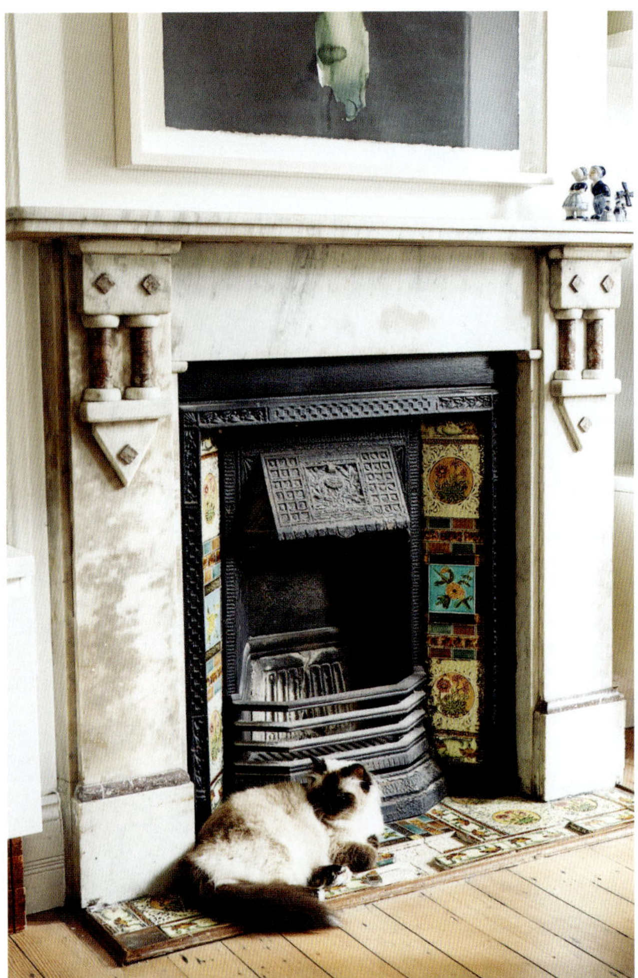

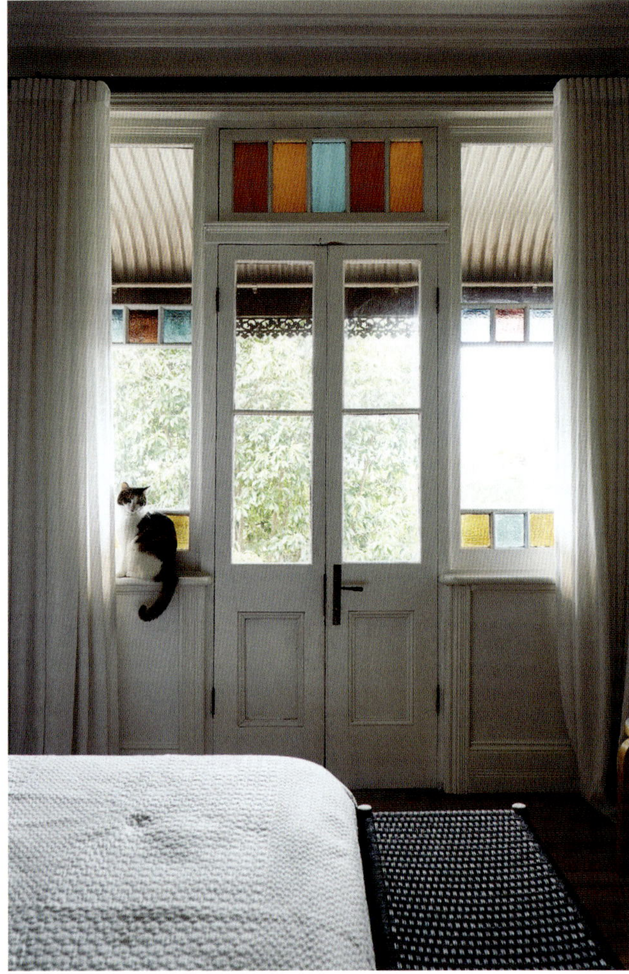

Architect: Emma Rees-Raaijmakers / Atelier DAU

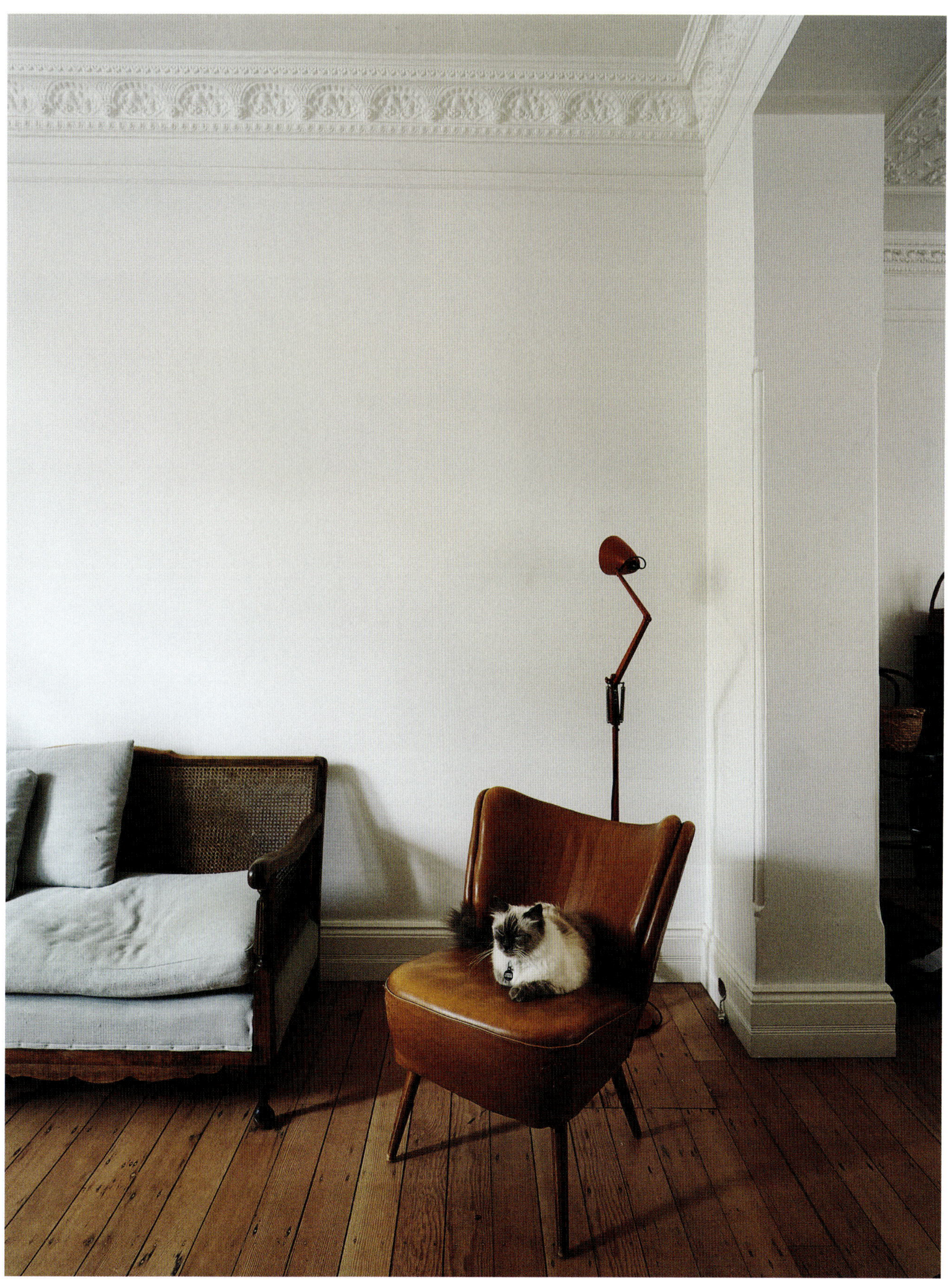

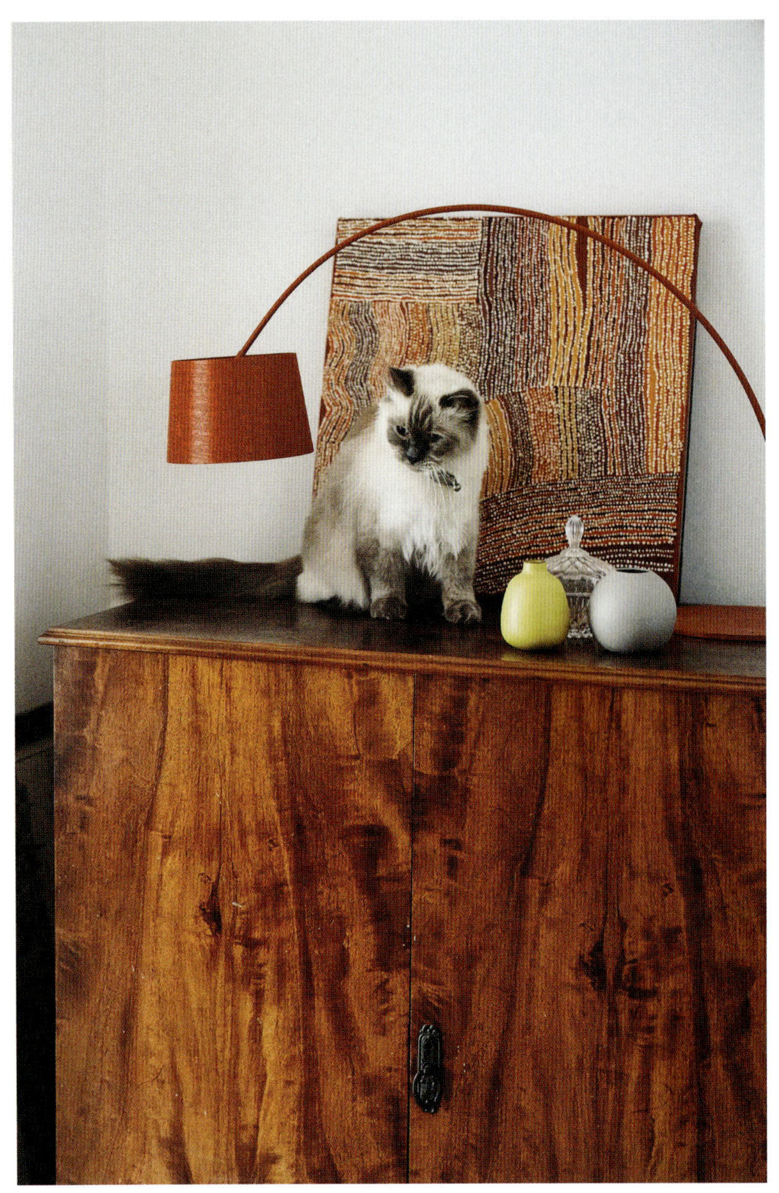

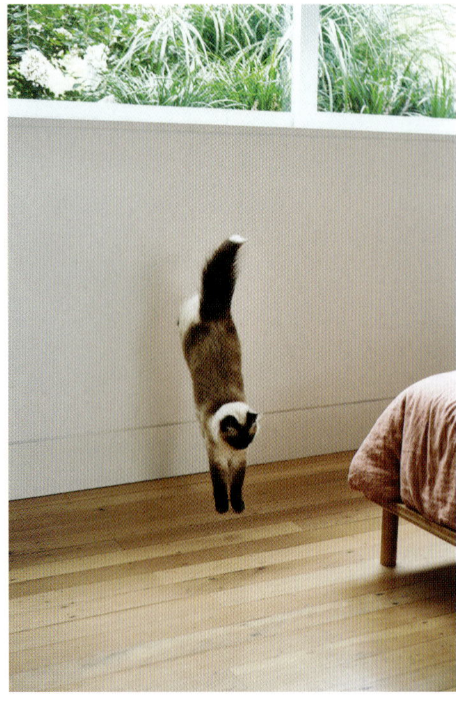

Architect: Emma Rees-Raaijmakers / Atelier DAU

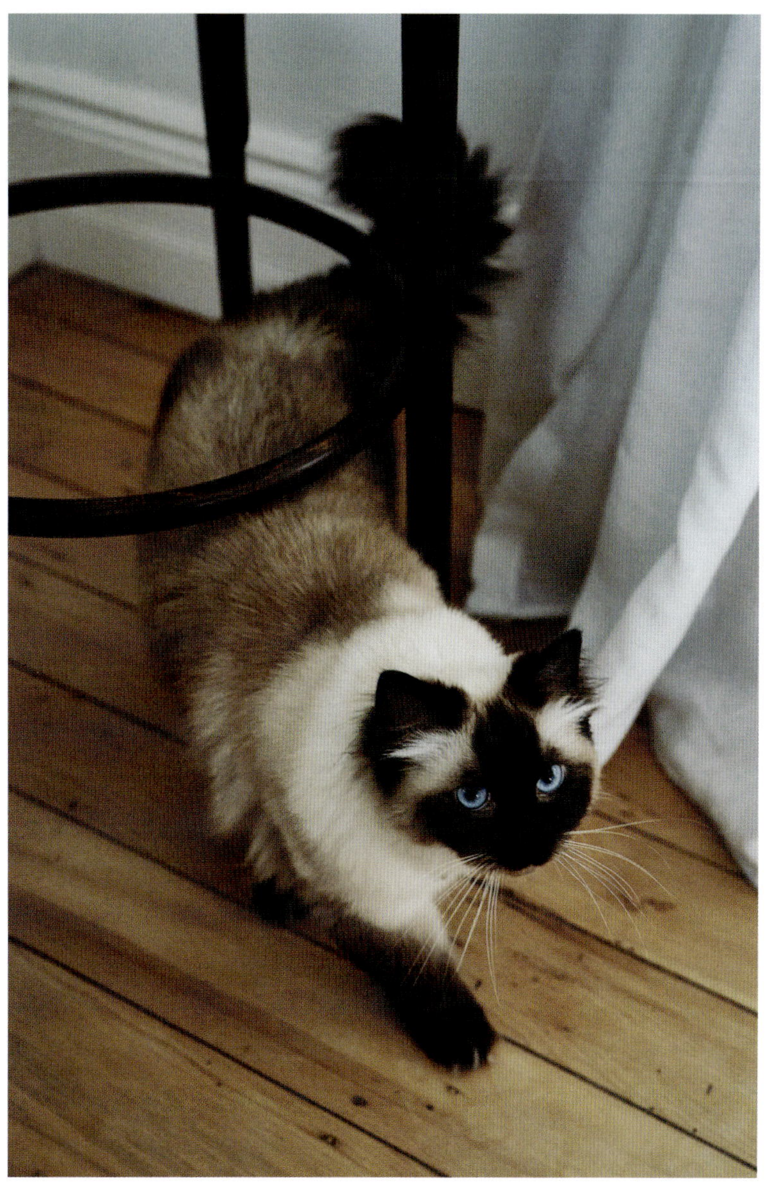

The home's palette is simple and timeless, providing an apt backdrop for a diverse collection of Australian and Dutch art and an eclectic assemblage of furniture. The place is brought to life by the sculptural spaces, the ornate detailing of the original terrace, the theatrics of the tall steel doors that open to the courtyard, and the views of nature at every turn.

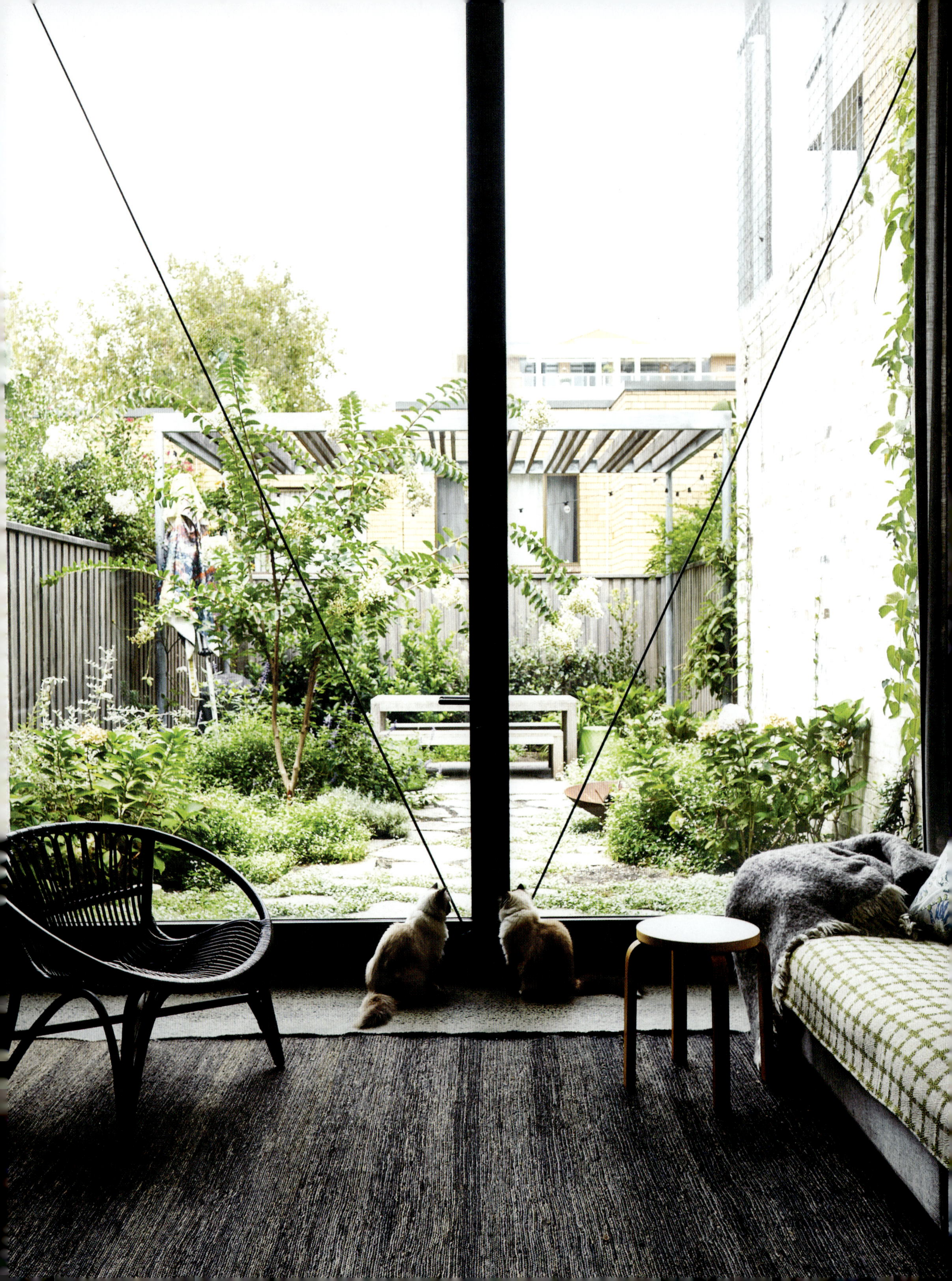

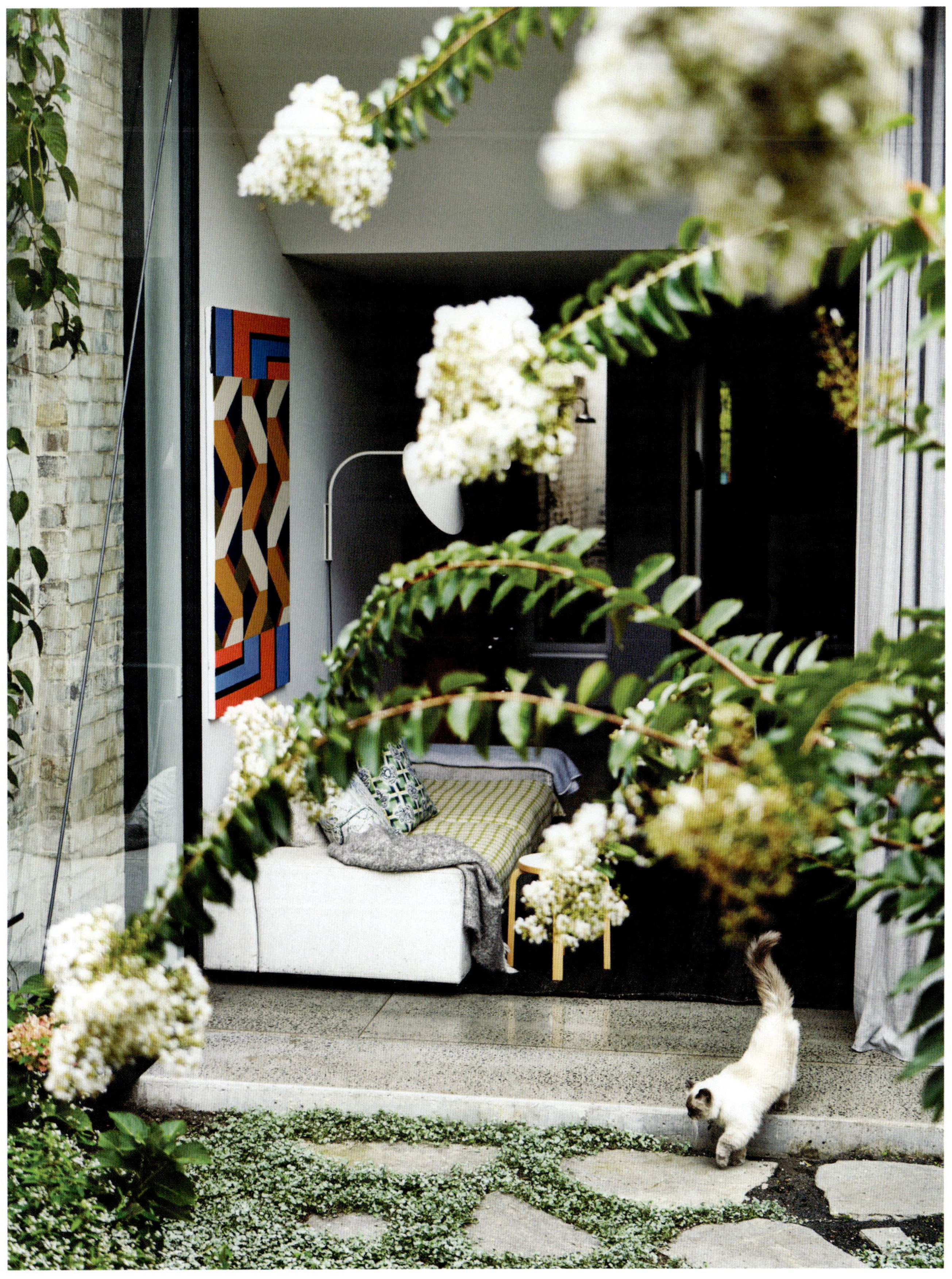

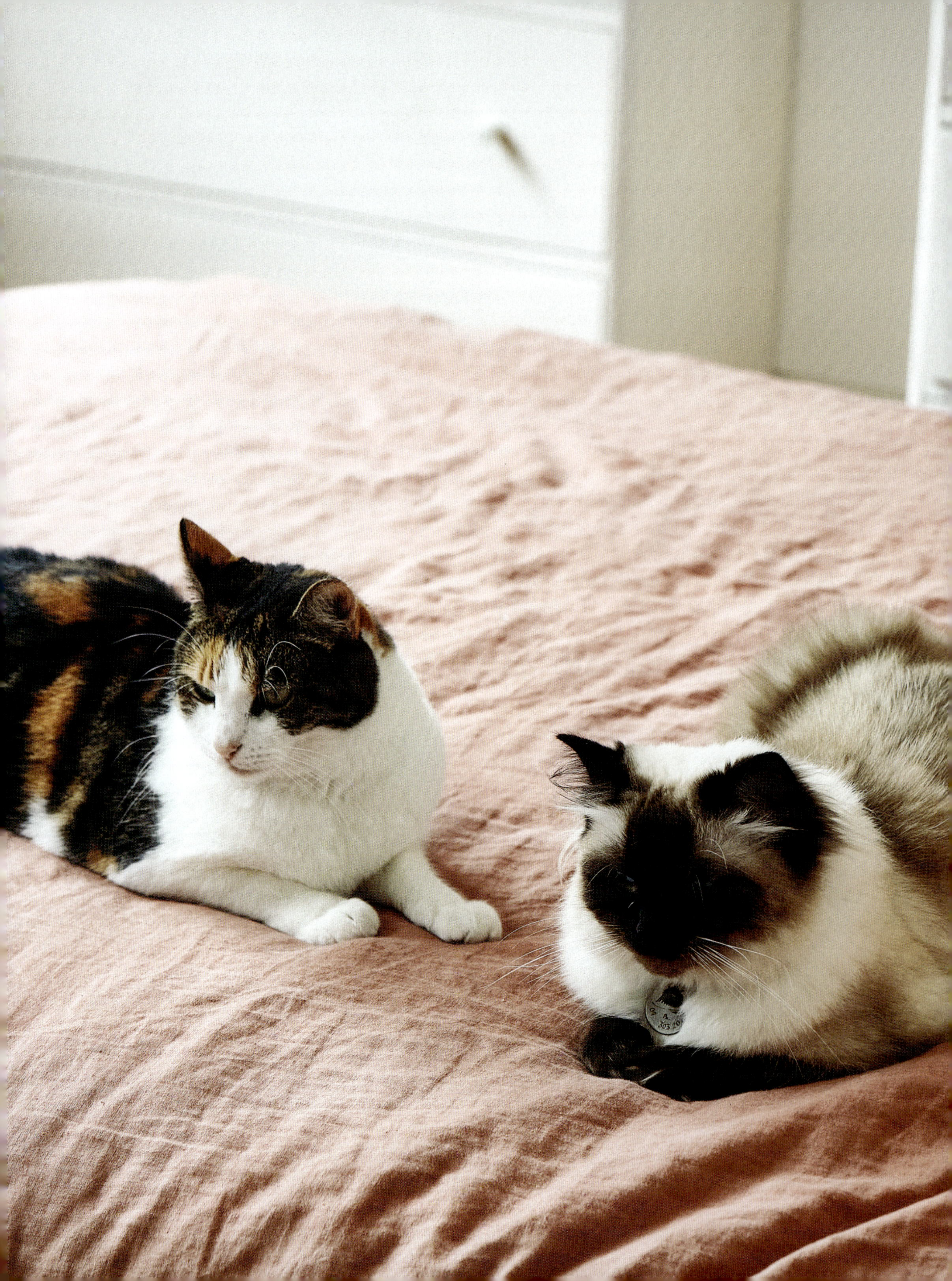

Q&A

DIVAS OR DEVOTED FRIENDS?
Devoted friends.

EXTROVERTS OR INTROVERTS?
Wolfgang: Extrovert. A bit too cool for school.
Minnie: More introvert. She's rather regal and aloof.
Zaza: Introvert. She was timid from day one.

LAP CATS OR NOT?
Wolfgang: Lap cat. A real floppy doll.
Minnie: Lap cat – but only when she wants.
Zaza: Not. Though she's happy to sit beside you.

OLD SOULS OR KITTENS AT HEART?
Wolfgang: Old soul, but very playful.
Minnie: Old soul. She is super serious and won't tolerate silly antics from anyone.
Zaza: Old soul. She's wise, but has an air of vulnerability.

EXPLORERS OR HOMEBODIES?
Wolfgang: Explorer if he gets a chance to escape, but equally happy lounging about at home.
Minnie: Homebody.
Zaza: Occasionally escapes and goes off on an adventure.

LAZY OR ACTIVE?
Wolfgang: Bouts of both.
Minnie: Loves to sleep, but is not lazy as such.
Zaza: It's hard to be lazy when you're always on alert.

DOGS – FRIEND OR FOE?
Wolfgang: Friend. He enjoys a gentle rumble with Alfred (the dachshund).
Minnie: Foe-ish. She's just not interested in their antics.
Zaza: Foe. No, thank you very much.

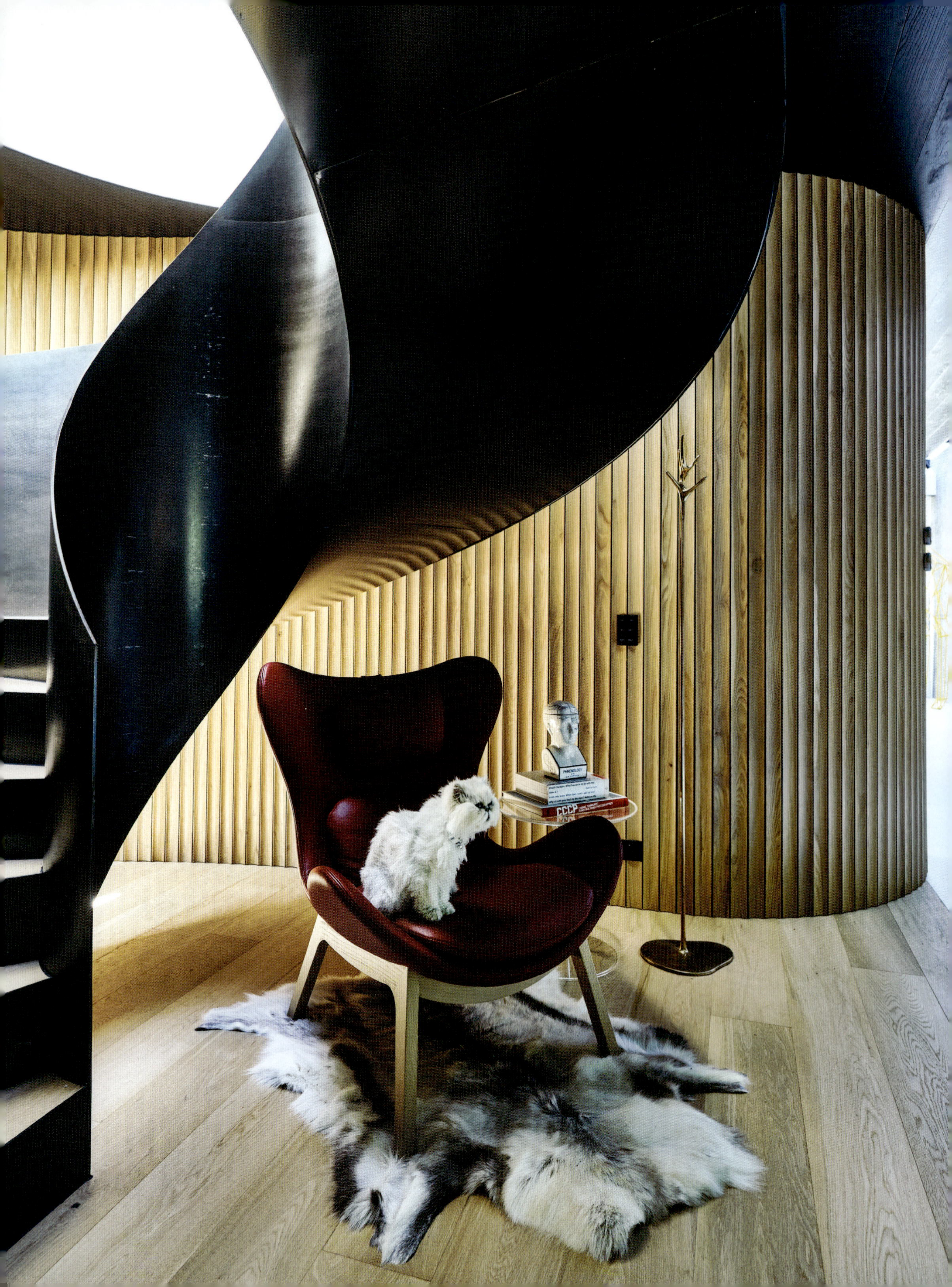

HERCULES

ARCHITECT: BILLY KAVELLARIS / KAVELLARIS URBAN DESIGN (KUD)

Hercules was a gift for his owner's thirty-fifth birthday. Collectively, the family decided that they needed the love of a cat – specifically, a cat who also wanted to be loved. This led them to select a chinchilla, a Persian breed that has silky silvery hair, green eyes, and a docile and affectionate nature. Now nine years old, Hercules is happy to have time and space to himself when the family is out, but he is equally content to lounge with them on the couch when they are home. He often seeks out the security and warmth of his owner and enjoys nothing better than lying on his chest, relishing the feel of his human's heartbeat.

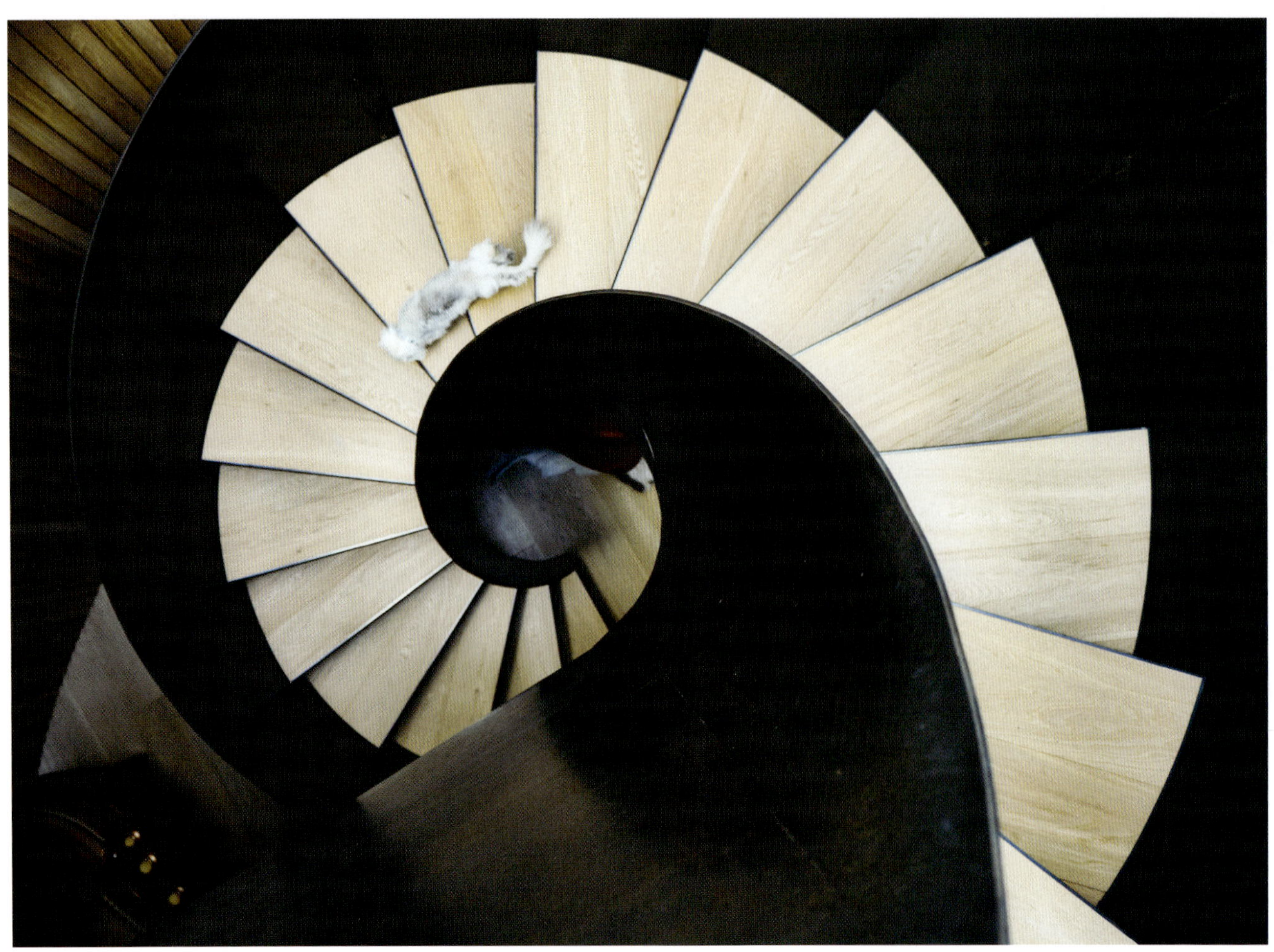

The owner of this home is also the building's architect. He wanted to design a house that reflected his family's values and aspirations; where they not only live among the art they have collected, but where the architecture itself is a work of liveable art. There are plenty of nooks for Hercules to explore and inhabit.

Architect: Billy Kavellaris / Kavellaris Urban Design (KUD)

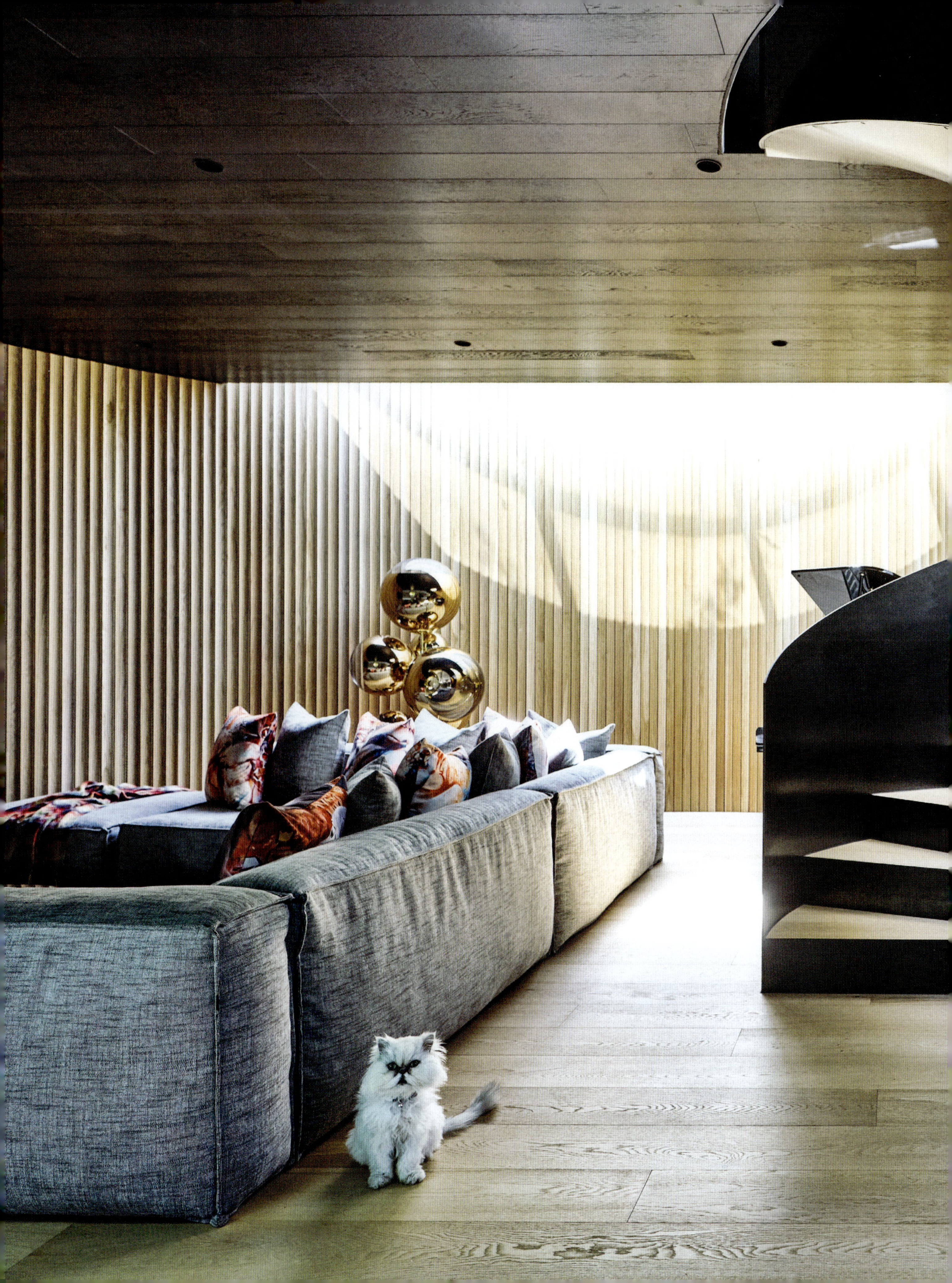

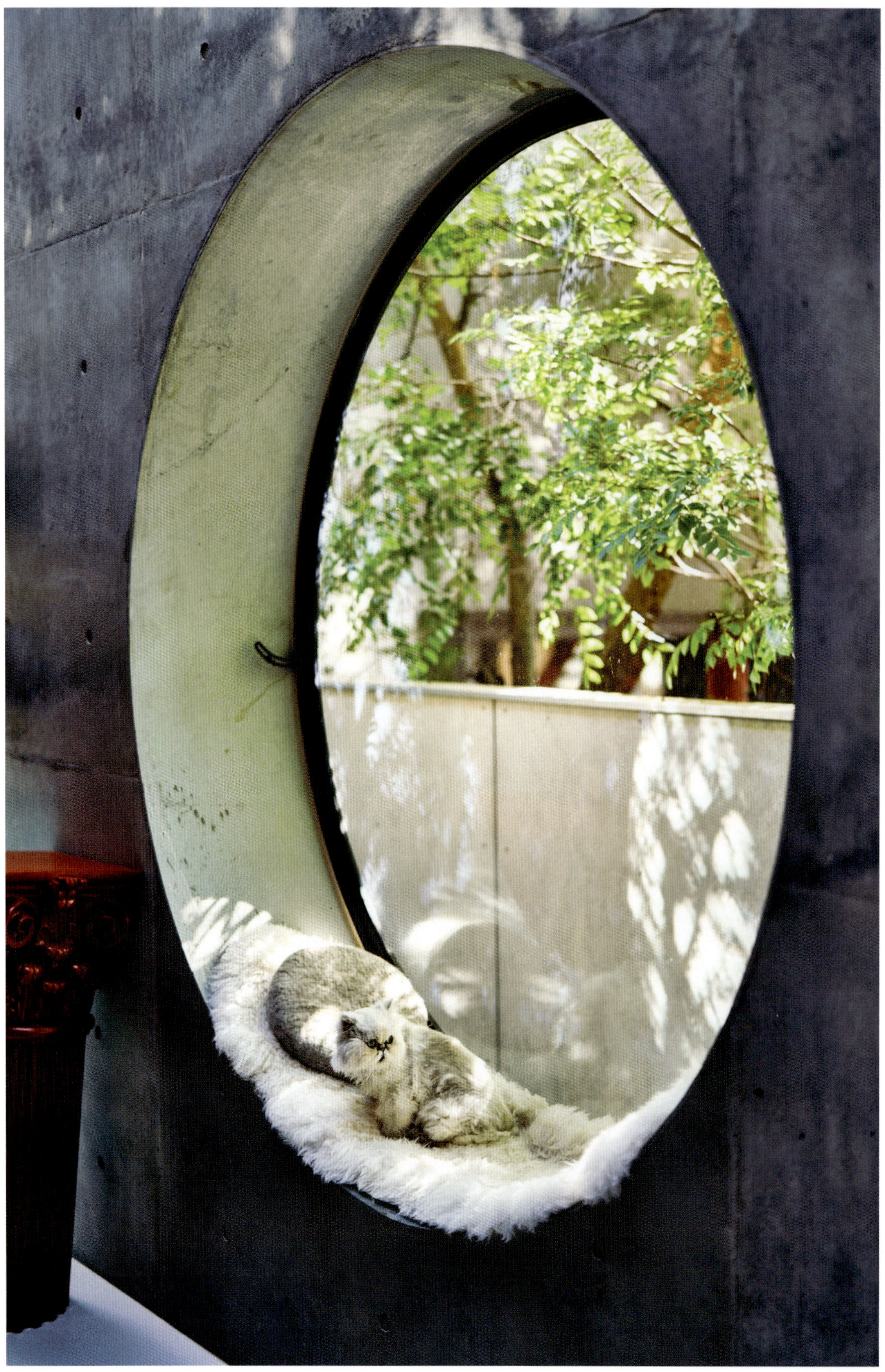

Architect: Billy Kavellaris / Kavellaris Urban Design (KUD)

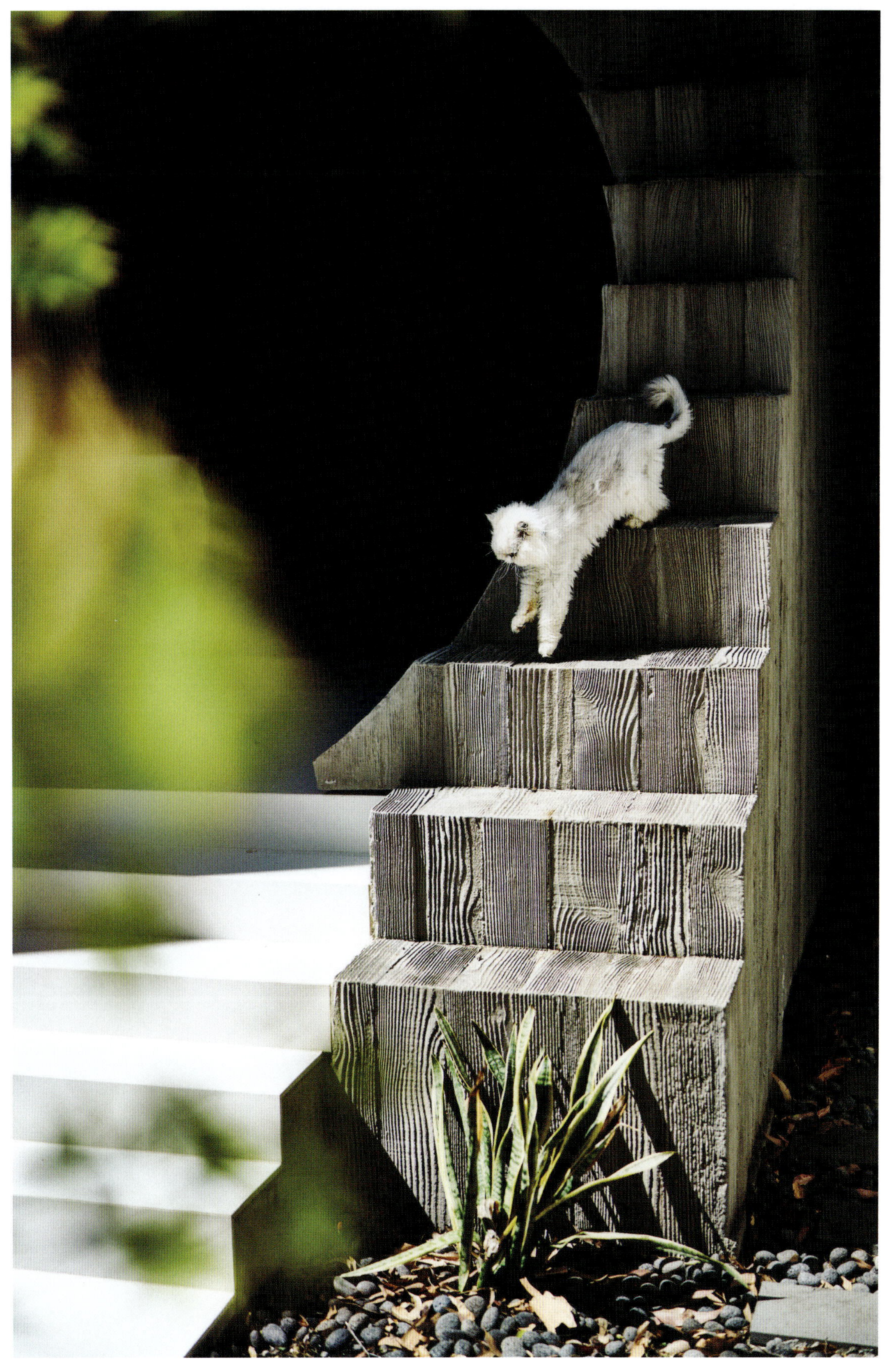

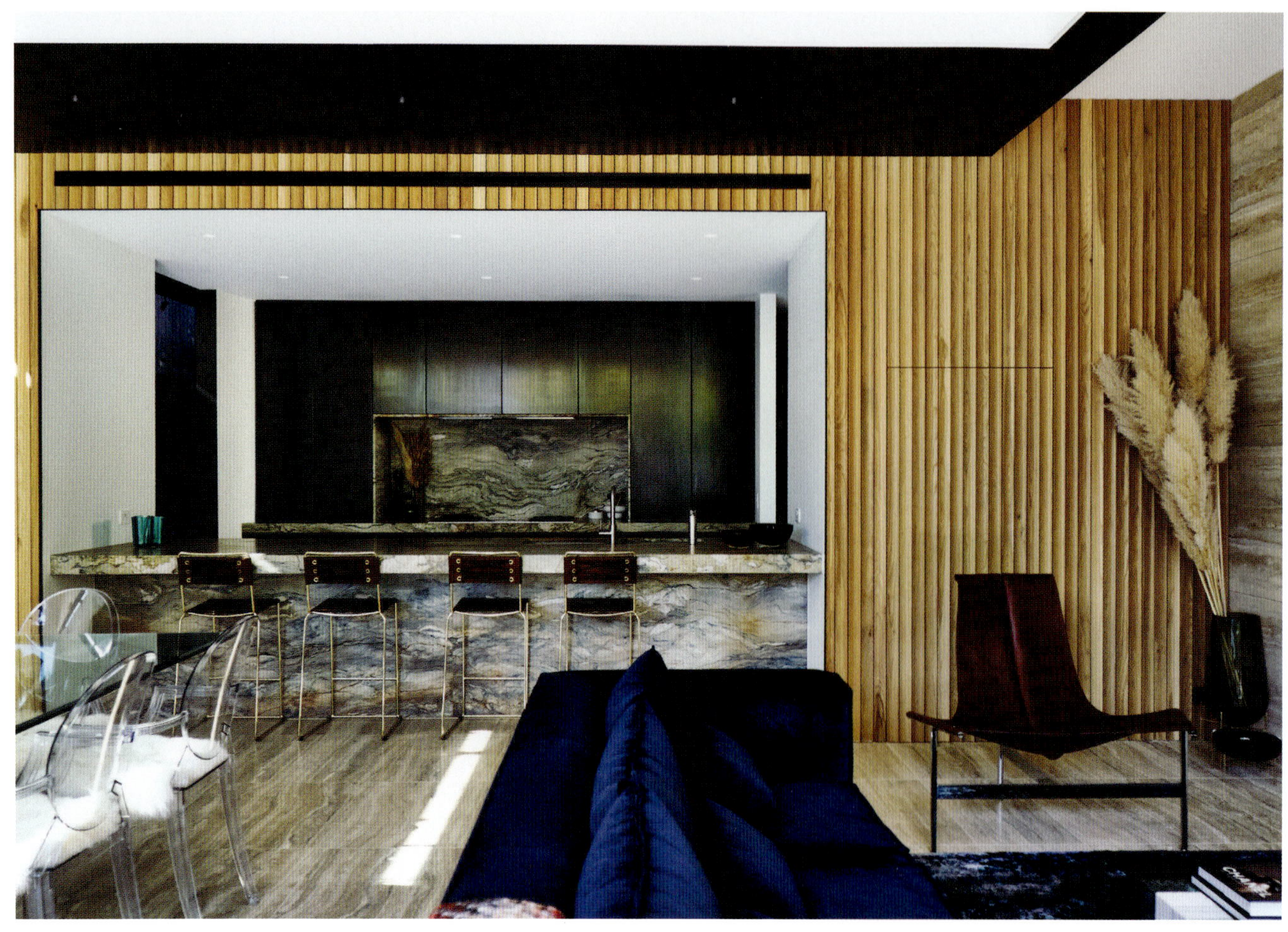

In choosing materials for the home, the owner wanted to enhance and balance the tension between contrasting elements – organic and industrial, textured and smooth, tactile and abstract – in order to create an engaging space and building.

Architect: Billy Kavellaris / Kavellaris Urban Design (KUD)

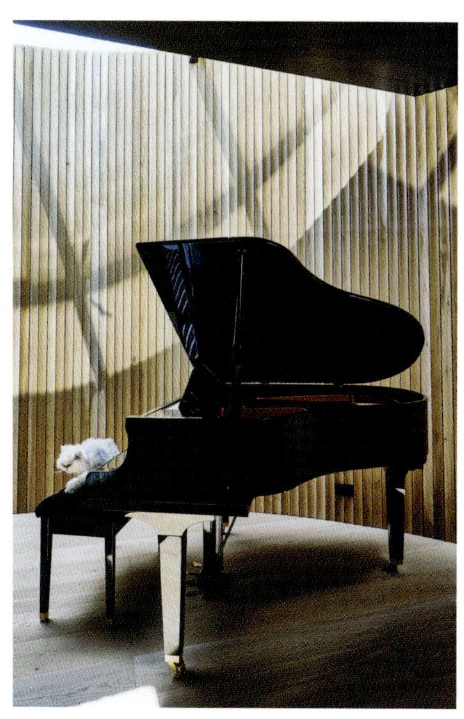

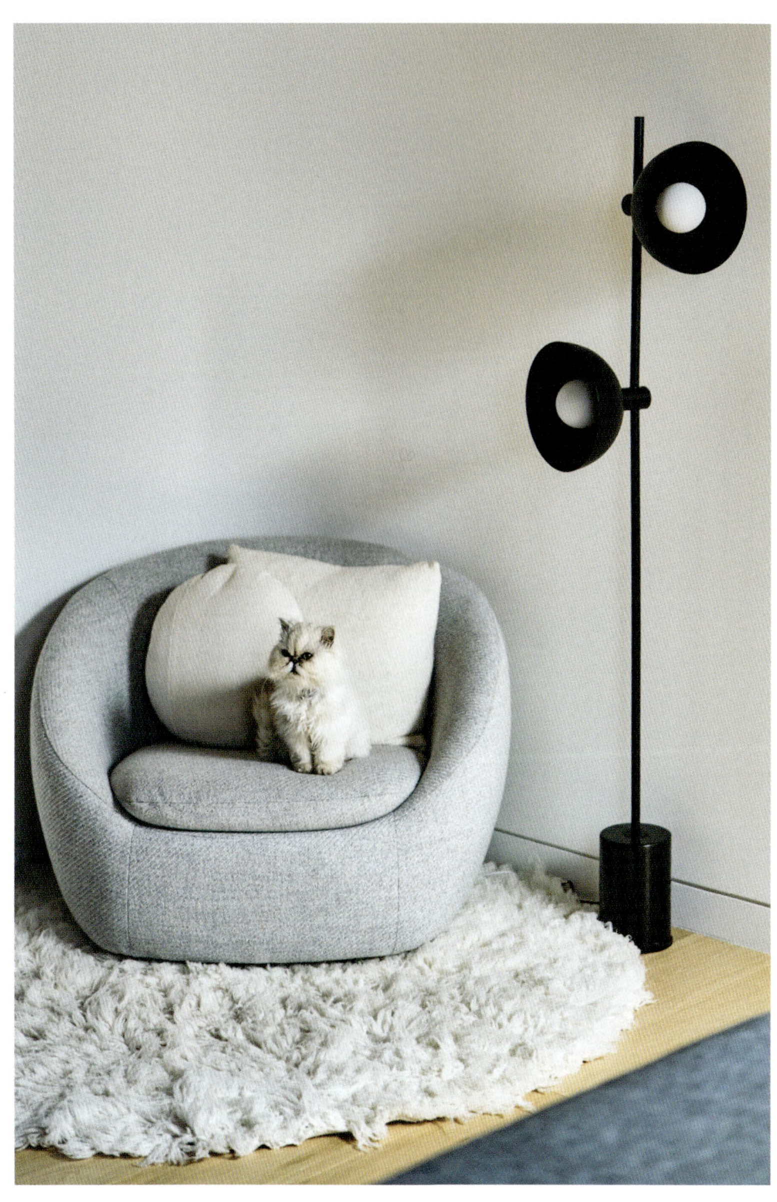

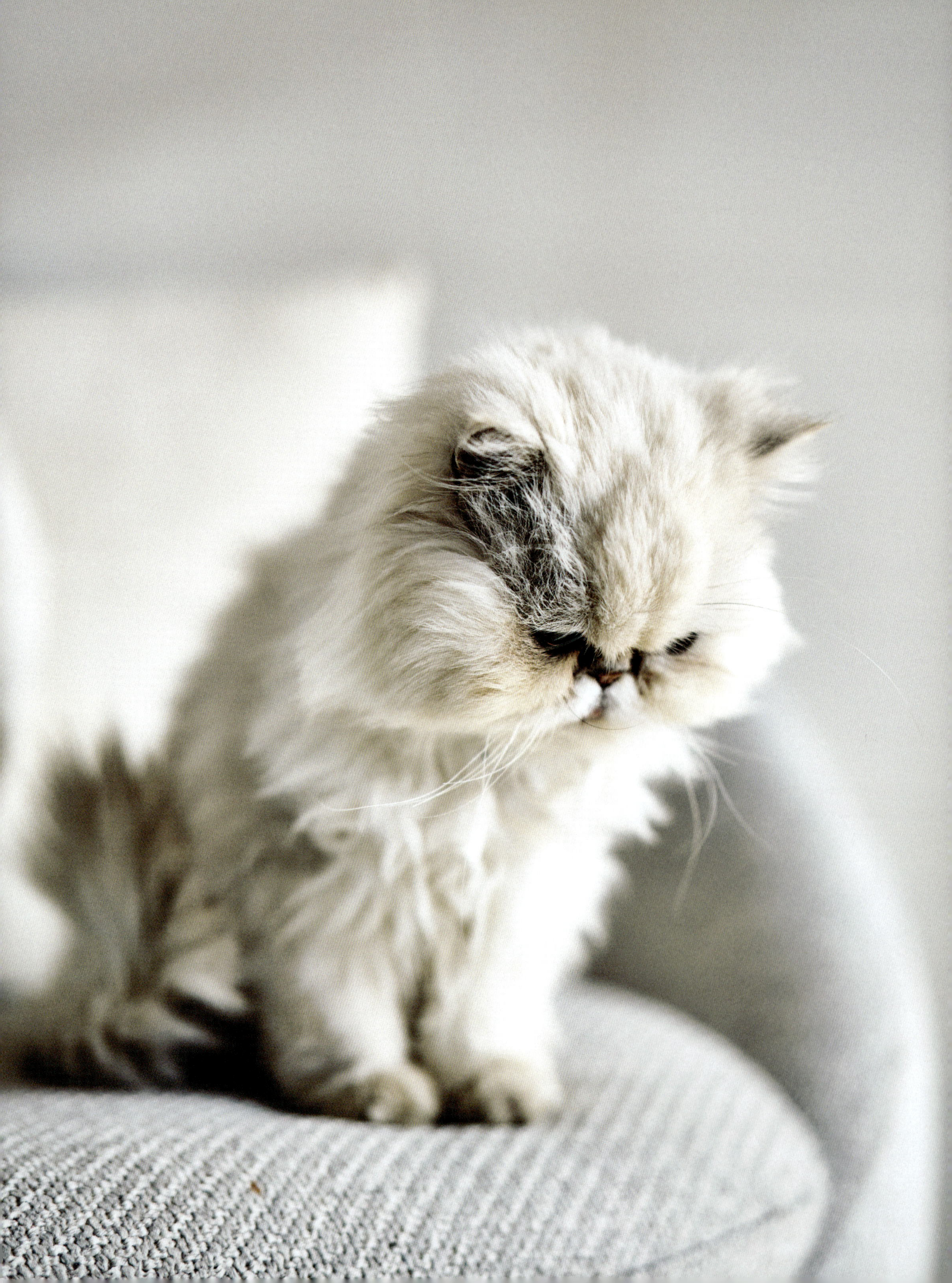

Q&A

DIVA OR DEVOTED FRIEND?
Devoted friend.

EXTROVERT OR INTROVERT?
Introvert.

LAP CAT OR NOT?
Lap cat.

OLD SOUL OR KITTEN AT HEART?
Old soul.

EXPLORER OR HOMEBODY?
Homebody.

LAZY OR ACTIVE?
Lazy.

DOGS – FRIEND OR FOE?
Friend.

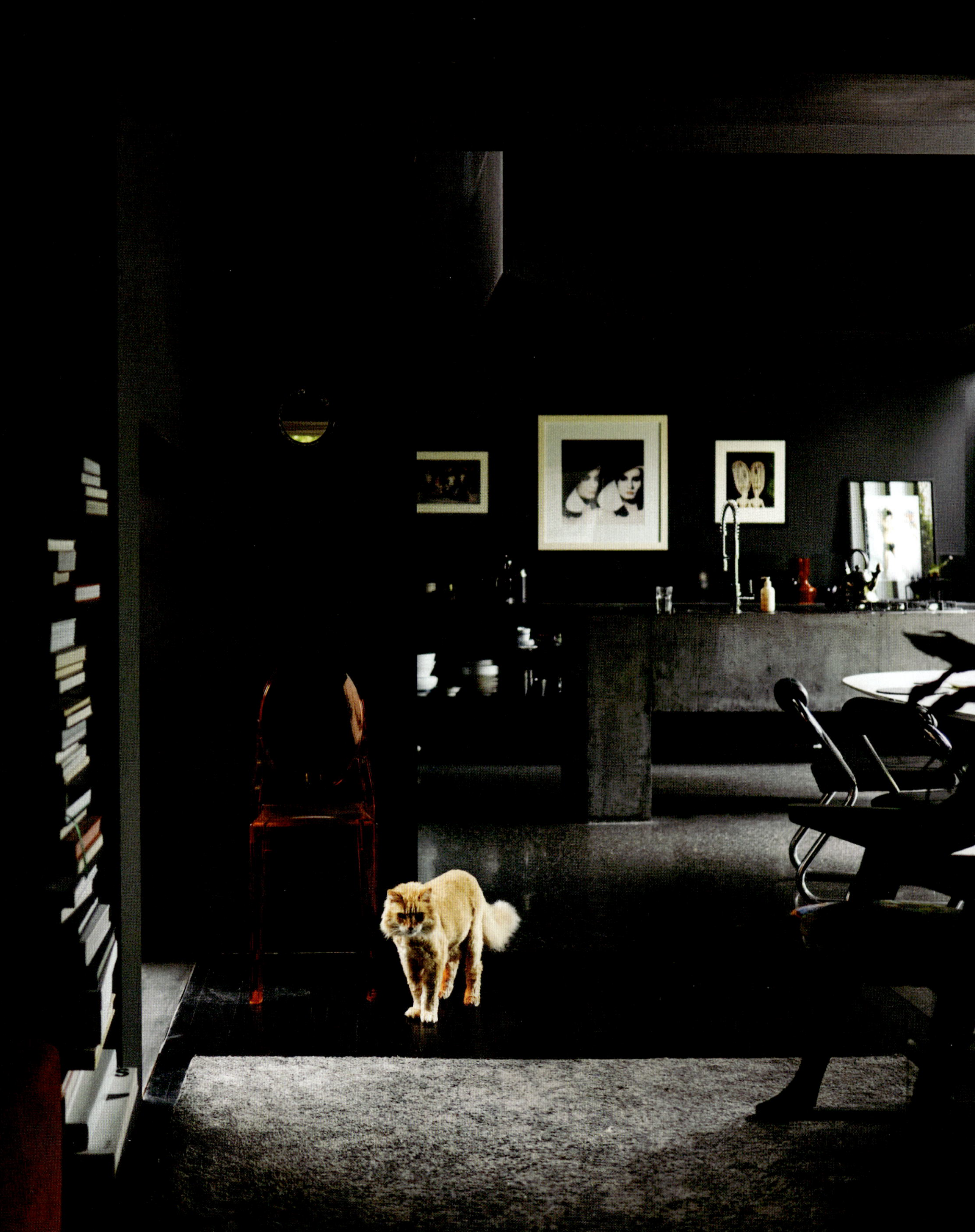

HARVEY CRAFTI

ARCHITECT: ROBERT SIMEONI / ROBERT SIMEONI ARCHITECTS

Harvey Crafti's owners inherited him from their son after he moved to Berlin, and Harvey quickly became a beloved member of his new household. He is affectionately referred to as a Canadian mountain cat because of his impressive mane, but he is, in fact, a domestic ginger tabby whose domain is exclusively indoors. Nowadays, Harvey prefers to hang out on the couch in the living room, but will dash to the kitchen if he hears someone opening the door of the pantry where his treats are kept. Harvey and his owners are perfectly suited: he tends to sleep a lot, as do they.

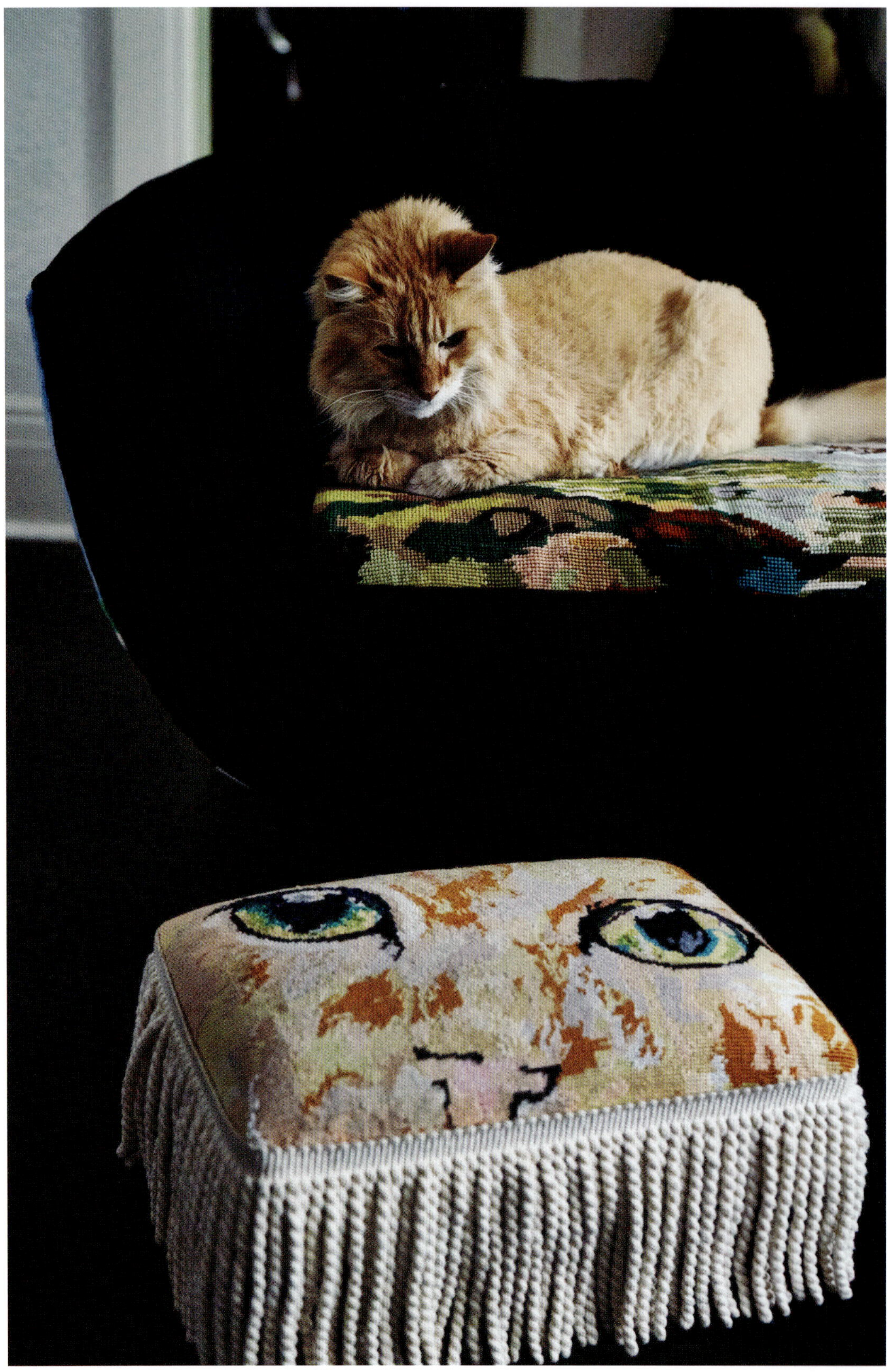

Architect: Robert Simeoni / Robert Simeoni Architects

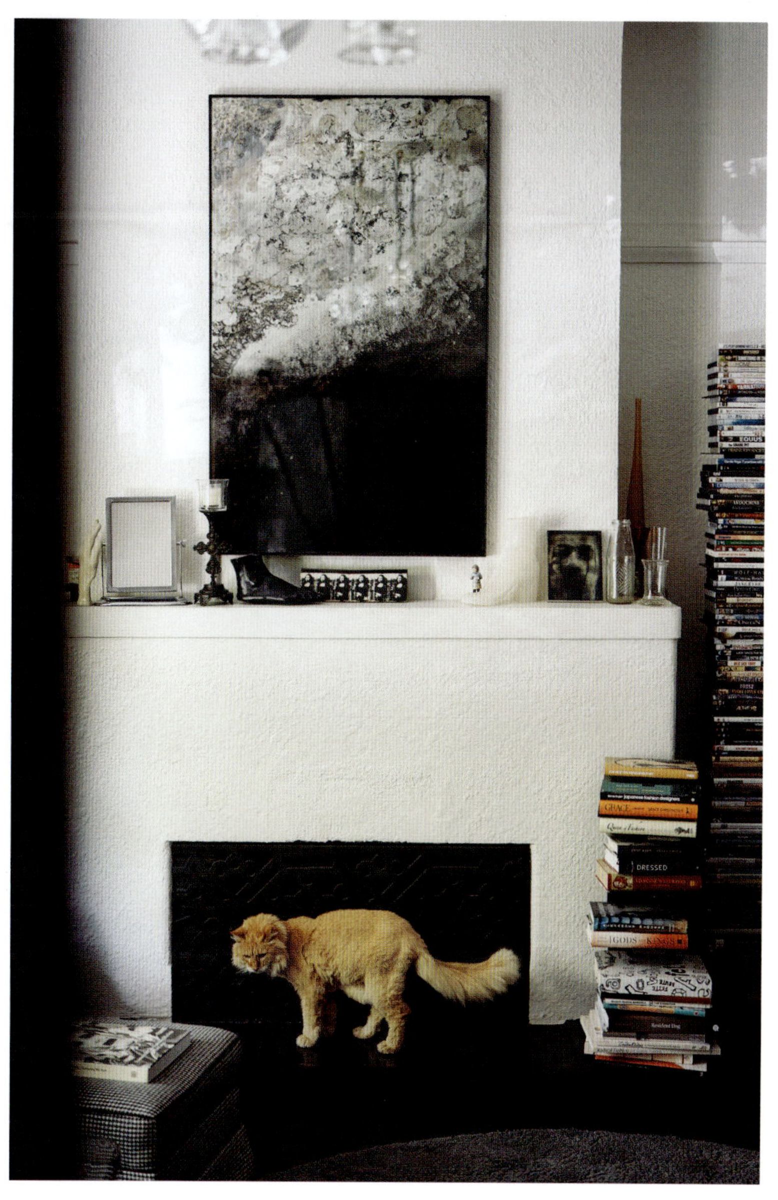

The owner of this home – an architecture writer – converted the original mid-1930s duplex into a single residence. The style is very European, with touches of Milan and Antwerp.

Harvey's likeness is featured on several items around the home, even appearing on a custom ottoman designed by Suzie Stanford.

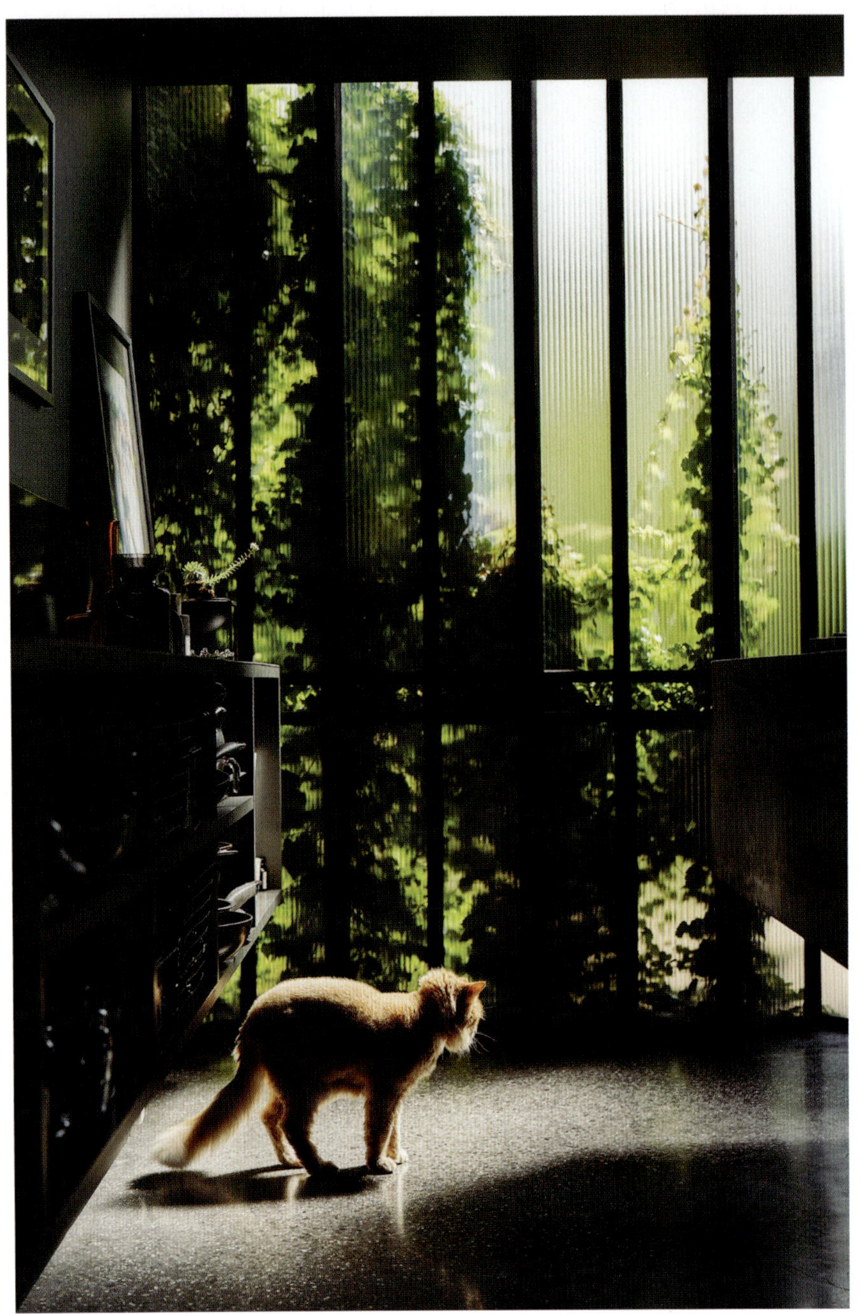

The striking windows were inspired by Pierre Chareau's *Maison de Verre* (House of Glass). The dark and moody interiors call attention to the verdant garden on the other side of the glass.

Architect: Robert Simeoni / Robert Simeoni Architects

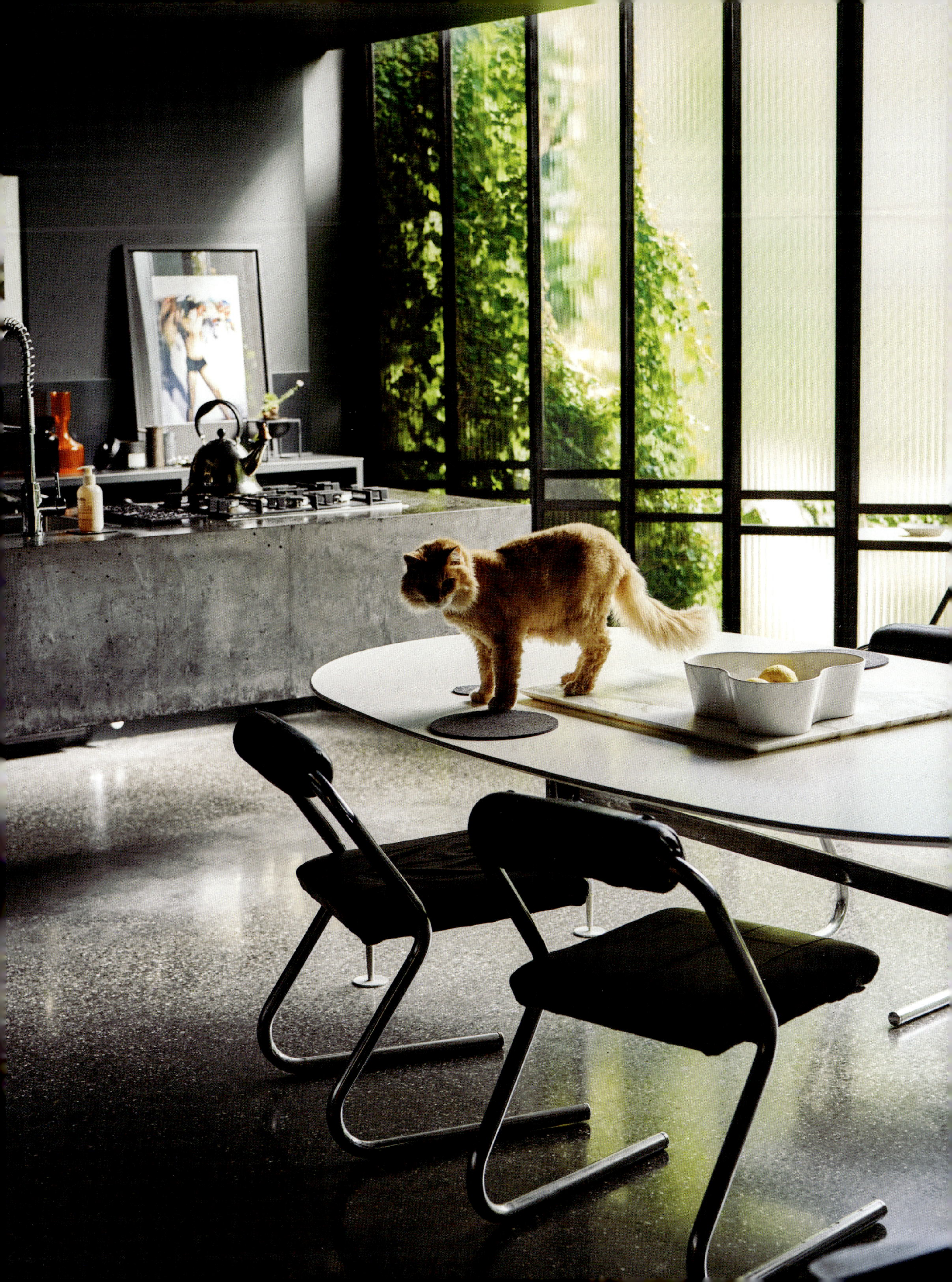

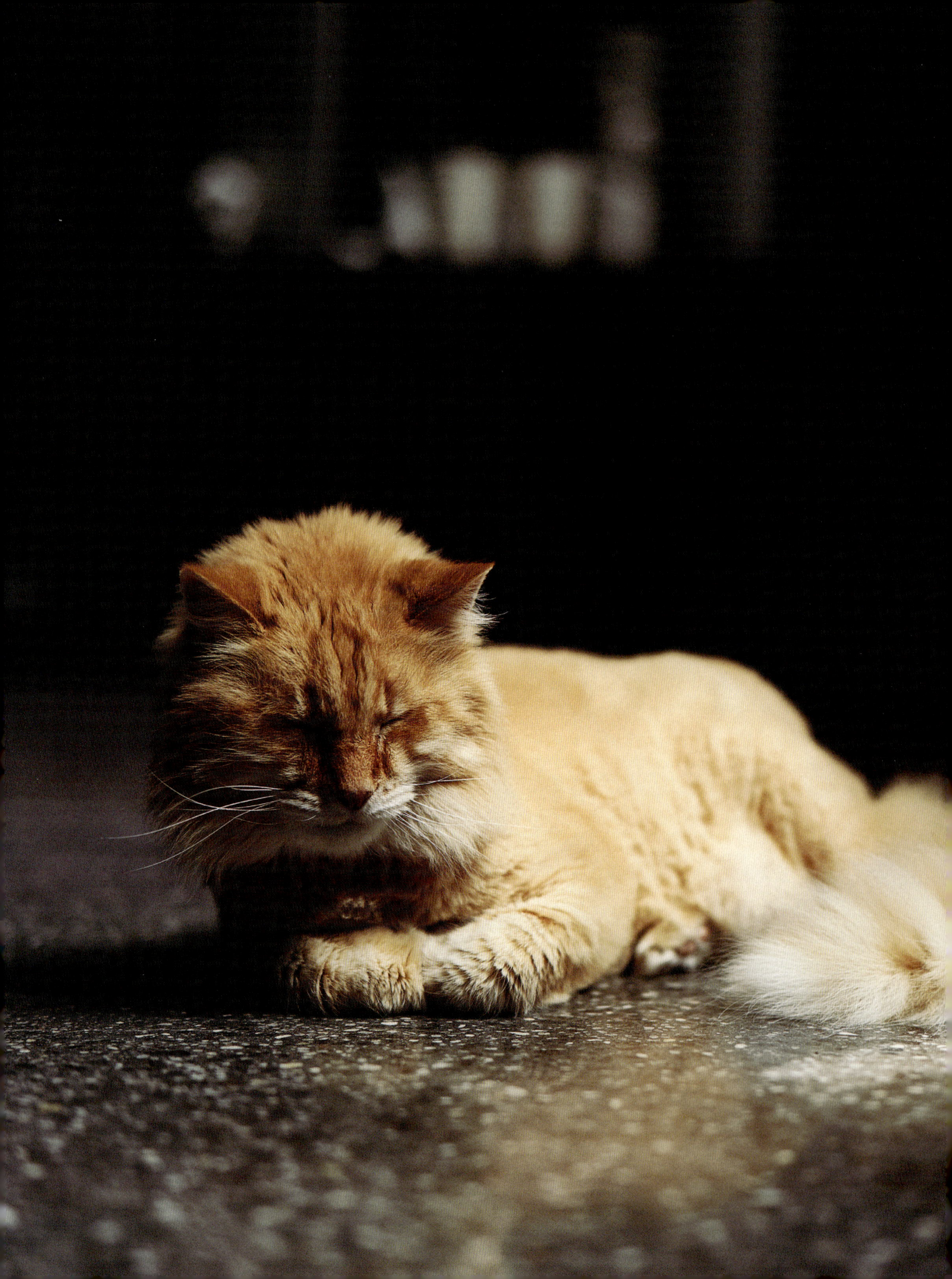

Q&A

DIVA OR DEVOTED FRIEND?
Devoted friend.

EXTROVERT OR INTROVERT?
Fairly extroverted, particularly when friends and family come over. He loves attention and tends to wait until the guests are all seated around the dining table before making his grand entrance.

LAP CAT OR NOT?
Generally not, but he loves cuddling up when his owner is lying on the couch.

OLD SOUL OR KITTEN AT HEART?
Kitten at heart.

EXPLORER OR HOMEBODY?
Homebody – he never goes outside.

LAZY OR ACTIVE?
Fairly lazy.

DOGS – FRIEND OR FOE?
Unknown. He hasn't seen a dog since he came to live with his current family.

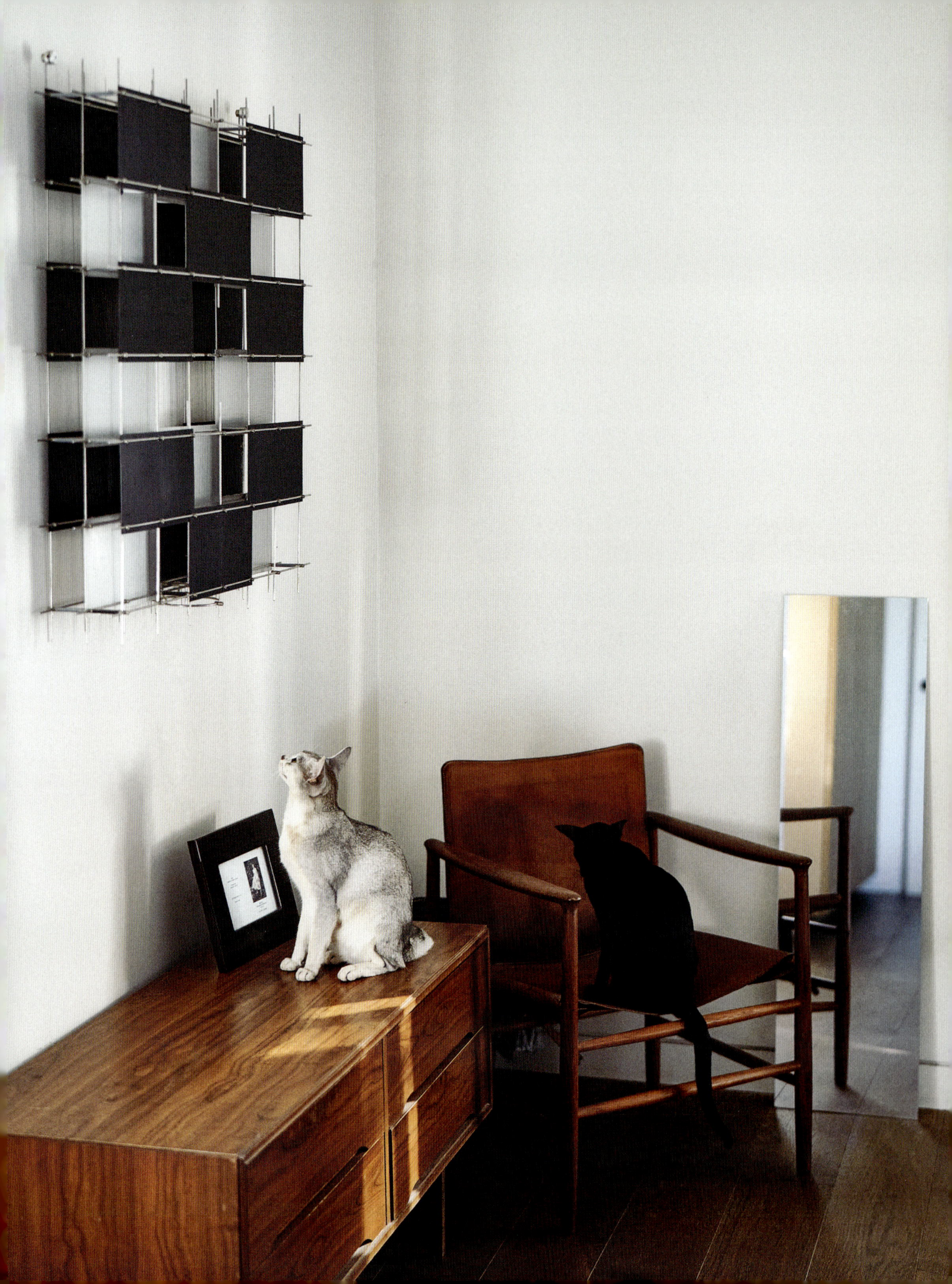

CAROL AND LUTHER

ARCHITECTS: TELLY THEODORE AND ANDY MACDONALD / ALLIED_OFFICE

Carol and Luther have their own distinct personalities, yet they are inseparable. Luther, also known as Luthersaurus or The Oil Slick, is an oriental shorthair who has built himself somewhat of a reputation. He seems to think he's a dog and is so noisy it even annoys the neighbours. Carol, a grey Abyssinian, is more refined. She's not so keen on a cuddle but has a beautiful nature. Their owners are architects, so of course the cats match the decor – but they also happen to be low-maintenance bundles of joy.

Carol and Luther reside in a converted terrace house on the edge of Sydney Harbour. The home is light-filled, and the cats love exploring every nook and cranny.

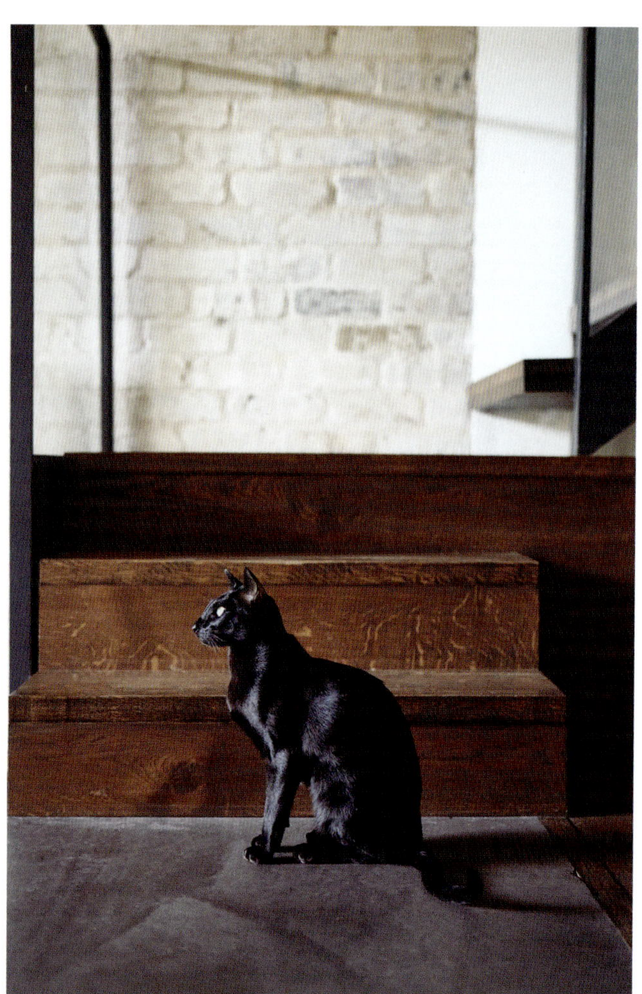

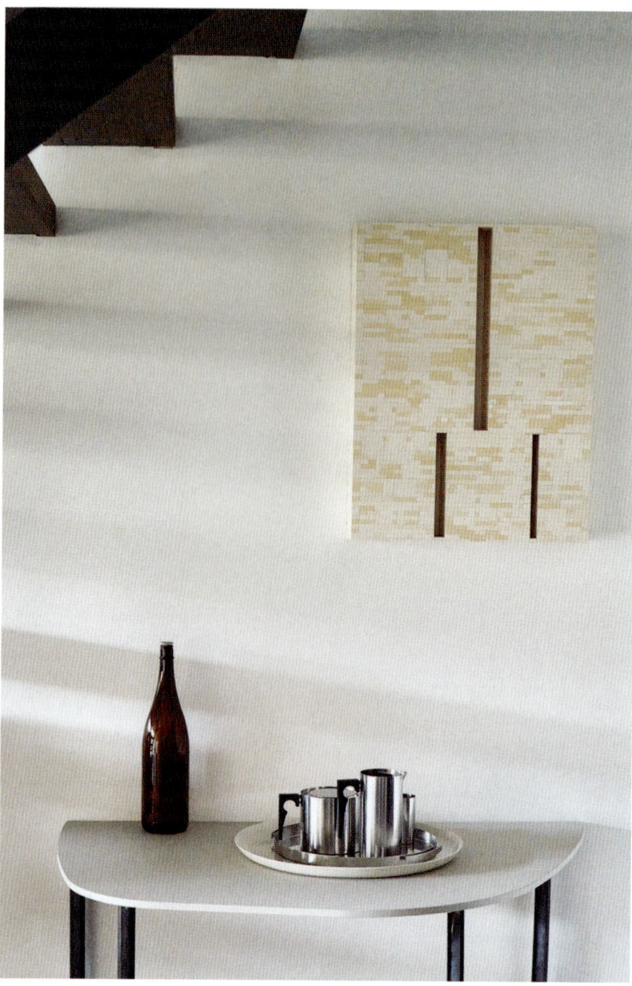

Architects: Telly Theodore and Andy Macdonald / Allied_Office

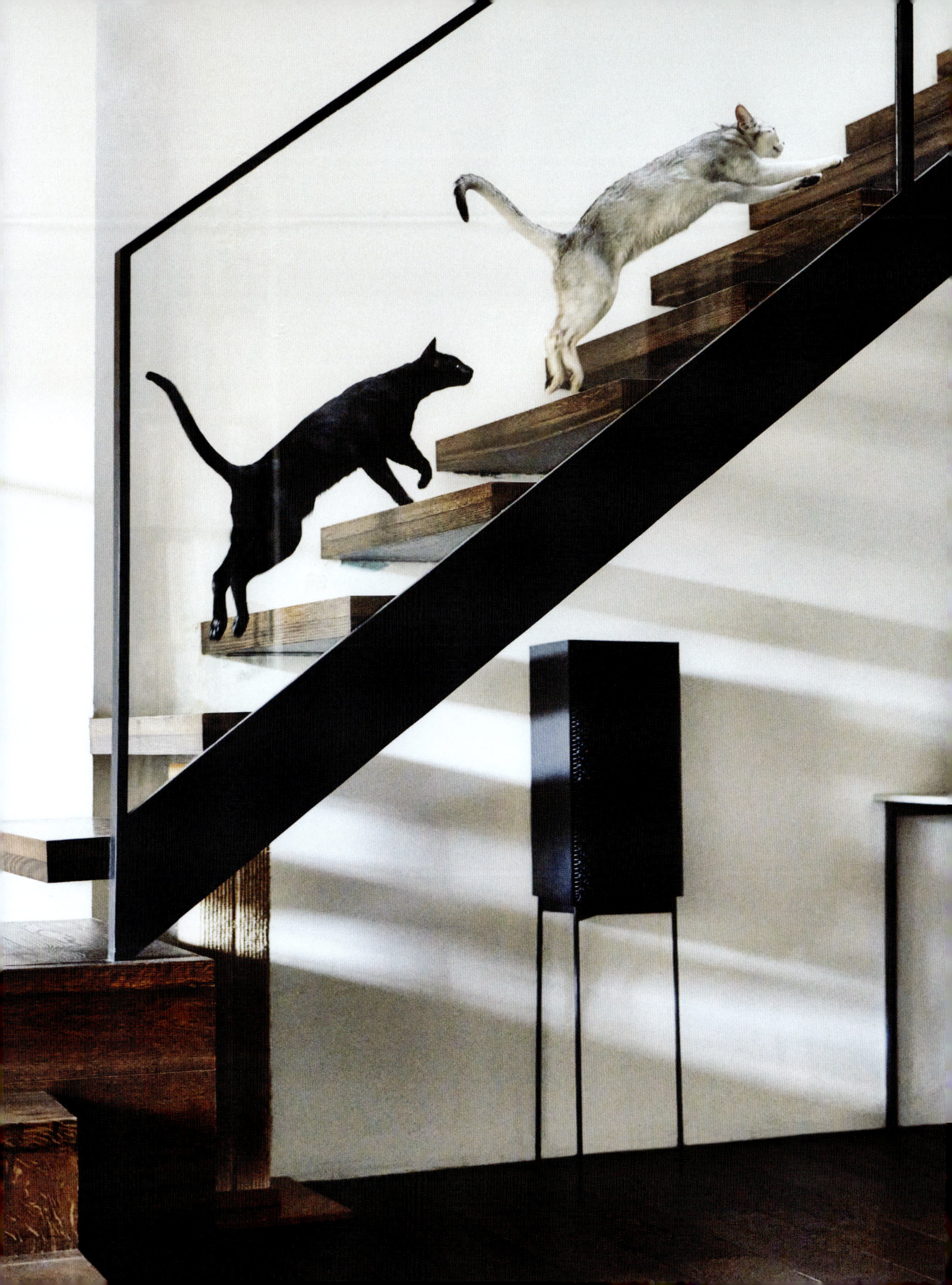

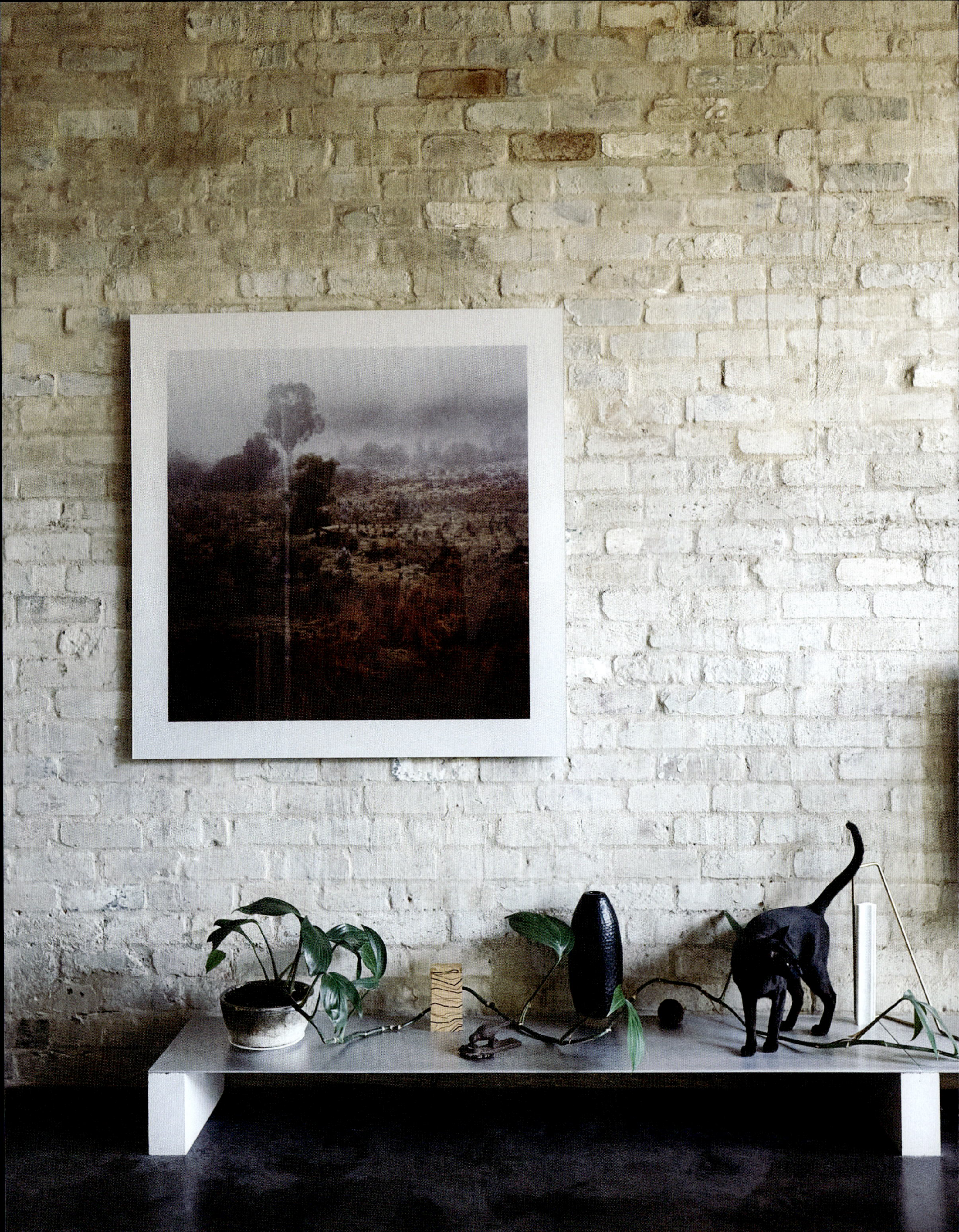

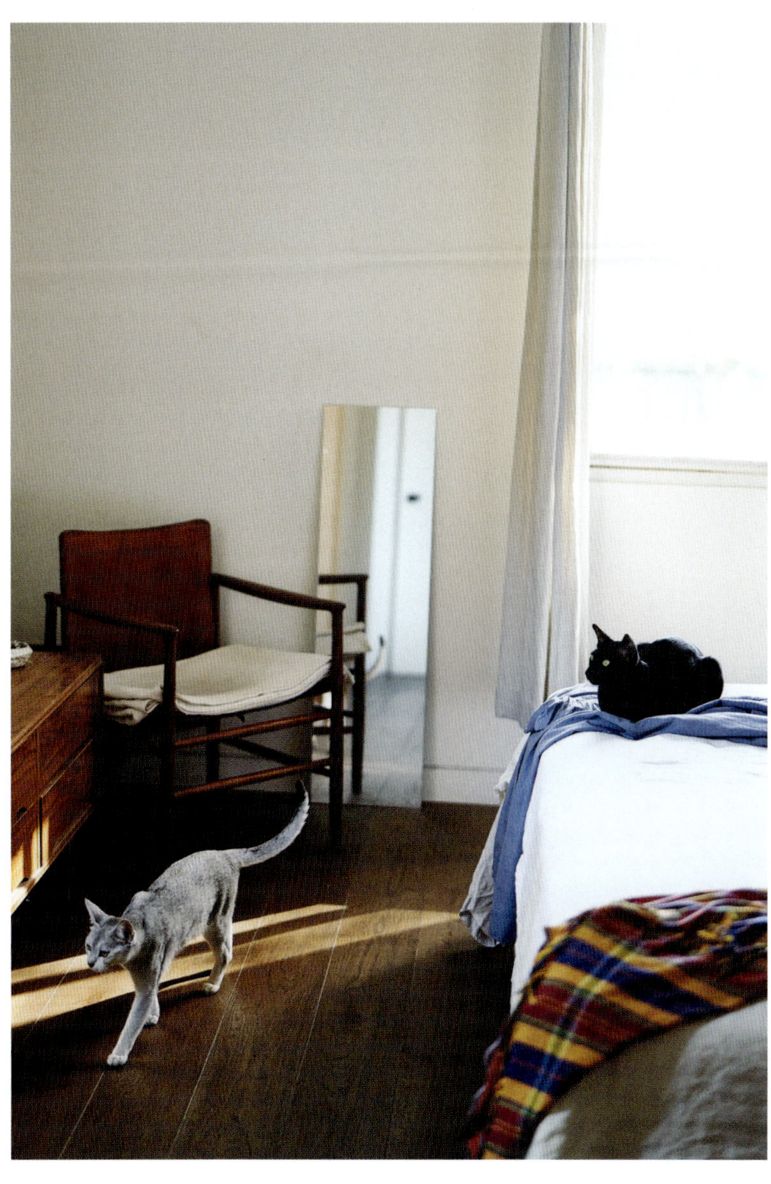

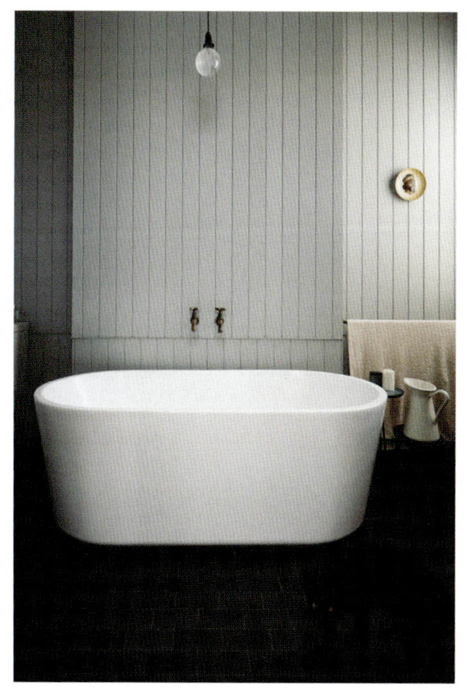

The home is great for both intimate gatherings and large parties – though Carol and Luther generally prefer to avoid the latter by taking refuge in the bedroom.

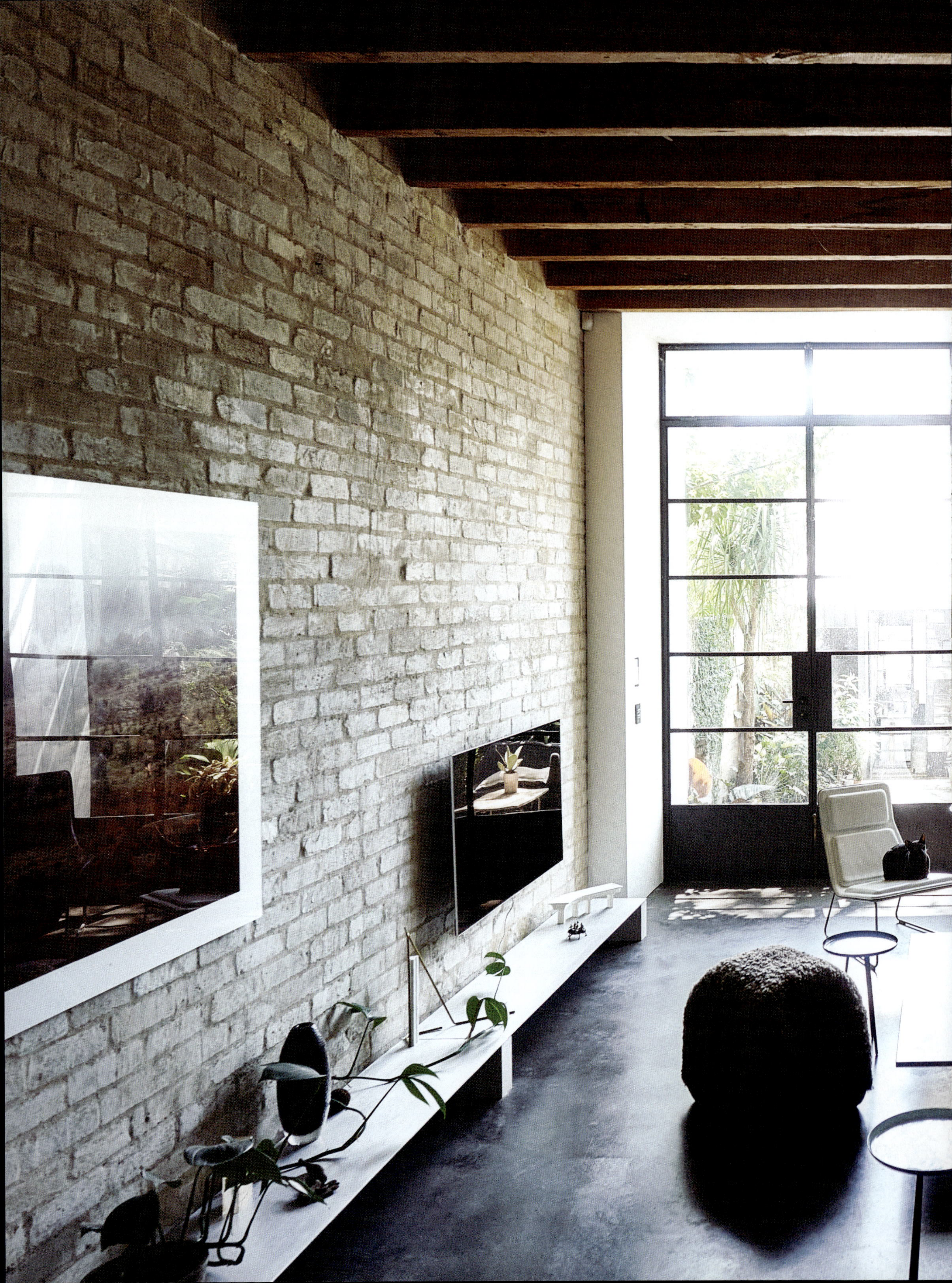

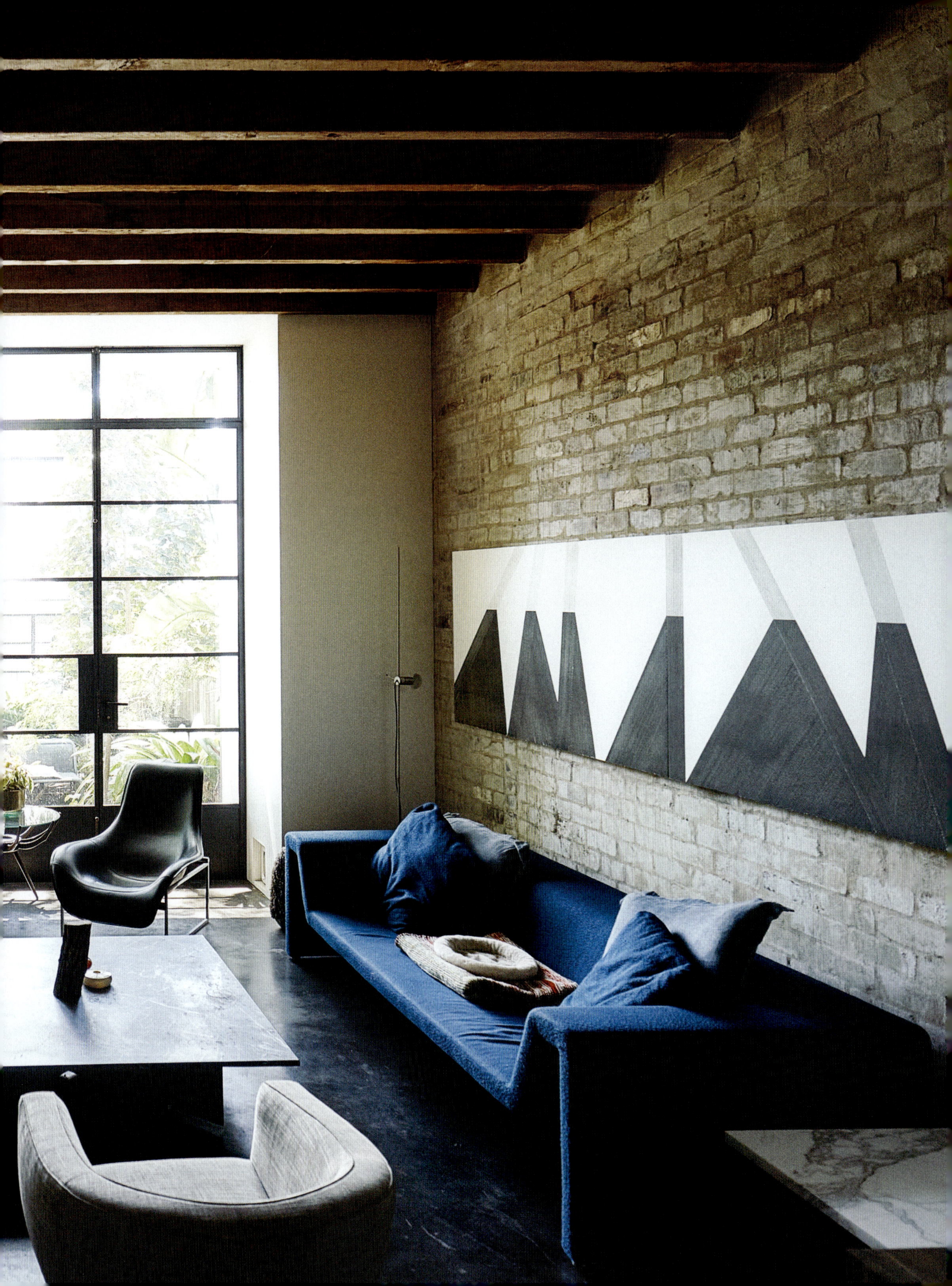

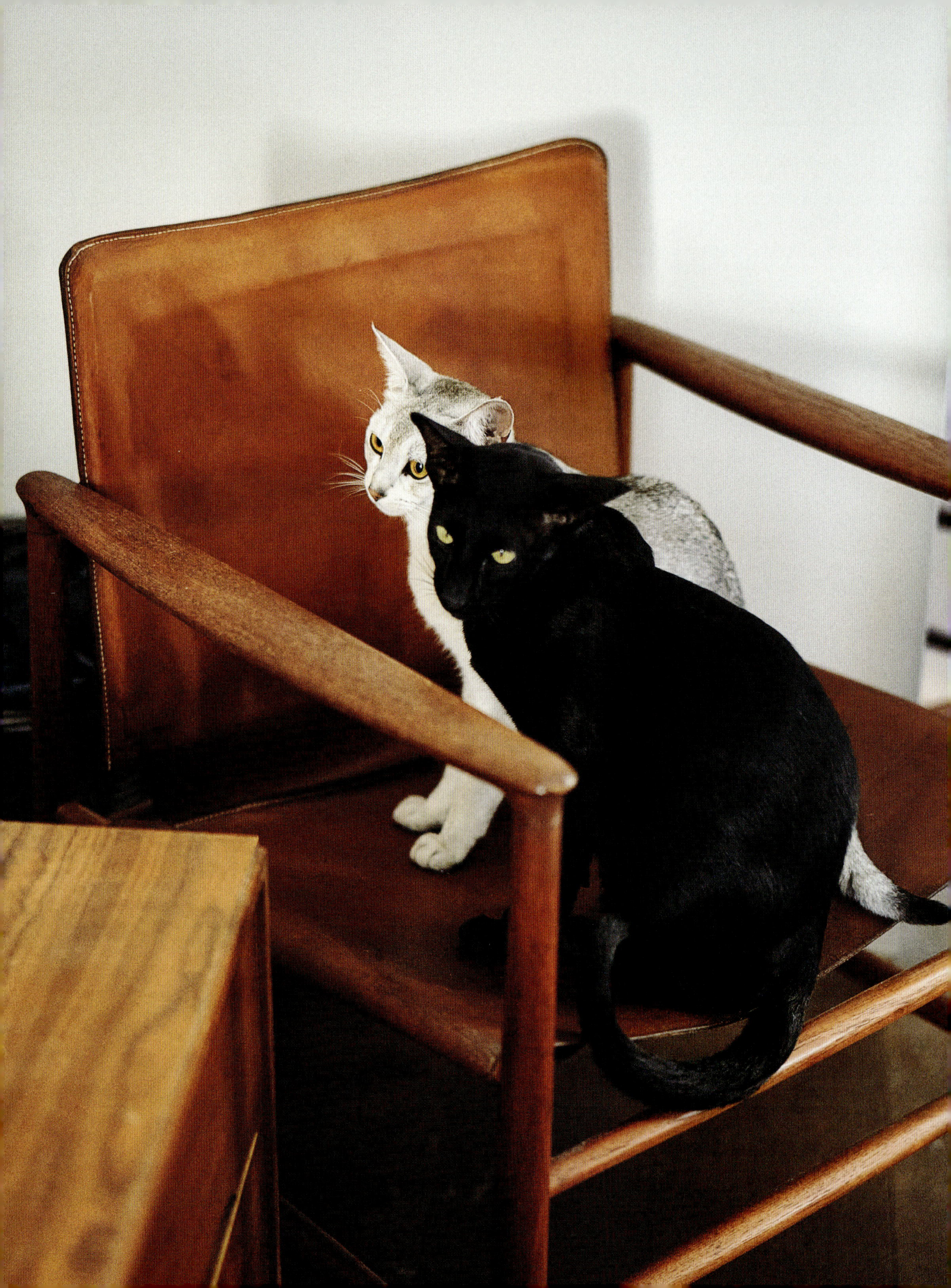

Q&A

DIVAS OR DEVOTED FRIENDS?
Devoted friends – they follow their owners around the house.

EXTROVERTS OR INTROVERTS?
Luther is an extrovert and Carol is an introvert.

LAP CATS OR NOT?
He's a lap cat. She's more like, 'Mmmmmmaybe ... nah ... ok ... nah.'

OLD SOULS OR KITTENS AT HEART?
Luther has the soul of a canine! Carol's probably 'been around the block' a few times.

EXPLORERS OR HOMEBODIES?
Both super explorers!

LAZY OR ACTIVE?
Luther is active, while Carol is really lazy.

DOGS – FRIEND OR FOE?
Foe. Luther actually growls like a dog ... at dogs.

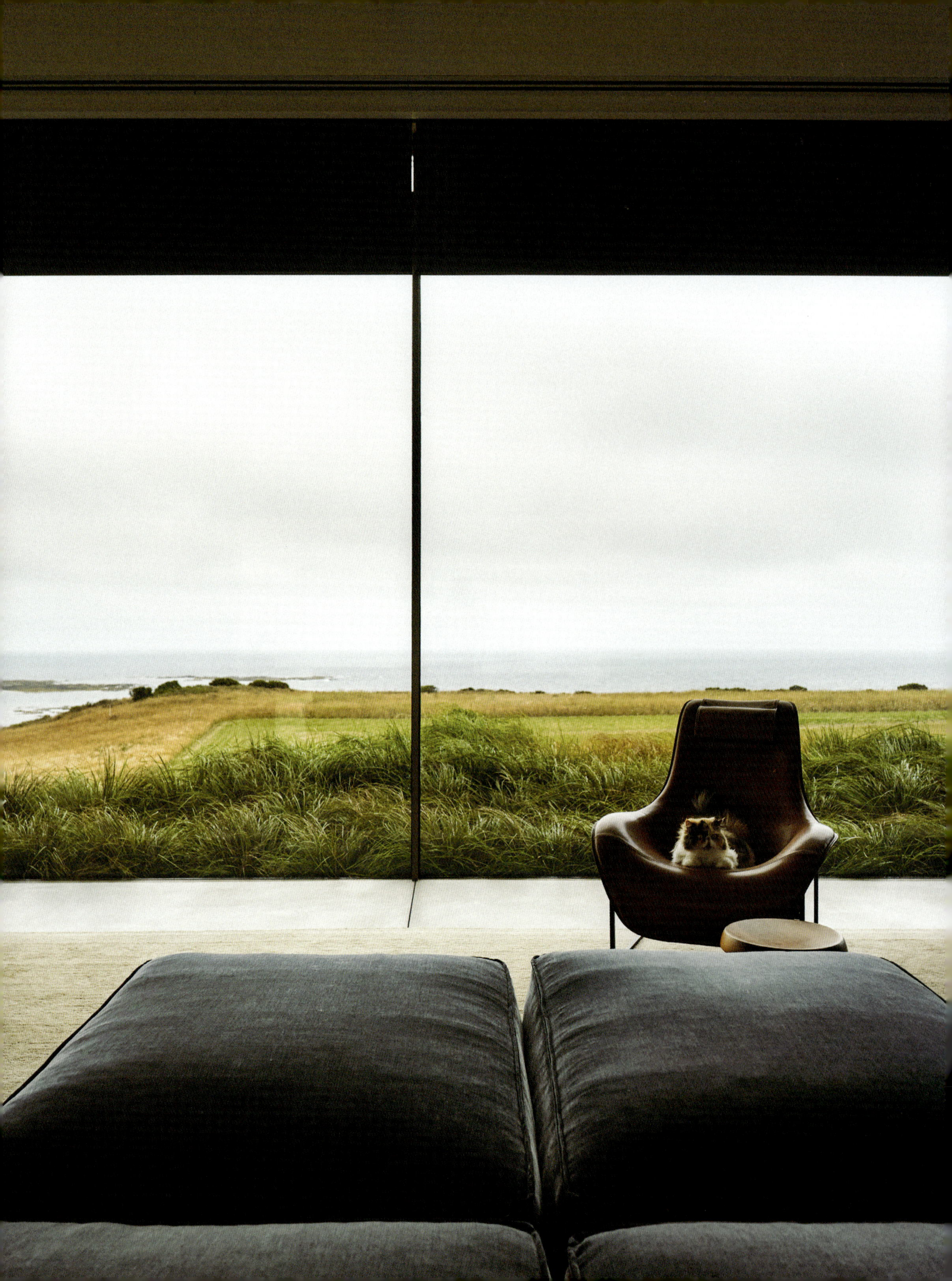

ESMERALDA

ARCHITECT: SUE CARR / CARR

Esmeralda fills the large gap left in this family by the passing of their previous cat, who had a big personality. Esmeralda is a tortoiseshell Persian who is seven years old and full of mystique. For a small cat, she has a lot of presence. She fits perfectly into the household, as she is easygoing and not highly excitable – she is content to luxuriate in her surroundings on her own. Of course, it's not hard to maintain a relaxed disposition when you live in a modern farmhouse with boundless ocean views. The cat flap she uses to let herself in and out of the dwelling is even microchipped, so other animals can't invade her sanctuary.

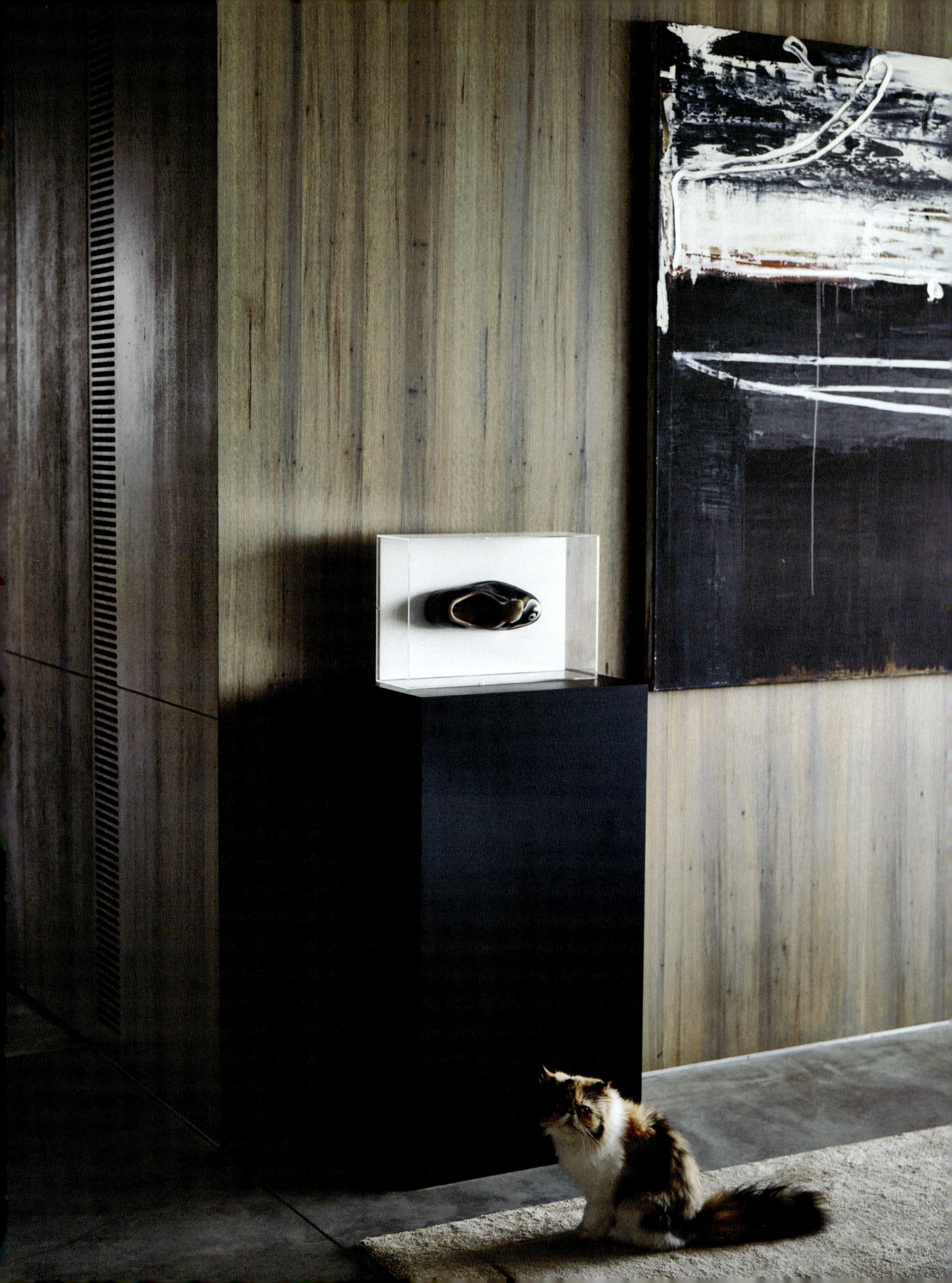

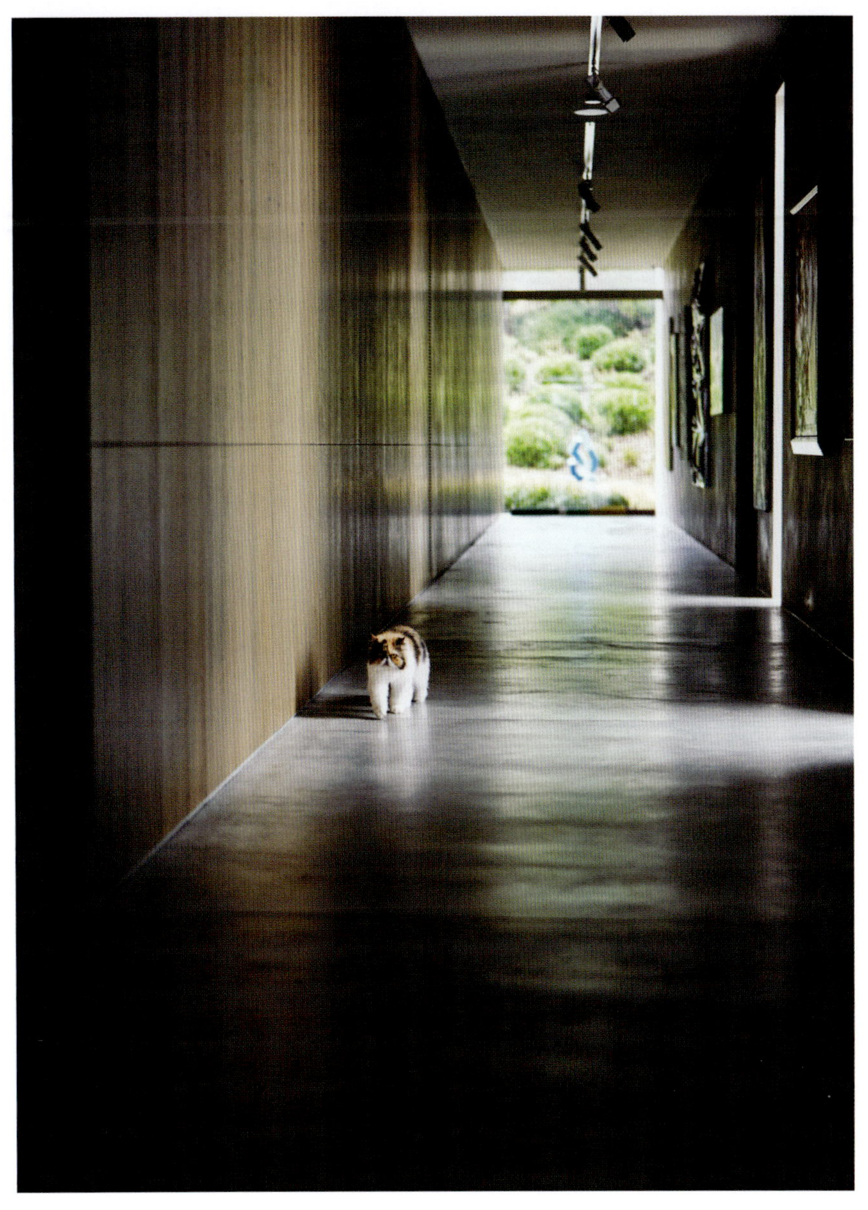

Esmeralda's owners wanted their home to be a simple structure with high ceilings and an orientation that would maximise every view. Numerous spaces have been dedicated to the display of their extensive art collection, including a gallery hall.

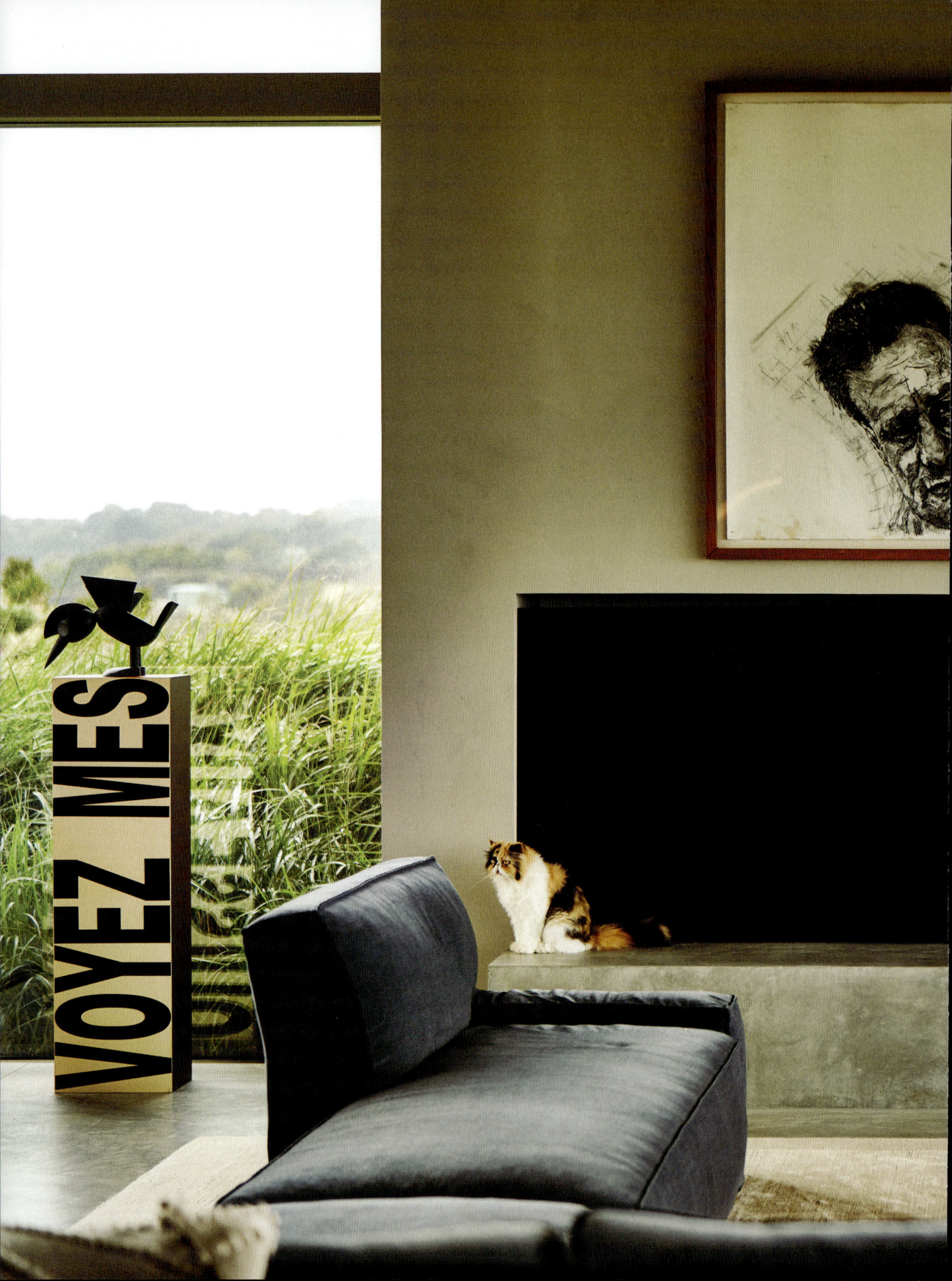
VOYEZ MES

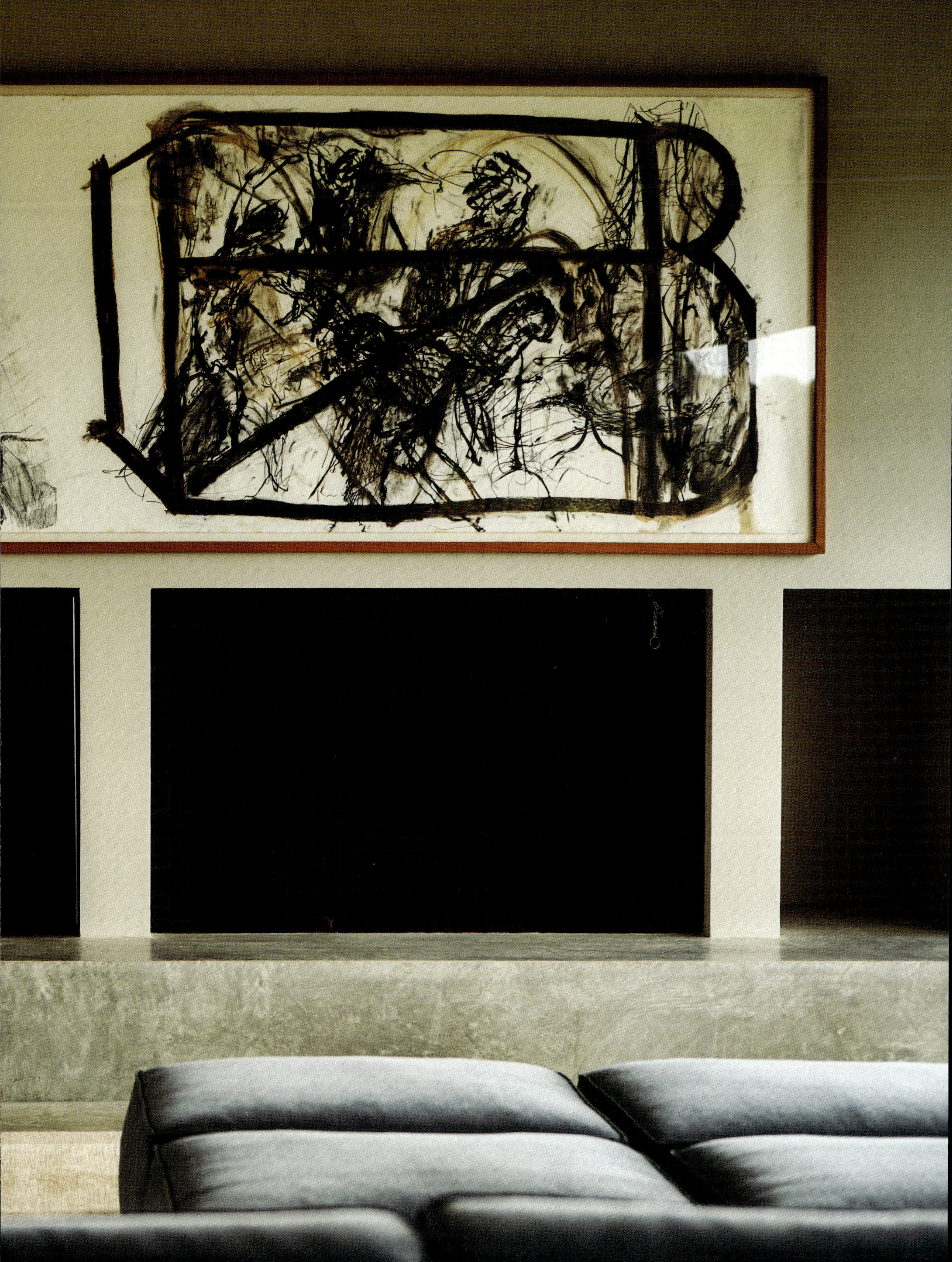

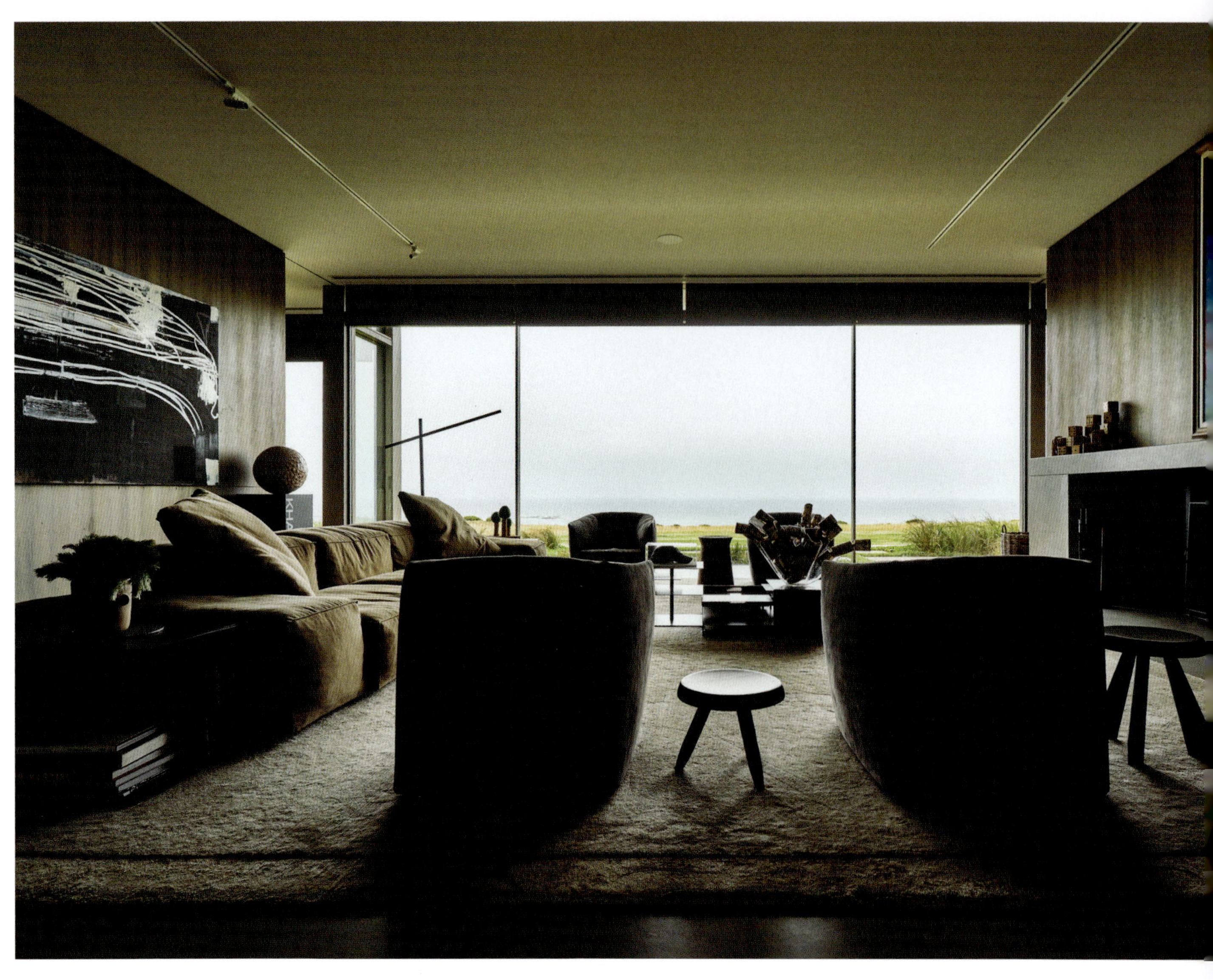

The home has large windows that frame panoramic coastal scenes, which shift and change with the tides.

Architect: Sue Carr / Carr

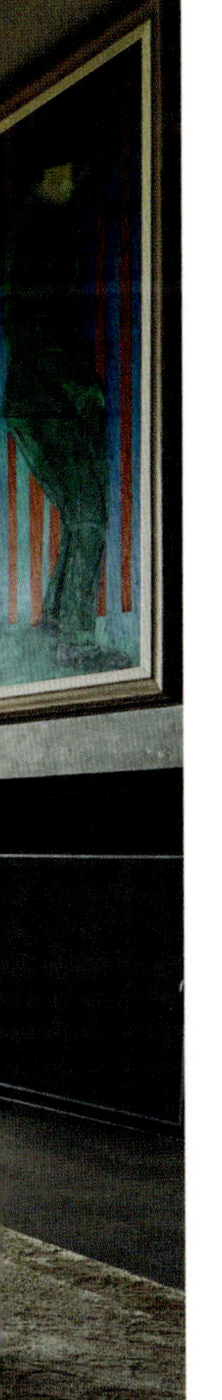

Esmeralda's only indulgence is eating six tins of seafood a day.

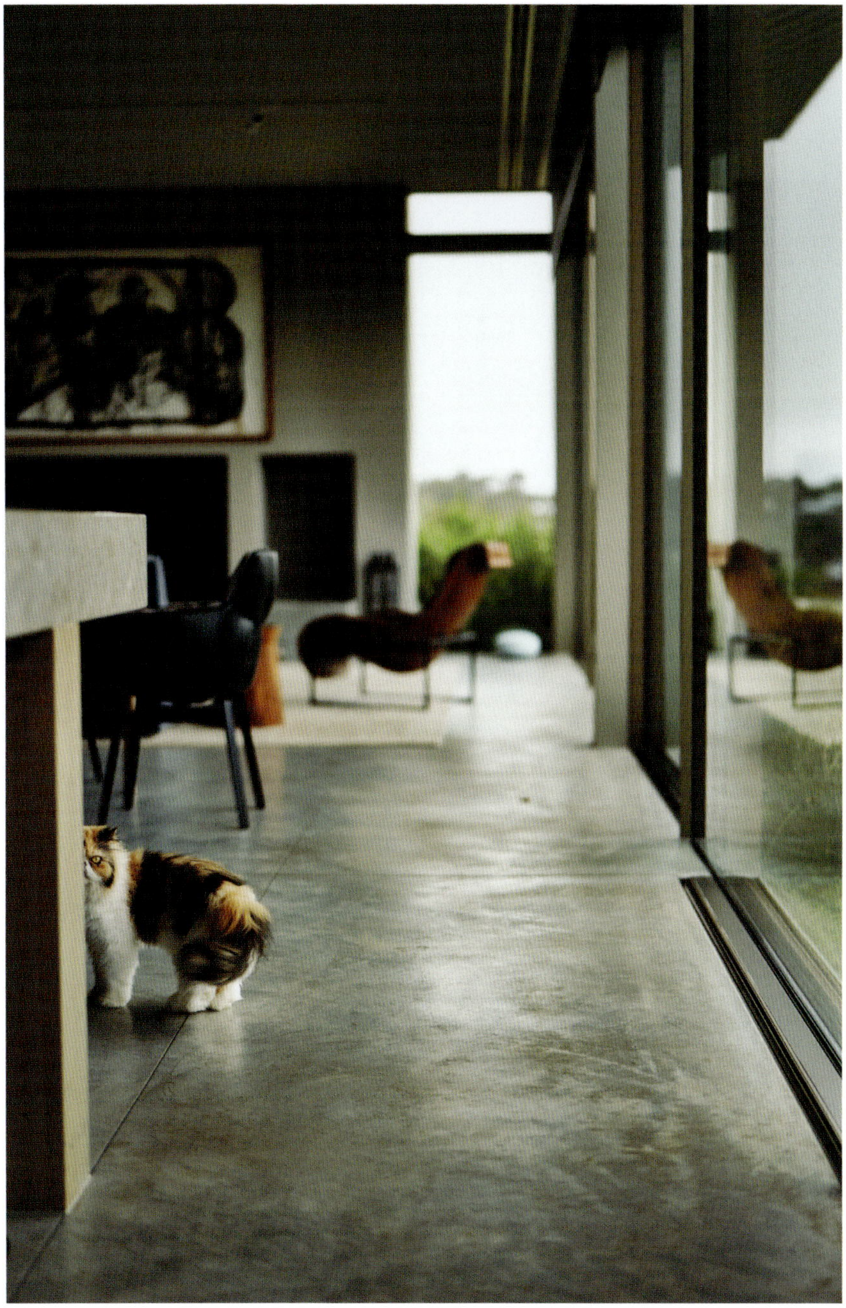

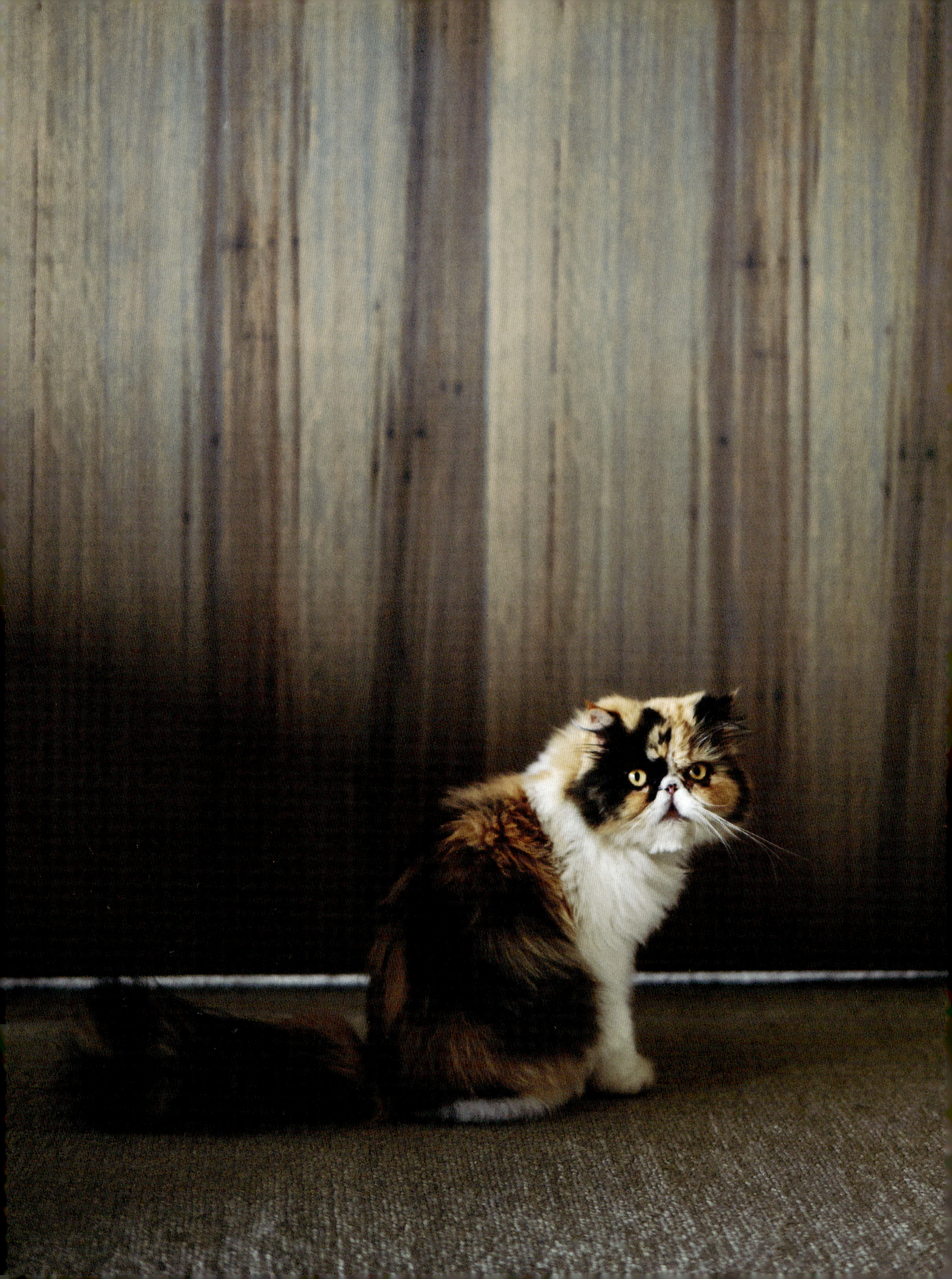

Q&A

DIVA OR DEVOTED FRIEND?
Diva.

EXTROVERT OR INTROVERT?
Introvert.

LAP CAT OR NOT?
Only when she wants something.

OLD SOUL OR KITTEN AT HEART?
Kitten at heart.

EXPLORER OR HOMEBODY?
Homebody – she goes literally nowhere.

LAZY OR ACTIVE?
Lazy.

DOGS – FRIEND OR FOE?
She rules the house – the family's dogs are just her guests.

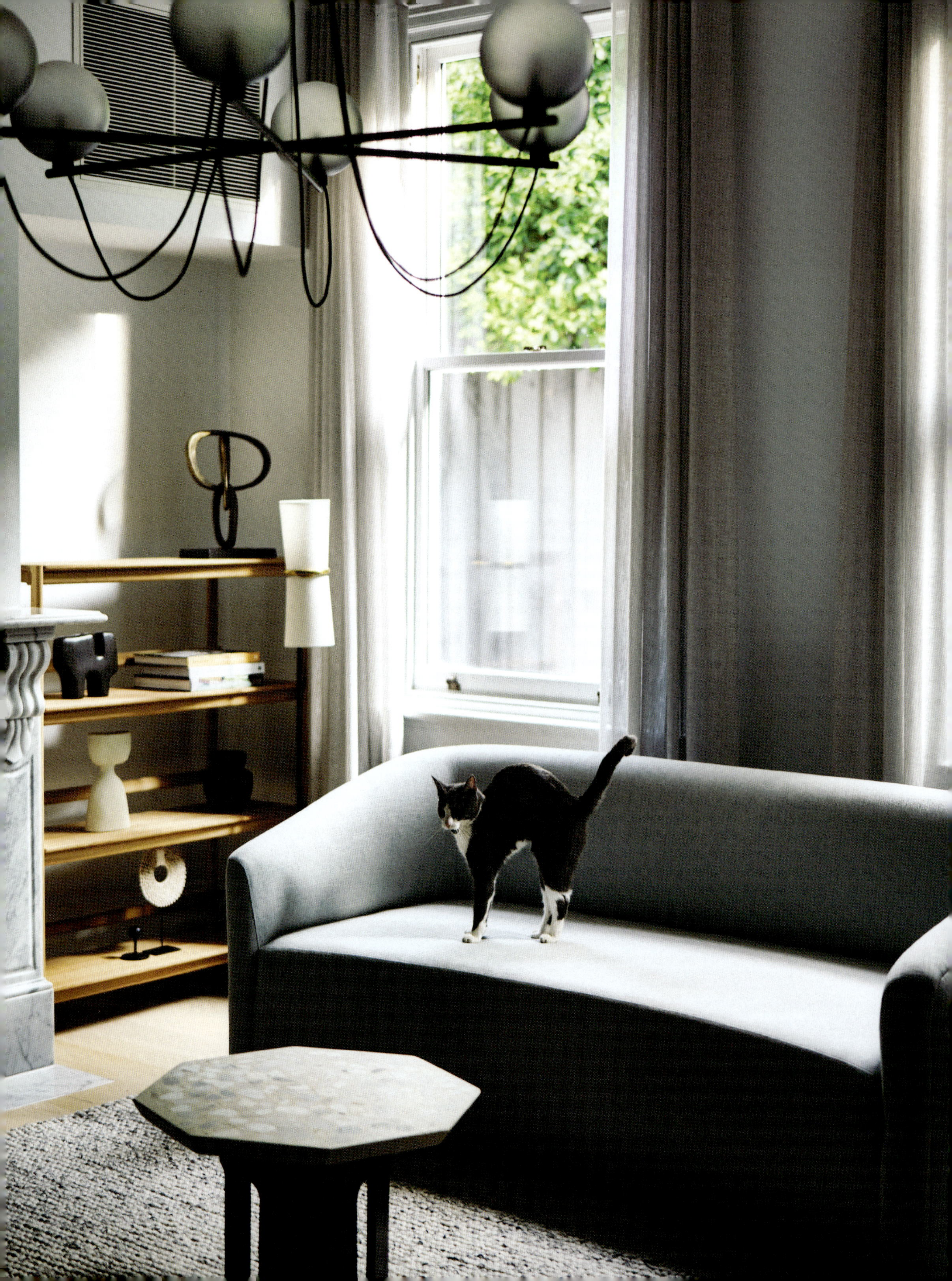

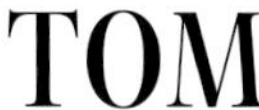

TOM

INTERIOR CURATION: SIMONE HAAG AND SARAH SHINNERS / SIMONE HAAG

Tom, a confident and energetic two-year-old rescue cat, is what you would call a 'bitser' – he is a bit of this and a bit of that! He got off to a bit of a wobbly start in life. When Tom was still a kitten, his first adoptive family returned him to the shelter because they thought he was too boisterous. His second adoptive family adored him – but their purebred British shorthair did not. It was third time lucky for Tom when he became a cherished part of this household at just seven months old.

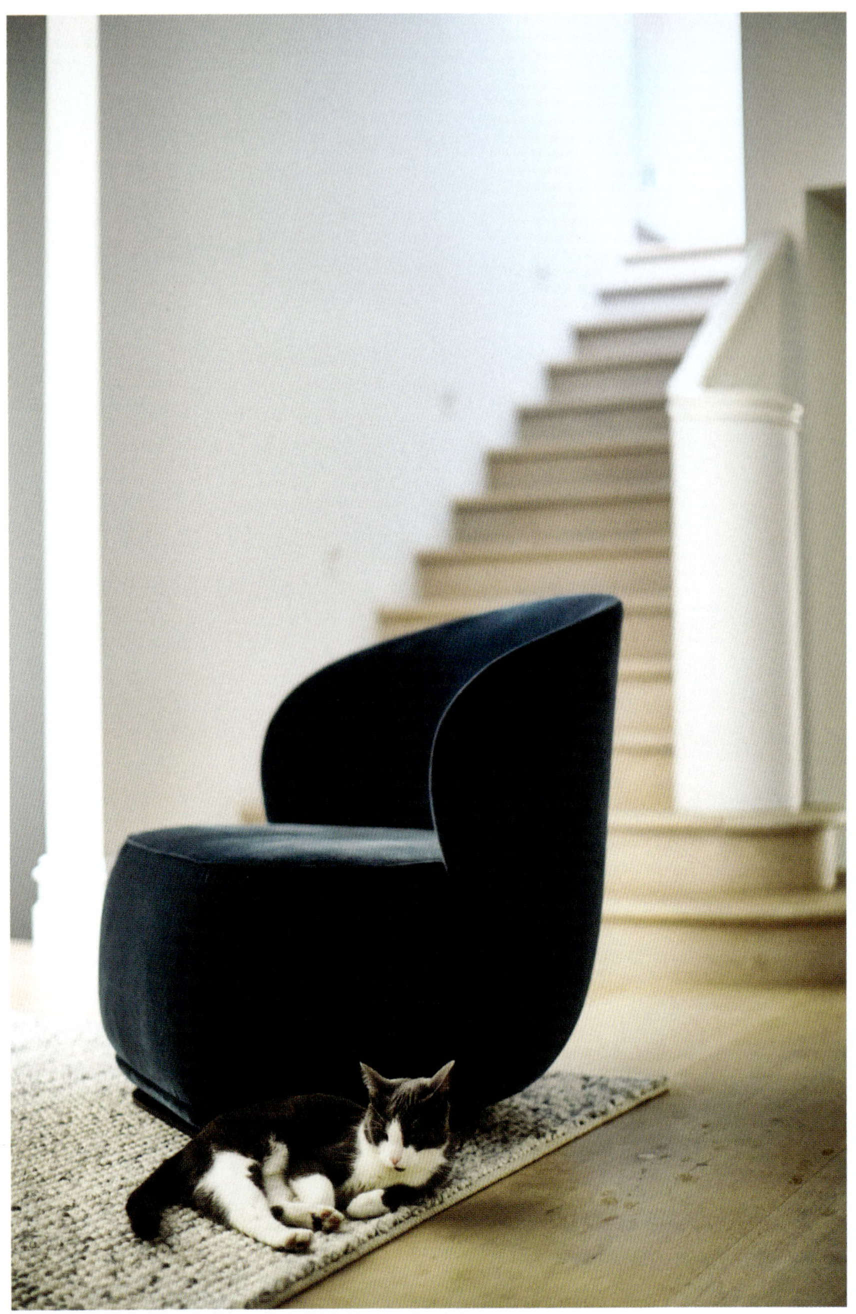

Tom has made himself at home in this renovated double-fronted Victorian Italianate. Tackling 120 years of wear and tear, his owners restored the house to its former glory while judiciously integrating modern updates. The wide Dinesen oak floorboards give the space a sense of peace and tranquillity.

Interior curation: Simone Haag and Sarah Shinners / Simone Haag

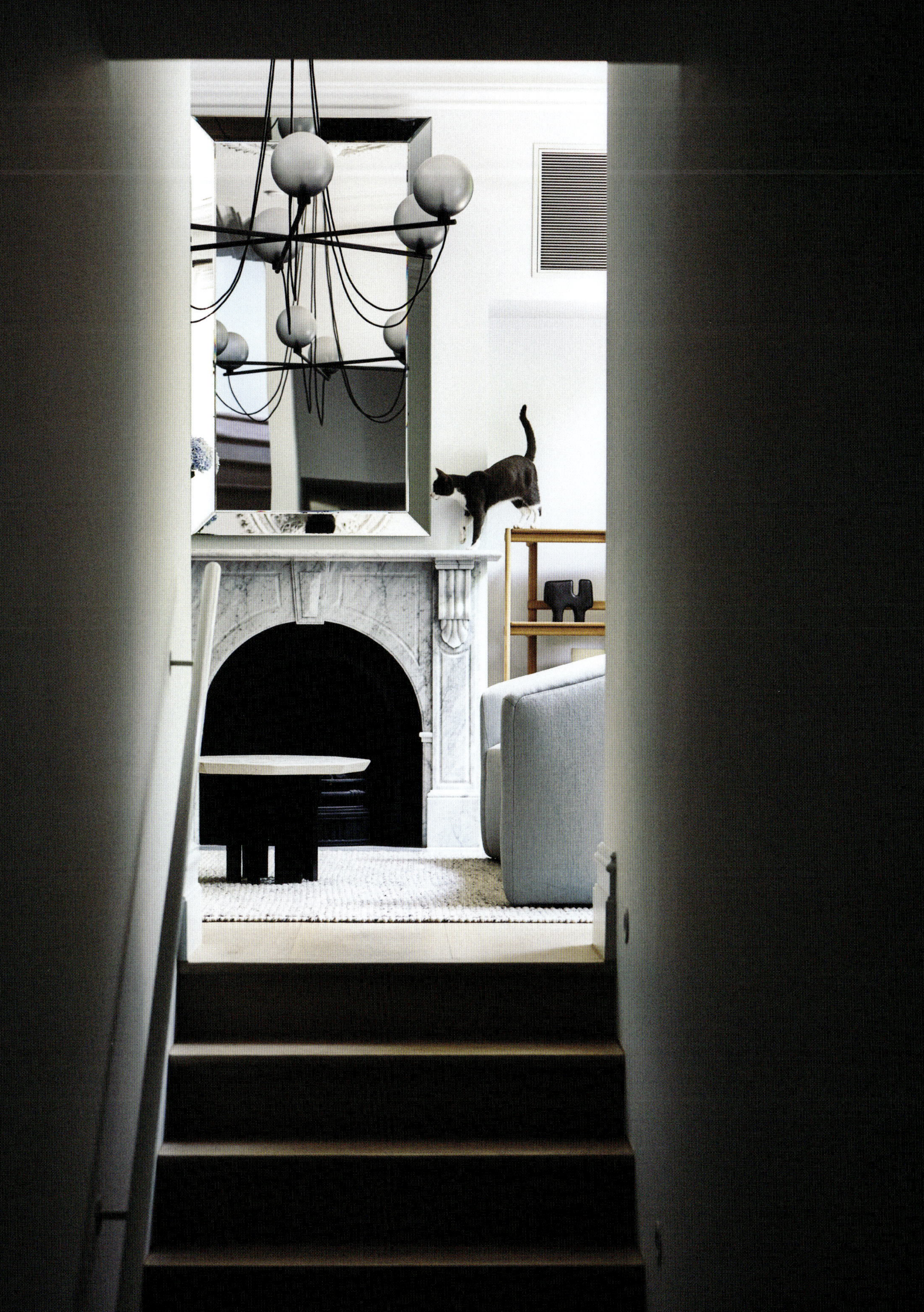

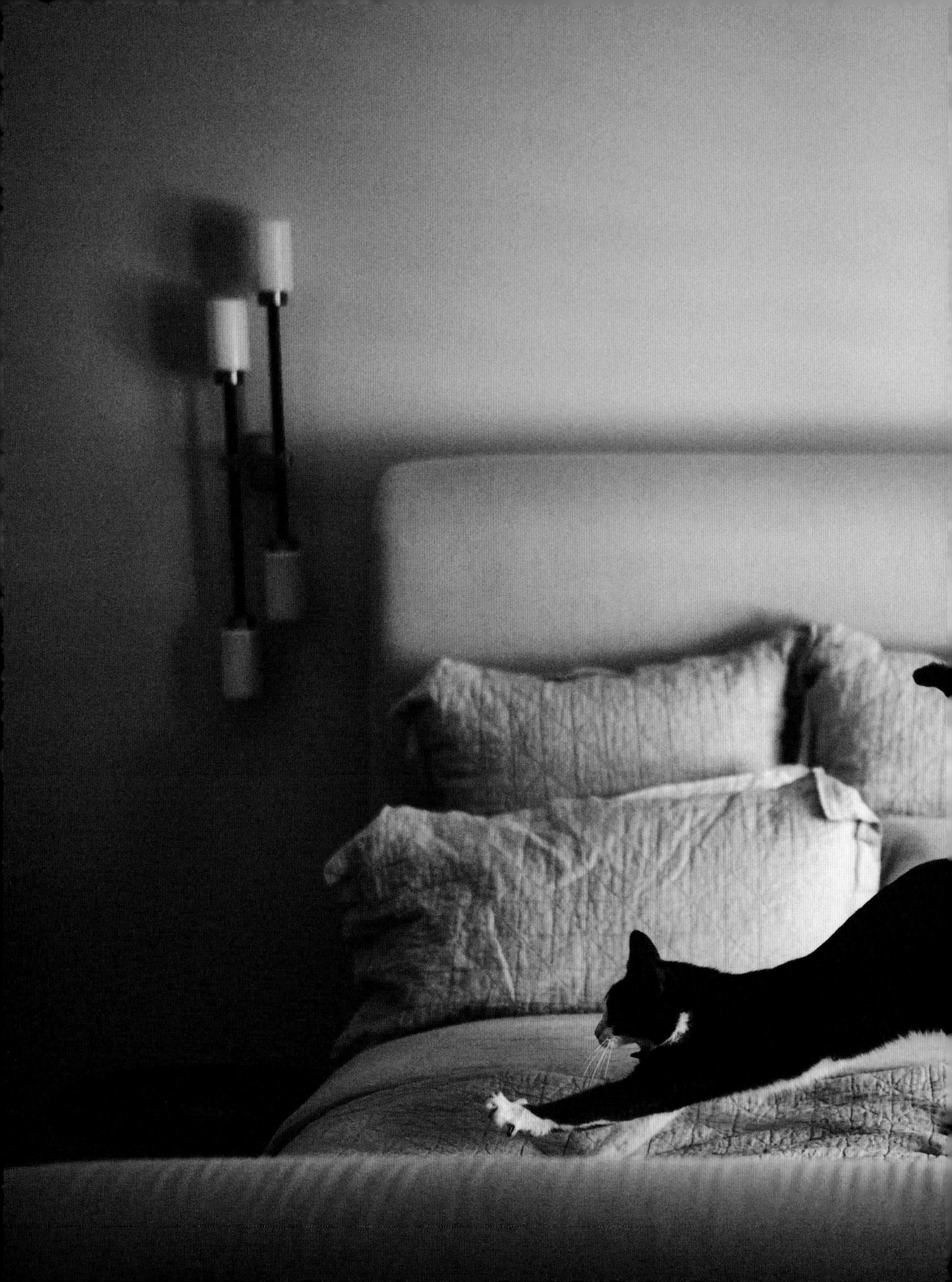

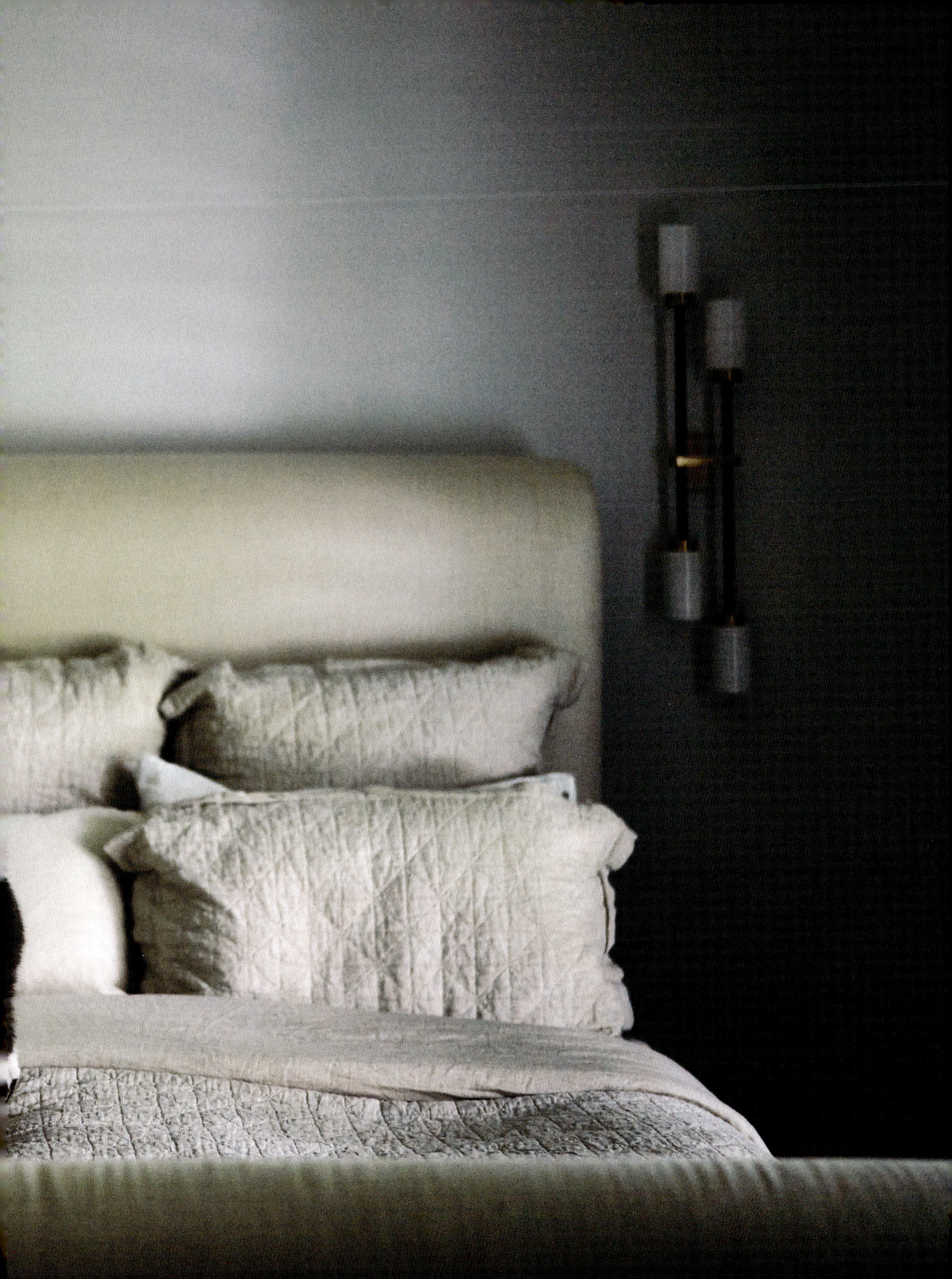

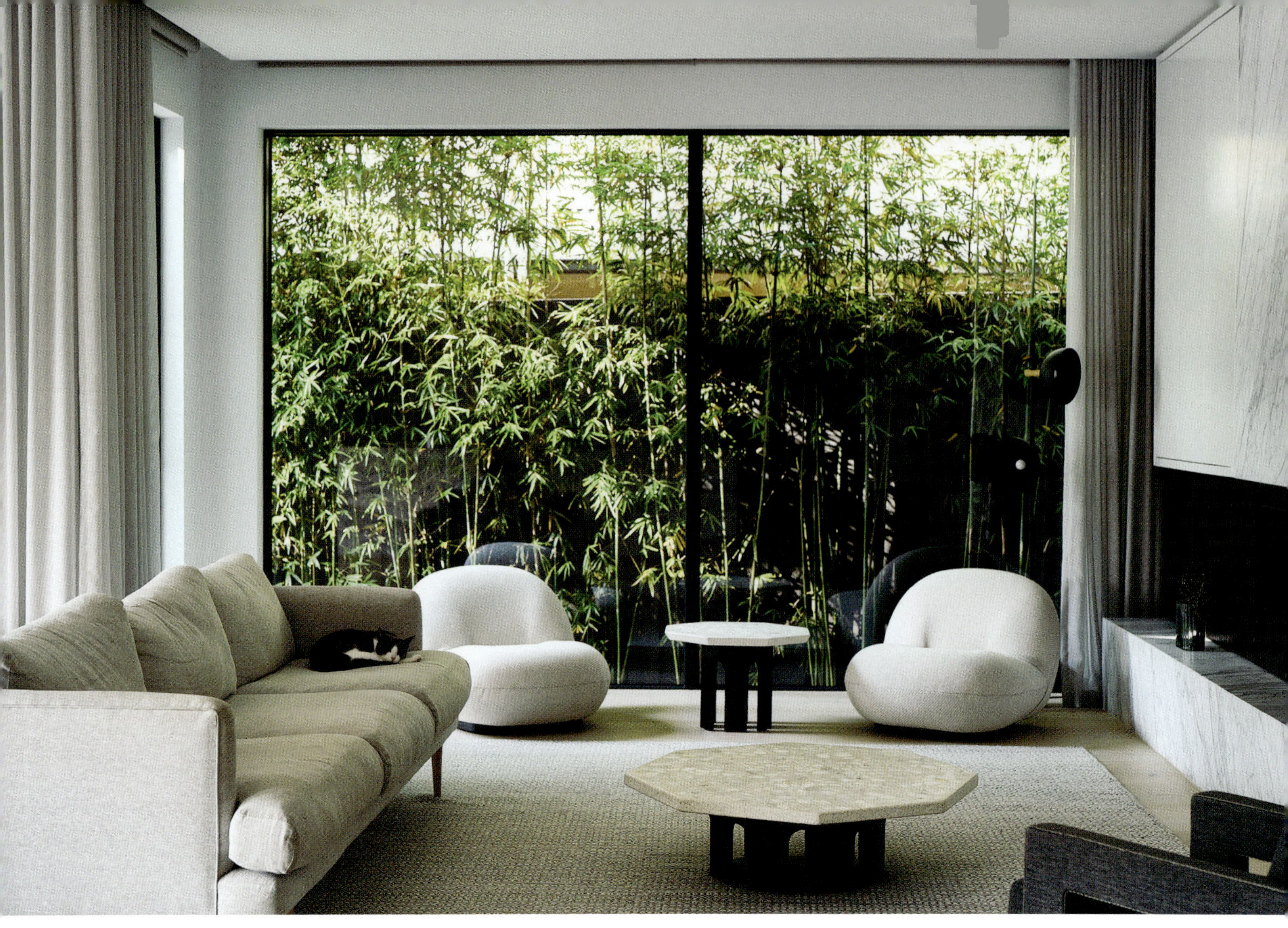

By day, Tom comes and goes through his cat door; at night he is kept inside to protect the local wildlife – and to keep him safe from the resident fox. He picks who he sleeps with in the evening, but gives everyone enough head rubs to keep him in their good books.

Interior curation: Simone Haag and Sarah Shinners / Simone Haag

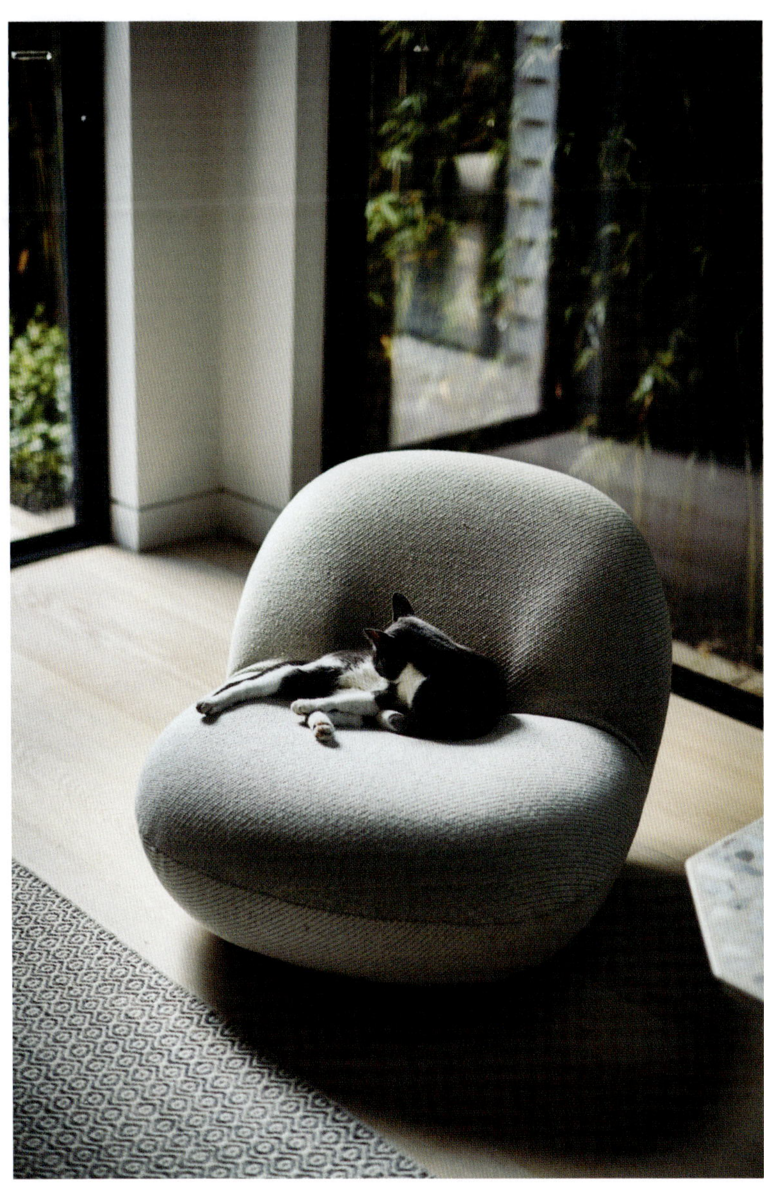

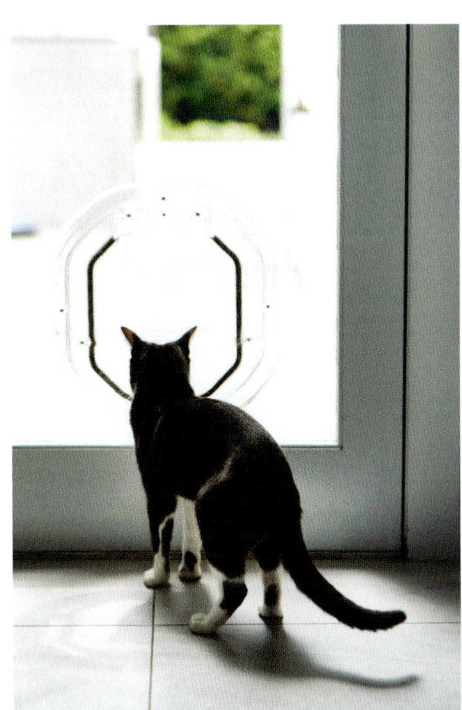

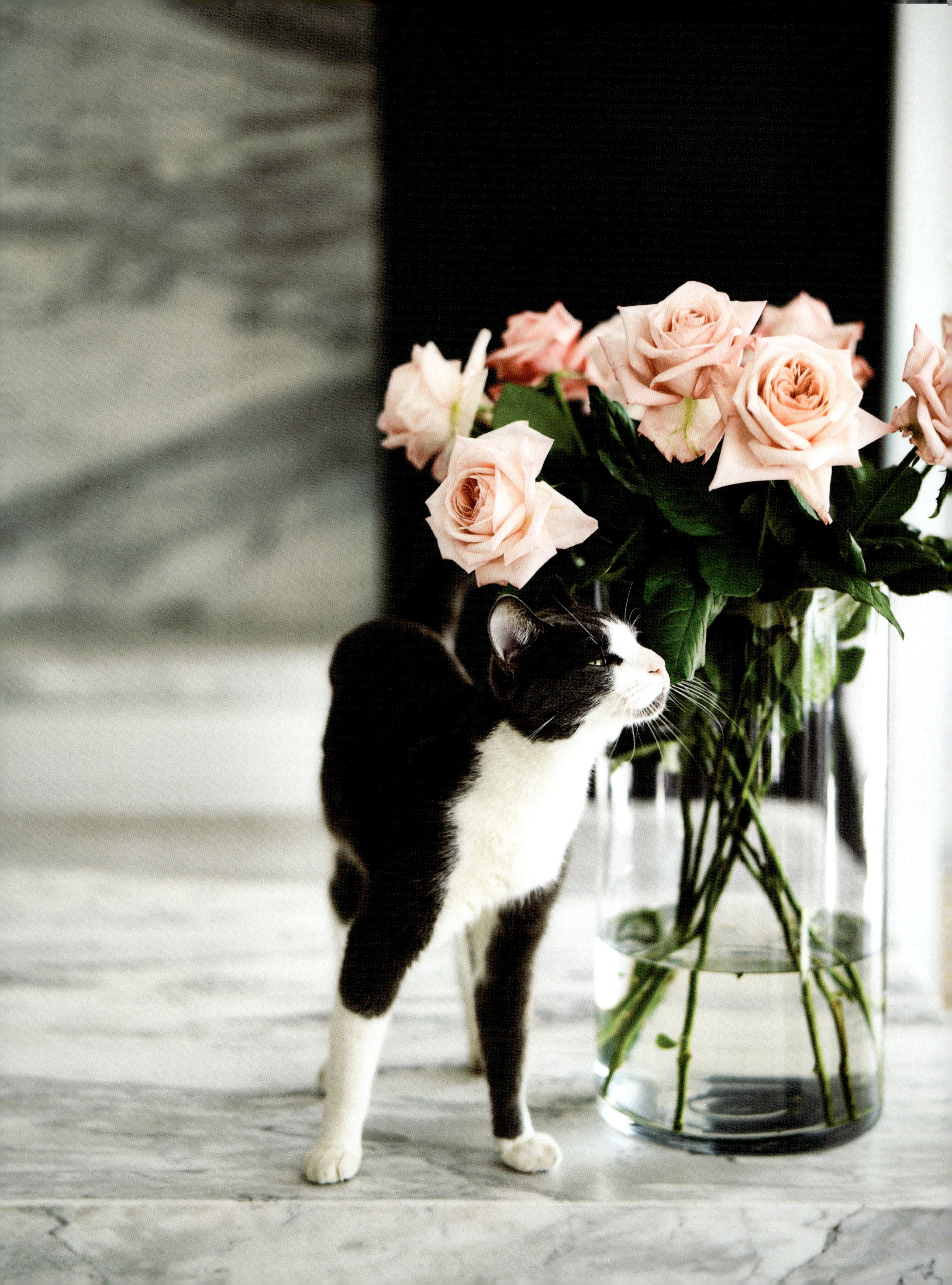

Q&A

DIVA OR DEVOTED FRIEND?
Devoted friend.

EXTROVERT OR INTROVERT?
Introverted extrovert. He is full of curiosity and needs to know what is going on at all times. He follows his family from room to room until they settle somewhere to relax, which is Tom's cue to make himself comfortable only a short distance away.

LAP CAT OR NOT?
No laps, just head rubs.

OLD SOUL OR KITTEN AT HEART?
Kitten at heart.

EXPLORER OR HOMEBODY?
Tom has worked out how to access everyone's bedroom from the outside of his two-storey home. He will find his way onto the roof and cry at each child's bedroom window (upstairs). If they won't let him in, he will head to the main bedroom window (ground level) and try his luck there.

LAZY OR ACTIVE?
Active.

DOGS – FRIEND OR FOE?
Foe.

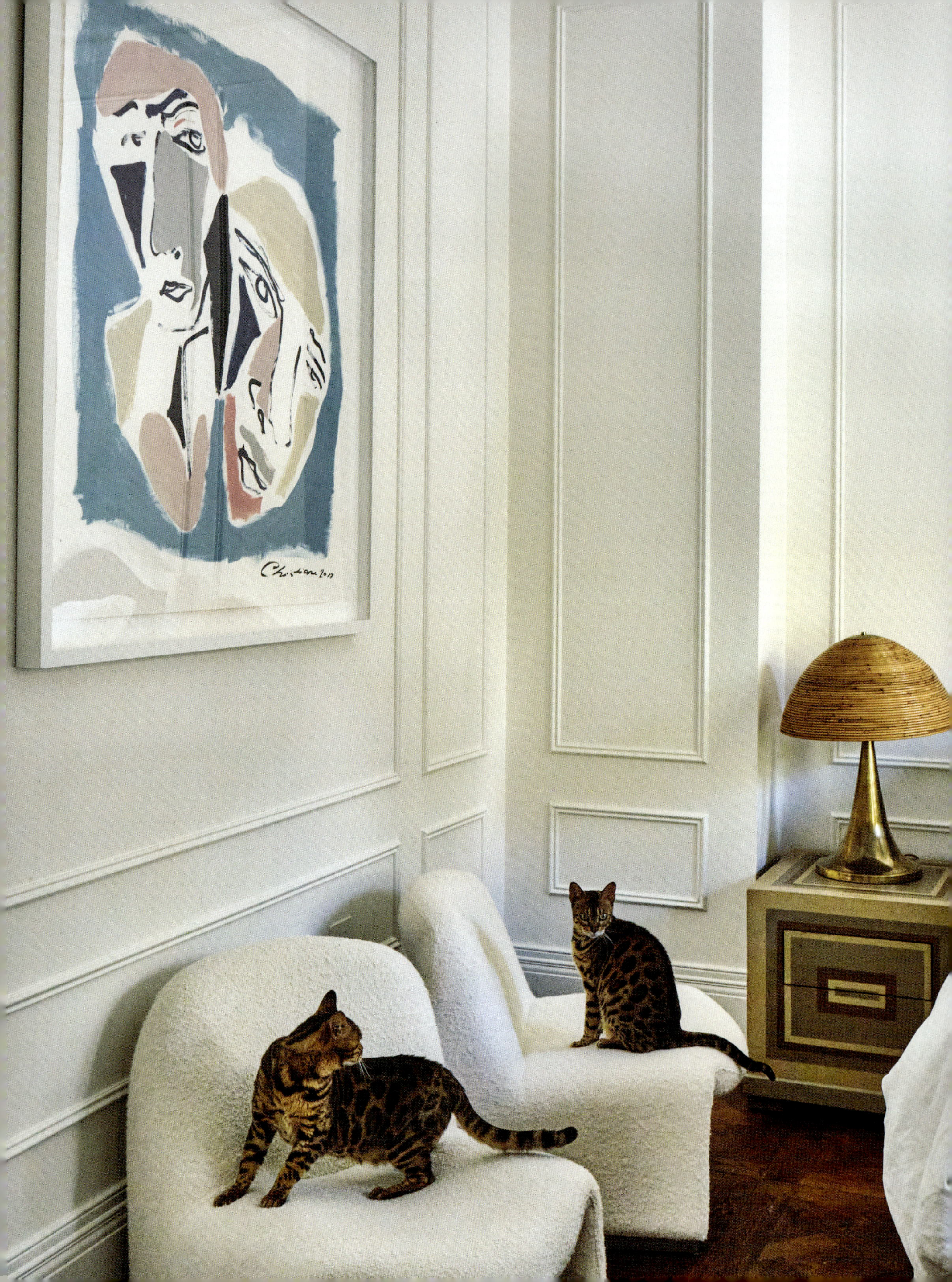

RAPHAEL AND FELLINI

DESIGNER: TAMSIN JOHNSON / TAMSIN JOHNSON INTERIOR DESIGN

Bengal cats are known to be highly intelligent and very social, with huge personalities – and a little crazy. Raphael and Fellini's owners decided that this was the perfect breed for them. Having had the two cats for four years now, they can confirm that the stereotypes are all true. Bengal cats are for level-ten expert cat owners only! In fact, they are more akin to young children than cats and are very high-maintenance. Then again, it's hard to stay annoyed at such cute kitties for long – and no matter what, they always end the day with a snuggle in bed. Raphael and Fellini's owners say that living with the cats was great training for parenthood.

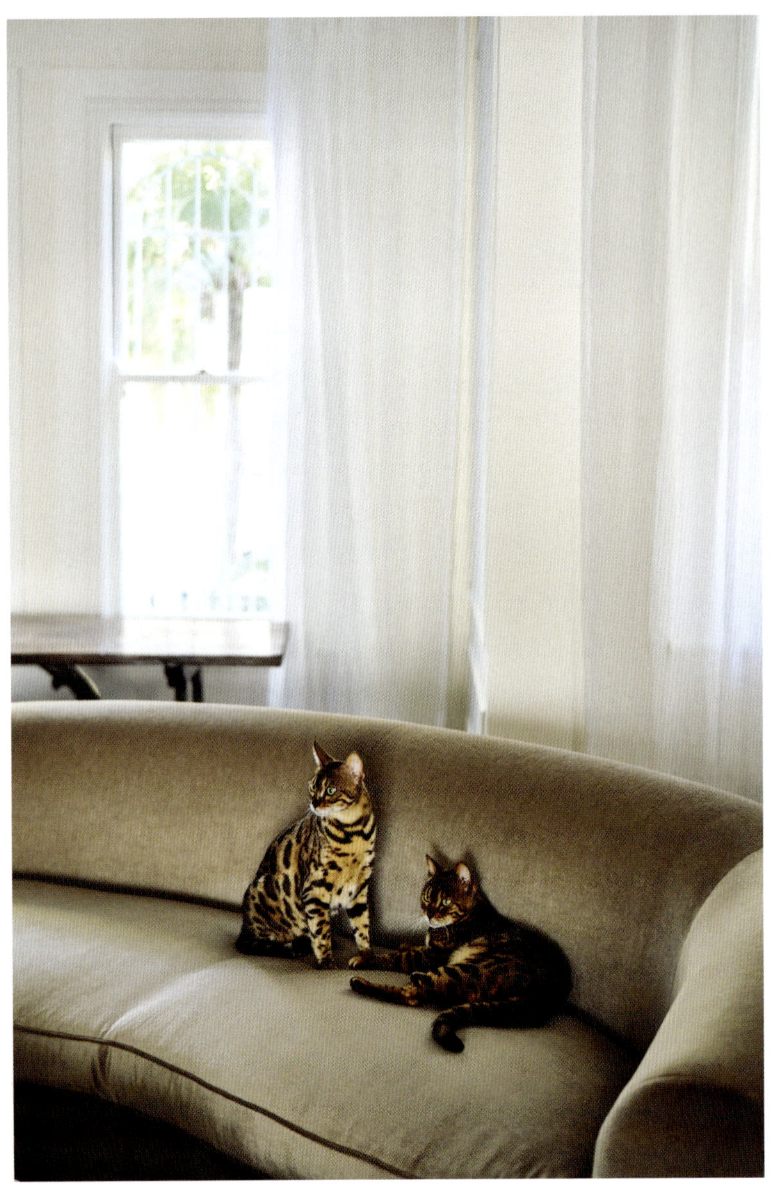

The owners of this Victorian terrace house, on one of Sydney's oldest streets, wanted their home to have a strong European influence, so they enlisted a designer with an eye for unique French and Italian antiques. Unfortunately, Raphael and Fellini are rather fond of scratching the furniture, so their owners have installed French doors between the kitchen and living area, for peace of mind when they are not home.

Designer: Tamsin Johnson / Tamsin Johnson Interior Design

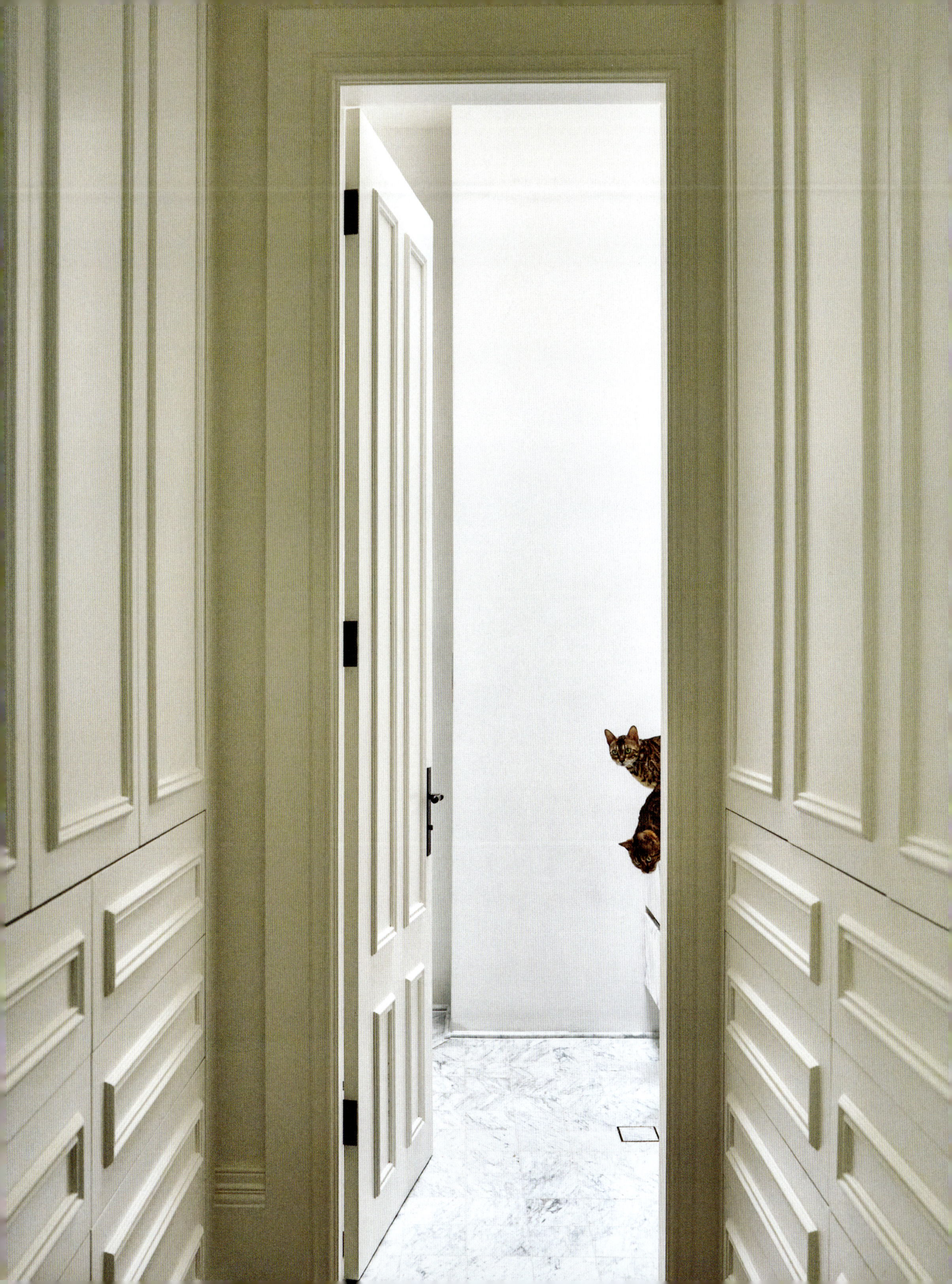

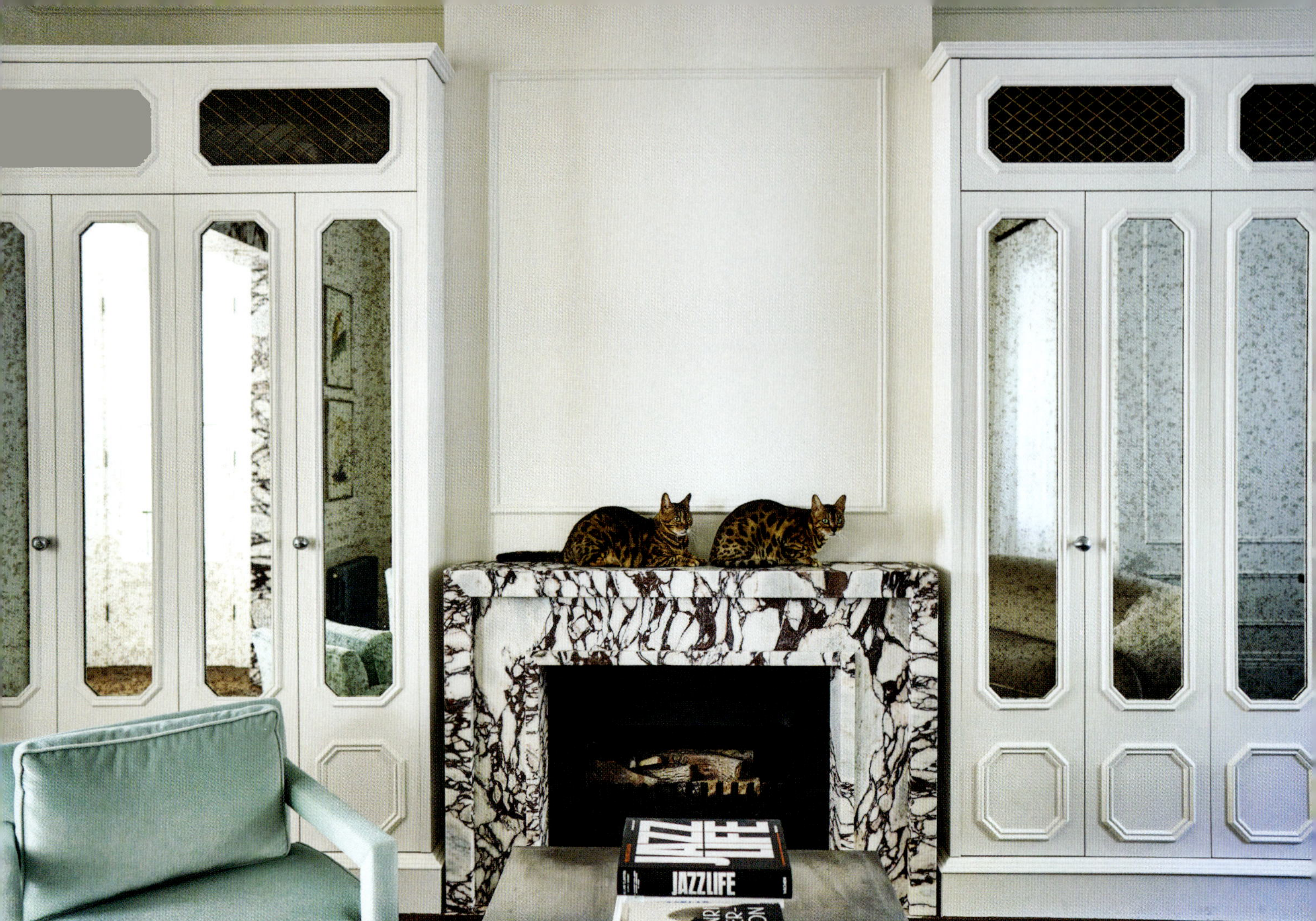

A grand villa at Lake Como and a Milanese-style pied-à-terre were the key influences behind the design of this home. The opulent interior features marble, parquetry and terrazzo, as well as detailed beading and antique Murano light fittings.

The marble staircase, with its wrought iron balustrade, is the perfect place for the cats to pounce on unsuspecting passers-by.

Designer: Tamsin Johnson / Tamsin Johnson Interior Design

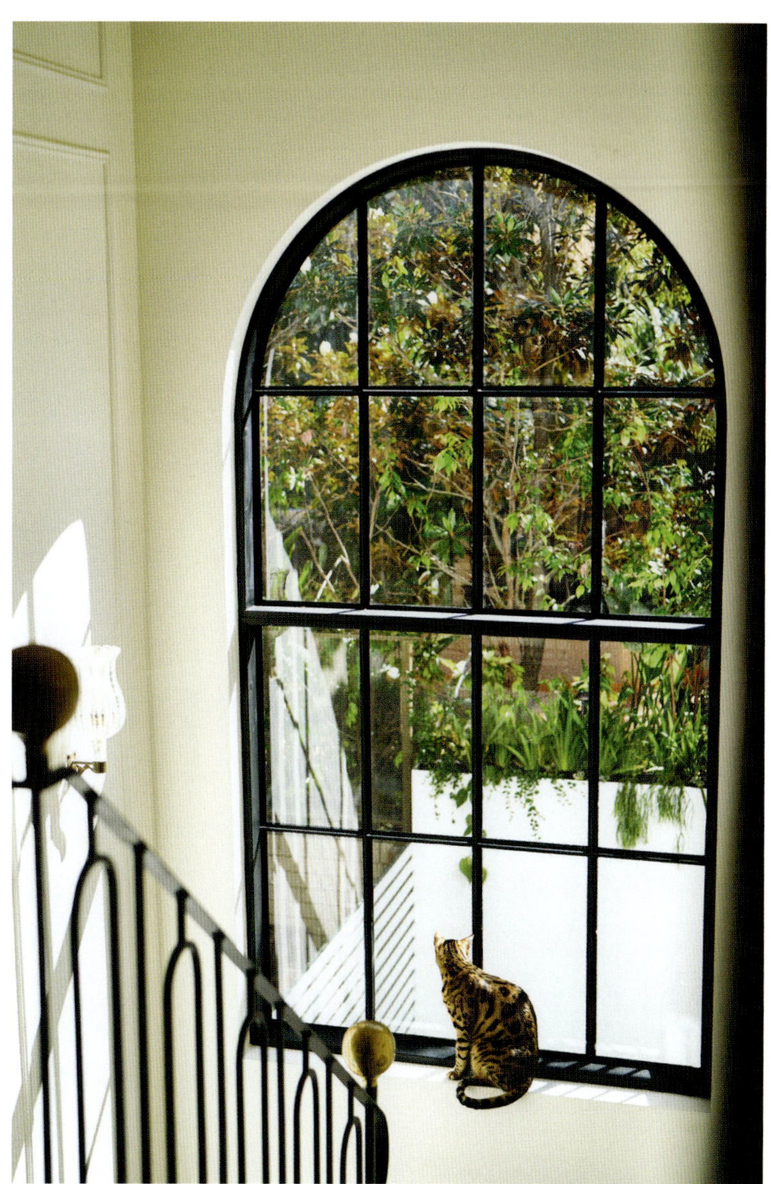

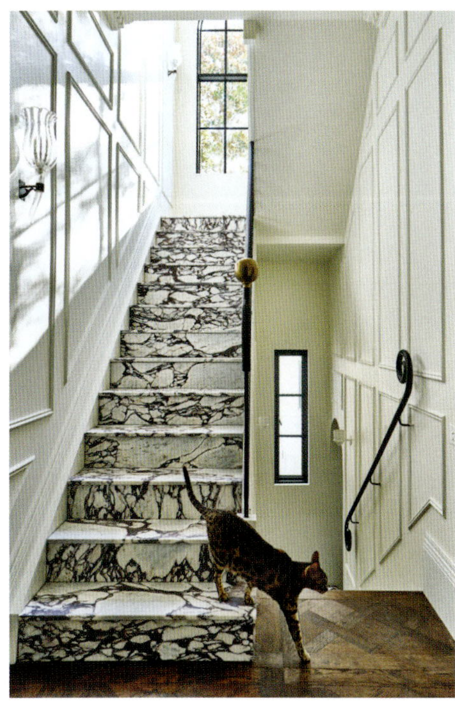

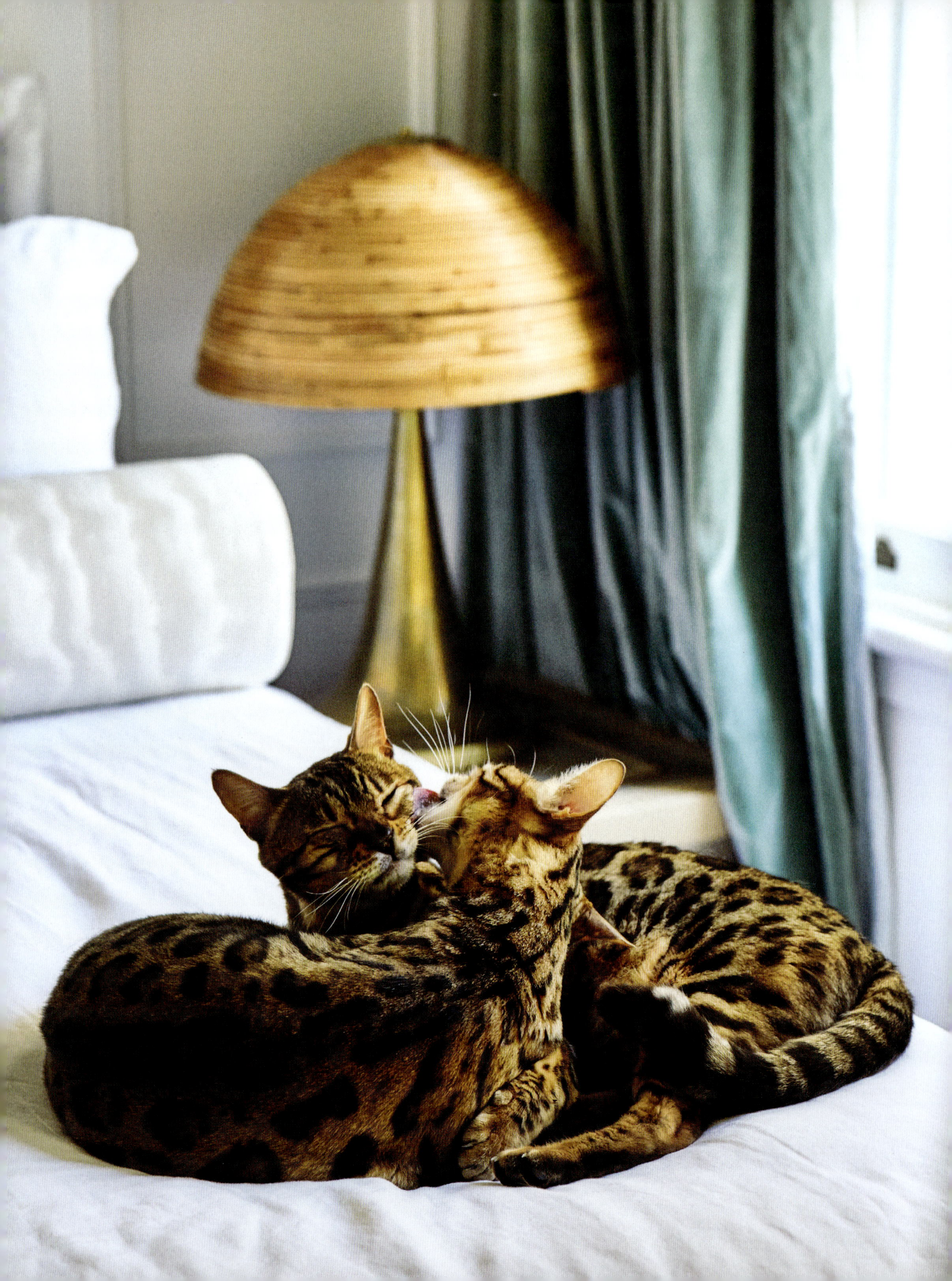

Q&A

DIVAS OR DEVOTED FRIENDS?
Total divas. If they aren't happy, they will let you know.

EXTROVERTS OR INTROVERTS?
Extroverts. Both of them.

LAP CATS OR NOT?
Depends on their mood. Raphael and Fellini are fiercely independent, but they also love attention and cuddles.

OLD SOULS OR KITTENS AT HEART?
Raphael is an old soul. Fellini is a kitten at heart.

EXPLORERS OR HOMEBODIES?
They are indoor cats, but would-be explorers. On day one, the vet warned their owners: 'Never let them outside – they will kill everything in their path.'

LAZY OR ACTIVE?
Active. Their favourite game is 'stair monster': they will hide on the stairs and pounce on anyone who walks by.

DOGS – FRIEND OR FOE?
Never been tested, but foe seems most likely.

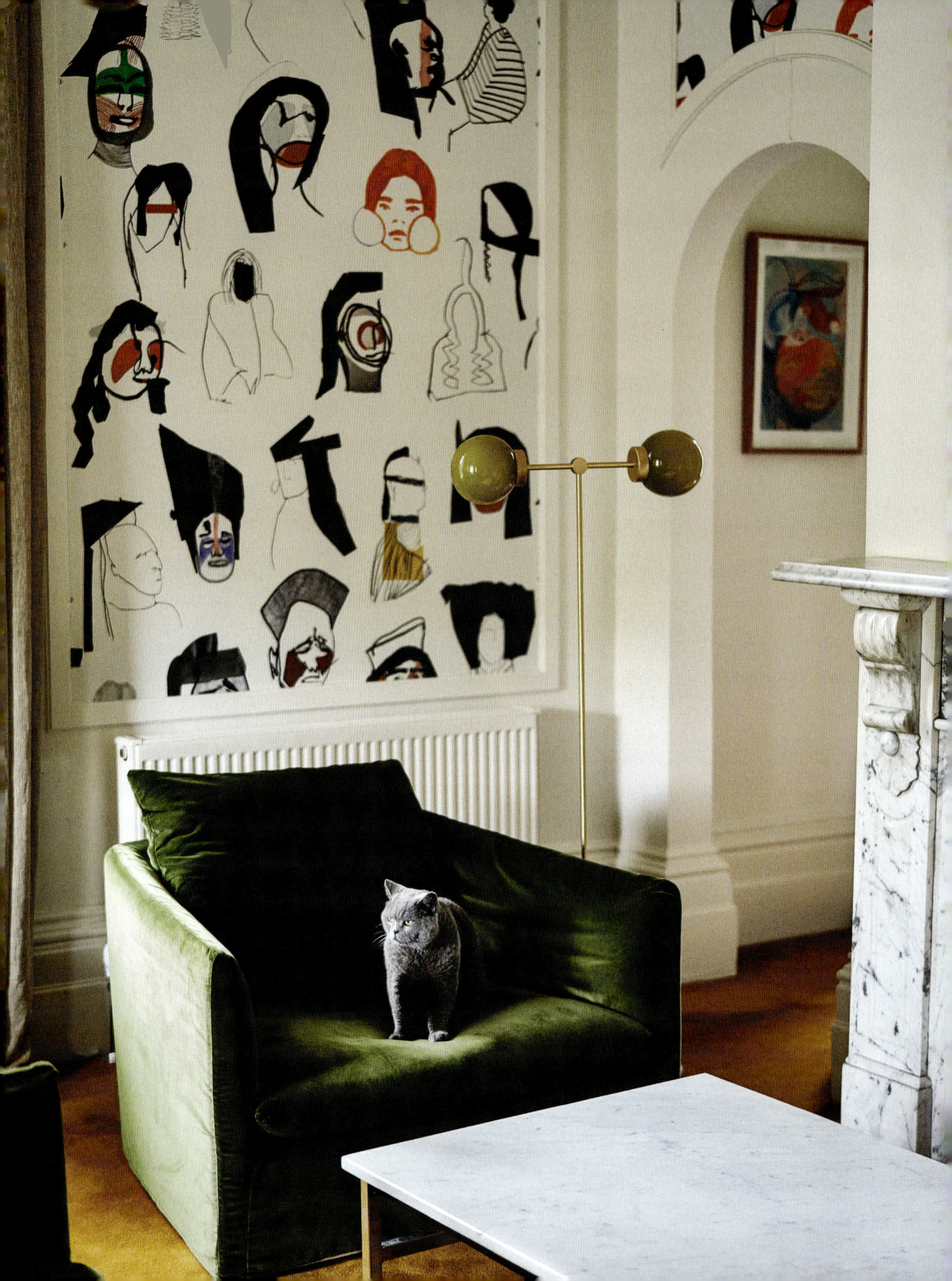

MOLLY

ARCHITECT: KENNEDY NOLAN

Molly, a ten-year-old British shorthair, was actually a surprise birthday gift for this family's eight-year-old son, and they've bonded ever since. She was once so tiny, she could almost fit in the palm of his hand. Now, a decade later, the much bigger Molly mostly lazes around her home, but she still ends each day by visiting her favourite person's room before bedtime to get her fill of love and affection.

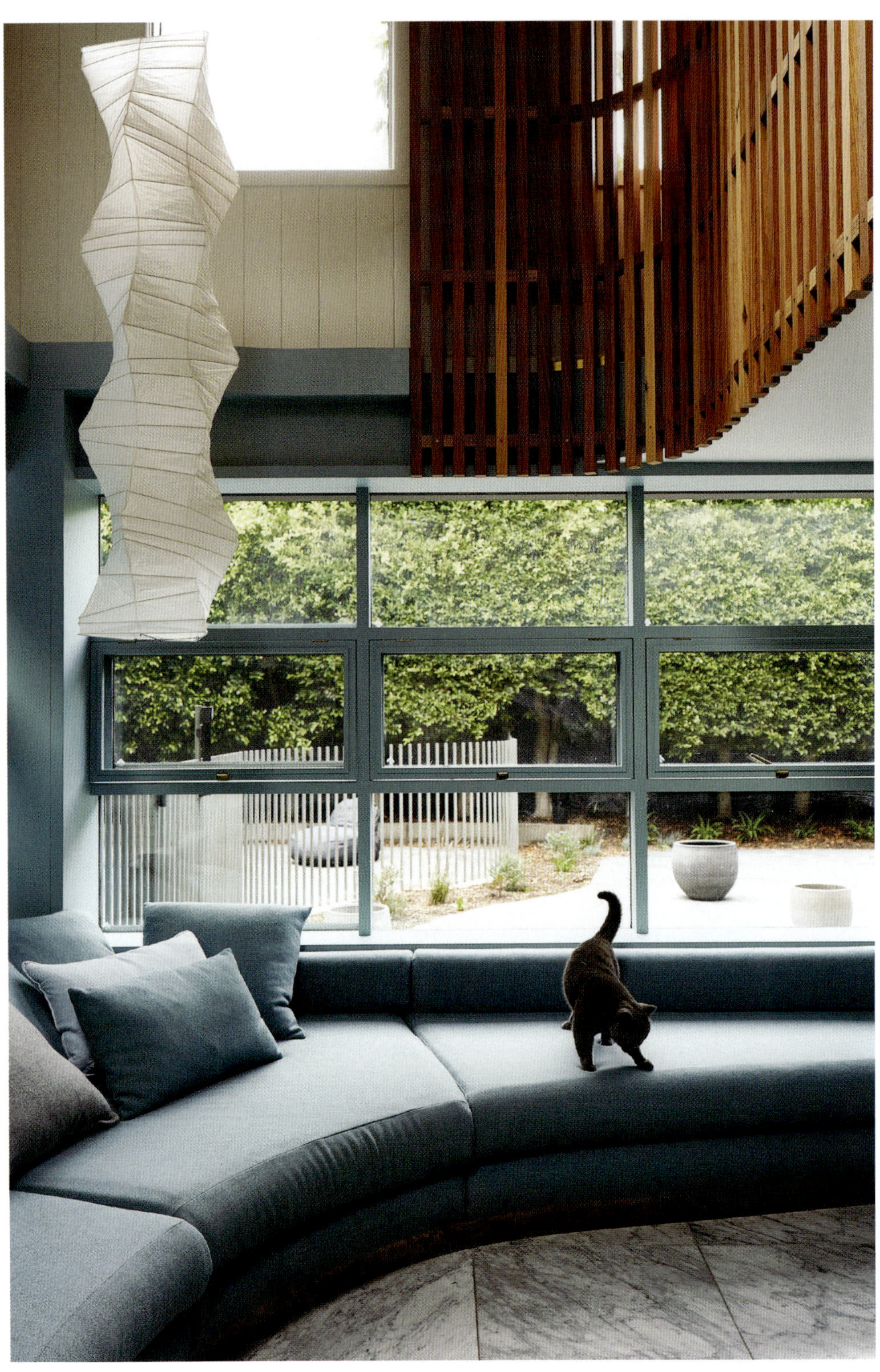

Architect: Kennedy Nolan

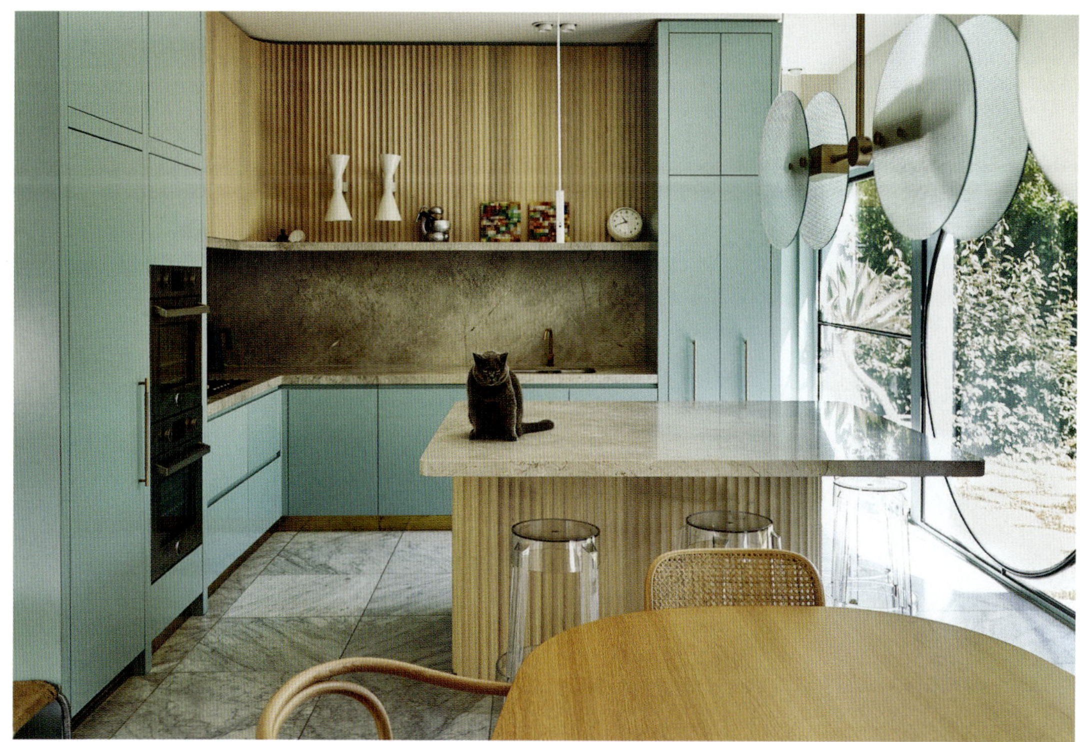

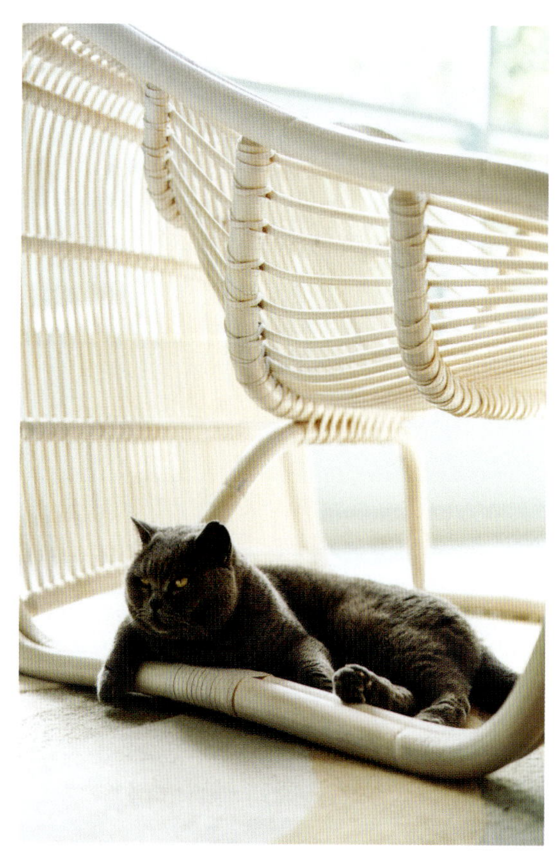

The transformation to Molly's home – a classic Victorian-period dwelling with additions made in the 1980s – was achieved through careful editing and intervention. Colour and texture were used wherever possible, along with bold, graphic gestures, to serve as a counterpoint to the more traditional features of the architecture.

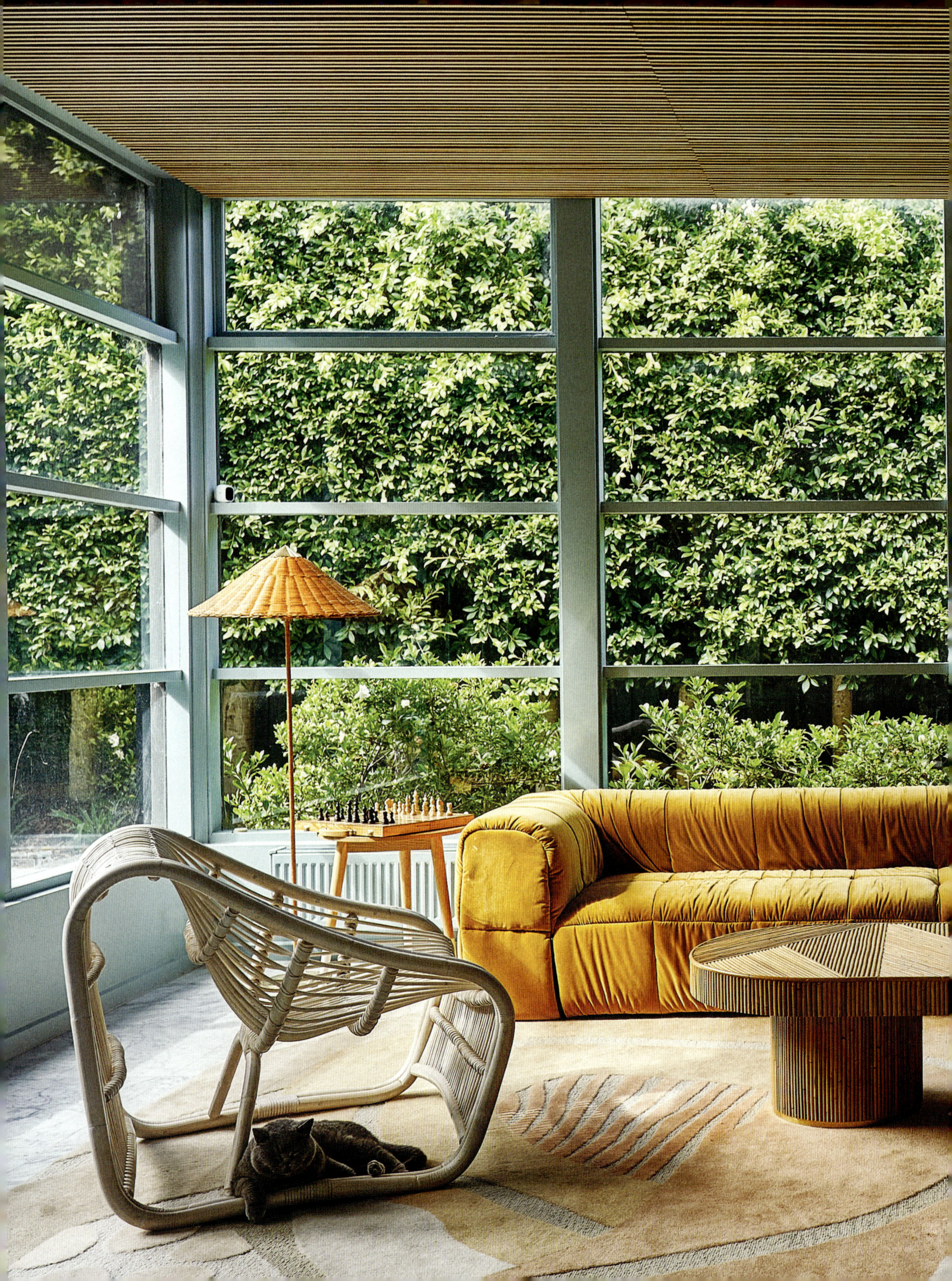

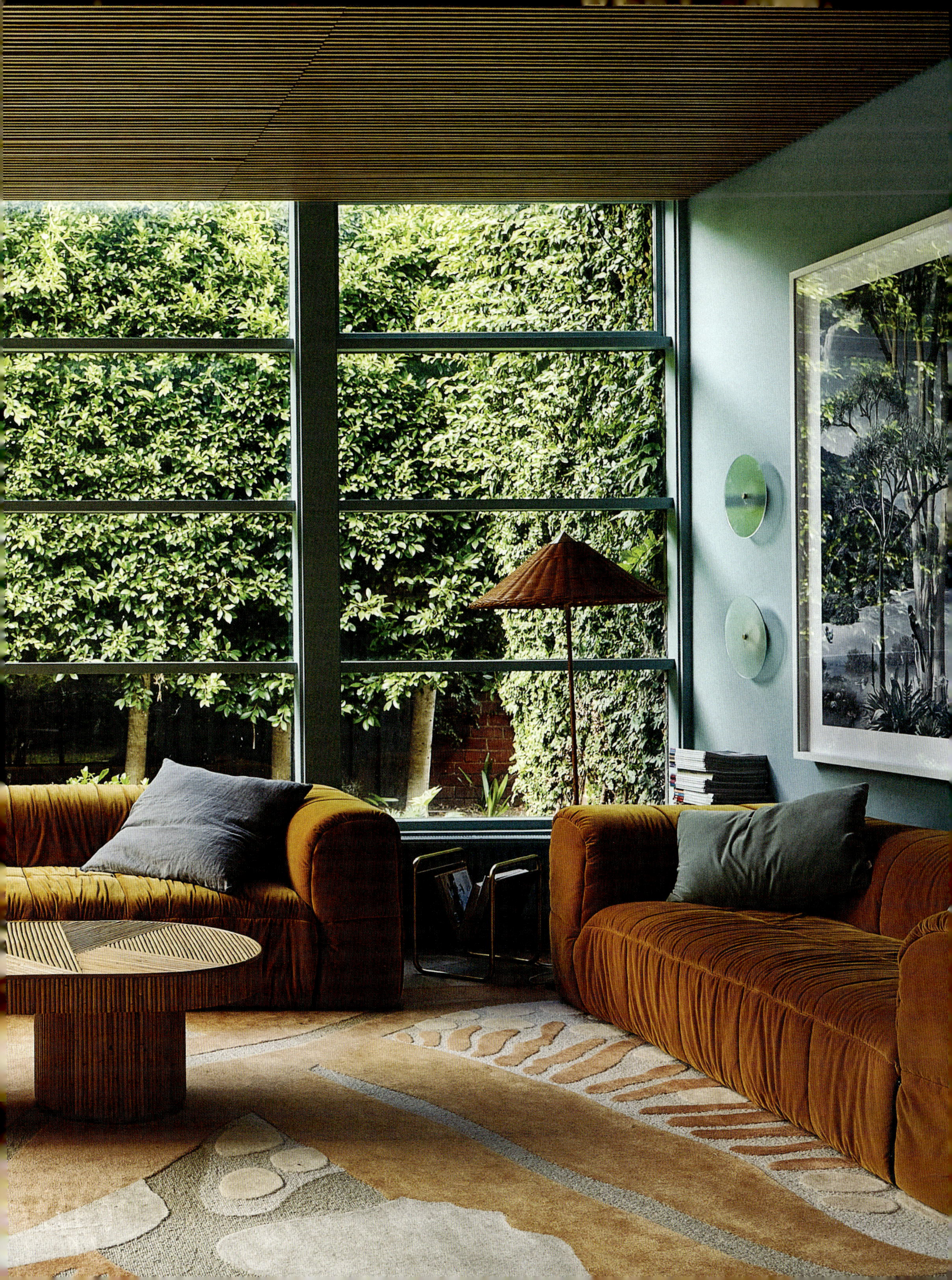

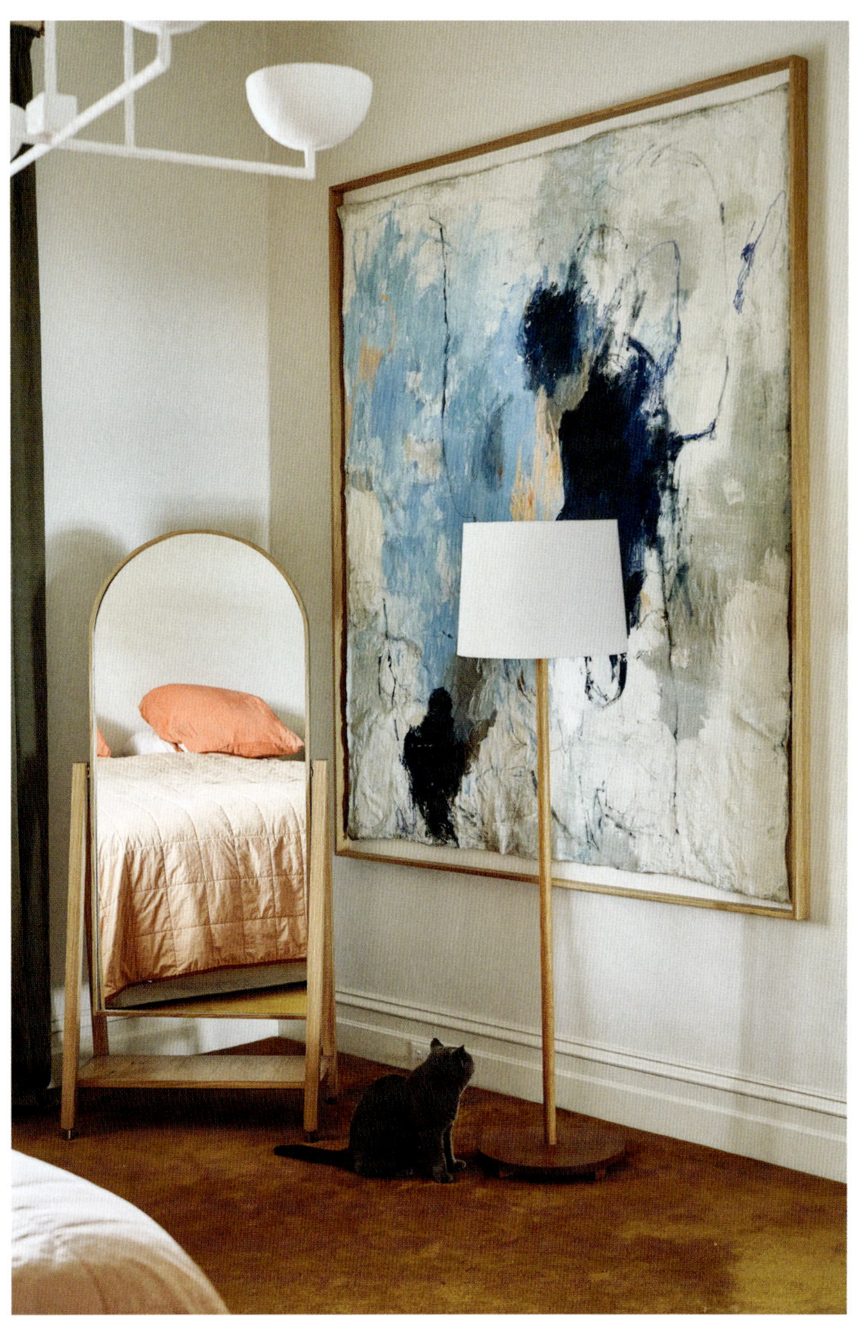

The colour palette, which strongly references the Swedish Gustavian style – cool and quiet, but with added playfulness – ensures the various parts of the home feel unified.

Architect: Kennedy Nolan

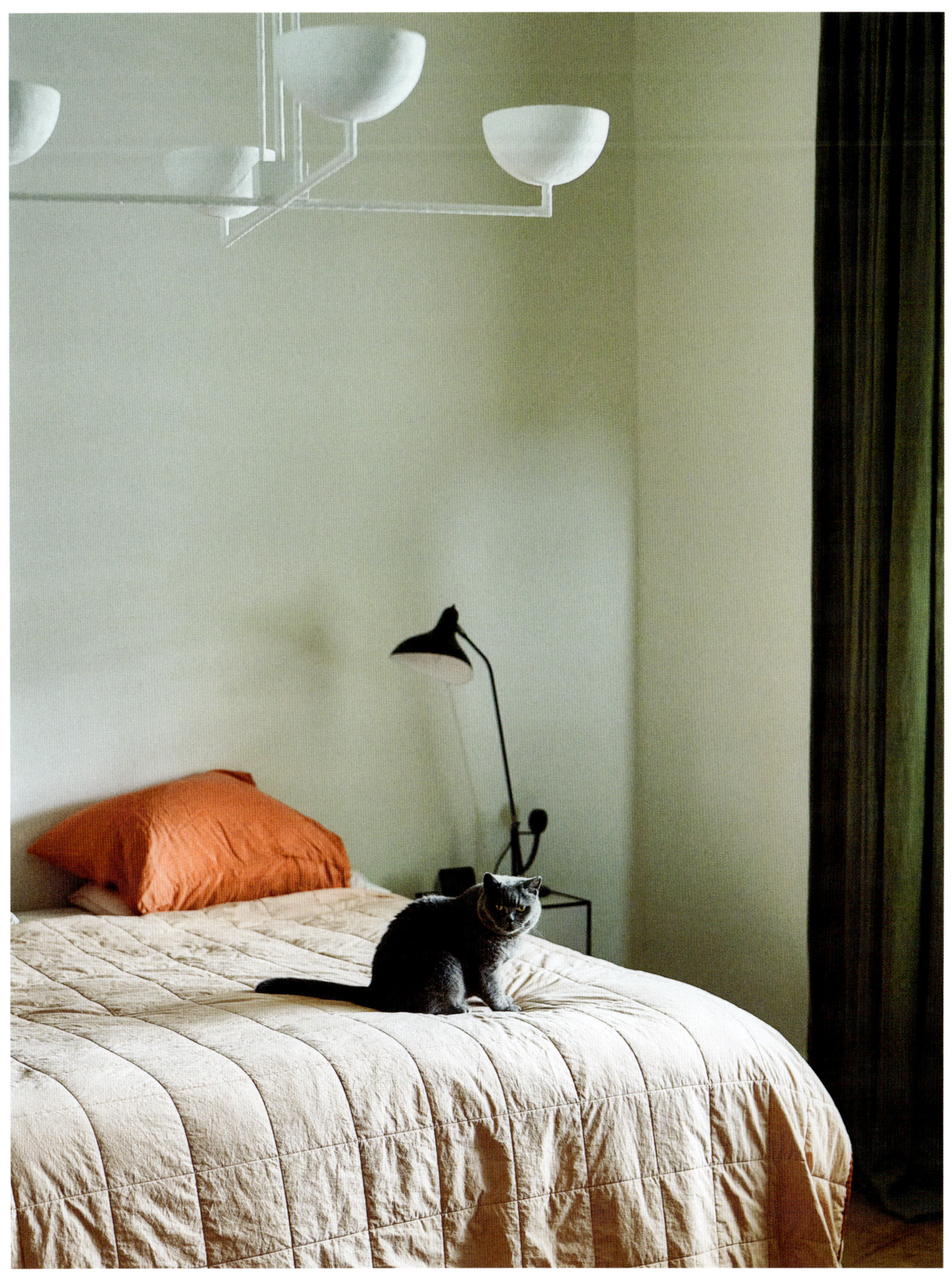

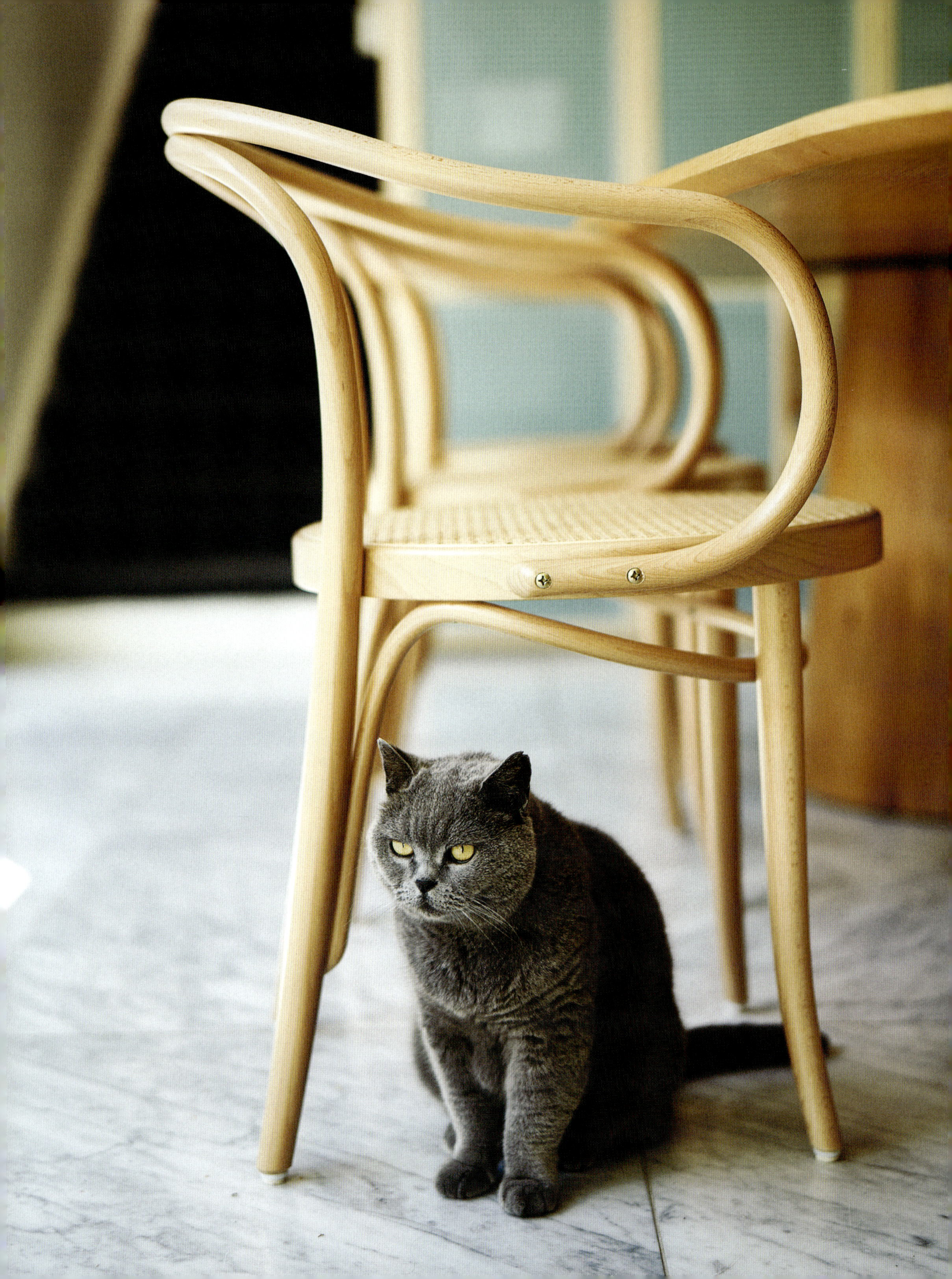

Q&A

DIVA OR DEVOTED FRIEND?

Diva.

EXTROVERT OR INTROVERT?

Introvert.

LAP CAT OR NOT?

Not.

OLD SOUL OR KITTEN AT HEART?

Old soul – there's not a lot of play going on.

EXPLORER OR HOMEBODY?

Homebody.

LAZY OR ACTIVE?

Both.

DOGS – FRIEND OR FOE?

She has complete contempt for the family's sweet-natured dog.

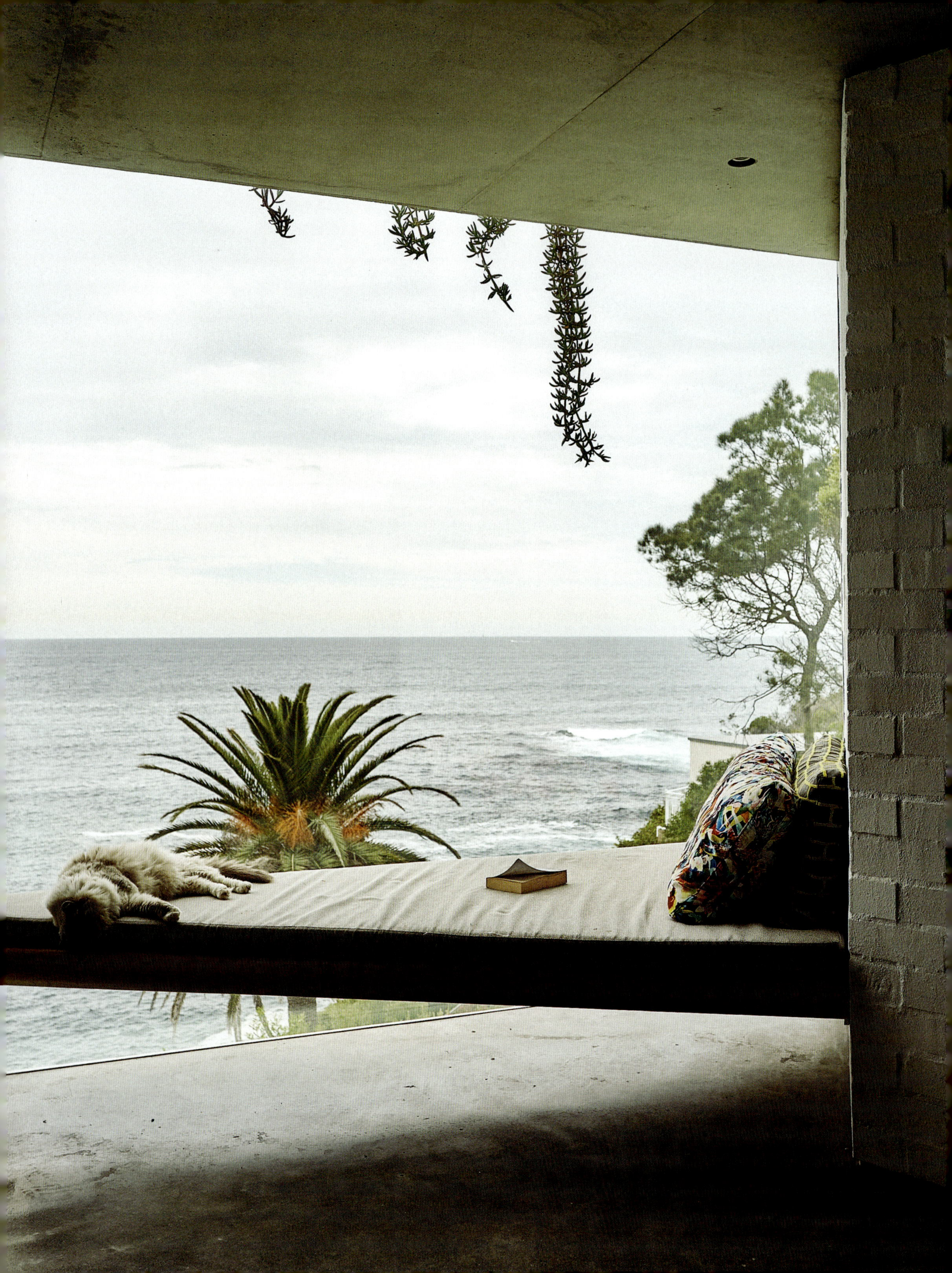

LULU

ARCHITECT: RENATO D'ETTORRE / RENATO D'ETTORRE ARCHITECTS

Lulu, a ragdoll, was just a kitten when she was brought home to be a companion for her family's ten-year-old daughter. These days, Lulu enjoys a charmed life, residing in a house on a cliff that overlooks an idyllic and secluded bay. From her vantage point, she watches the seabirds soaring on the updrafts – it's an endless source of entertainment.

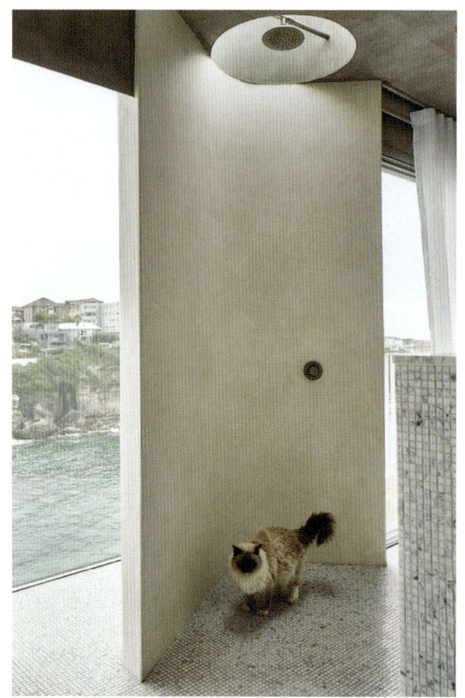

This home, located along a busy stretch of coastline, was designed to provide a sense of seclusion. Lookouts have been cleverly integrated, without compromising on privacy, so that Lulu and her family can take full advantage of the constantly changing panorama of bay, ocean and surf break.

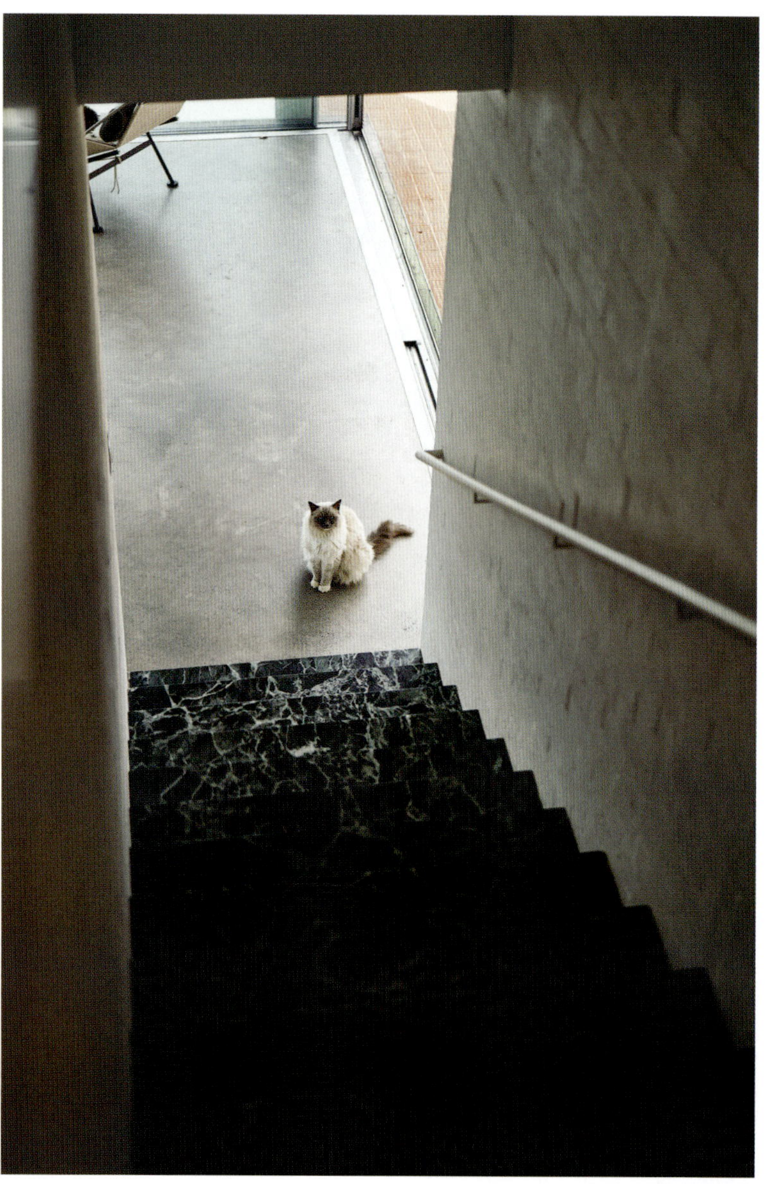

Architect: Renato D'Ettorre / Renato D'Ettorre Architects

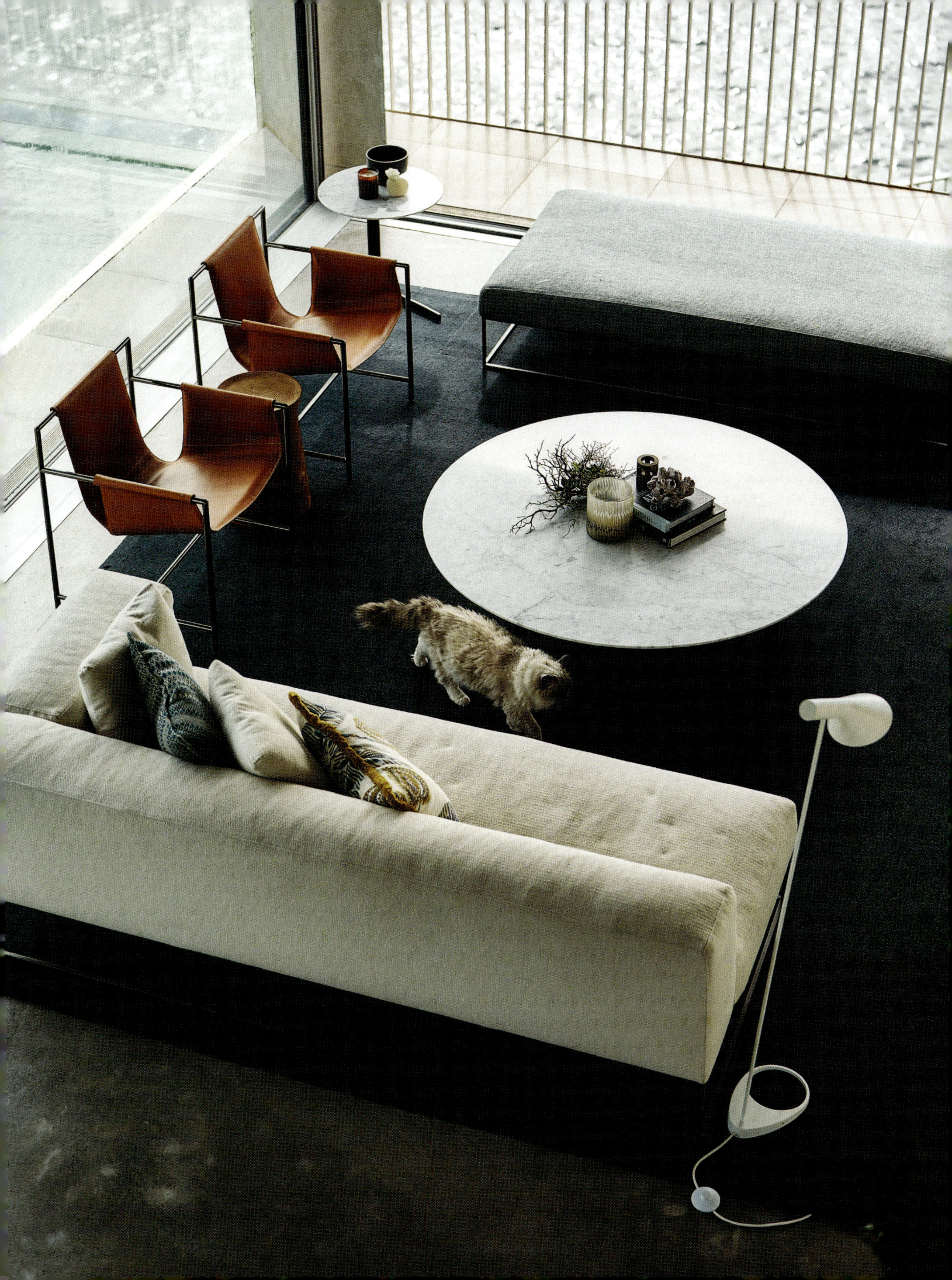

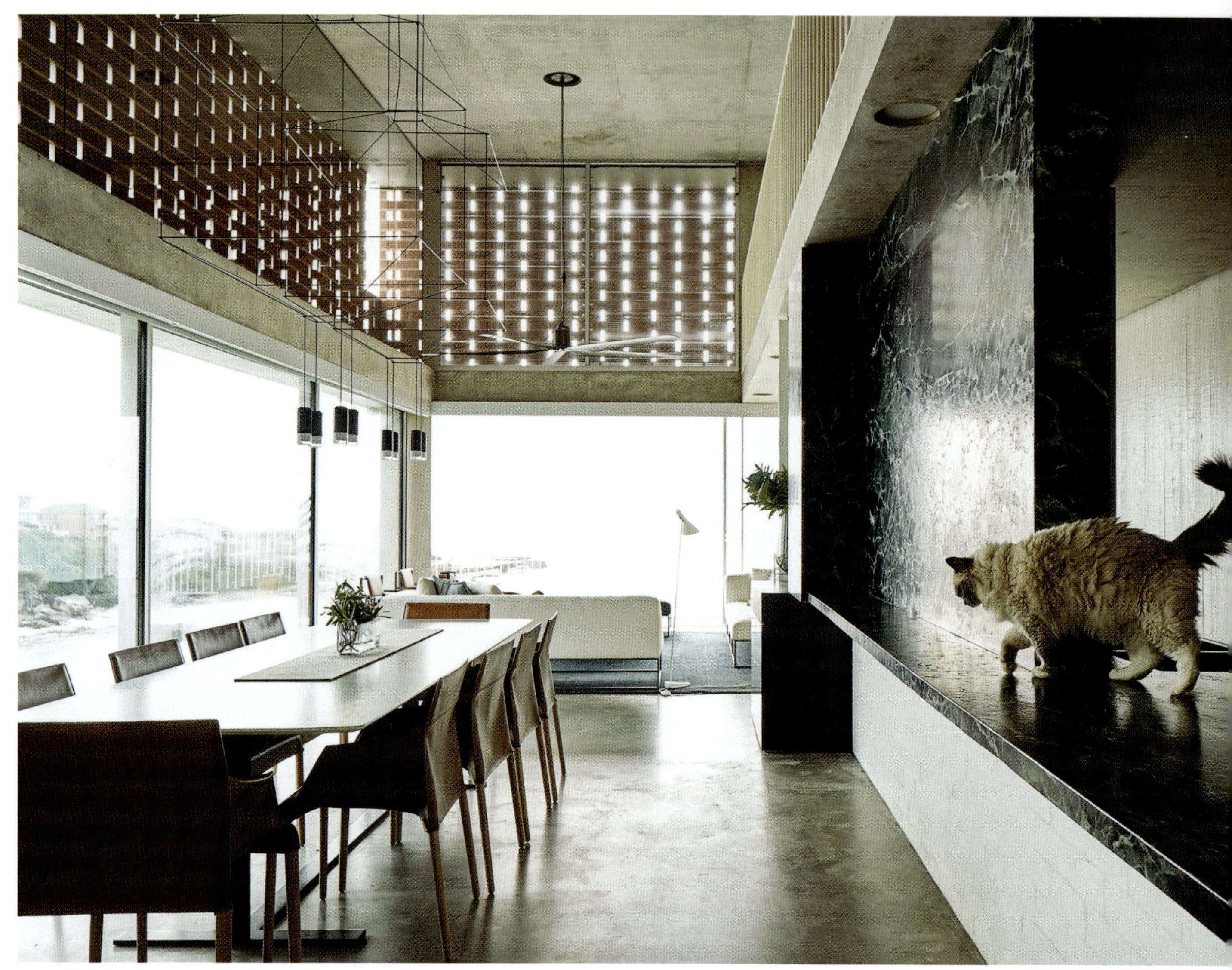

Rugged and simple materials like brick and concrete were chosen to suit the craggy location of the house as well as the practicalities of family life. Green marble surfaces evoke the bay below.

Architect: Renato D'Ettorre / Renato D'Ettorre Architects

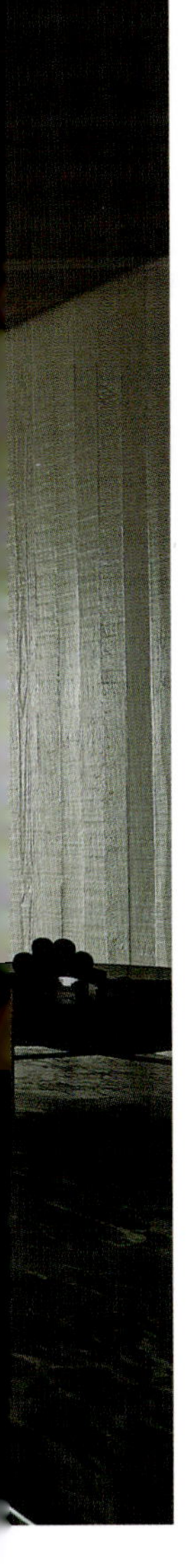

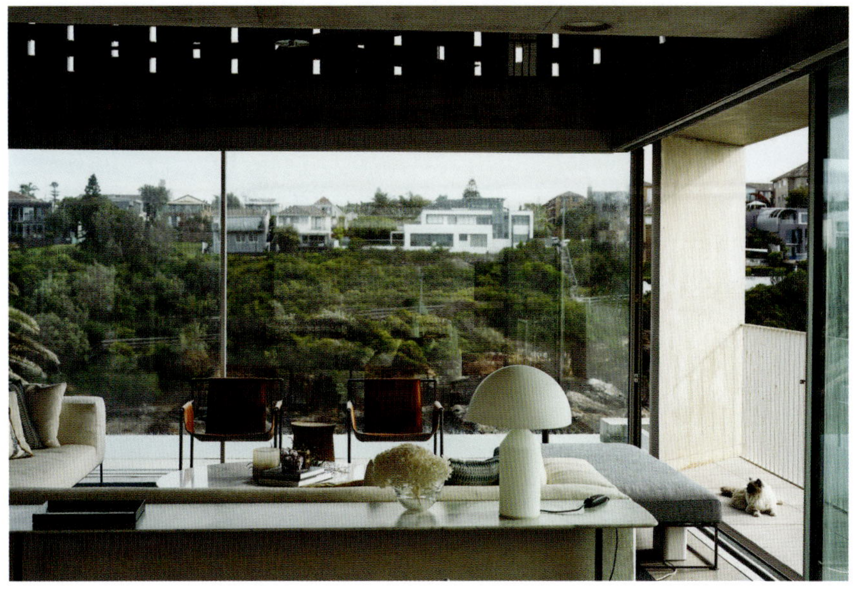

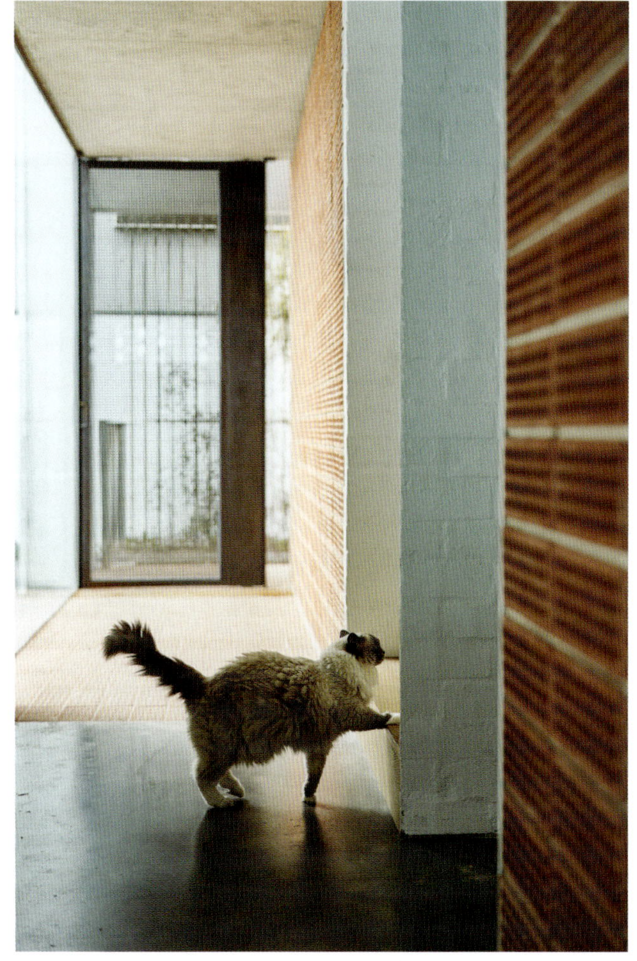

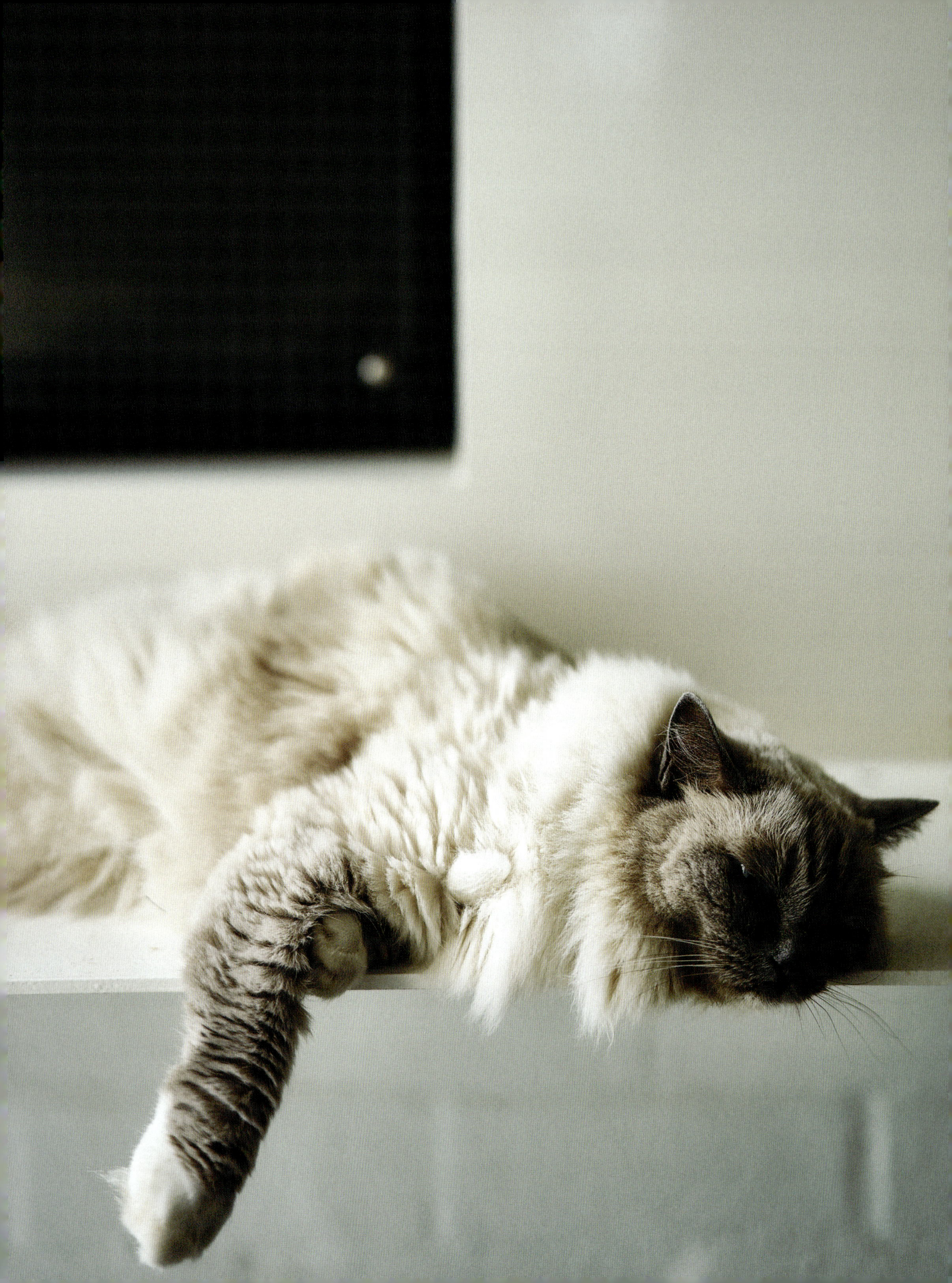

Q&A

DIVA OR DEVOTED FRIEND?
Diva.

EXTROVERT OR INTROVERT?
Introvert.

LAP CAT OR NOT?
Not.

OLD SOUL OR KITTEN AT HEART?
Old soul.

EXPLORER OR HOMEBODY?
Homebody.

LAZY OR ACTIVE?
Lazy.

DOGS – FRIEND OR FOE?
Definitely foe.

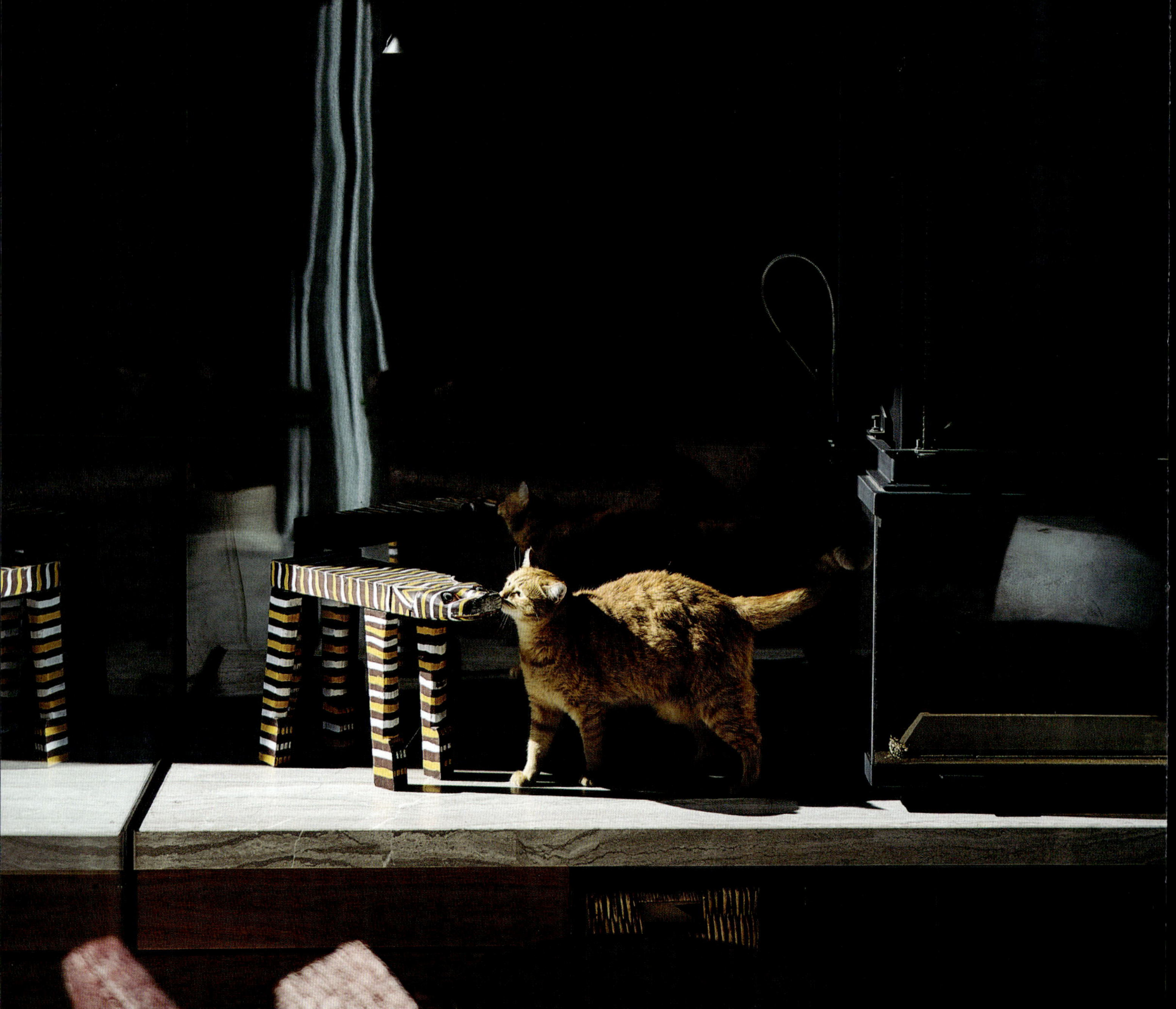

PRUDENCE GINGER, AKA PRU PRU

ARCHITECTS: ASHA NICHOLAS AND CHRIS STANLEY / SPLINTER SOCIETY ARCHITECTURE

Prudence Ginger, aka Pru Pru, was chosen – at the behest of the family's daughter – to balance the male-to-female ratio in the household (at the time: dad, son and boy dog Charlie; mum and daughter). When the family called the local rescue shelter to enquire about adopting a cat, they were told that there was only one female kitten available. They drove over immediately to claim her and it was love at first sight. In a twist of fate, Pru Pru was a ginger cat – a rare colouring for a female – and she was just like the family's previous beloved cats, which made her even more special.

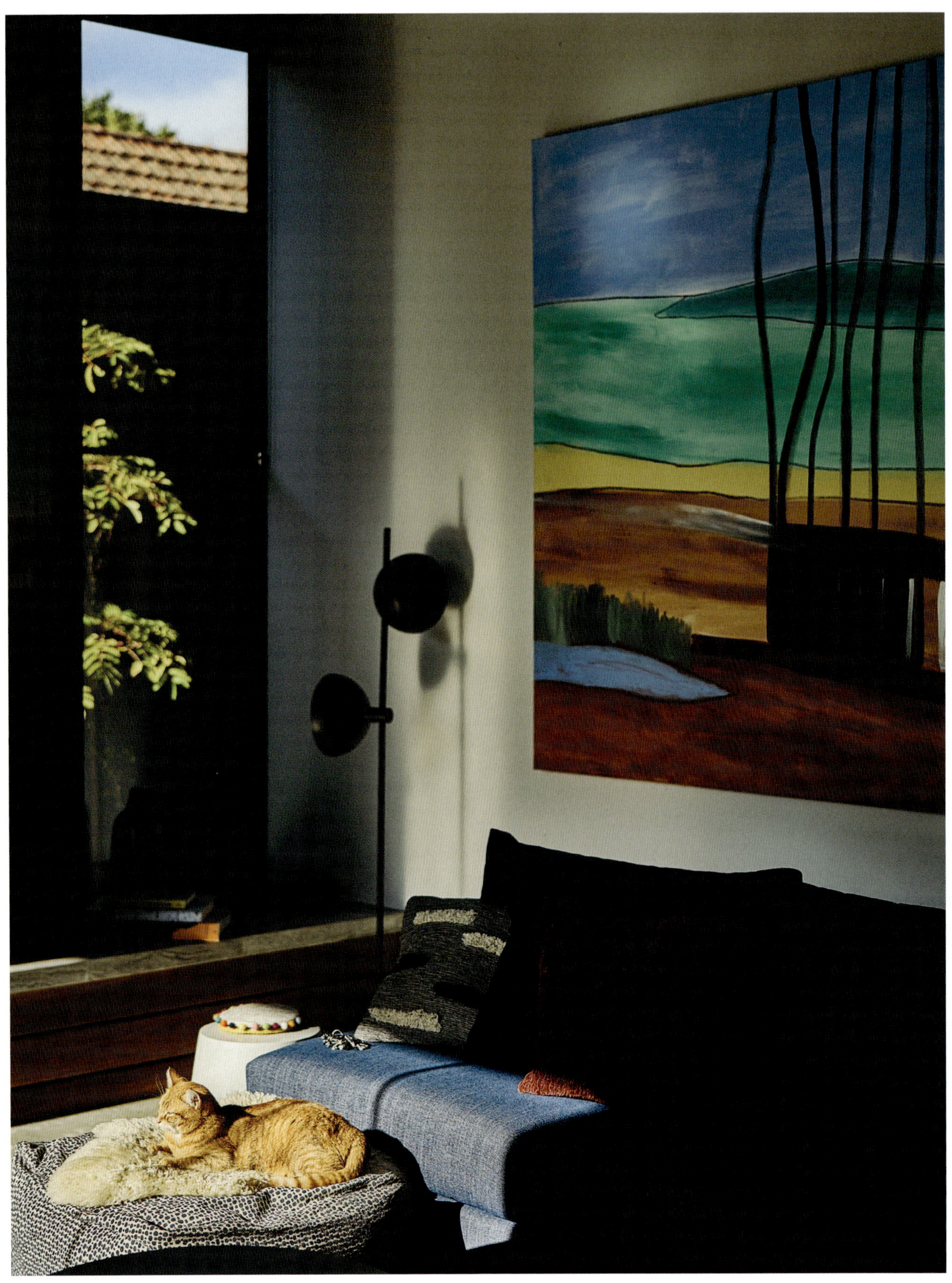

Architects: Asha Nicholas and Chris Stanley / Splinter Society Architecture

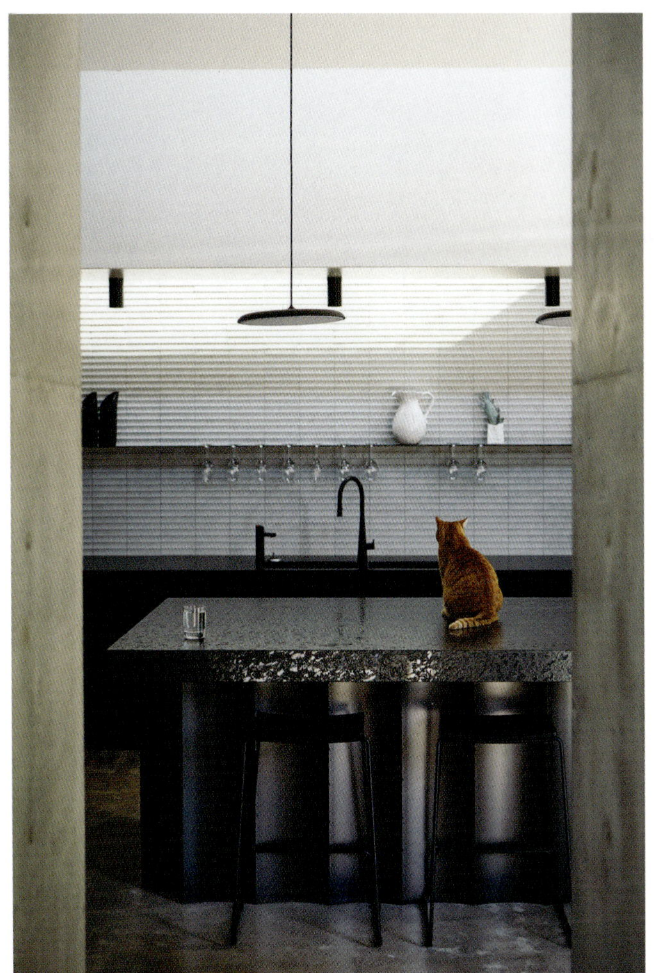

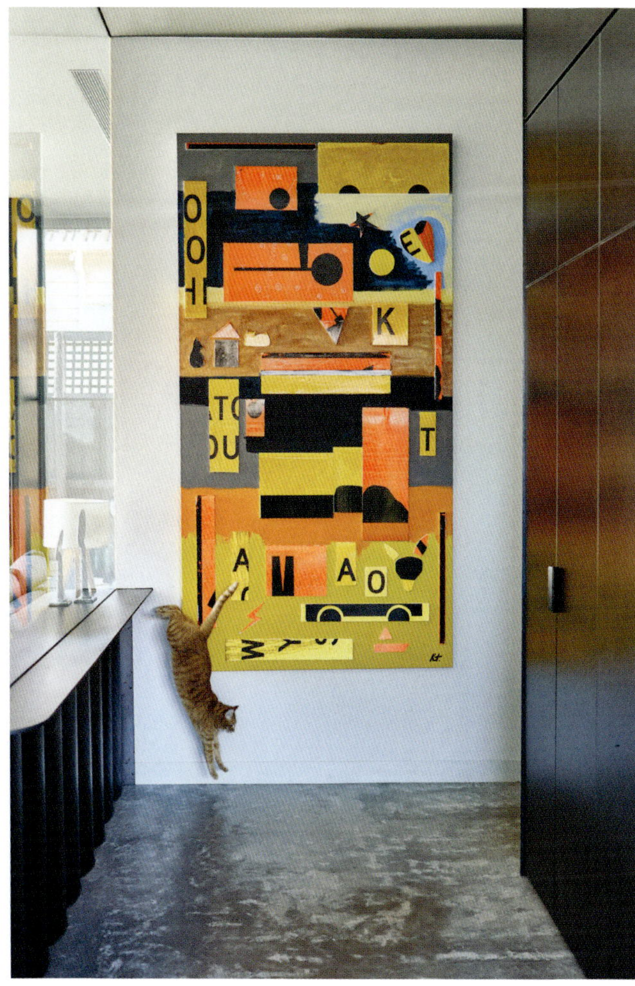

Pru Pru's family wanted to ensure that the extension to their Federation house paid respect to the original structure of the building, while still giving the home a modern take. The concrete columns are a distinctive feature that seamlessly link the old with the new. The wonderfully tactile granite island bench in the kitchen is where Pru Pru likes to drink her water – from a glass.

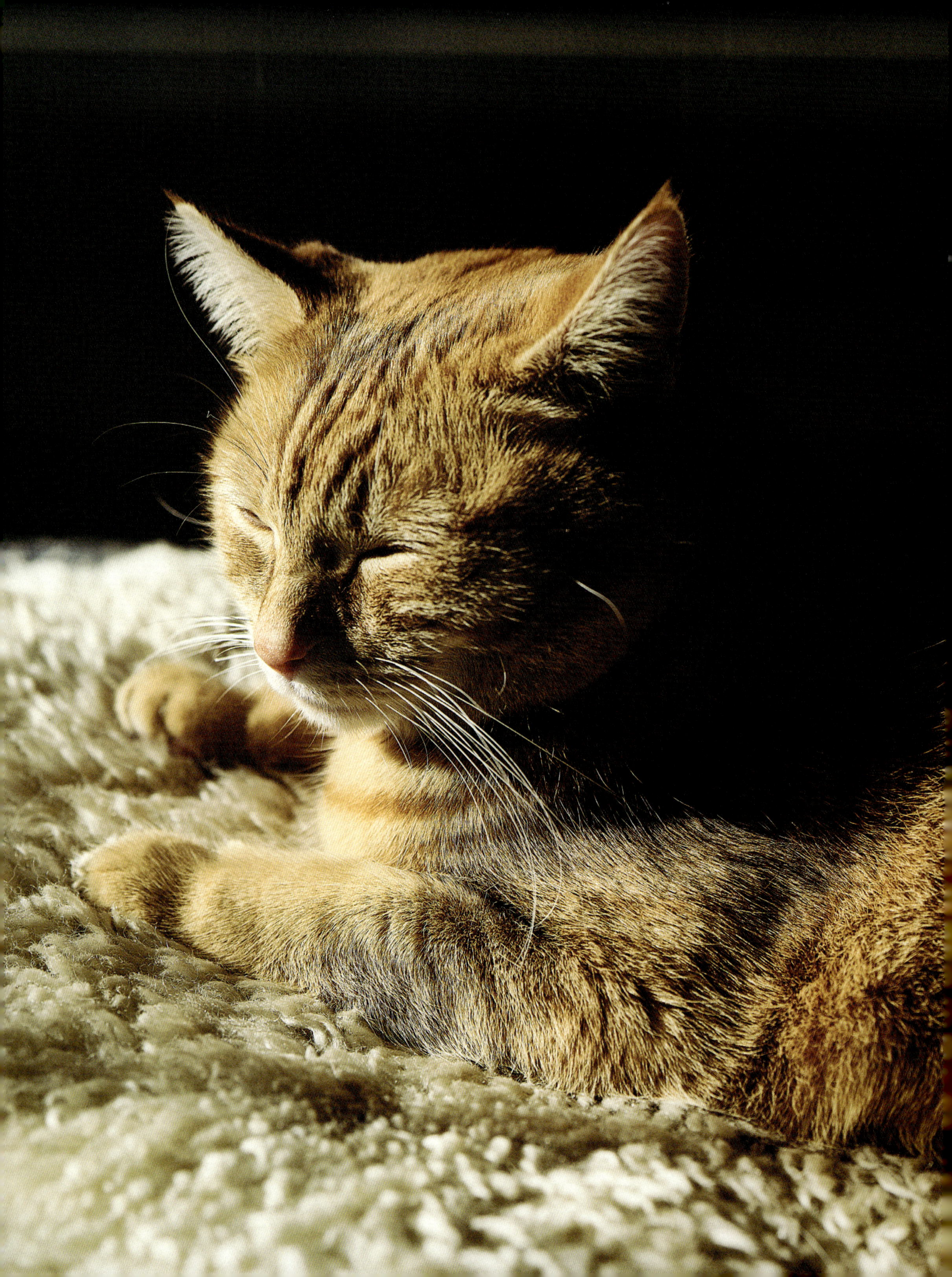

Q&A

DIVA OR DEVOTED FRIEND?

Can be both, but usually devoted friend.

EXTROVERT OR INTROVERT?

She is an extrovert and happy to be around people. You can even carry her around like a baby.

LAP CAT OR NOT?

Definitely a lap cat. She will sit on you and give you kisses, with her forehead resting on your forehead.

OLD SOUL OR KITTEN AT HEART?

Kitten at heart, although on the day the family first met her, they did feel a sense that she may be something of an old soul.

EXPLORER OR HOMEBODY?

Definitely an explorer, but never too far from home. She is horrified by travel and hates being out of her known environment.

LAZY OR ACTIVE?

She can fire up at times, running around erratically, climbing the fence and trees, and even venturing over to the neighbours for pats.

DOGS – FRIEND OR FOE?

She loves the family's dog, Charlie – he's like her nice older brother.

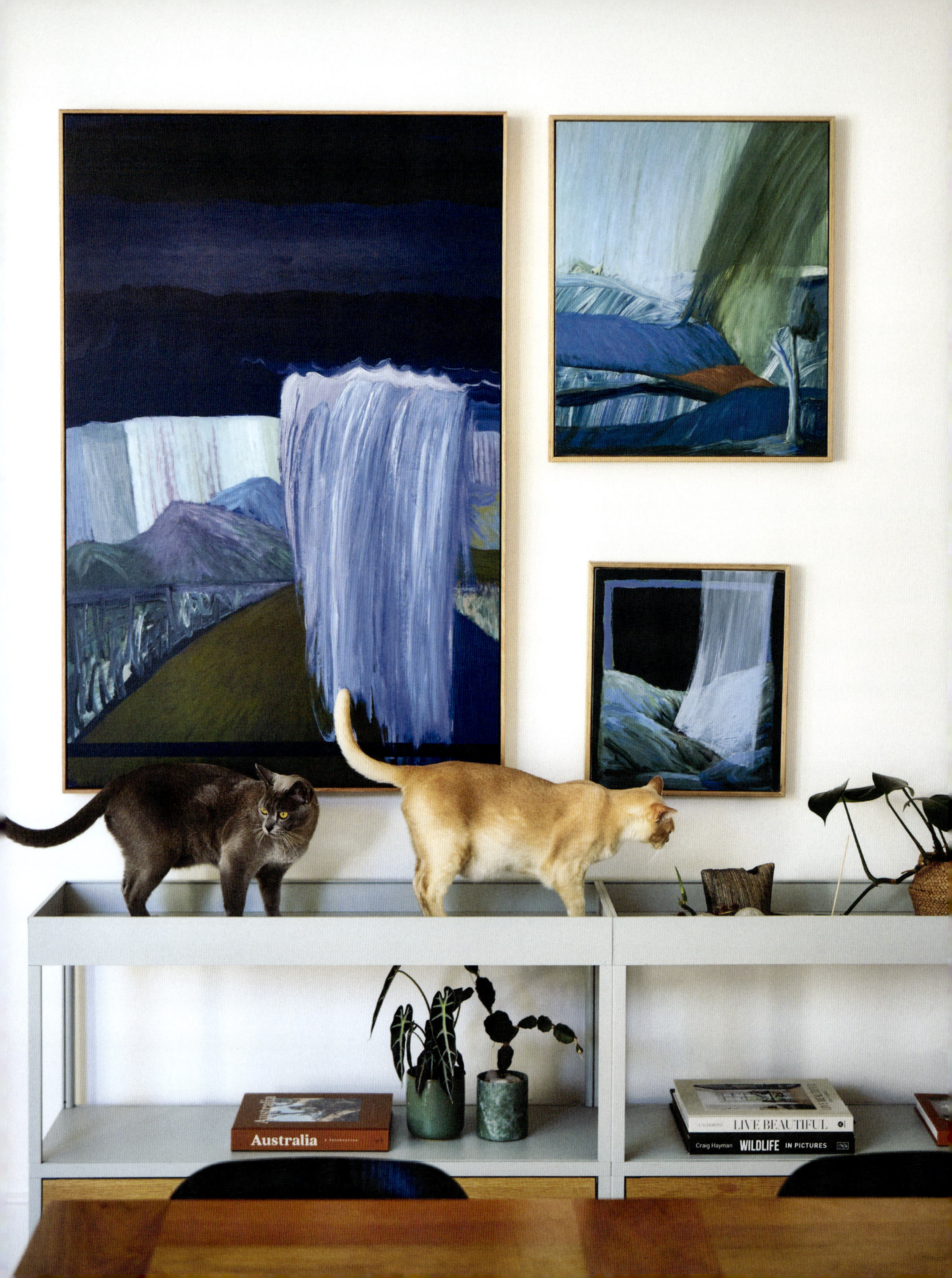

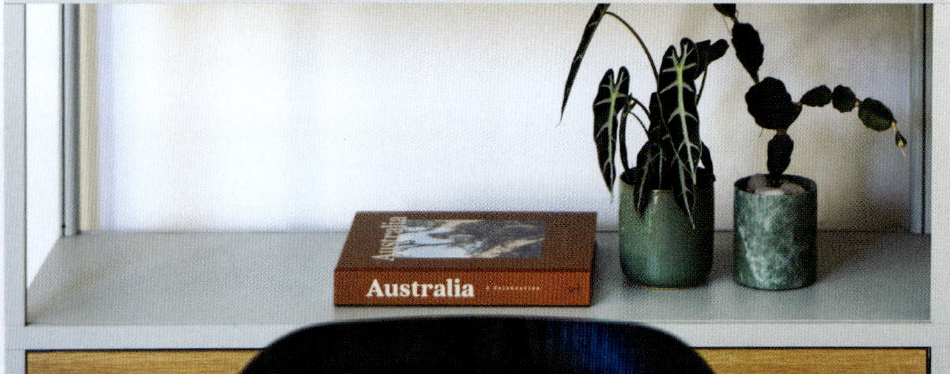
Australia

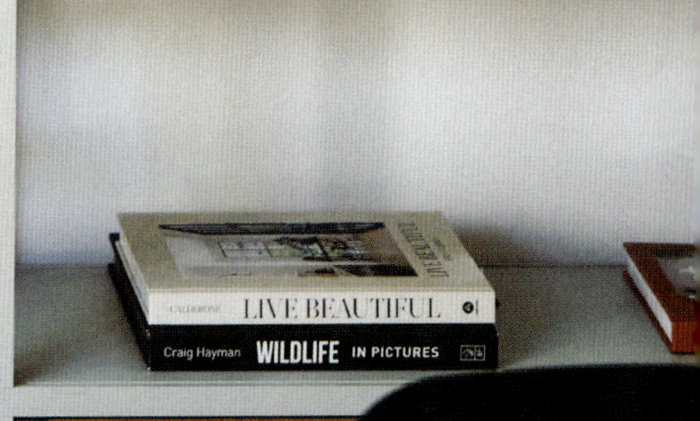
LIVE BEAUTIFUL
Craig Hayman WILDLIFE IN PICTURES

GUS AND FREDDIE

DESIGNER: SARAH-JANE PYKE / ARENT&PYKE
WITH VITALE DESIGN

Gus and Freddie are eighteen-month-old Burmese cats. They are supposedly from the same litter, but are so dissimilar in both appearance and personality that their family questions whether this can be true. Gus is grey and handsome, athletic and savvy. He is smart enough to get out of the way of the family's cockatoo when it's in a bad mood, and will make himself scarce if there are annoying kids around. Freddie, on the other hand, is cream and overweight. He is rather uncat-like in terms of his reflexes and falls off things all the time. He is friendly with other animals and doesn't even bother to move when the cockatoo pecks him – maybe he is easygoing, or perhaps just lazy. He likes to hang around whenever there are people present. Gus and Freddie's owners are animal lovers and believe that without pets, a home is just a house.

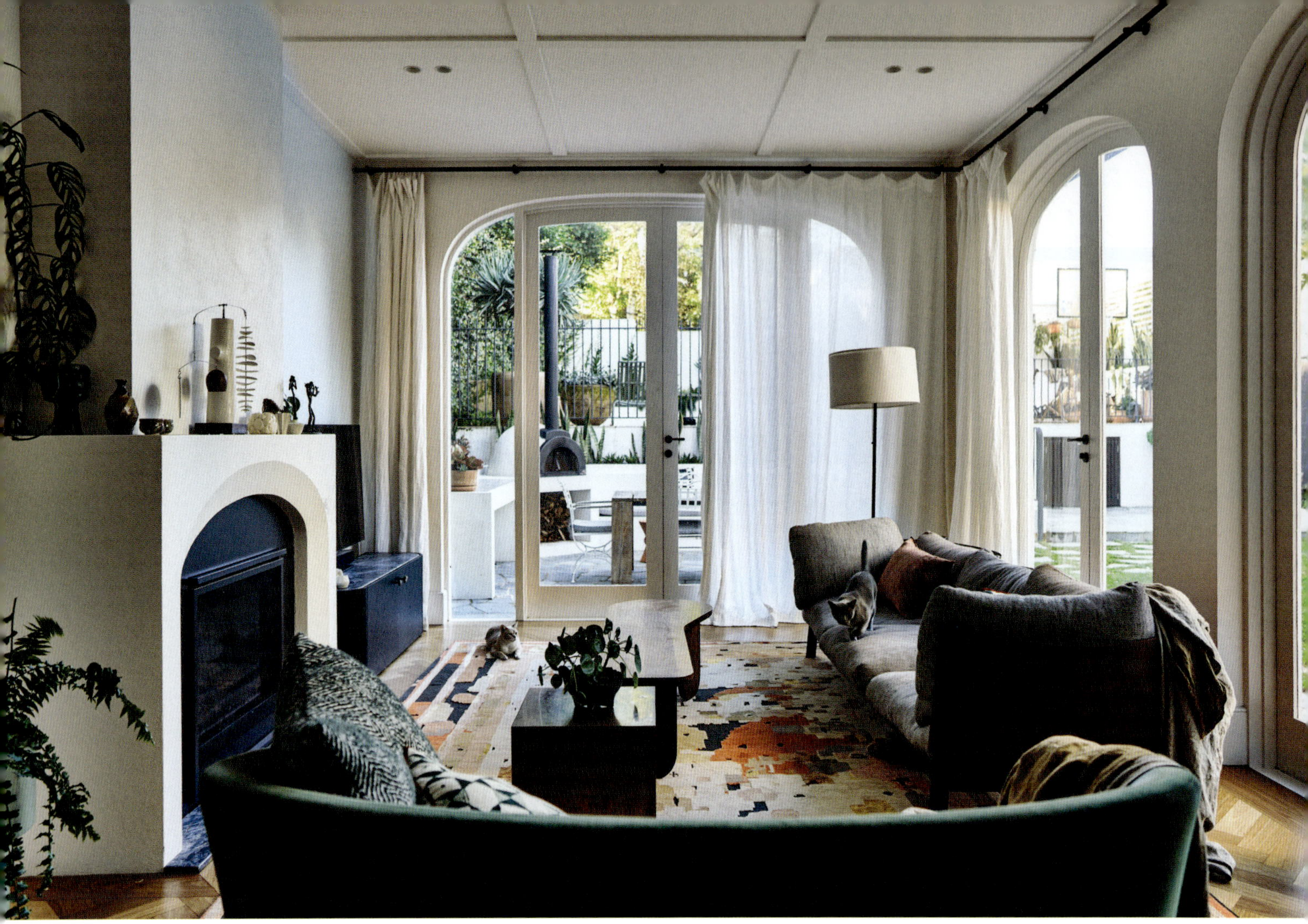

'Decorative modernism' was the design brief for the recent renovation of this heritage bungalow. The front three rooms are more traditional and intimate, but as you move through the house, the character builds as the spaces open up. The styling and use of colour throughout the home provides a sense of synergy.

Designer: Sarah-Jane Pyke / Arent&Pyke with Vitale Design

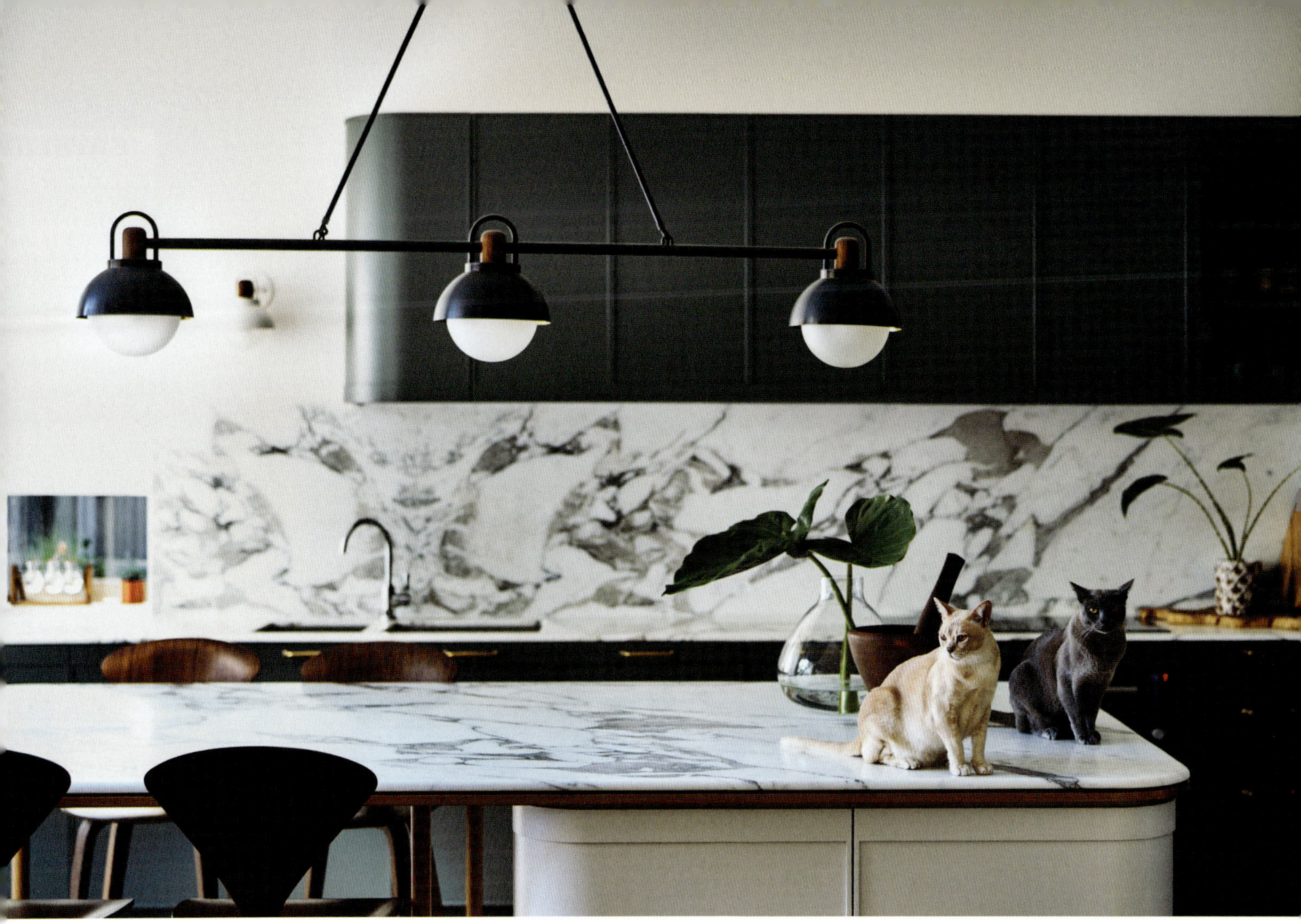

For Gus and Freddie's family, it was important to have a large kitchen bench with seating, as they love to cook and entertain.

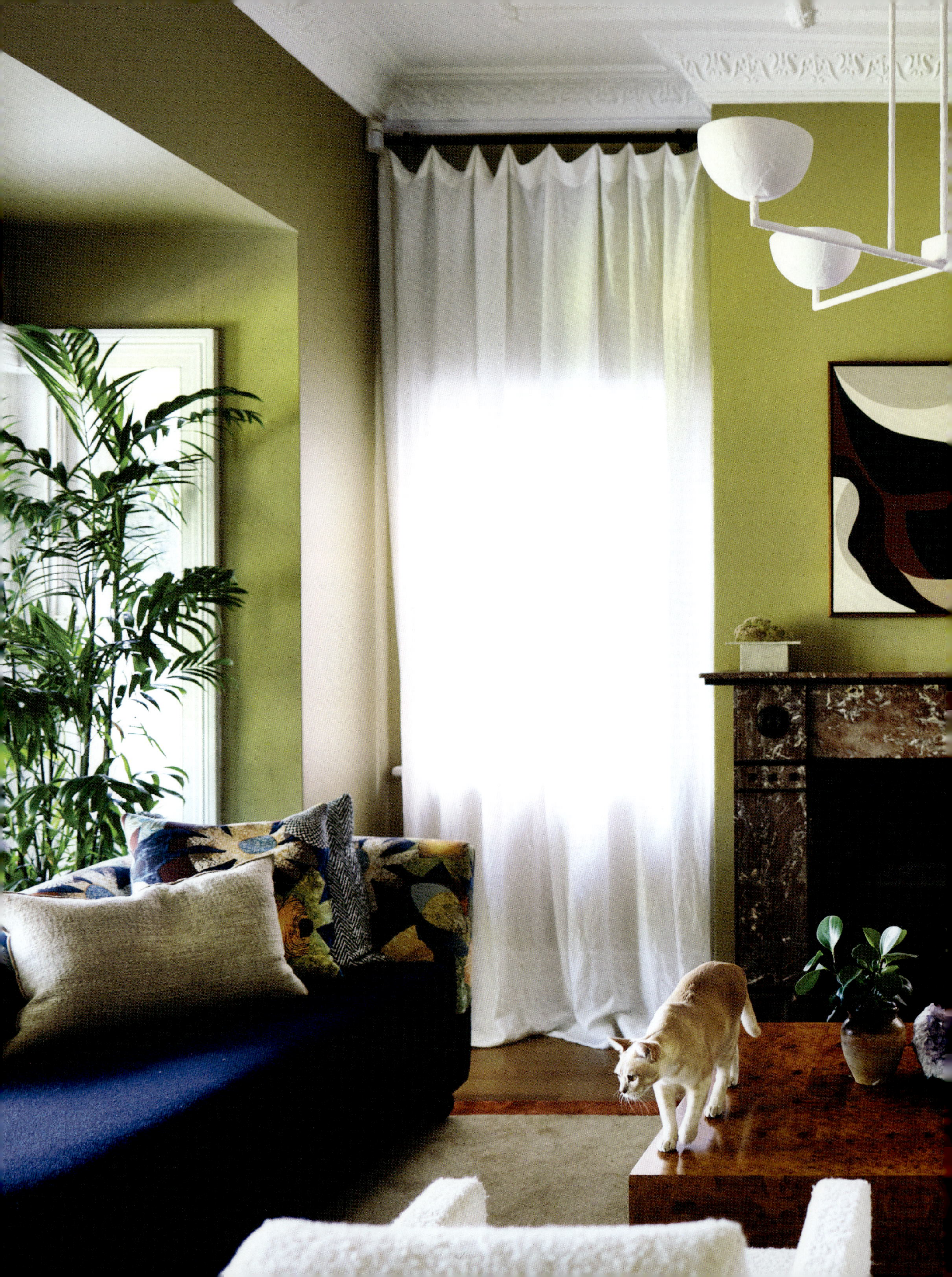

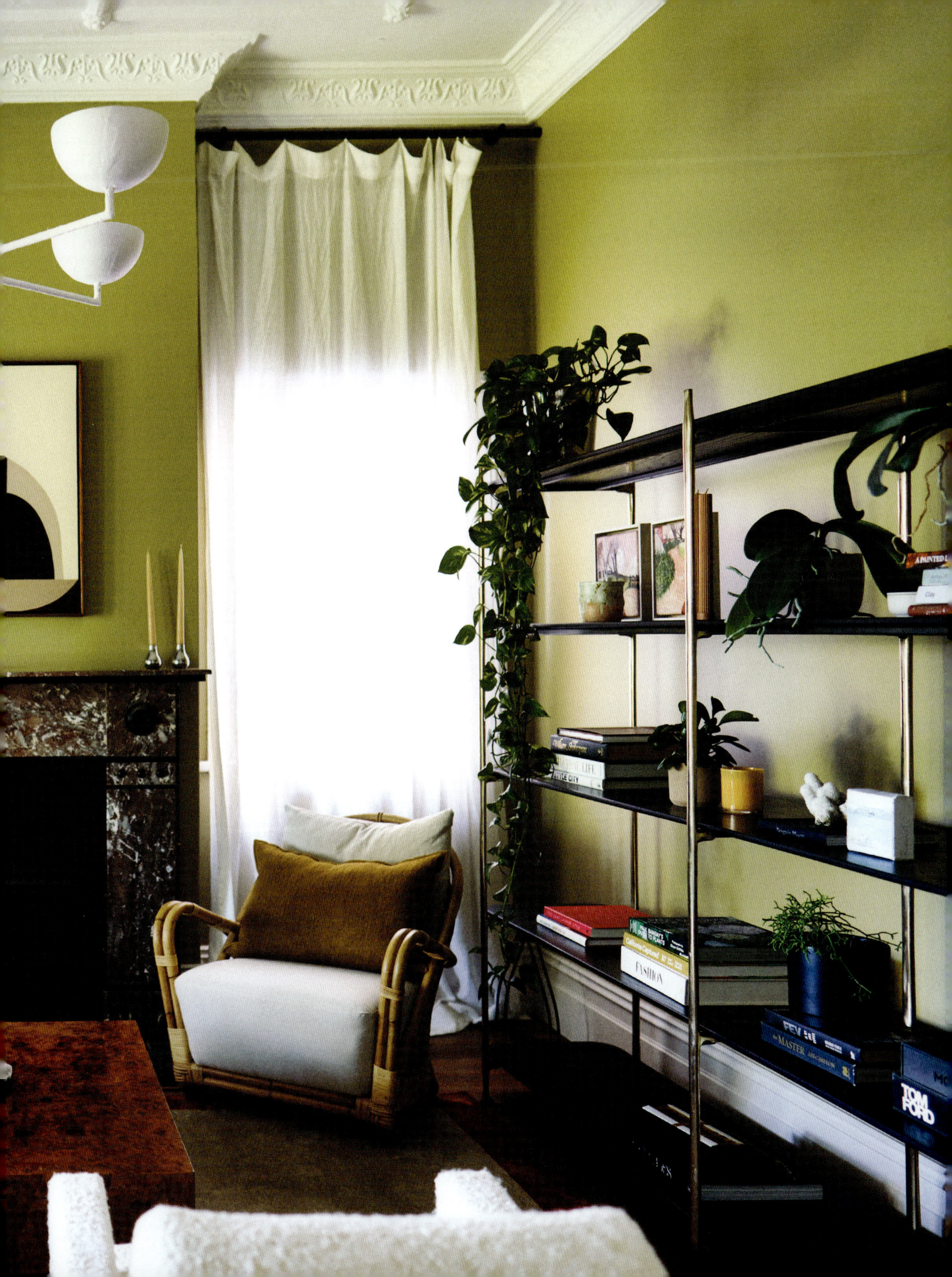
FASHION
TOM FORD

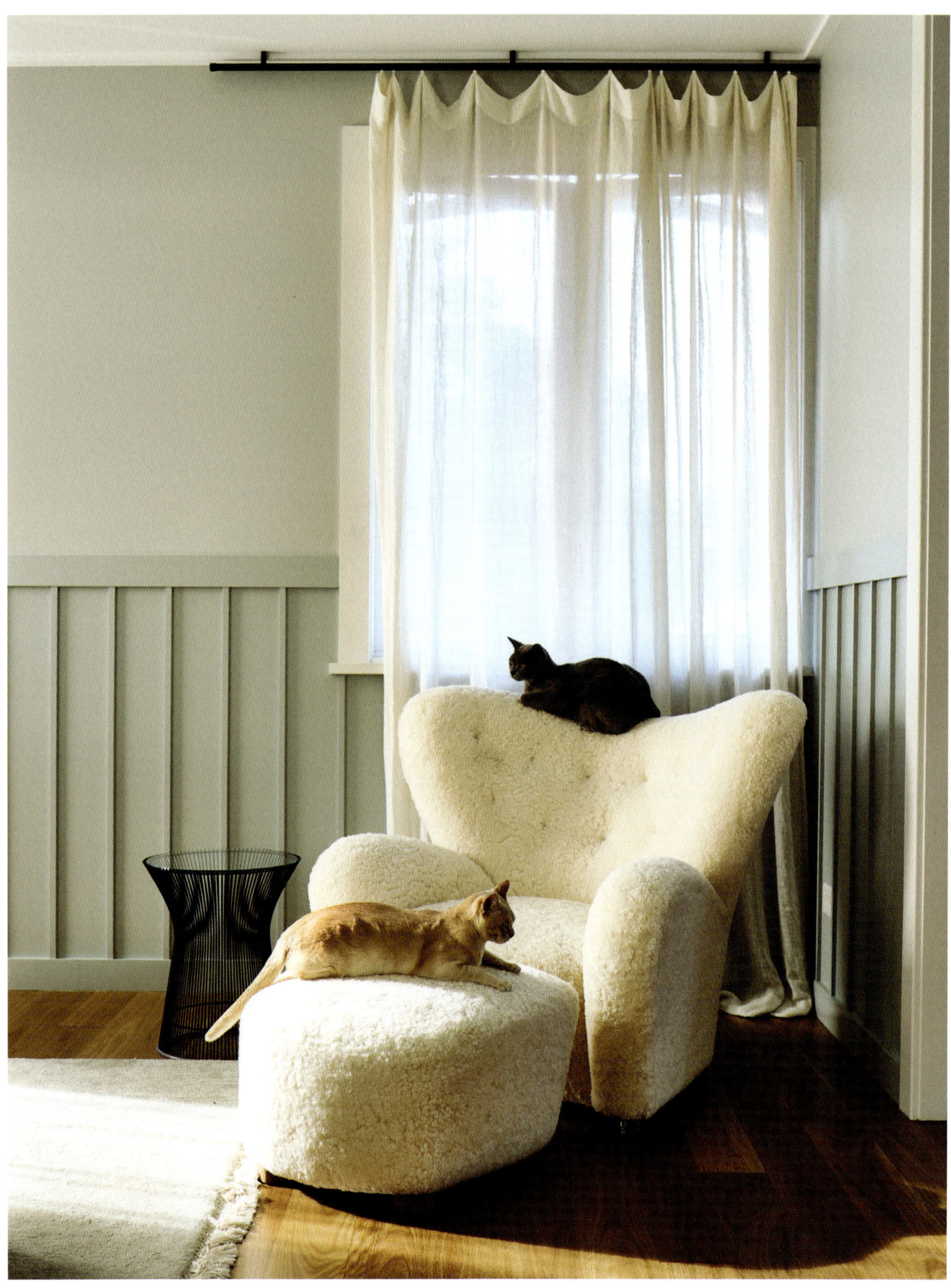

Designer: Sarah-Jane Pyke / Arent&Pyke with Vitale Design

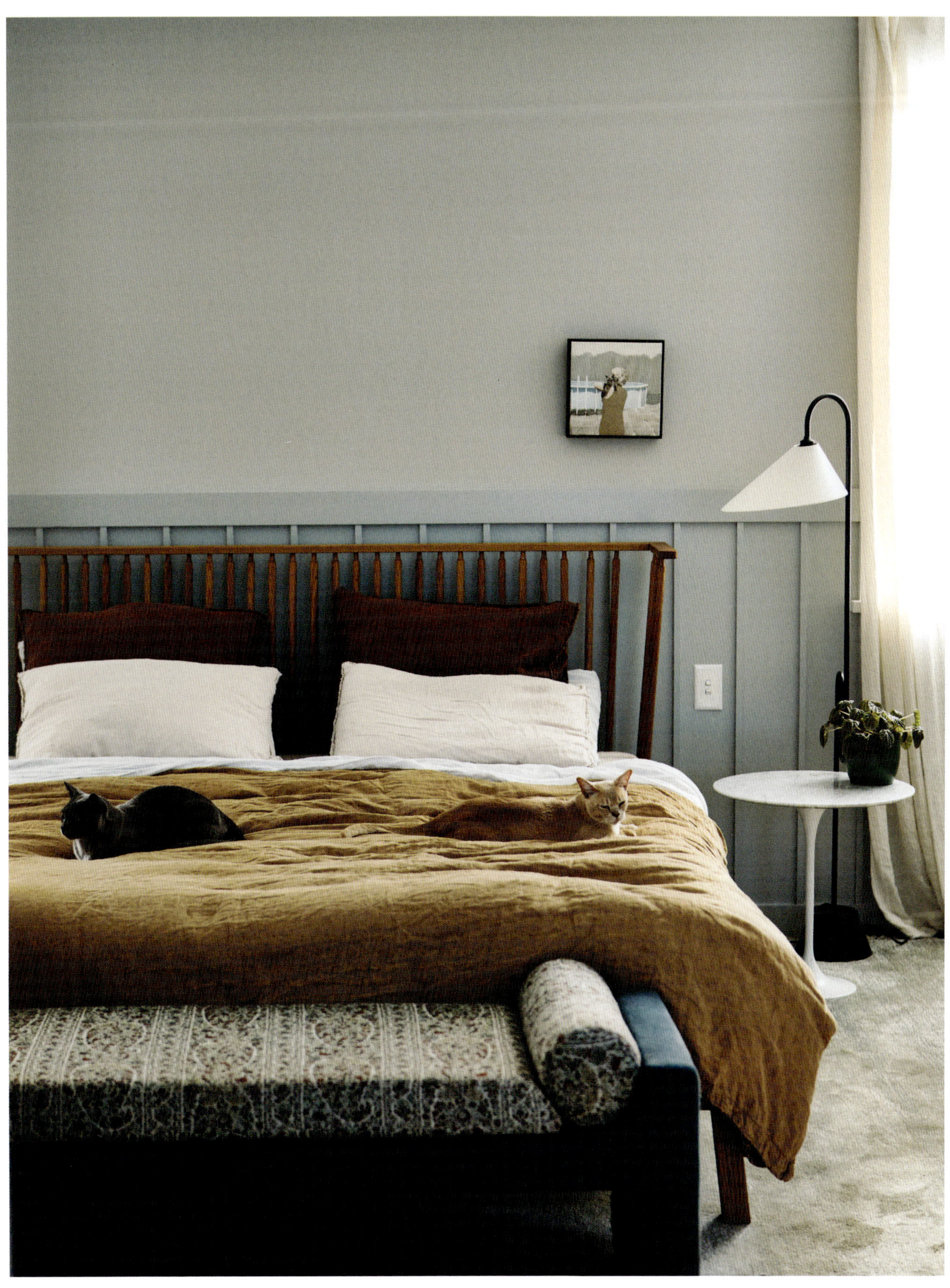

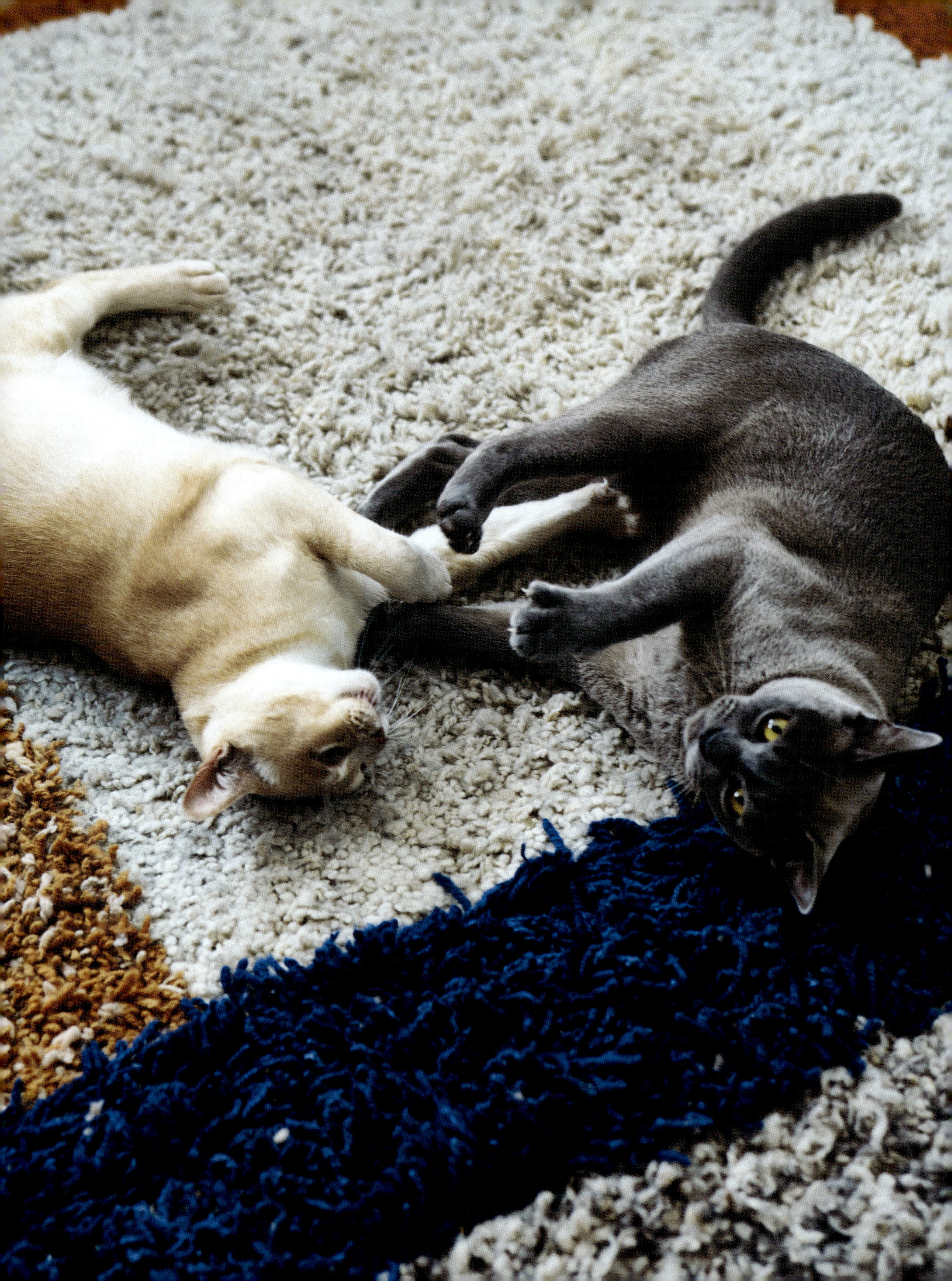

Q&A

DIVAS OR DEVOTED FRIENDS?
Devoted friends.

EXTROVERTS OR INTROVERTS?
Extroverts.

LAP CATS OR NOT?
Lap cats.

OLD SOULS OR KITTENS AT HEART?
Kittens at heart.

EXPLORERS OR HOMEBODIES?
Gus is a night explorer, while Freddie is a day explorer – but only within the house!

LAZY OR ACTIVE?
Lazy.

DOGS – FRIEND OR FOE?
Friend.

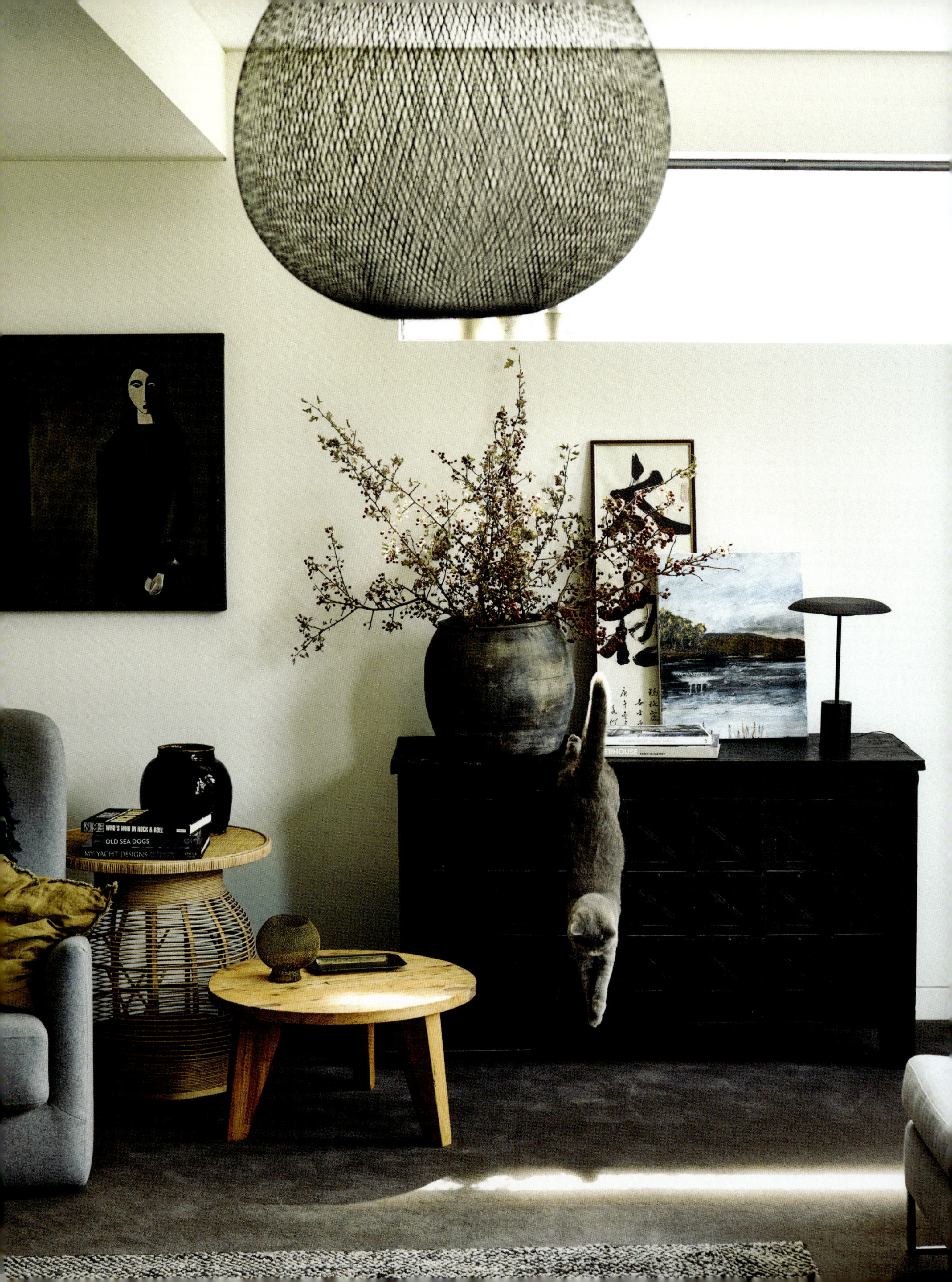
WHO'S WHO IN ROCK & ROLL
OLD SEA DOGS
MY YACHT DESIGNS

PIPPI AND TED

ARCHITECT: ANNE HINDLEY / HINDLEY & CO

Ted is the cheeky new kid on the block. He likes to jump on his wary and camera-shy companion, Pippi, and torment her. Pippi, almost ten years his senior, is much older and wiser and doesn't always want to play his games. However, this pair of British shorthairs do like to keep each other company when no one else is home.

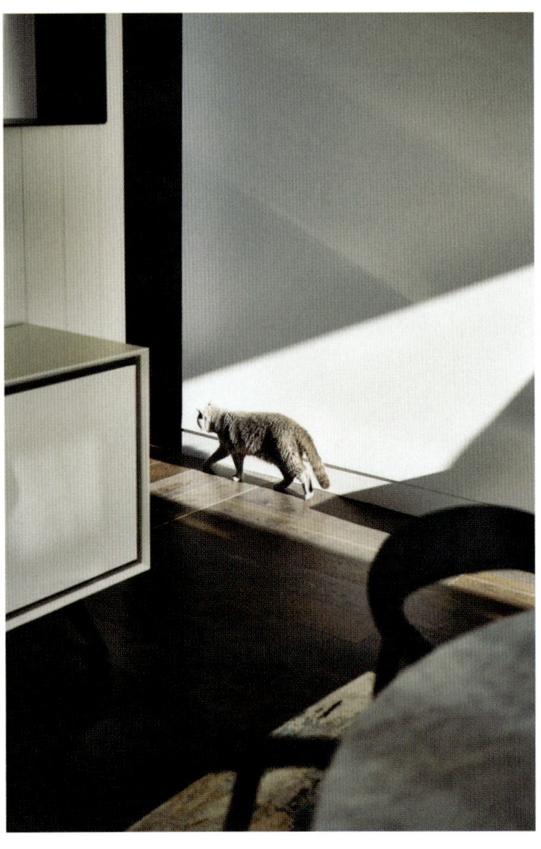

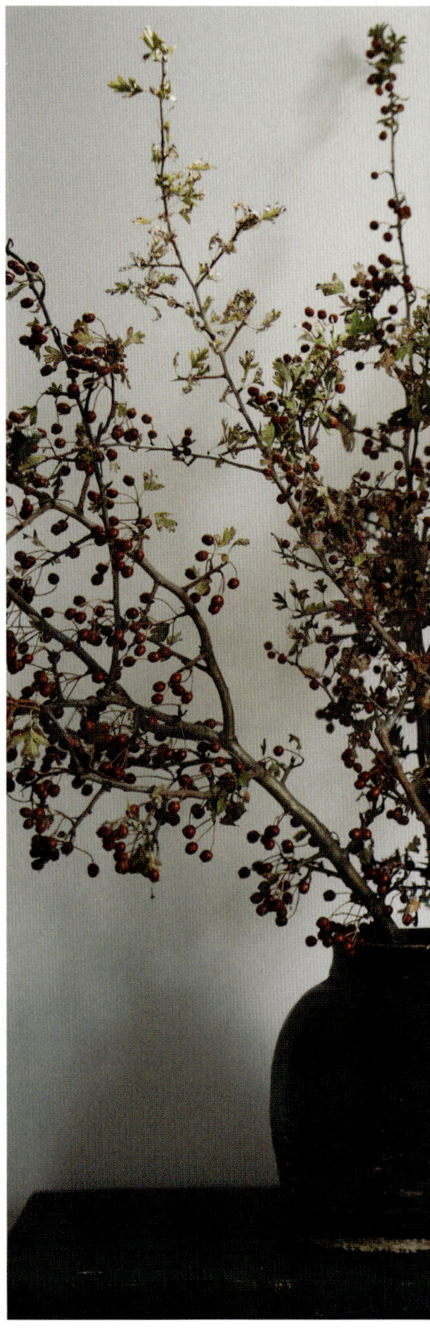

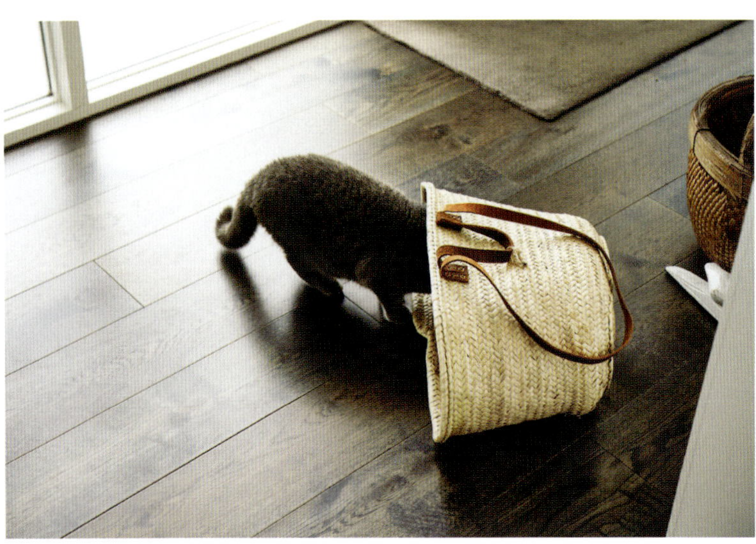

Architect: Anne Hindley / Hindley & Co

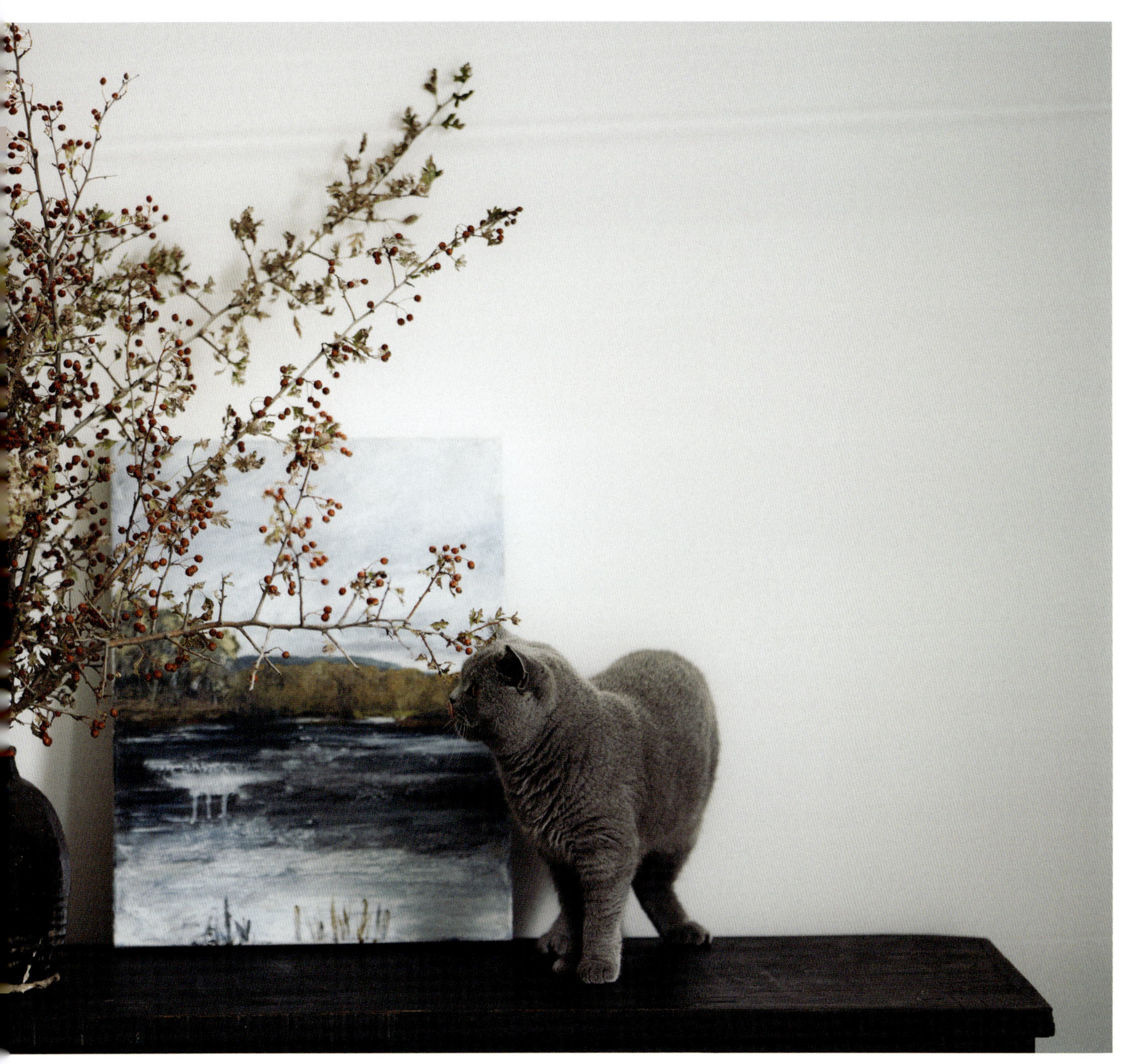

From the street, Pippi and Ted's home appears to be a simple 1960s dwelling, but the owners have added an eclectic extension at the back, designed primarily to allow more light into the house.

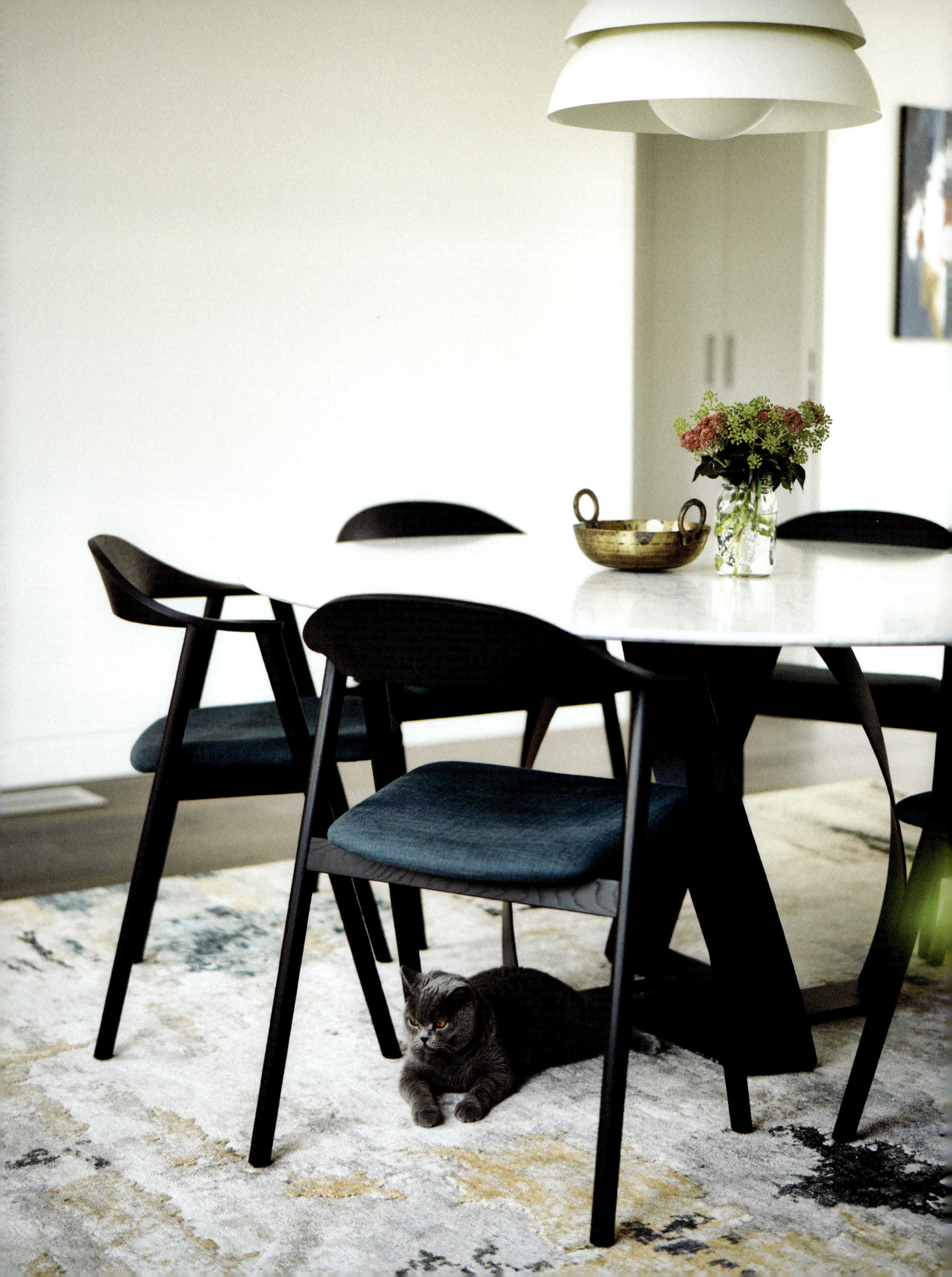

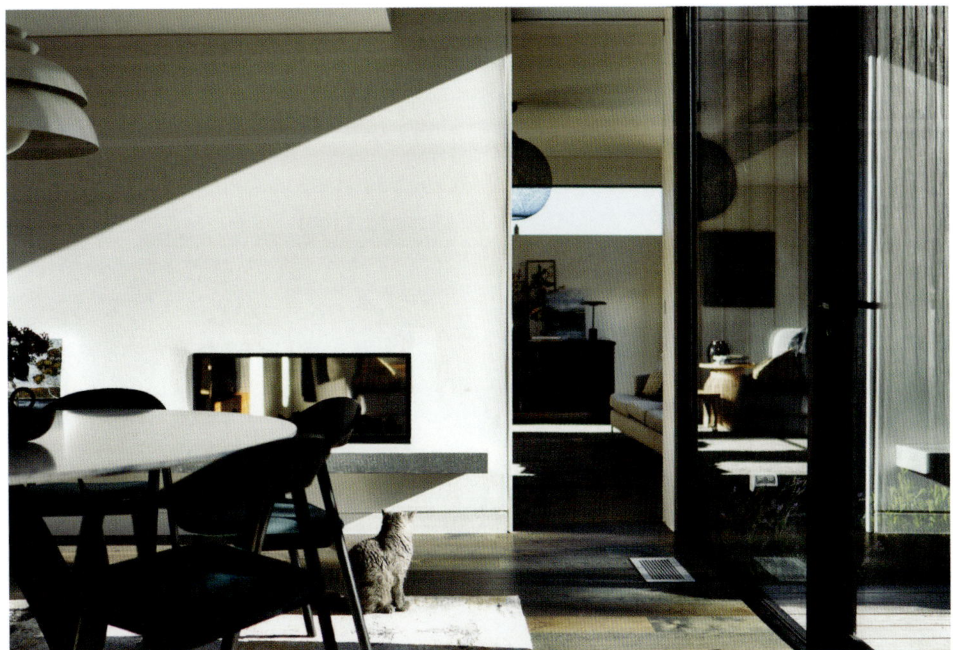

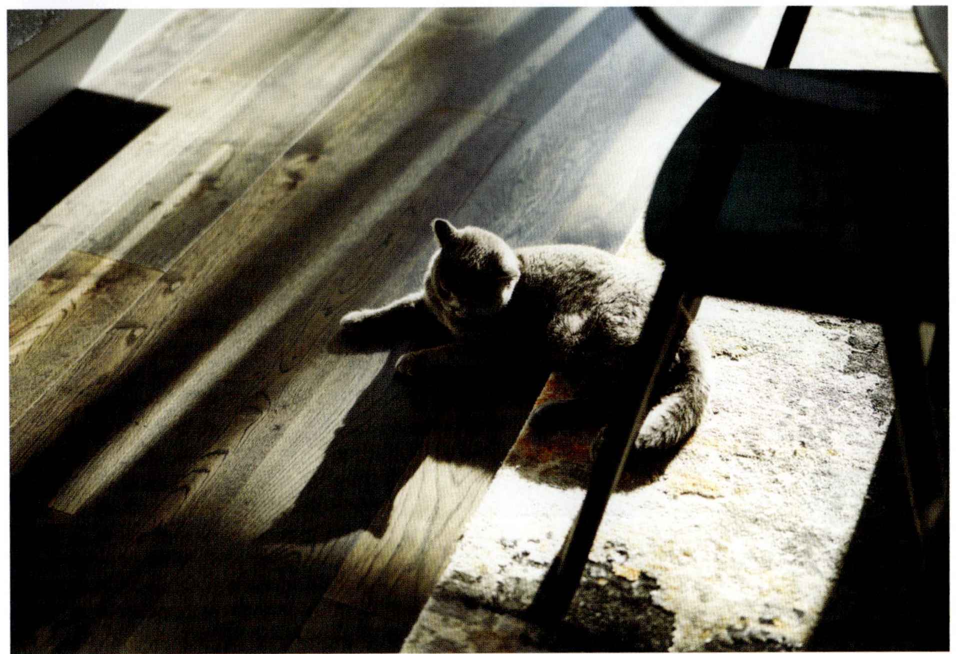

The Italian marble dining table takes pride of place in the dining room and was chosen for its style, quality and opulent feel.

At dinnertime, Ted hovers around hoping for any tidbits that may be on offer, but he rarely has any luck!

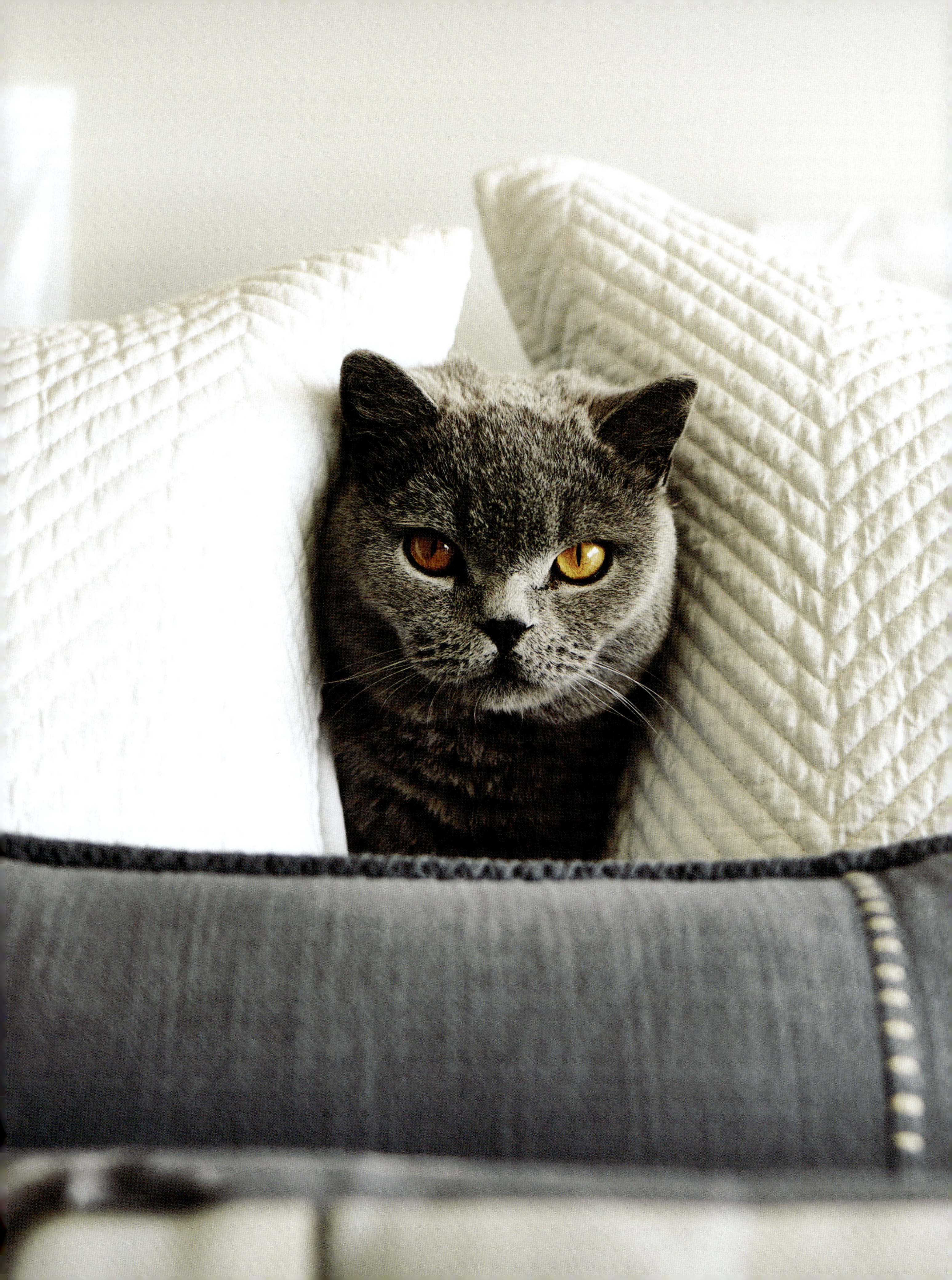

Q&A

DIVAS OR DEVOTED FRIENDS?
Devoted friends.

EXTROVERTS OR INTROVERTS?
Pippi is an introvert. Ted (pictured) is an extrovert.

LAP CATS OR NOT?
Pippi is a lap cat. Ted is not.

OLD SOULS OR KITTENS AT HEART?
Pippi is an old soul. Ted is very much a kitten.

EXPLORERS OR HOMEBODIES?
Pippi is a homebody. Ted is an explorer.

LAZY OR ACTIVE?
Pippi is lazy. Ted is active.

DOGS – FRIEND OR FOE?
Foe.

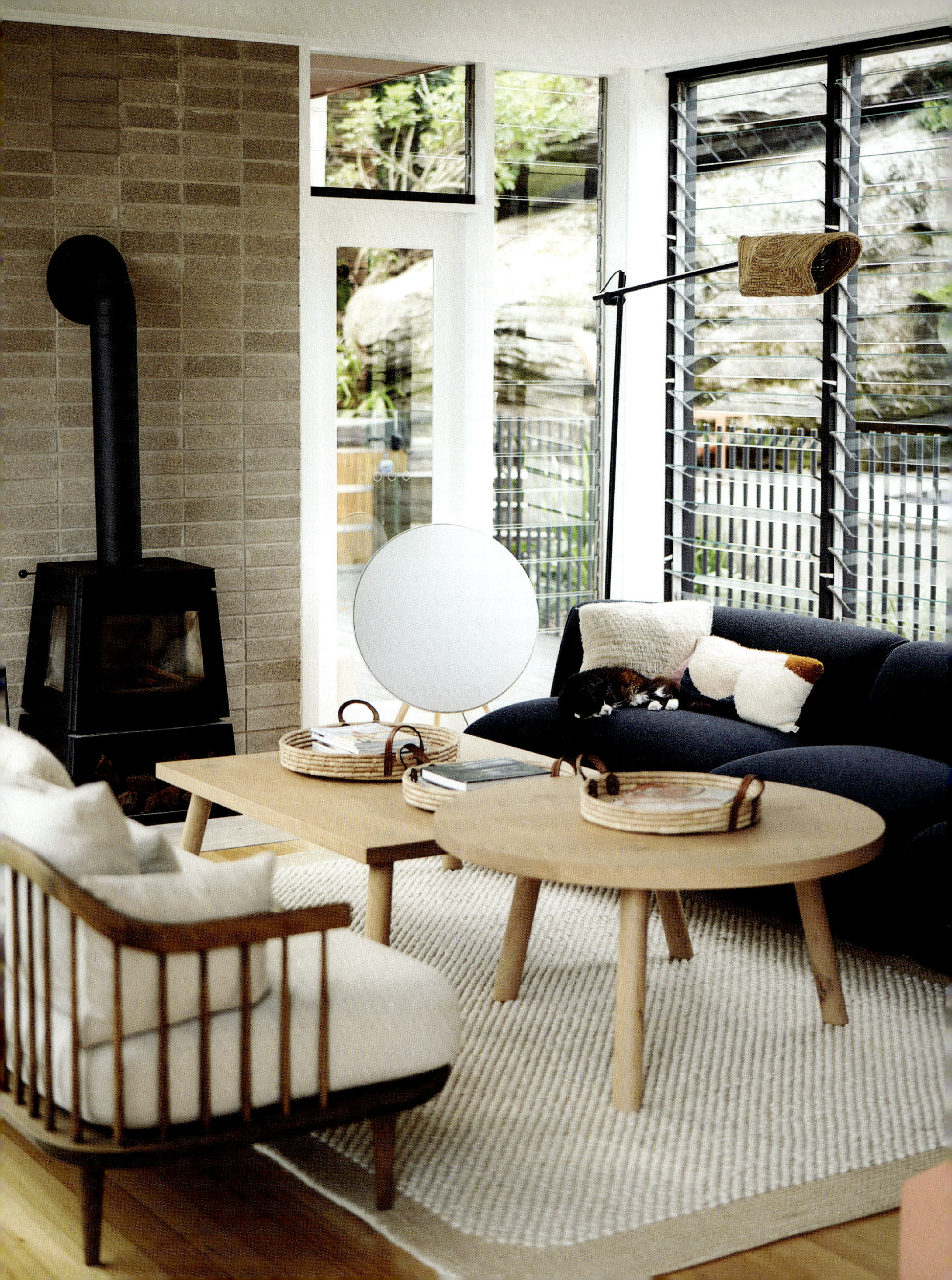

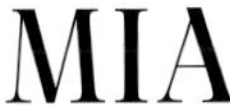

MIA

INTERIOR DESIGNER: CAROLE WHITING STUDIO FOR WILD LUXURY

Mia is a low-fuss, adventurous puss who loves to feel the wind in her fur. A long-haired mixed-breed, she was adopted by her owners from a rescue centre in Sydney. Mia has since lived with them in three different countries – she even has her own pet passport! On one memorable occasion, Mia joined the family on a scenic vaporetto ride along the Grand Canal in Venice on a snowy New Year's Day.

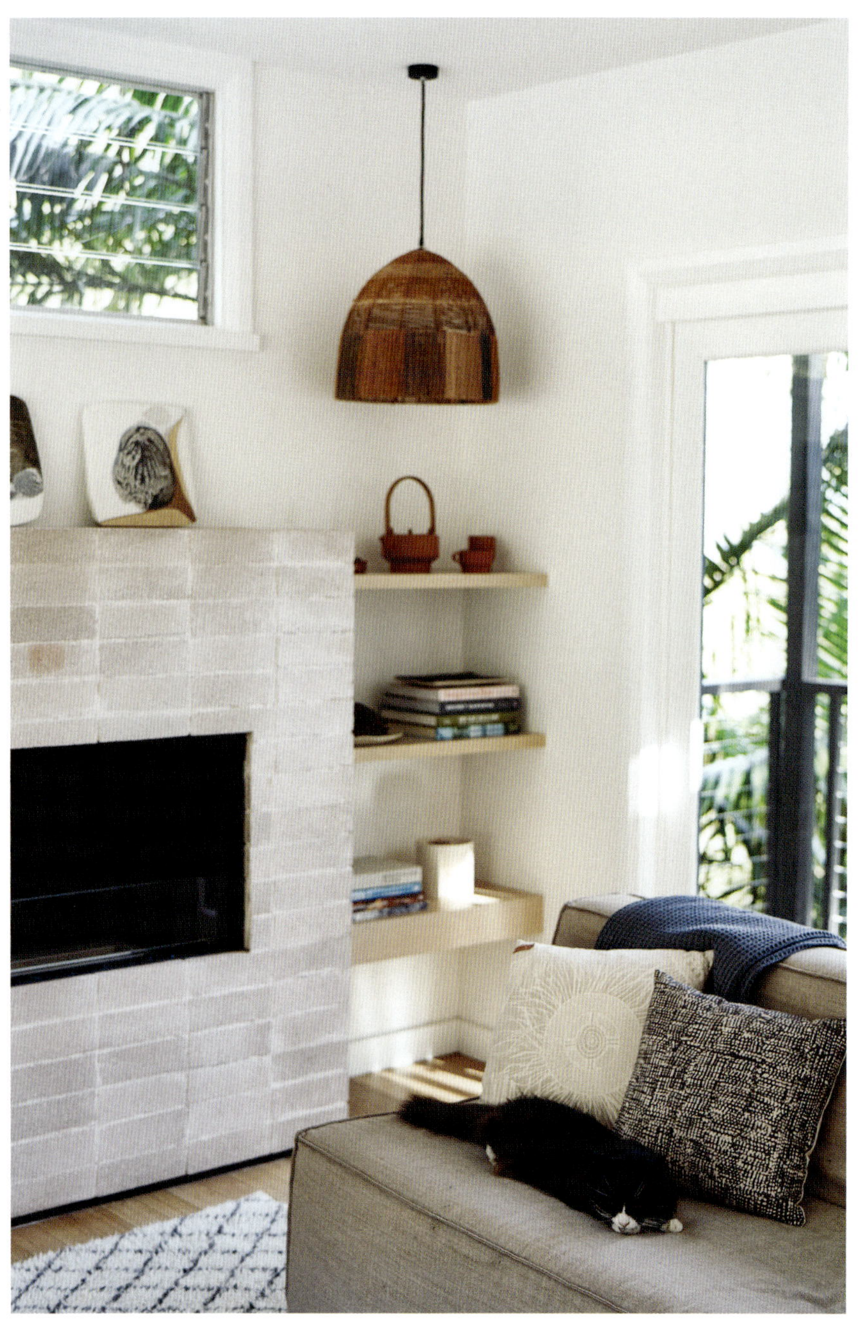

The home was designed as a weekender for Mia's family and no detail has been spared in creating this luxurious yet relaxed getaway. The owners took natural elements from the site as inspiration for the design narrative.

Interior designer: Carole Whiting Studio for Wild Luxury

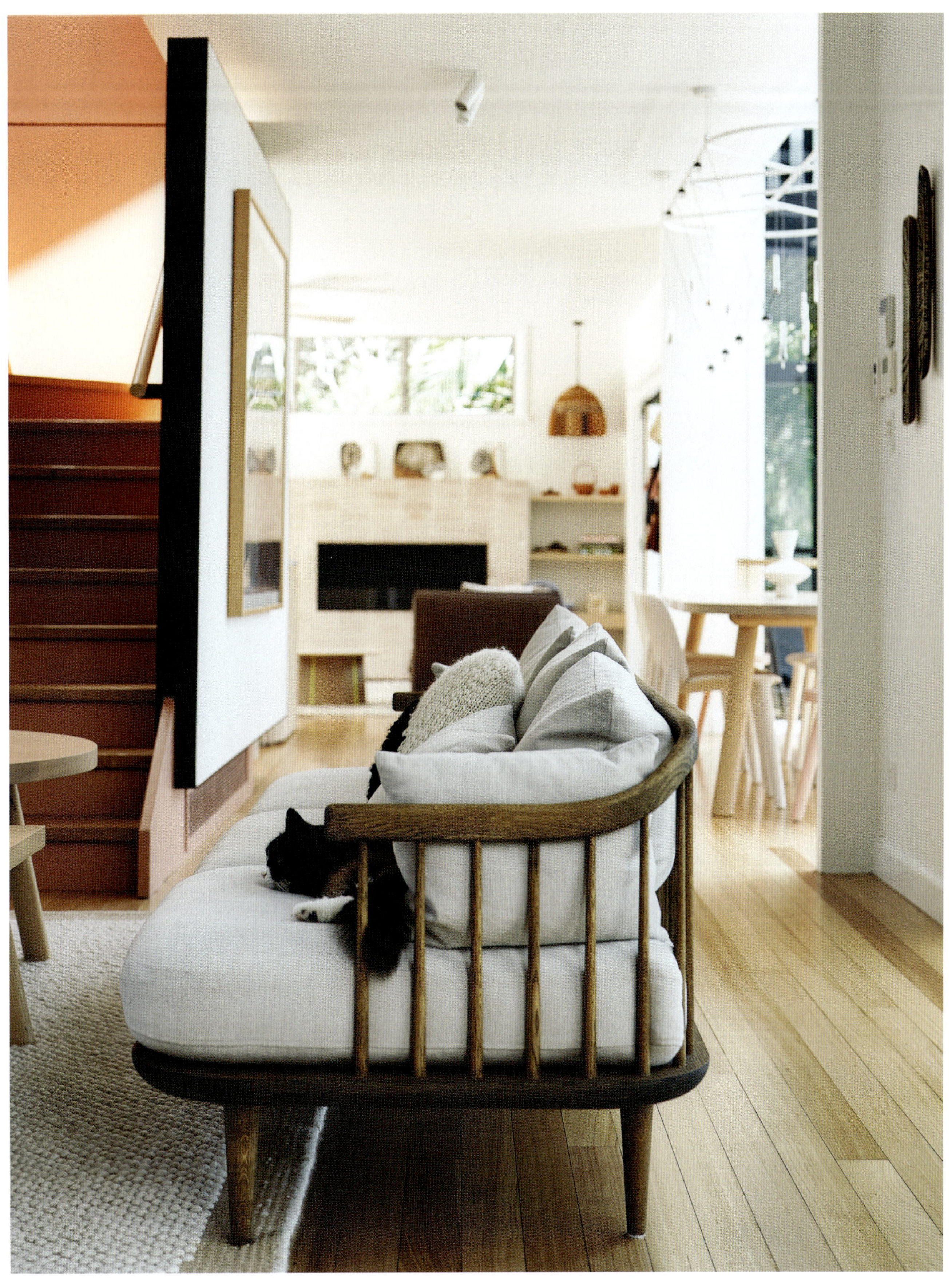

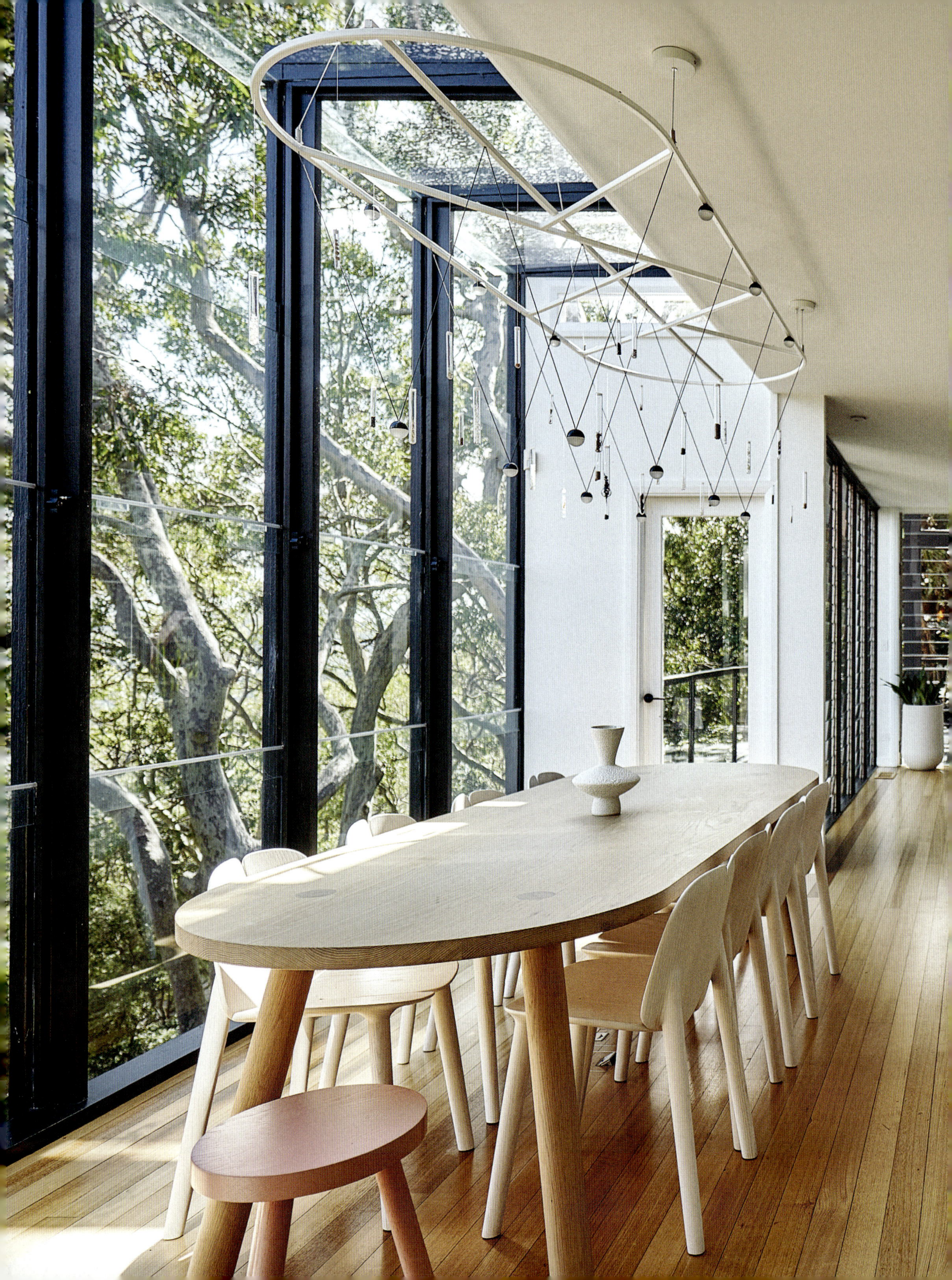

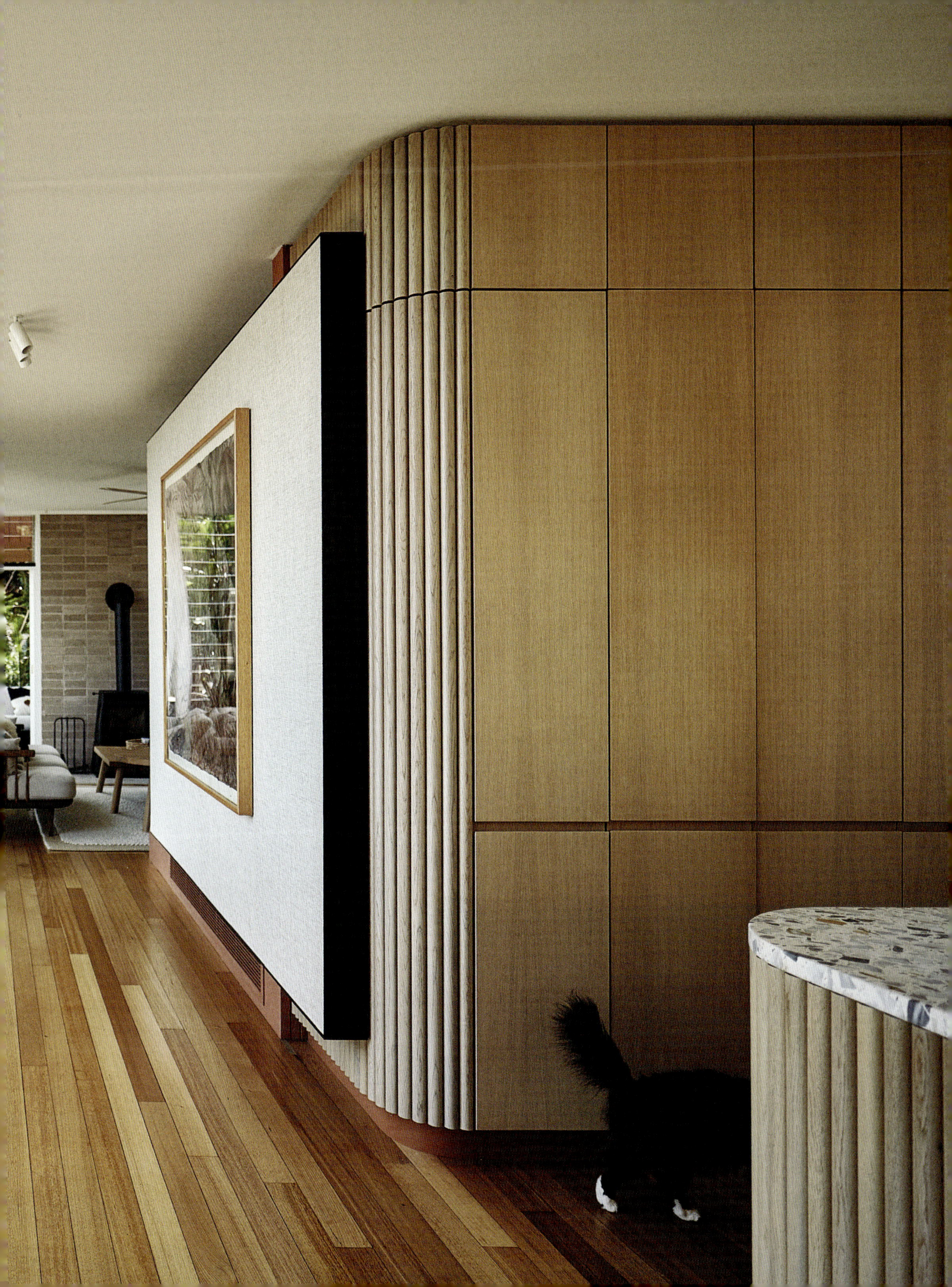

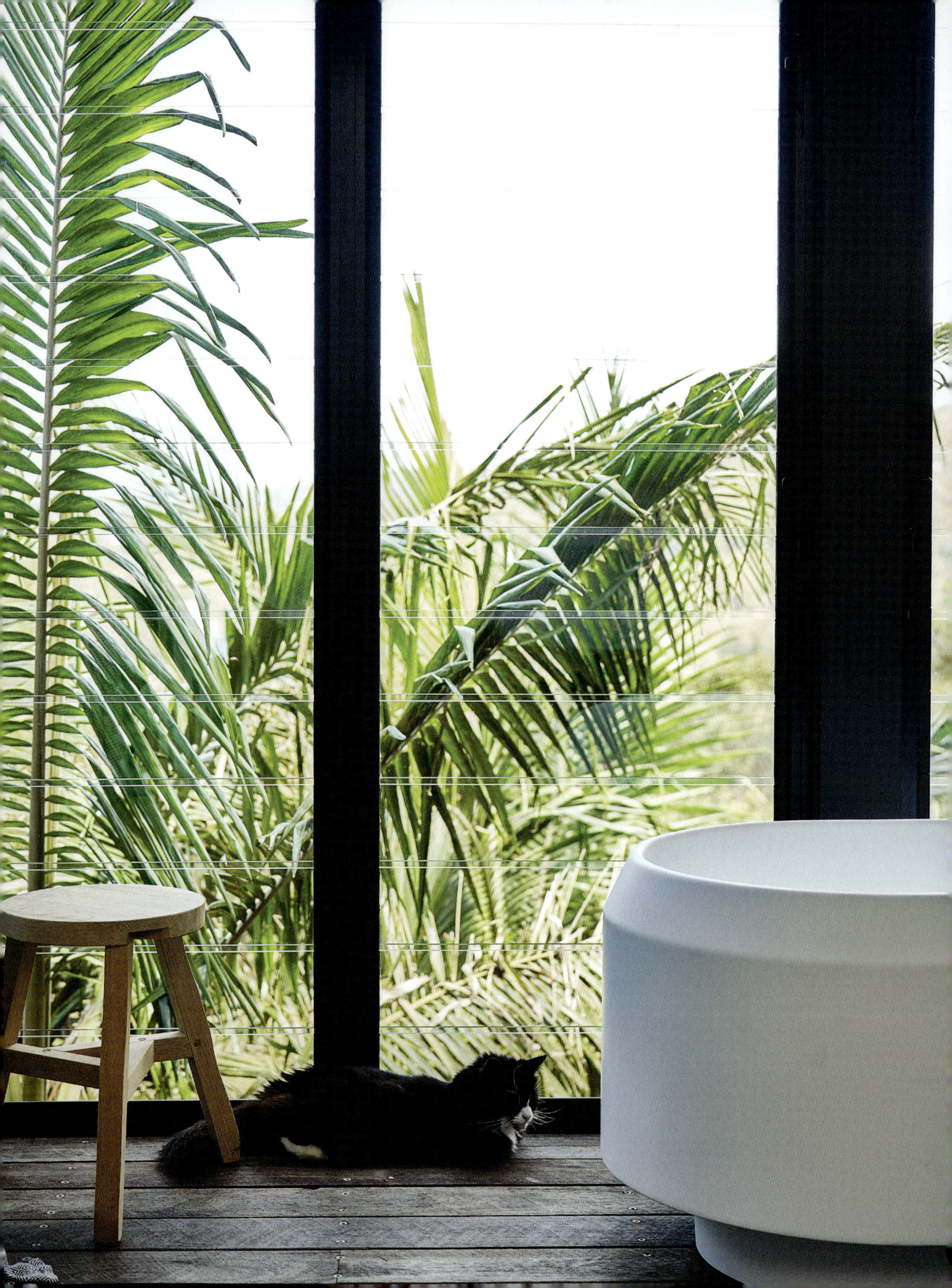

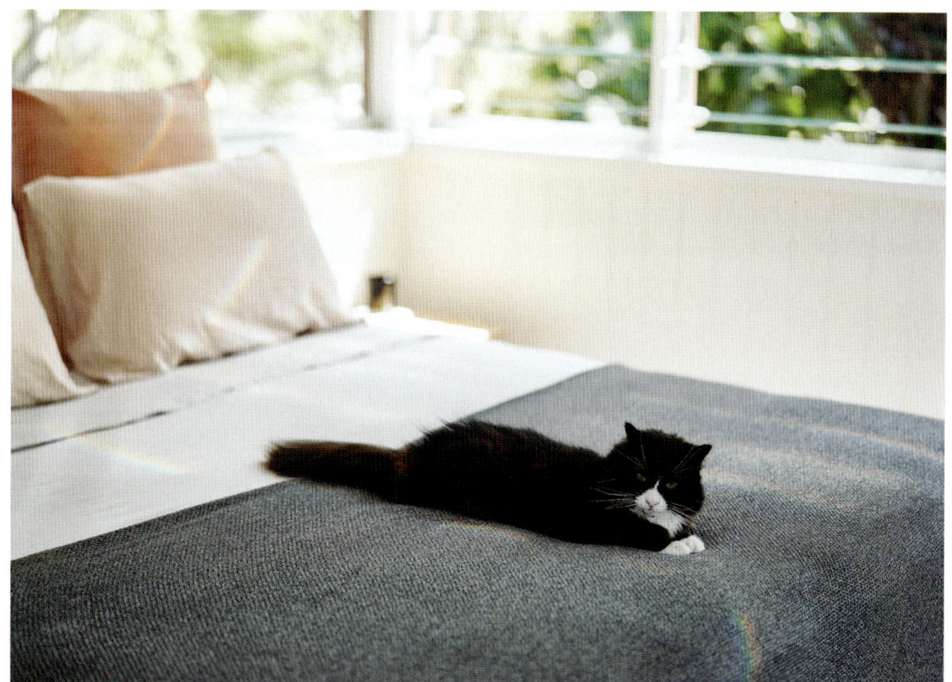

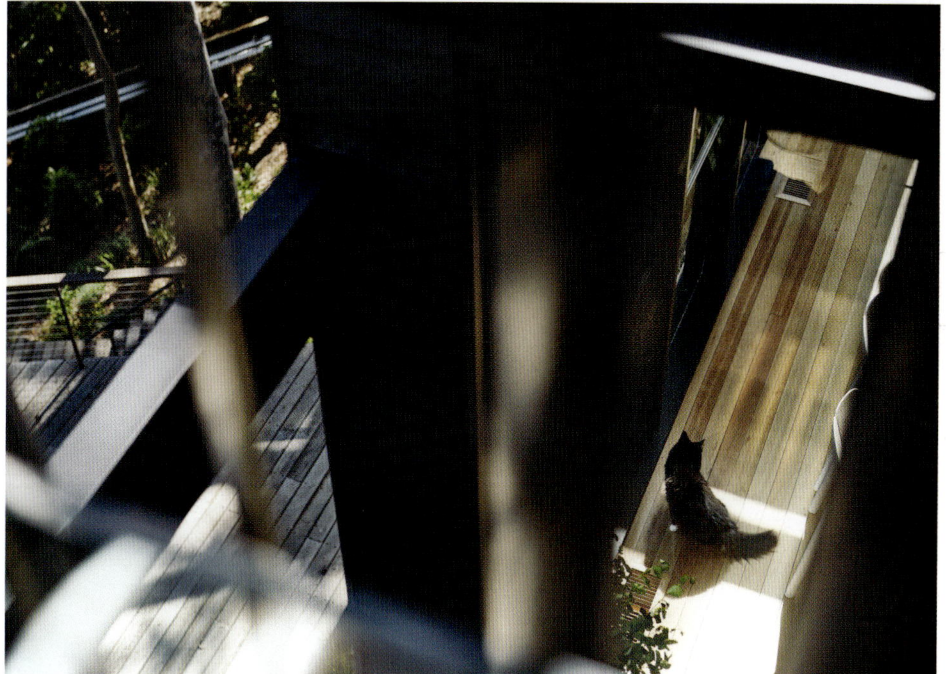

Mia loves to bask in the sun in the main bedroom; it's like her personal princess suite. The family takes after Mia in that they, too, love having a nice warm place to lounge: the house offers a choice of spaces with comfortable sofas and fireplaces, both indoors and out.

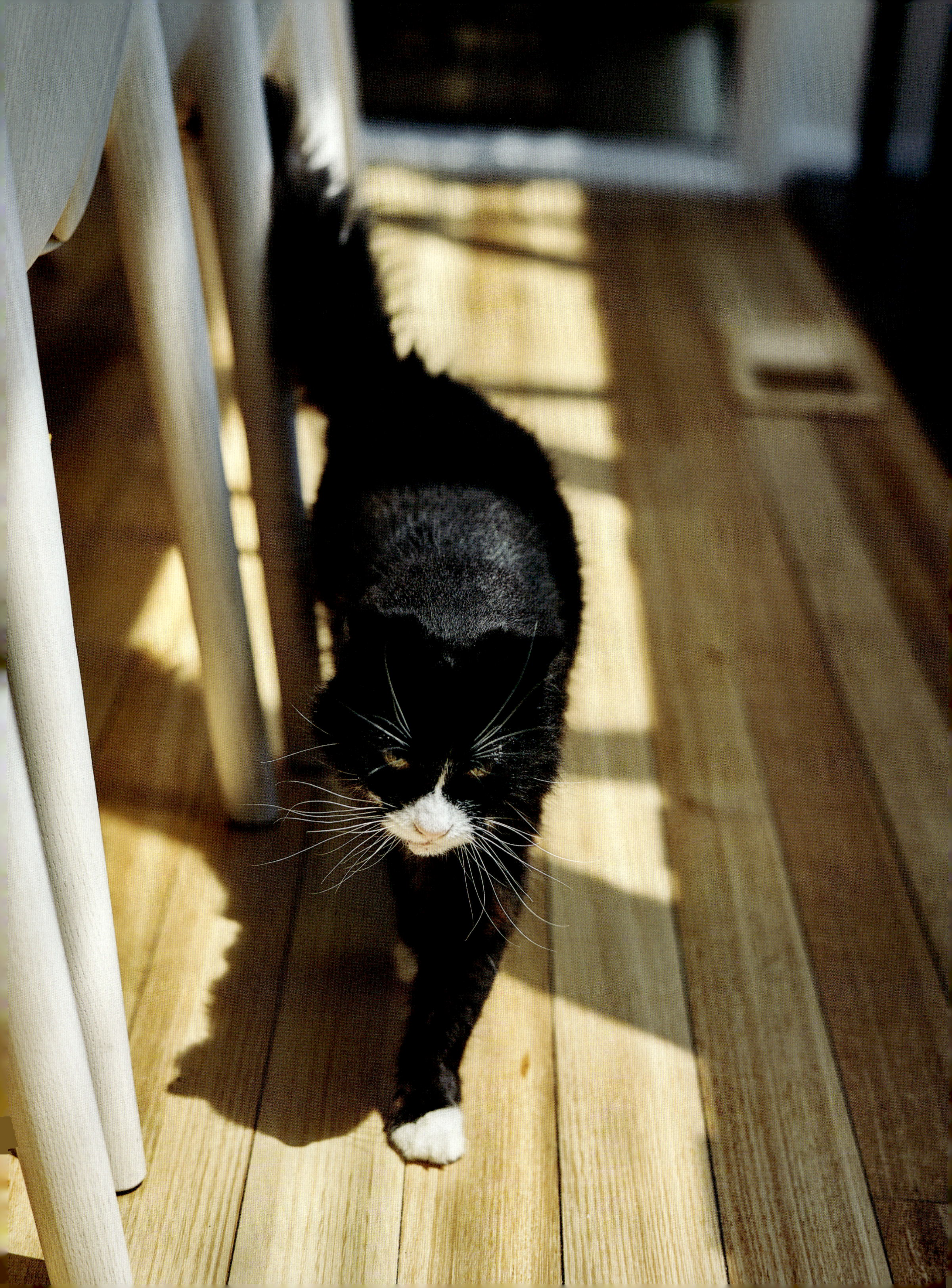

Q&A

DIVA OR DEVOTED FRIEND?

Devoted friend. Always up for a cuddle.

EXTROVERT OR INTROVERT?

Total show-off. Loves to flirt with males of the human species.

LAP CAT OR NOT?

Likes sitting on laps – and laptops.

OLD SOUL OR KITTEN AT HEART?

Until recently, there was still a smidge of kitten in her, but now that she's well into her second decade, she is slowing down and embracing her role as matriarch of the family.

EXPLORER OR HOMEBODY?

Loves her home and garden, but still happily travels by boat to the family's holiday home on the Hawkesbury River, north of Sydney, because she likes to be in their company. She's only gone missing twice in eighteen years.

LAZY OR ACTIVE?

Lazy – except for the occasional mysterious disappearance. Her family has never figured out what she gets up to on those days.

DOGS – FRIEND OR FOE?

Foe. The family's children would love to get a puppy, but Mia would never tolerate a dog in the home – she would not be shy about making her feelings known.

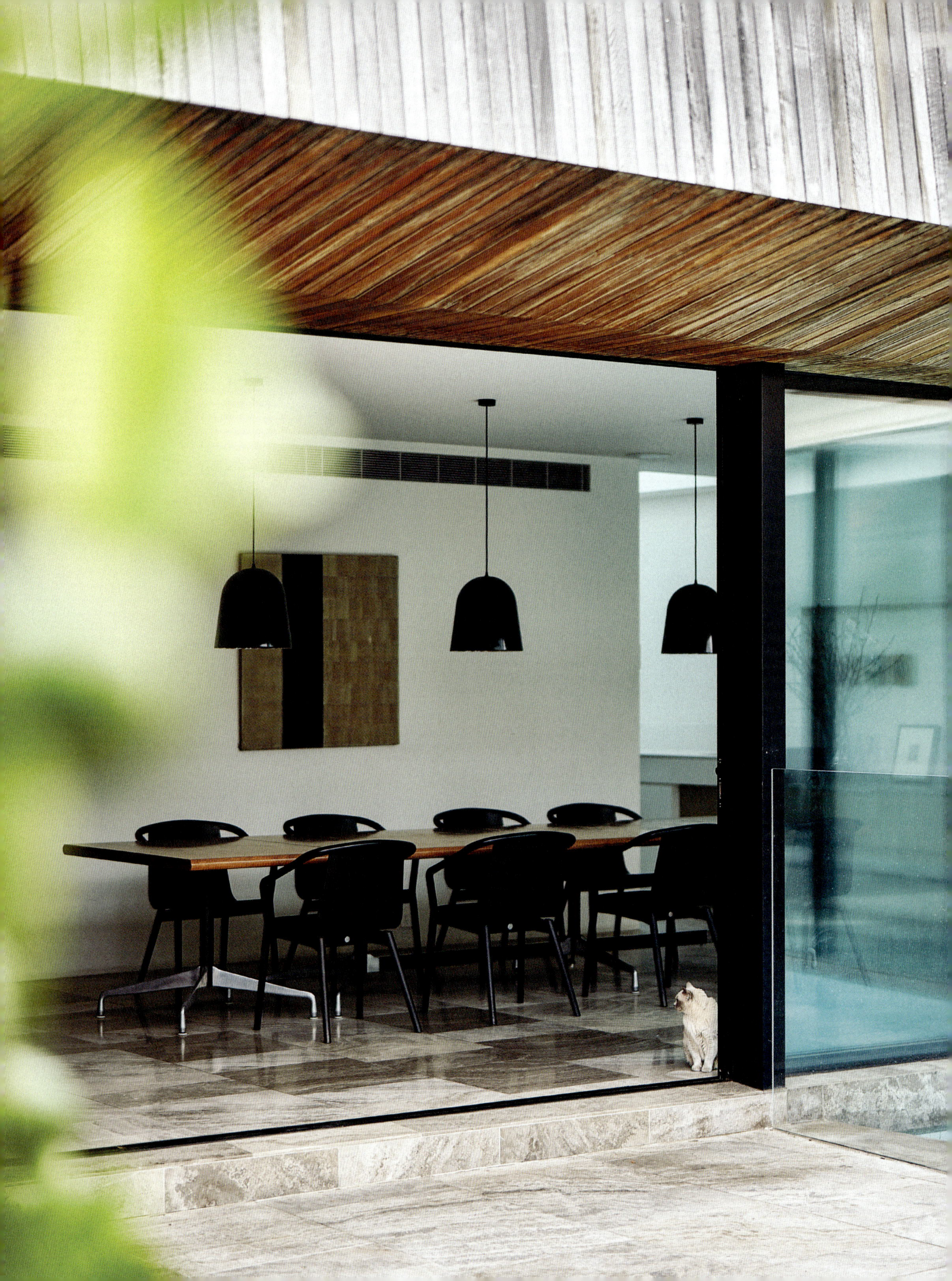

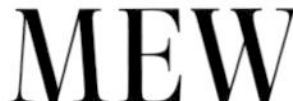

MEW

ARCHITECTS: GEORGE YIONTIS AND ROSA COY / COY YIONTIS ARCHITECTS

Mew's namesake is a very powerful, cat-like pink Pokémon. She was named by the family's older children, who were very much into the characters at the time. A twelve-year-old lilac Burmese, Mew can always find a sunny spot to nap in her family's renovated Victorian weatherboard house, often in a bedroom or in the corridor alongside the pool. She is well-suited to her family, as she likes to be up and about early, and she loves curling up by the fire or watching a movie with them in the evening.

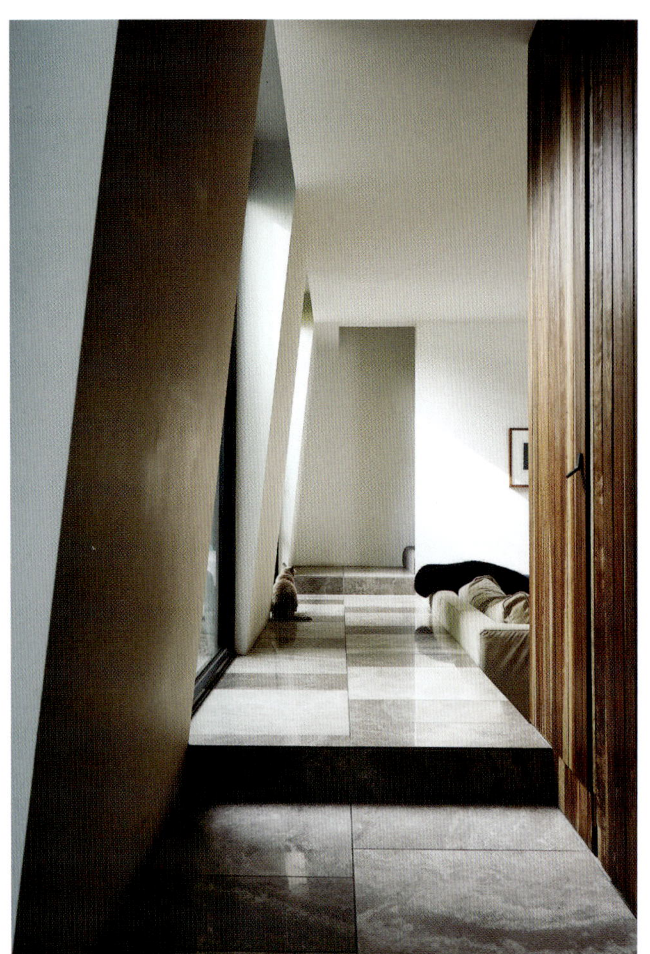

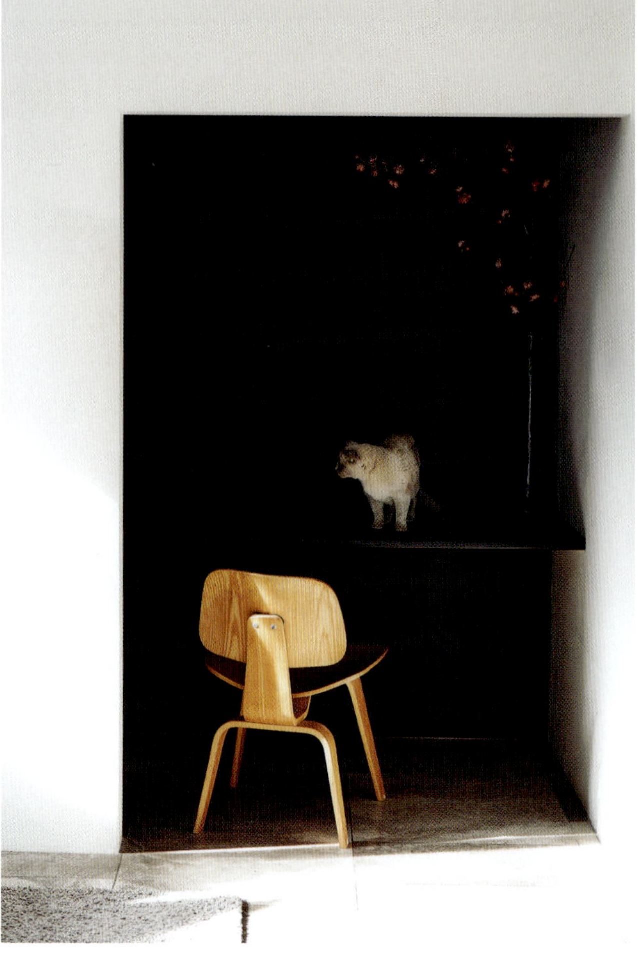

Mew's residence, built by a husband-and-wife team of architects for their family, is minimalist, calm and introspective. Light, and the way it moves through the spaces, is an important feature in this home.

Architects: George Yiontis and Rosa Coy / Coy Yiontis Architects

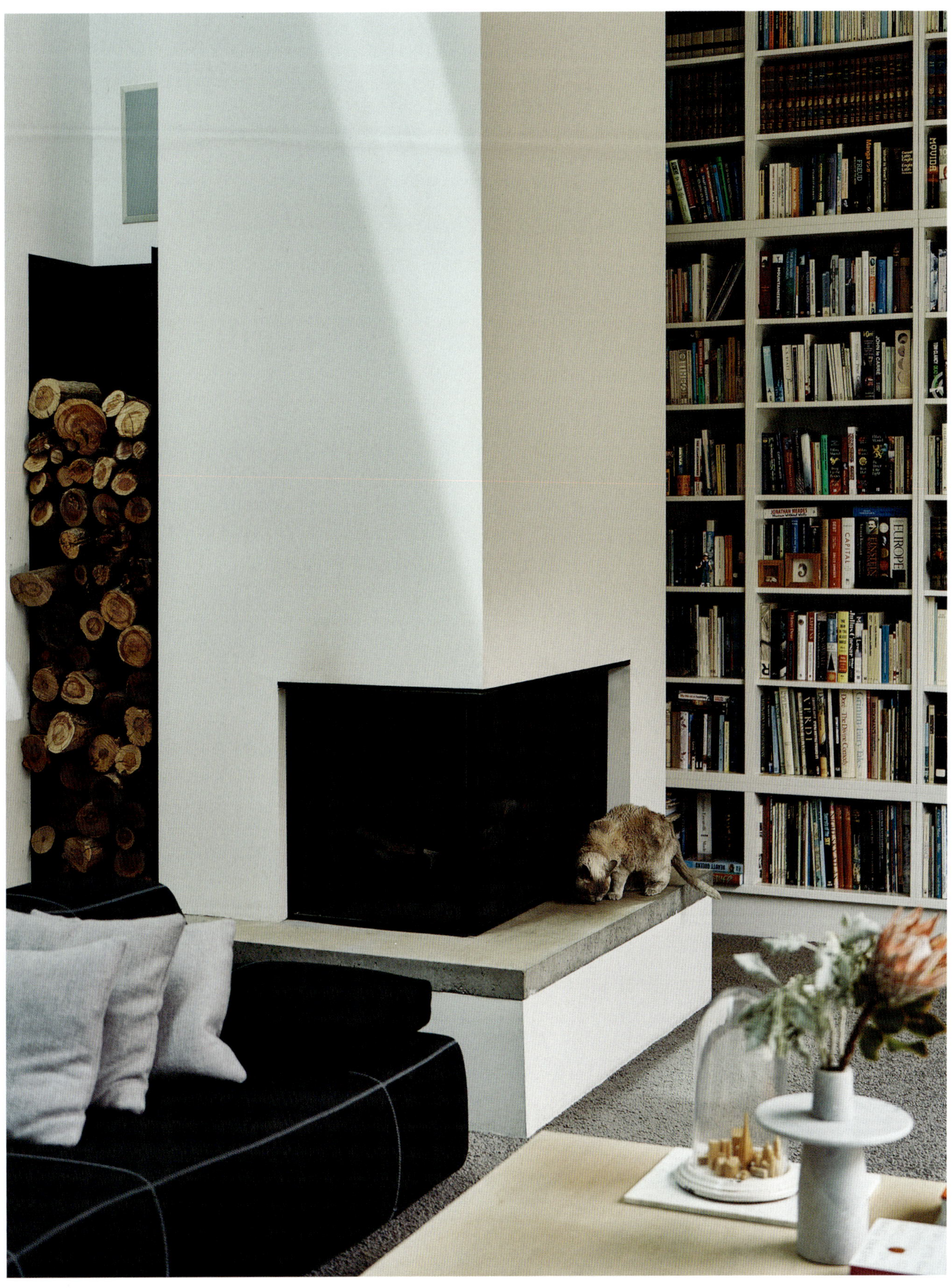

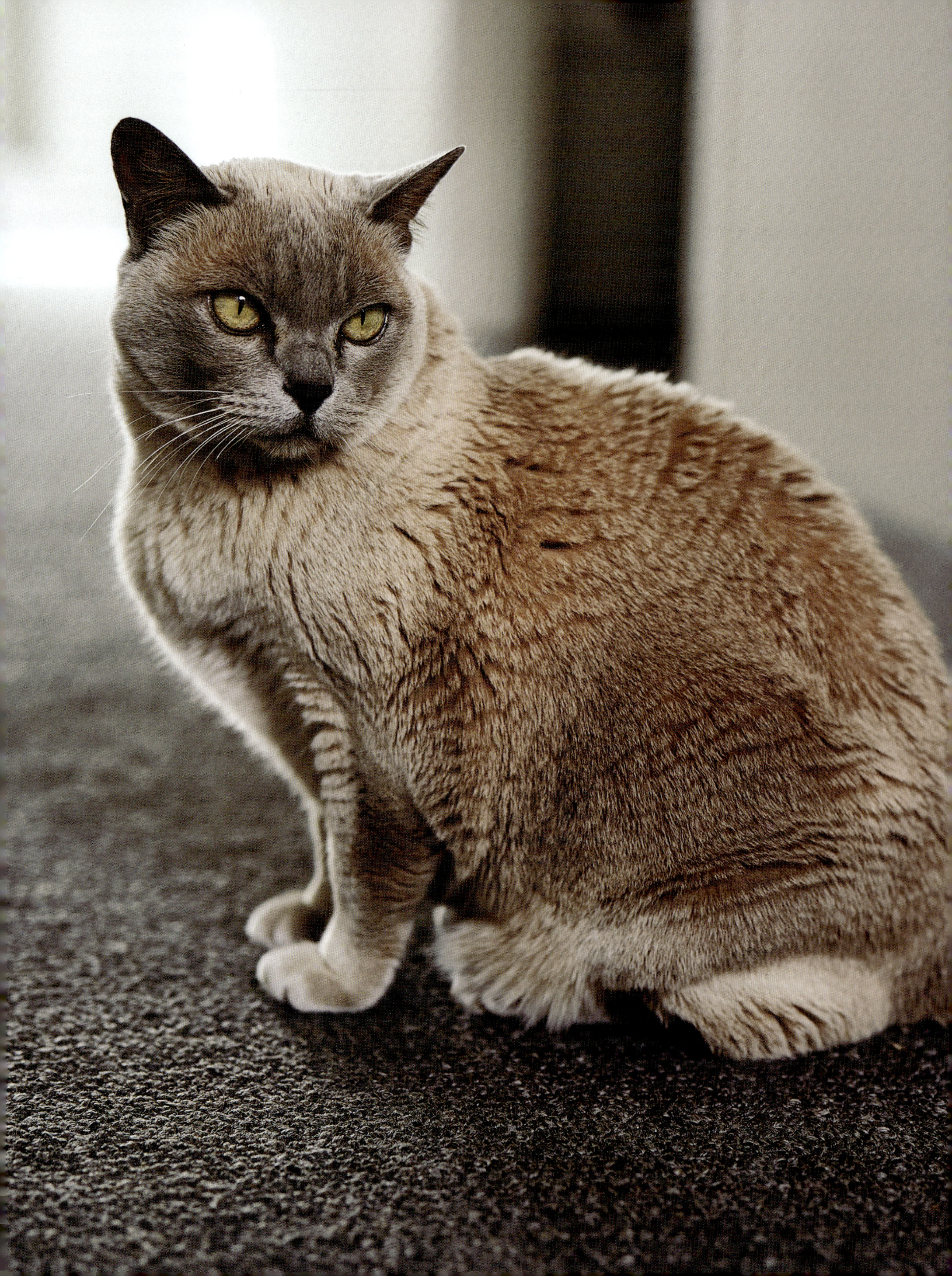

Q&A

DIVA OR DEVOTED FRIEND?

Diva. Mew will approach her family to be patted and fed, but will ignore them otherwise. She has no patience for time-wasters.

EXTROVERT OR INTROVERT?

Introvert.

LAP CAT OR NOT?

Not.

OLD SOUL OR KITTEN AT HEART?

Kitten at heart.

EXPLORER OR HOMEBODY?

Homebody.

LAZY OR ACTIVE?

Lazy.

DOGS – FRIEND OR FOE?

Foe. Mew is indignant that her family has brought a new puppy into her home, and after eighteen months, she still shows no sign of warming to him. She will hiss and attack if he encroaches on her personal space or if she finds him occupying her sunny spot. The dog has learnt to be very wary.

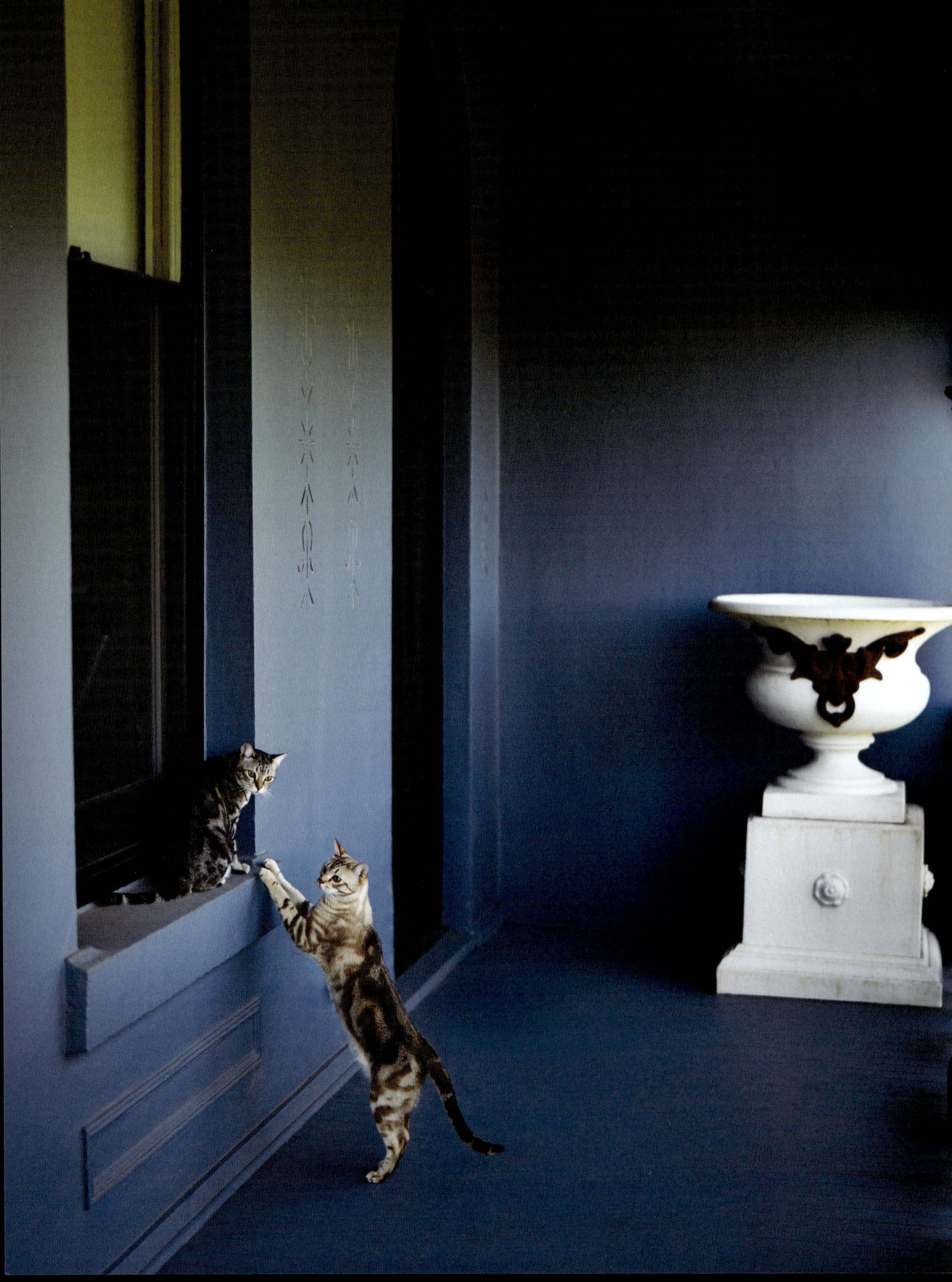

BILLIE AND TUCKER

ARCHITECT: ALEKSANDRA RAKOCEVIC / STAR ARCHITECTURE

Billie and Tucker are cheeky and inquisitive two-year-old Australian mists. They are brother and sister: Billie, the girl, is brown spotted, while Tucker is somewhat larger and lighter coloured. The breed is unique to Australia and originated in Sydney in the 1970s: it's a cross of Abyssinian, Burmese and tabby. This combination makes them very affectionate, chatty and sometimes too clever for their own paws. Billie and Tucker's owners were introduced to the breed by a dear friend over fifteen years ago, and this is their third pair of mists. The siblings have very individual personalities: Billie is a fearless adventurer, while Tucker is more laid-back.

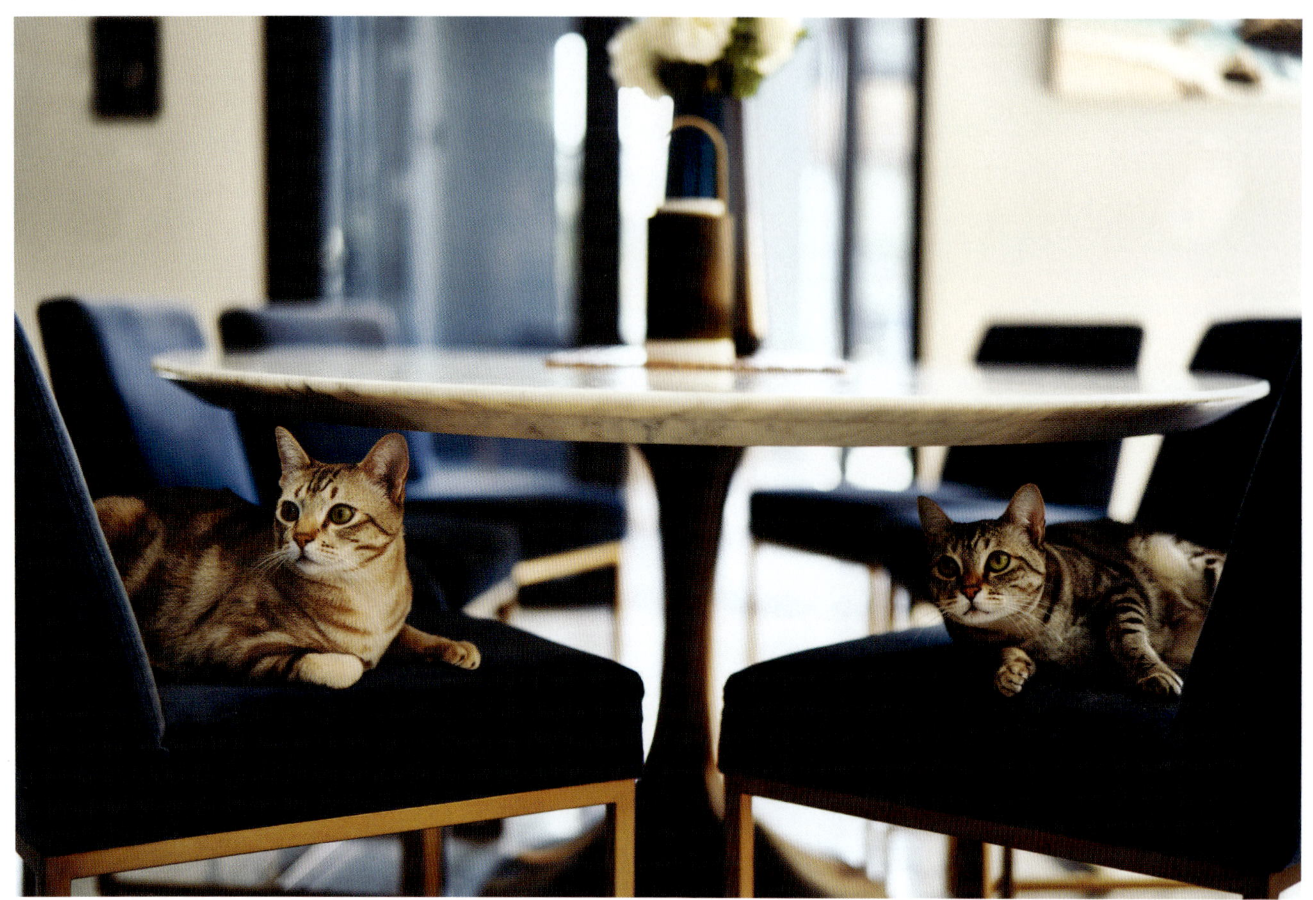

Billie and Tucker's home has a fascinating history, having once served as the Belgian consulate and, later, as a finishing school for young ladies. It was built in 1886, during Melbourne's land boom, on what was deemed to be the highest viewing hill in upmarket Hawthorn East.

The owners like to juxtapose unexpected elements and colour palettes in their interiors. They are sentimentalists at heart, and have incorporated elements of their personal history and origins into the home.

Architect: Aleksandra Rakocevic / STAR Architecture

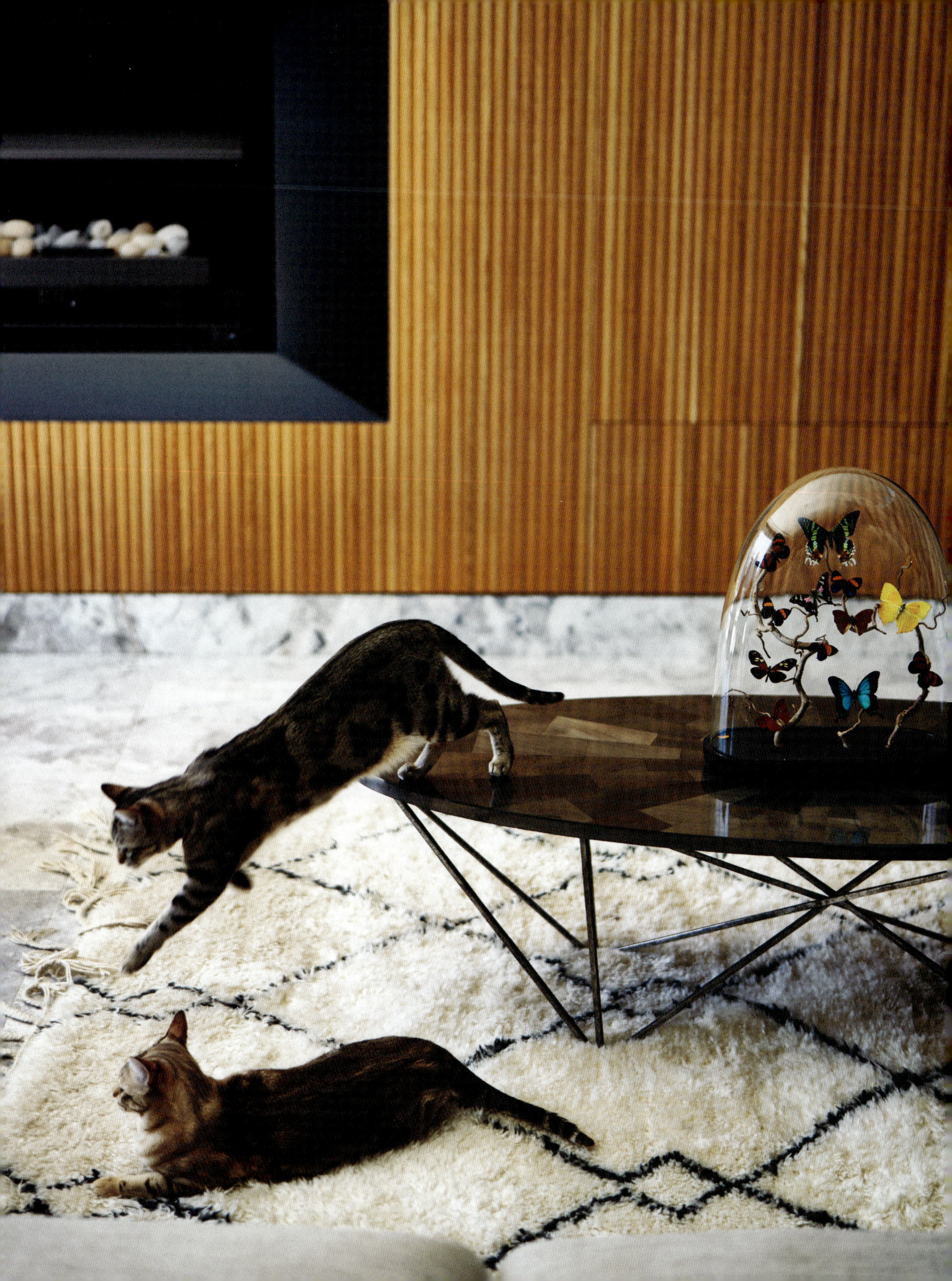

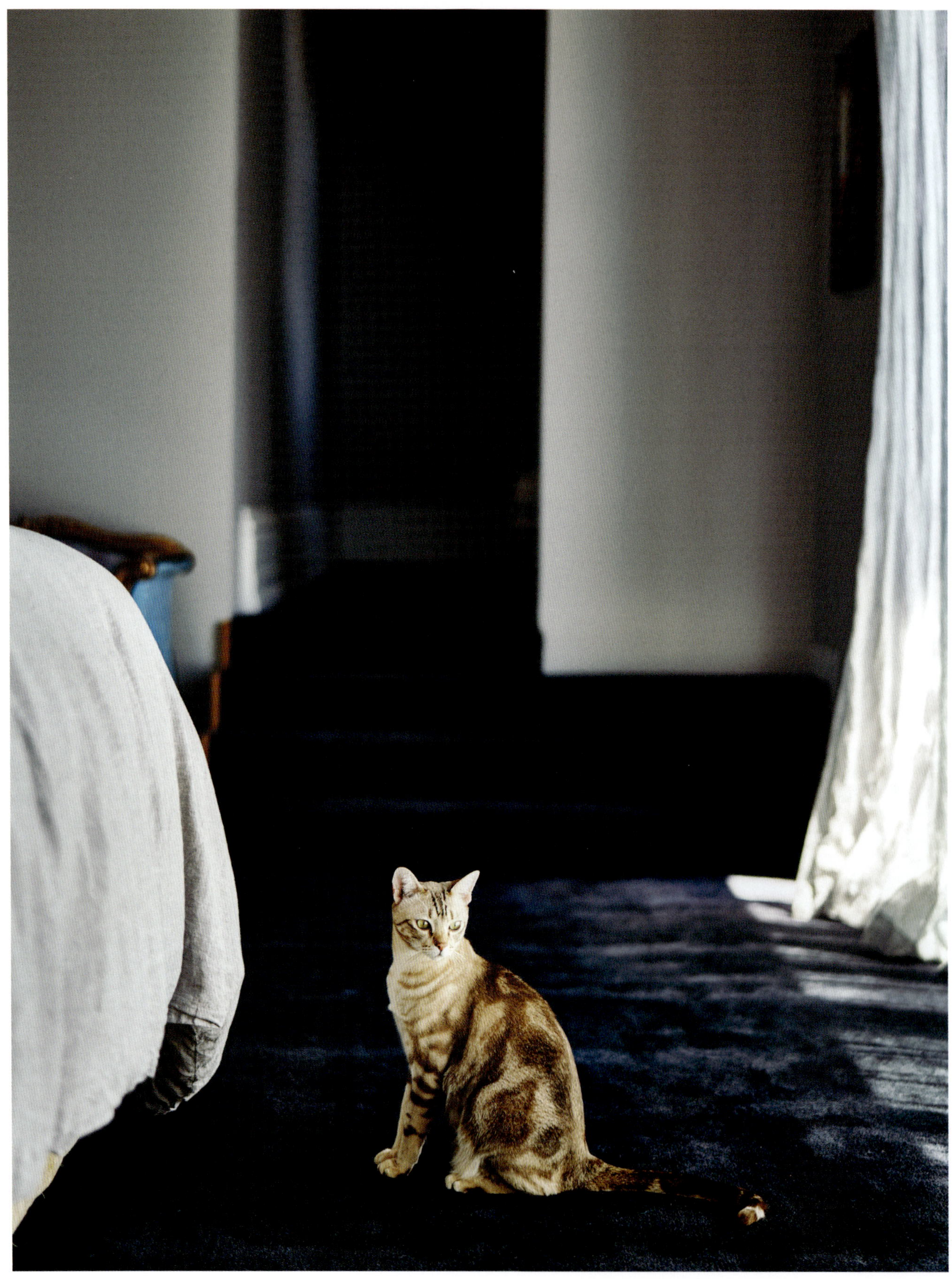

Architect: Aleksandra Rakocevic / STAR Architecture

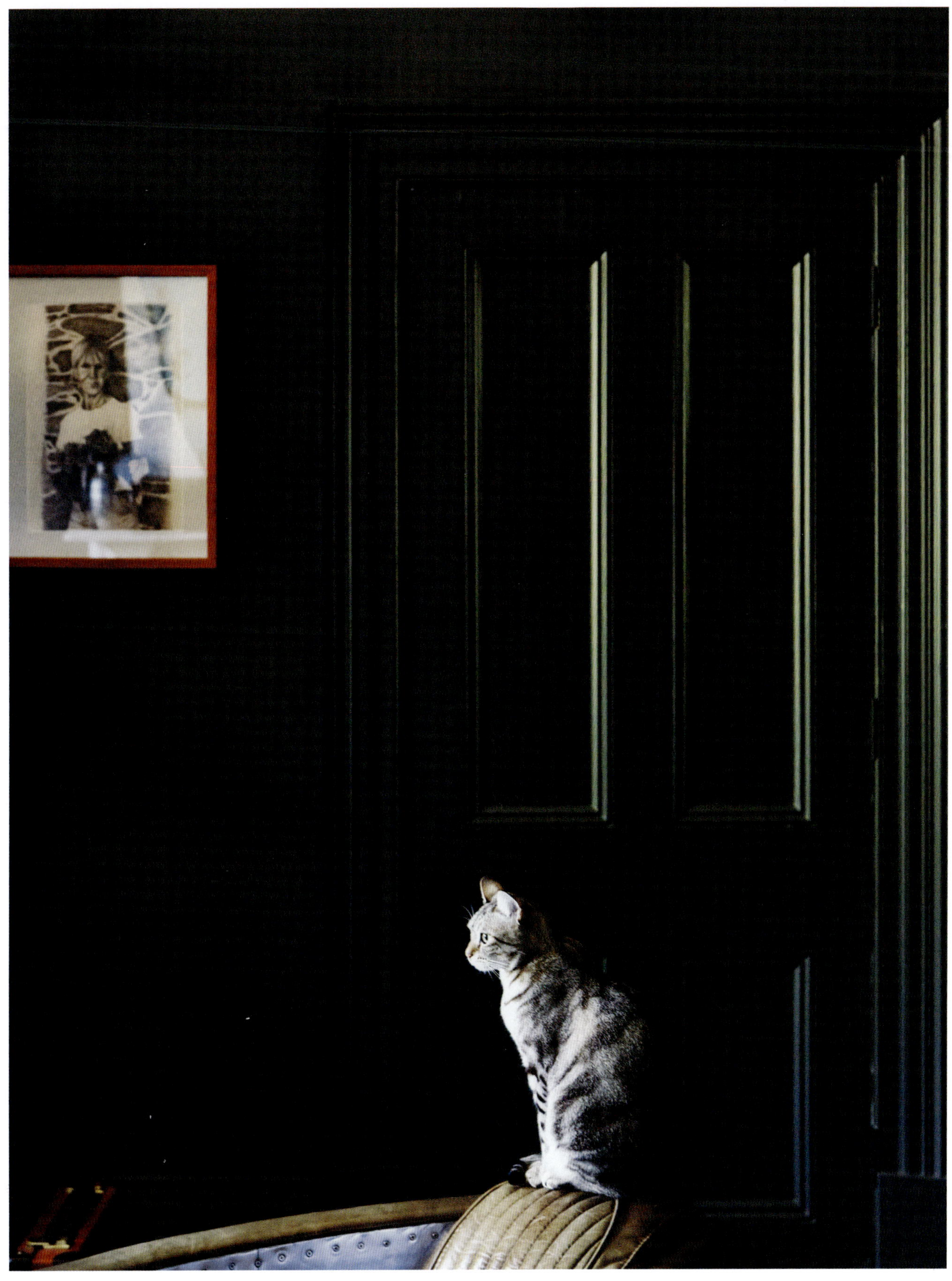

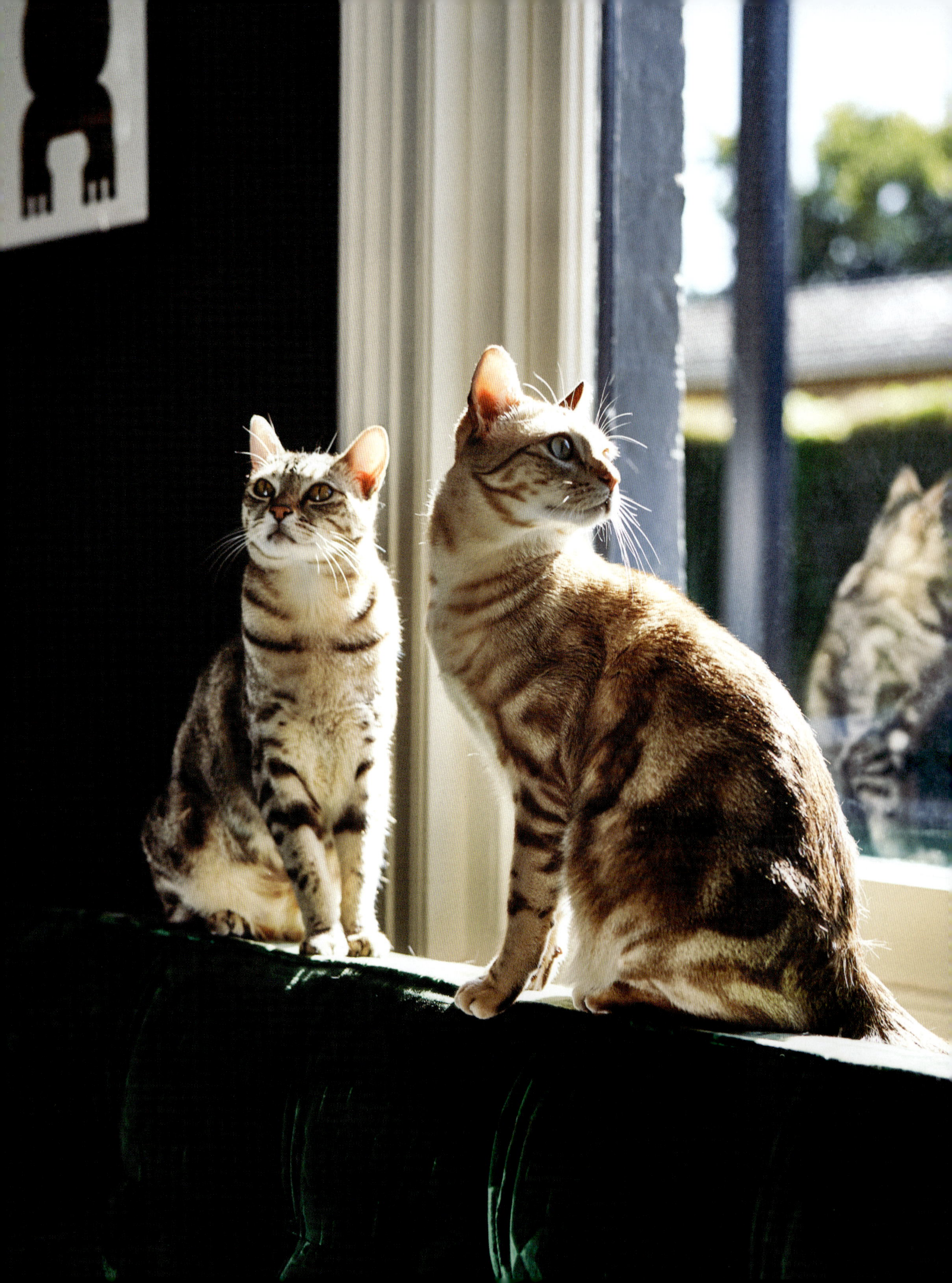

Q&A

DIVAS OR DEVOTED FRIENDS?
Billie is a diva for sure: she would win Best in Show in the 'I'm so unimpressed with you right now' facial-expression category. Tucker is the devoted but emotionally needy boyfriend.

EXTROVERTS OR INTROVERTS?
Billie is an introverted adventurer. Tucker is an extroverted charmer.

LAP CATS OR NOT?
Yes, yes and more yes. The breed is renowned for this trait, but Billie and Tucker are next level and unafraid to sit on the lap of any visitor they like.

OLD SOULS OR KITTENS AT HEART?
Tucker is an old soul, who is loving, kind and gentle. Billie is more independent and wistful, but ever so sweet.

EXPLORERS OR HOMEBODIES?
Billie is an inquisitive explorer. She will race through the house, just for a change of scene. Tucker is her cheerleader – from the couch. He prefers to view his sister's shenanigans from the comfort of a lap.

LAZY OR ACTIVE?
Both Billie and Tucker are very active during the day – and delightfully lazy at night.

DOGS – FRIEND OR FOE?
Any dogs that visit this pair's home are left in no doubt as to who are the king and queen in residence.

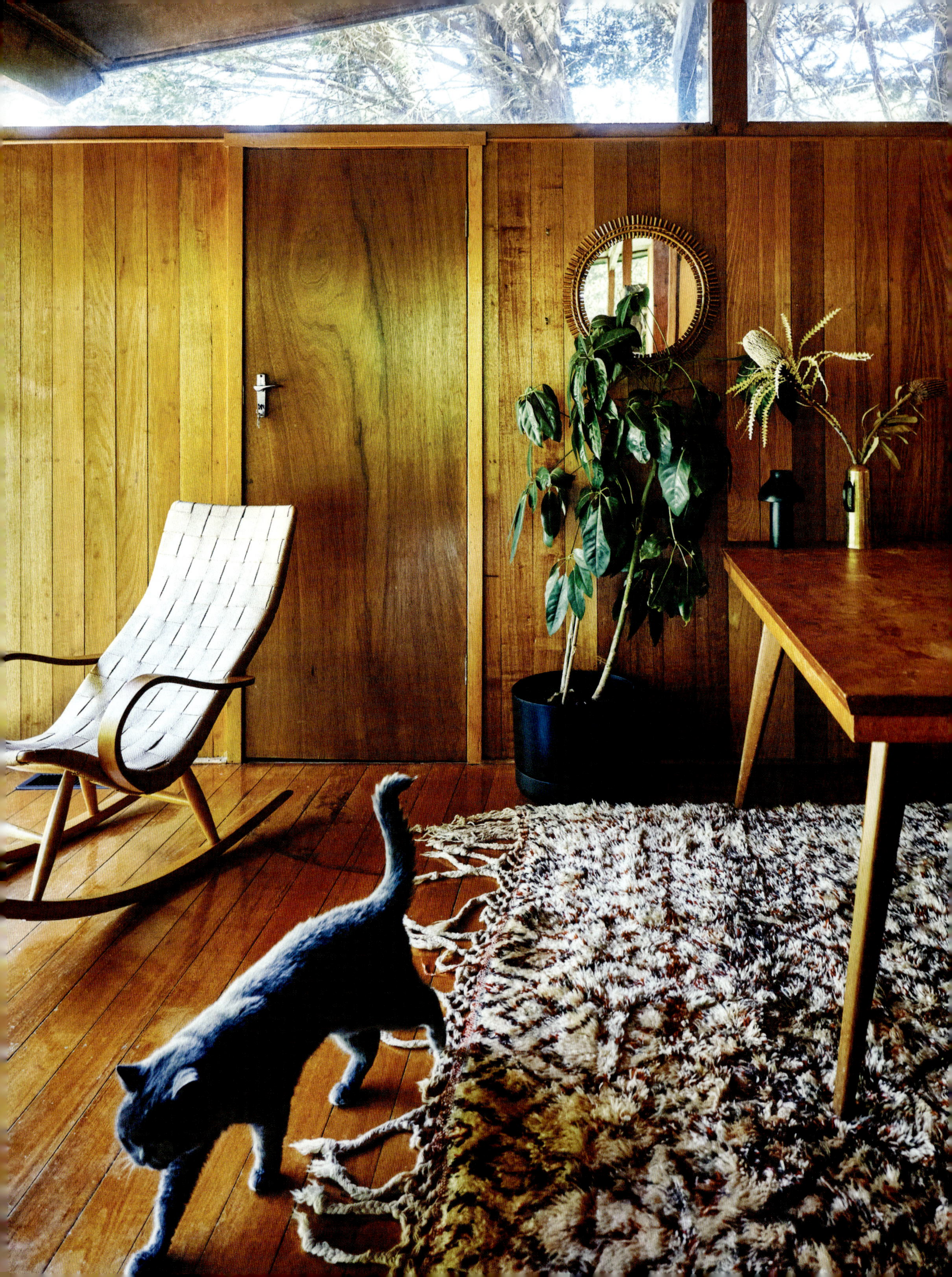

GUSTOV

ARCHITECT: ROBERT VAN ROMPAEY / BARLOW, VAN ROMPAEY & KERR

It was after meeting Gustov's cousin, and falling in love with him, that Gustov's owners decided to purchase a British shorthair from the very same breeder. When they finally got to pick him up, they were instantly enamoured of the tiny, fluffy, twelve-week-old kitten. Some cats don't like to leave the house or go in the car, but not Gusty – a weekend away is something he has always greatly enjoyed. He is now eight years old, and although his family sometimes spends months away from home, he remains as adaptable as ever – happily staying with friends during the family's absences and always ready to embrace new adventures and new people.

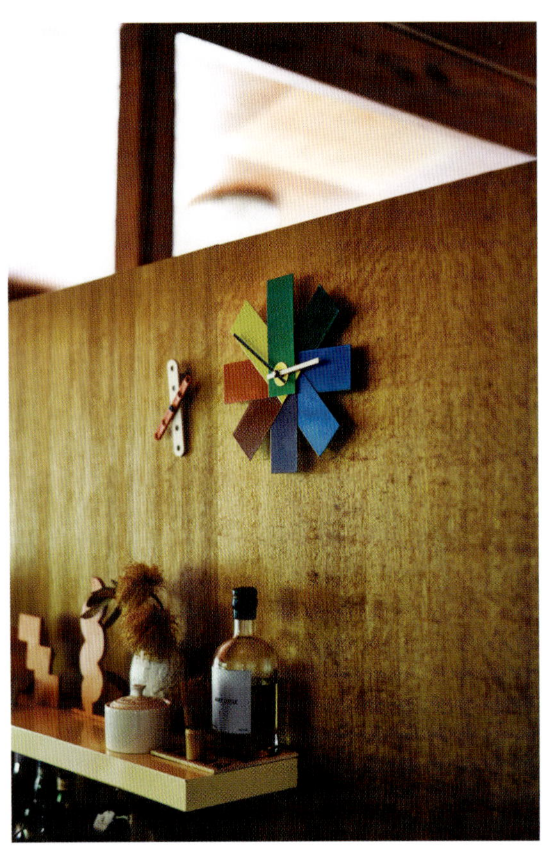

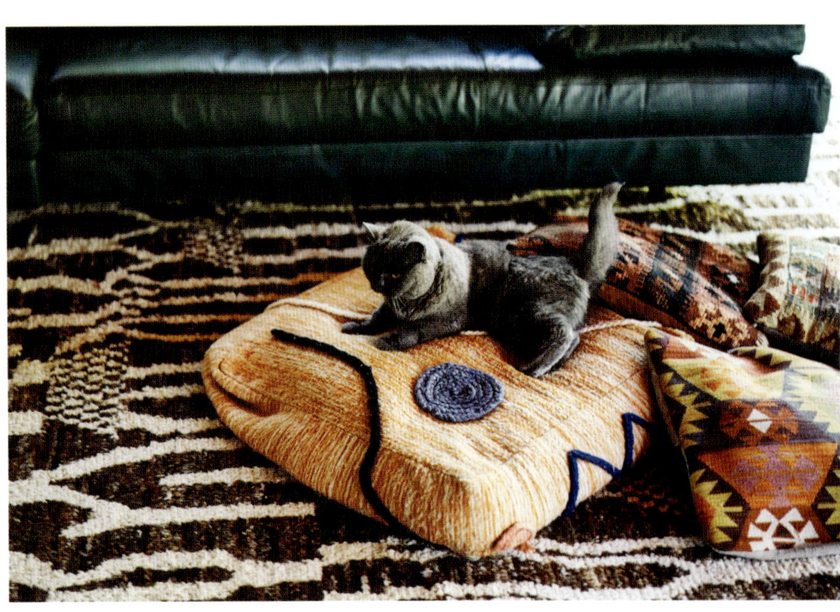

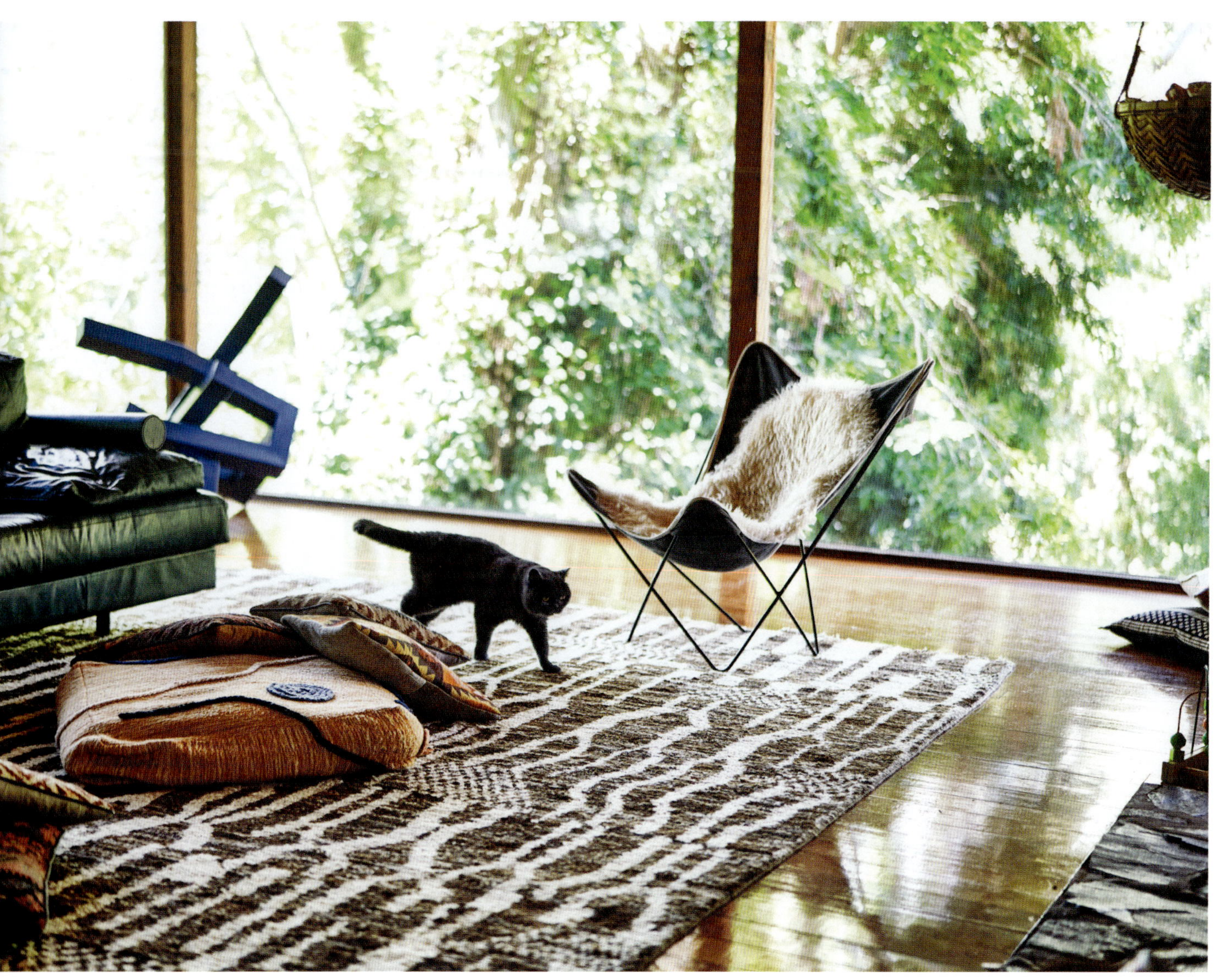

Gustov's home was built in 1958 by architect Robert Van Rompaey, as a weekender for his family. In the 1970s, Rompaey decided to sell all of his possessions, including the house, and move to Europe. The home had only one subsequent owner. When the property finally came up for sale again in 2015, the current owners couldn't pass up the opportunity to purchase such a well-preserved piece of Australian architectural history.

The home is made from timber and glass, elevated from the ground and immersed in a vibrant green canopy.

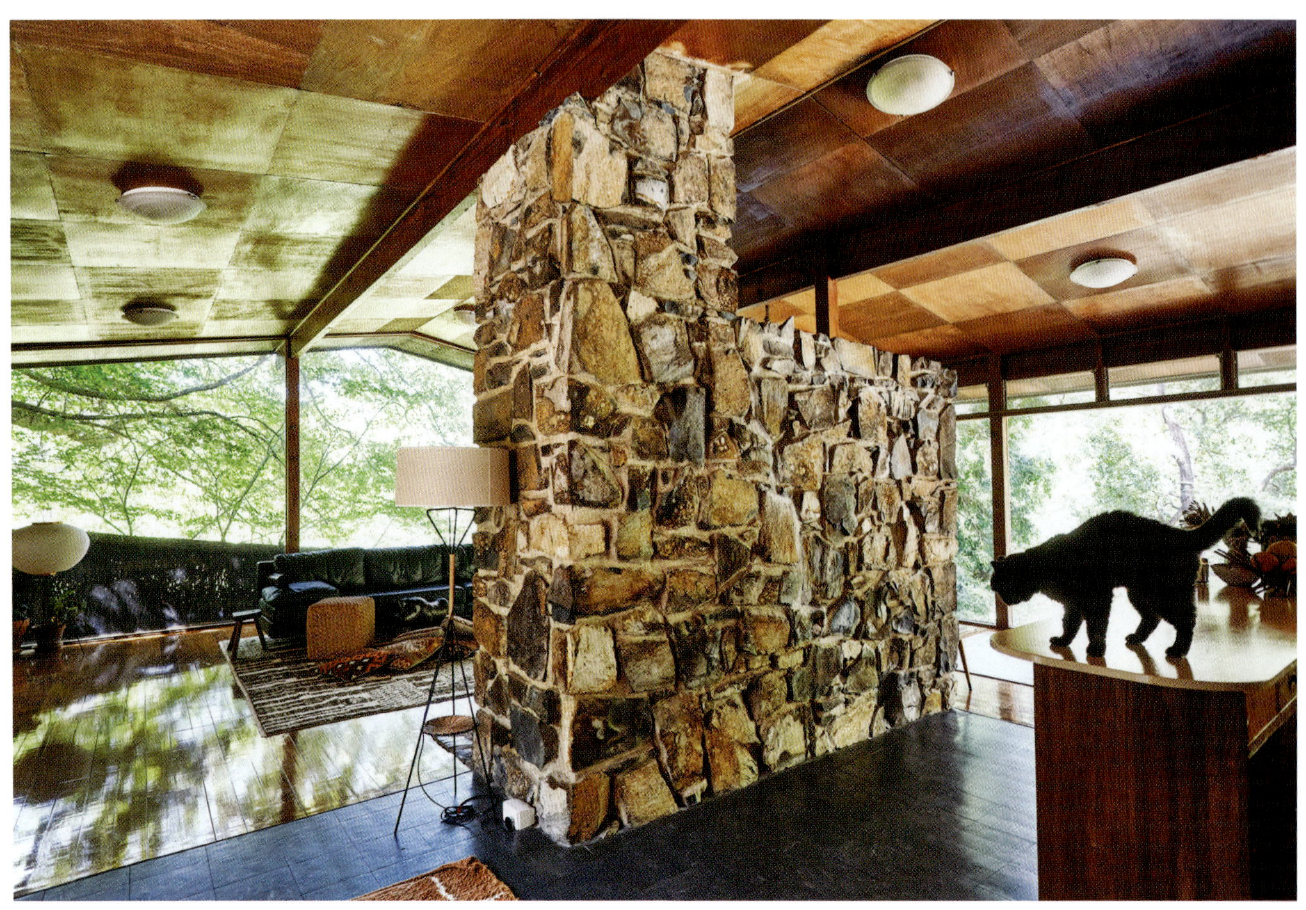

Apart from minor refurbishments, the house remains almost entirely as it was when originally built.

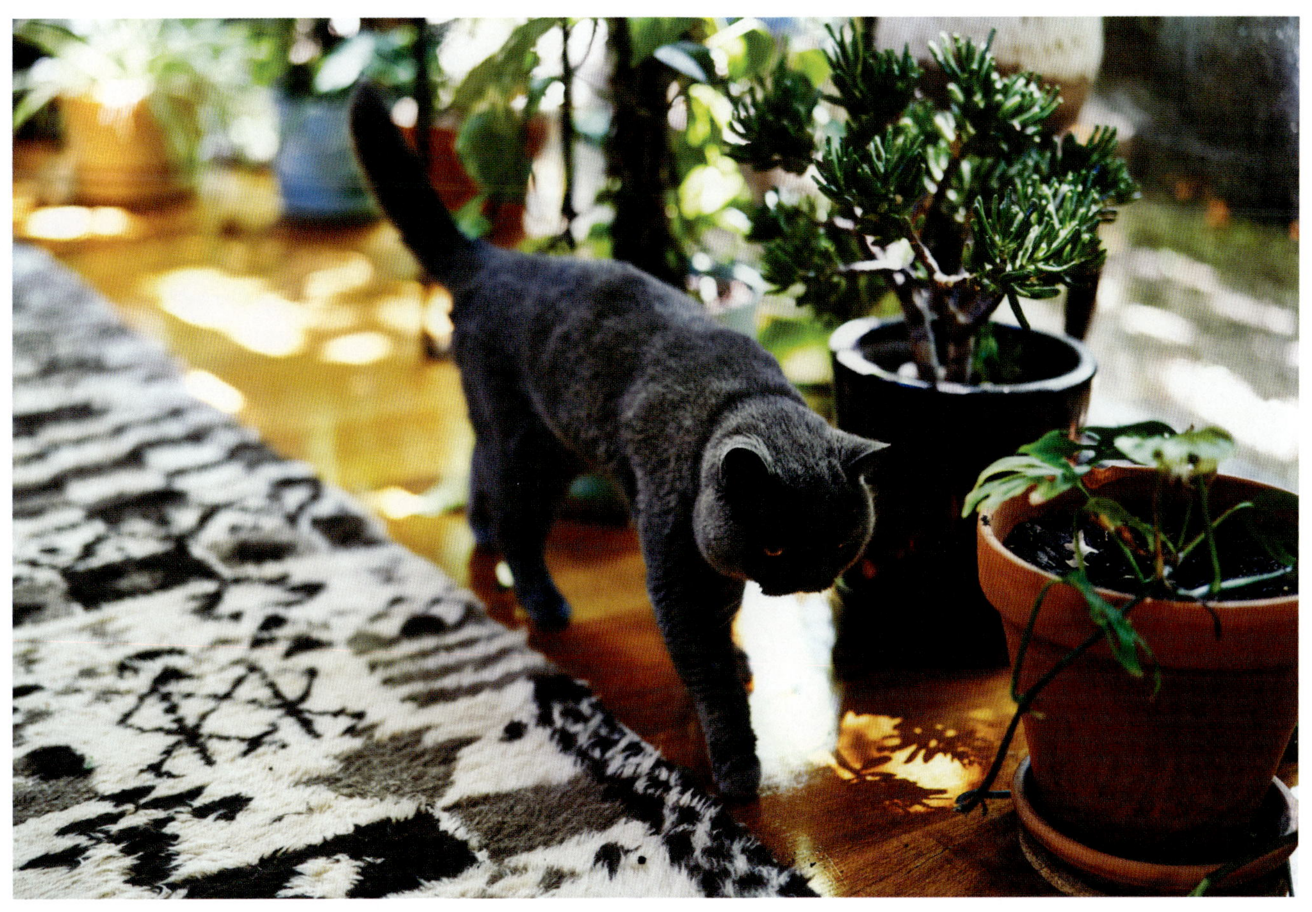

Gustov likes to hang out anywhere that has sunlight streaming in through the windows – ideally with a view of some bugs or birds. If moths or flies find their way inside, he will chase them around the house, although he rarely catches them!

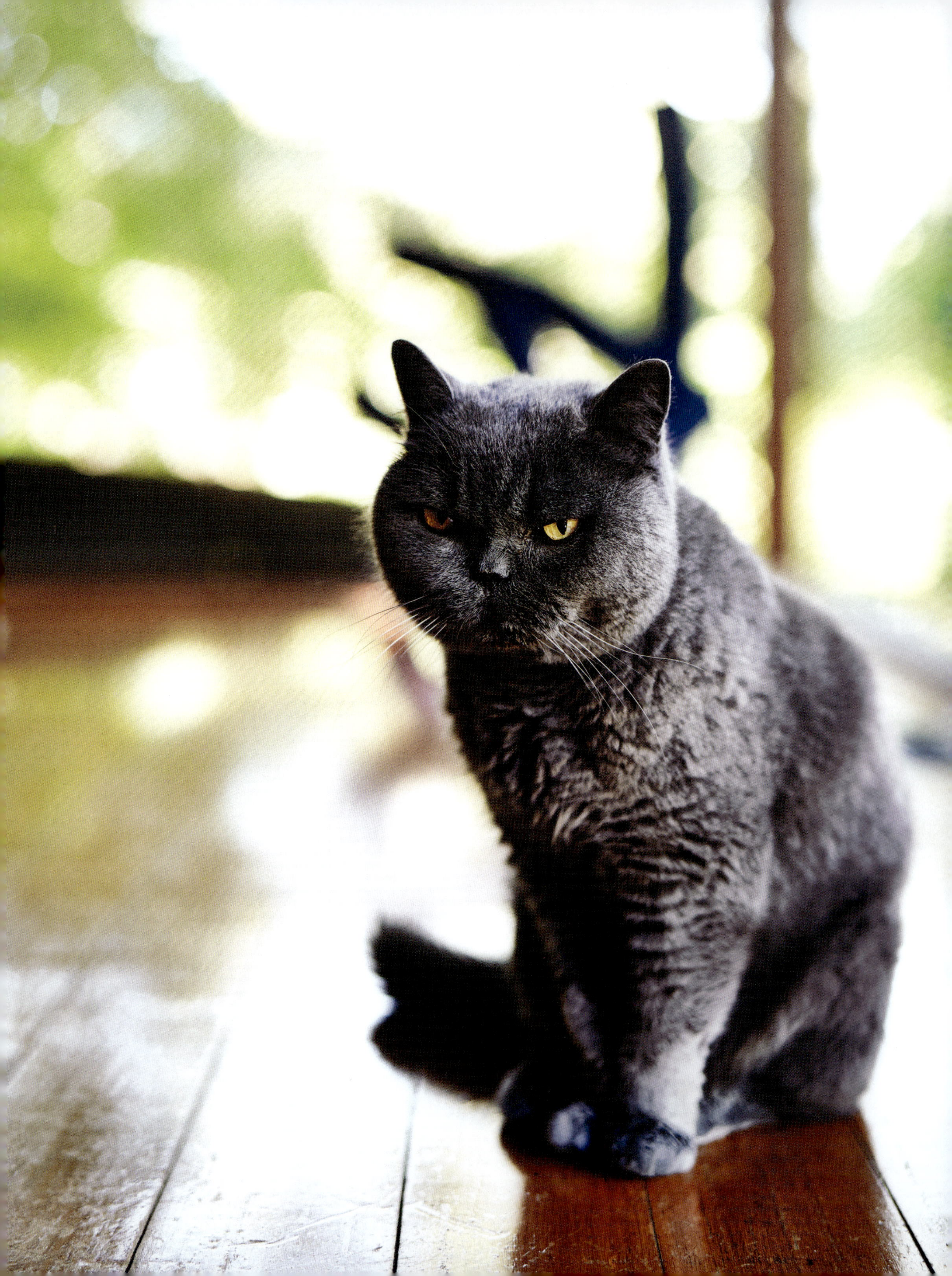

Q&A

DIVA OR DEVOTED FRIEND?

Devoted friend.

EXTROVERT OR INTROVERT?

Introvert.

LAP CAT OR NOT?

Lap cat – but only for the father of the household.

OLD SOUL OR KITTEN AT HEART?

Old soul, with occasional spurts of kitten.

EXPLORER OR HOMEBODY?

Homebody.

LAZY OR ACTIVE?

Lazy for 23.5 hours a day. Active for 0.5 hours!

DOGS – FRIEND OR FOE?

Foe.

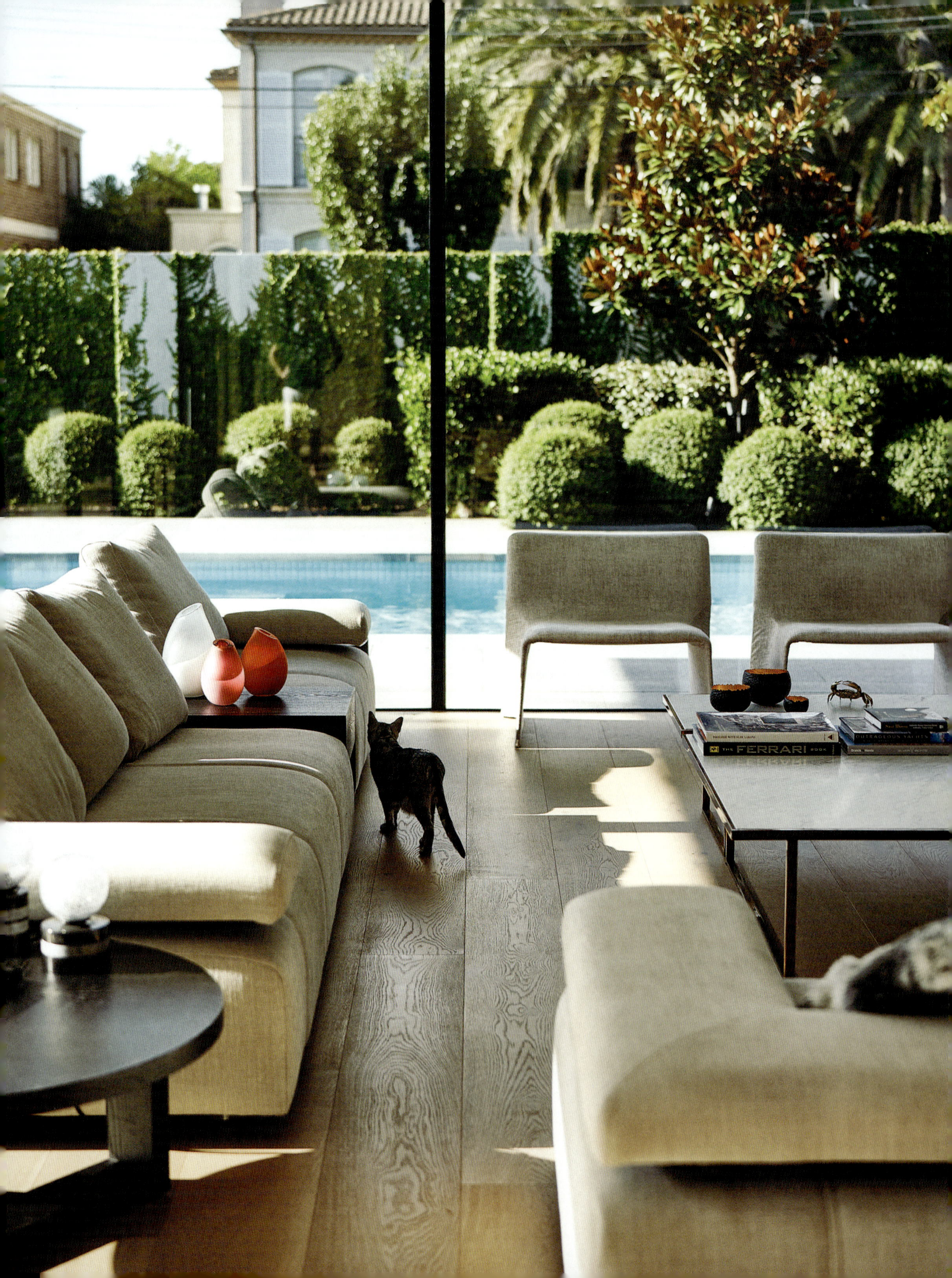
THE FERRARI BOOK
OUTRAGEOUS YACHTS

BUDDY

ARCHITECT: BEAR AGUSHI / AGUSHI

An independent and kooky cat, Buddy is a five-year-old silver Bengal who lives with her big, blended family of seven humans (dad with his three children; mum with her twins). When the two families moved in together, Buddy was initially indifferent to most members of her new household and very choosy about who deserved her devotion. She does have a few favourites, though, and is particularly fond of the mother of the family: Buddy is always eager to greet her when she comes home from work and is her faithful shadow around the house.

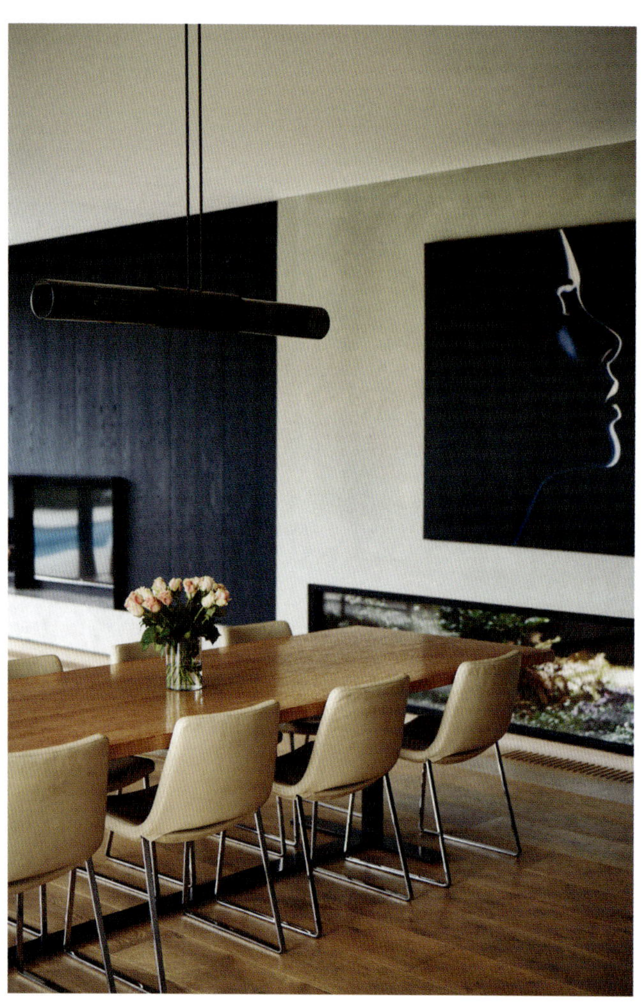

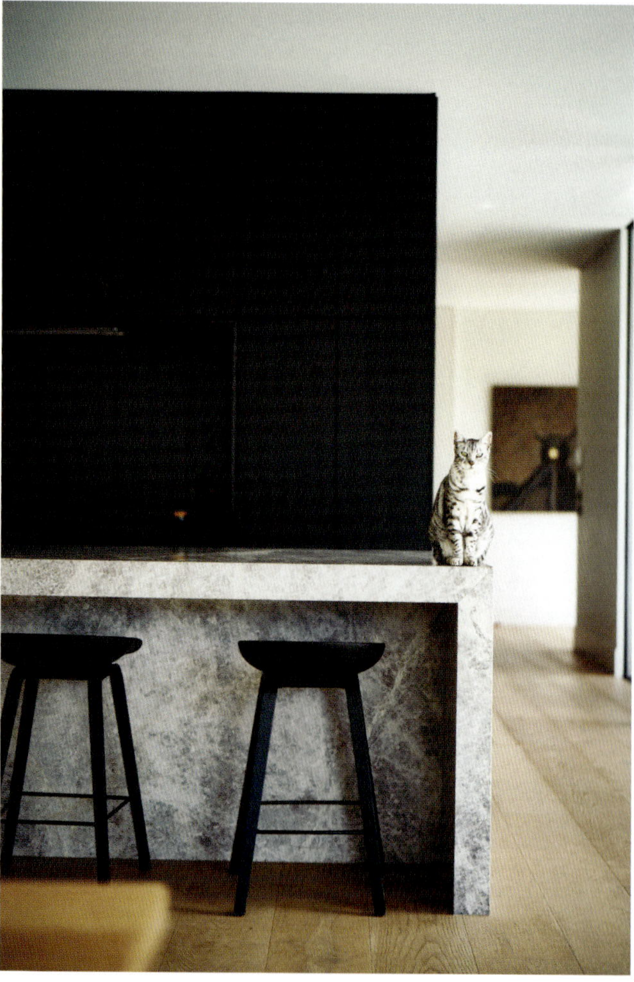

Buddy lives in a bright yet bold modern family home. The house was designed to provide unobstructed views of the entire outside area from the kitchen, living and dining spaces.

Architect: Bear Agushi / AGUSHI

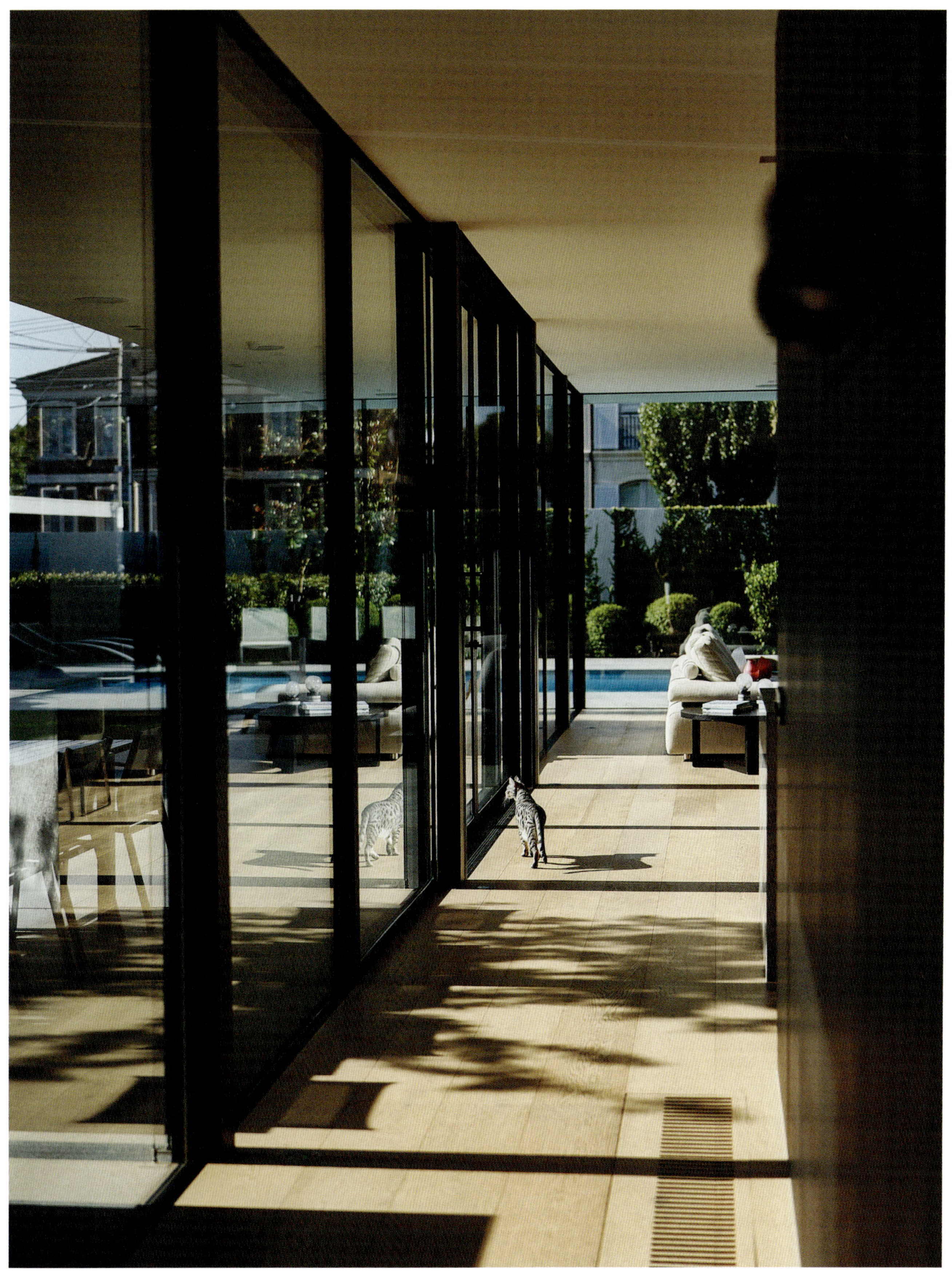

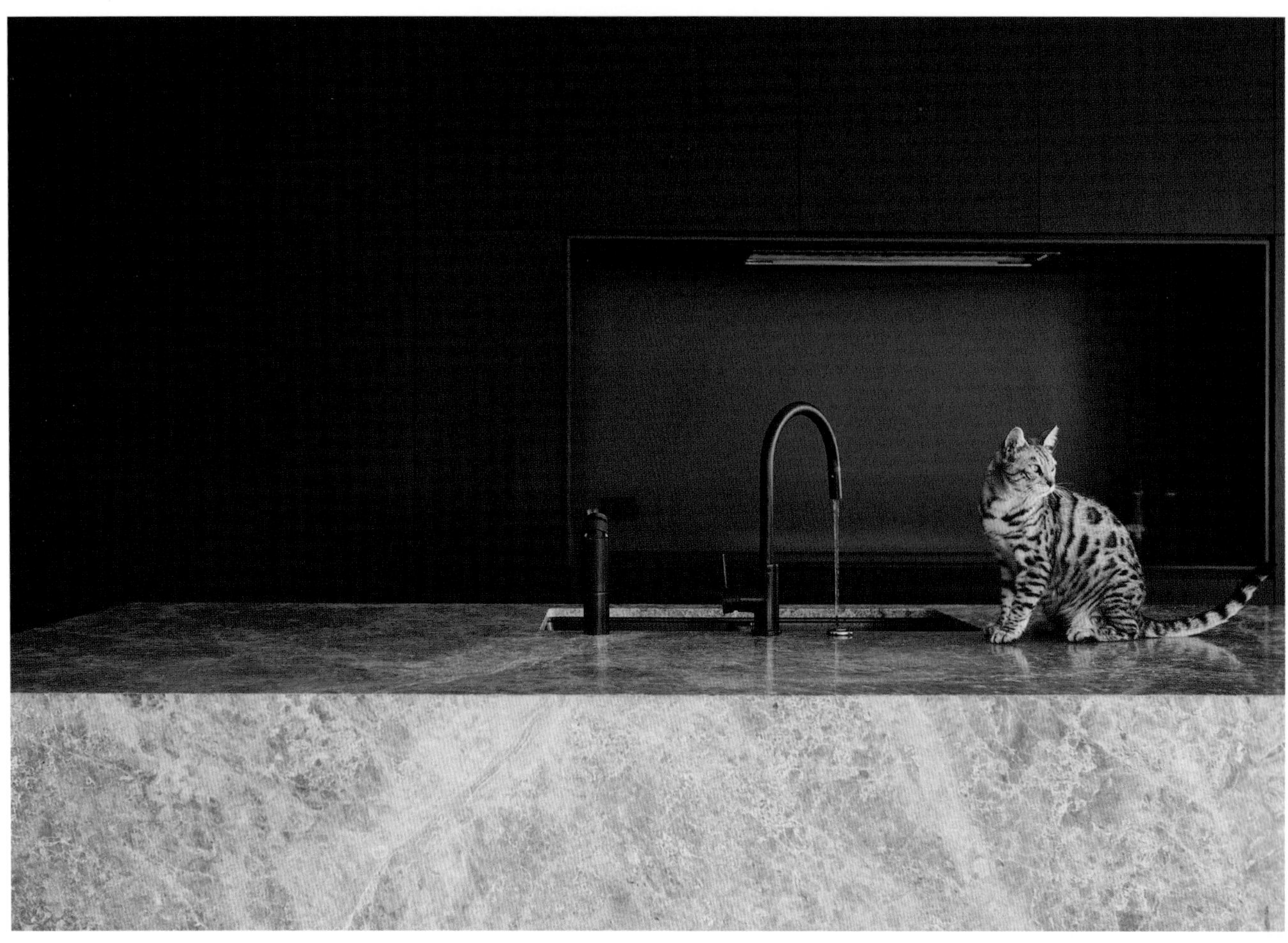

The owners wanted a home full of texture and with an abundance of warmth. Rendered concrete, black timber panelling and stone combine to create a luxurious and inviting mood.

Architect: Bear Agushi / AGUSHI

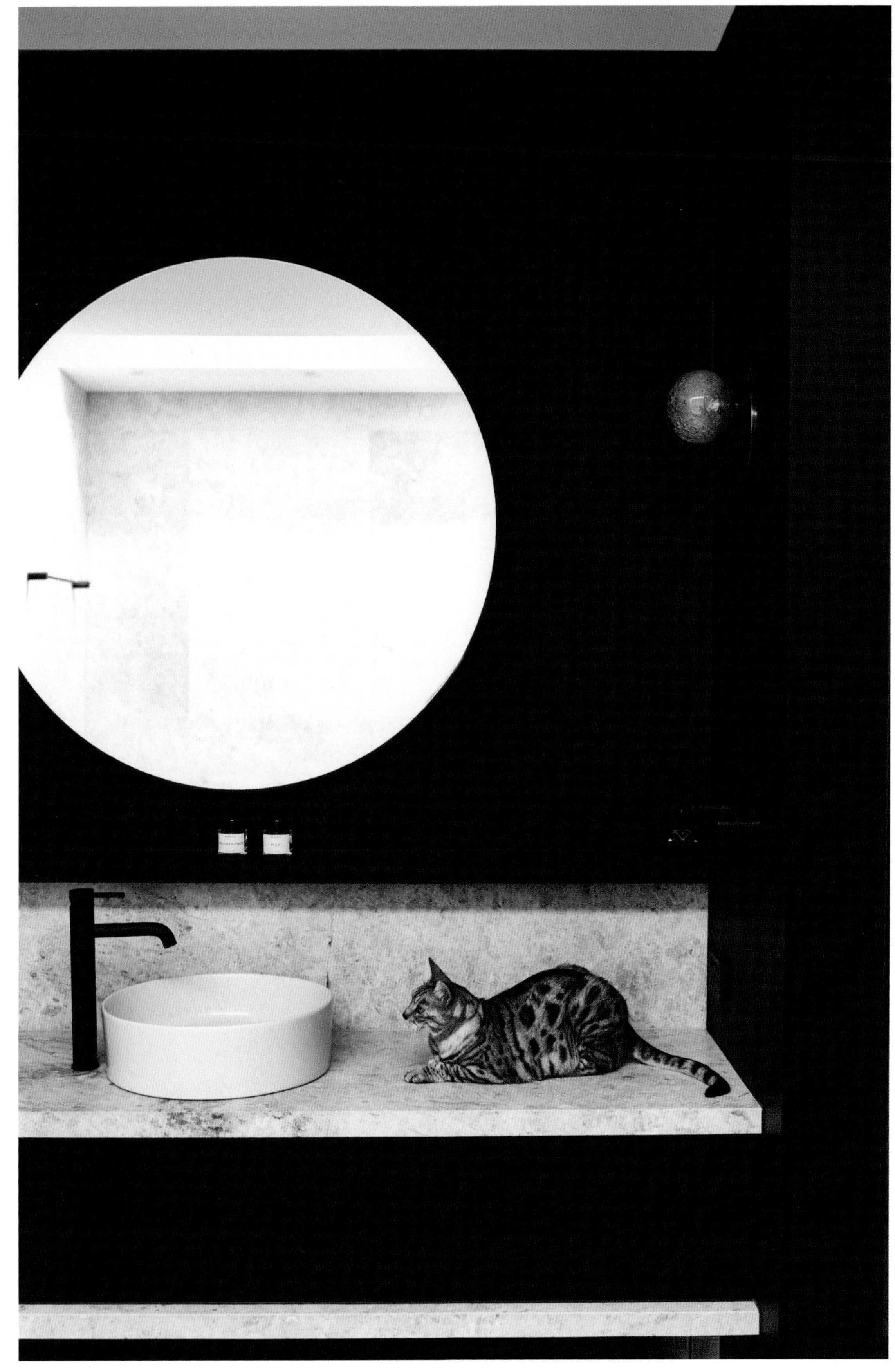

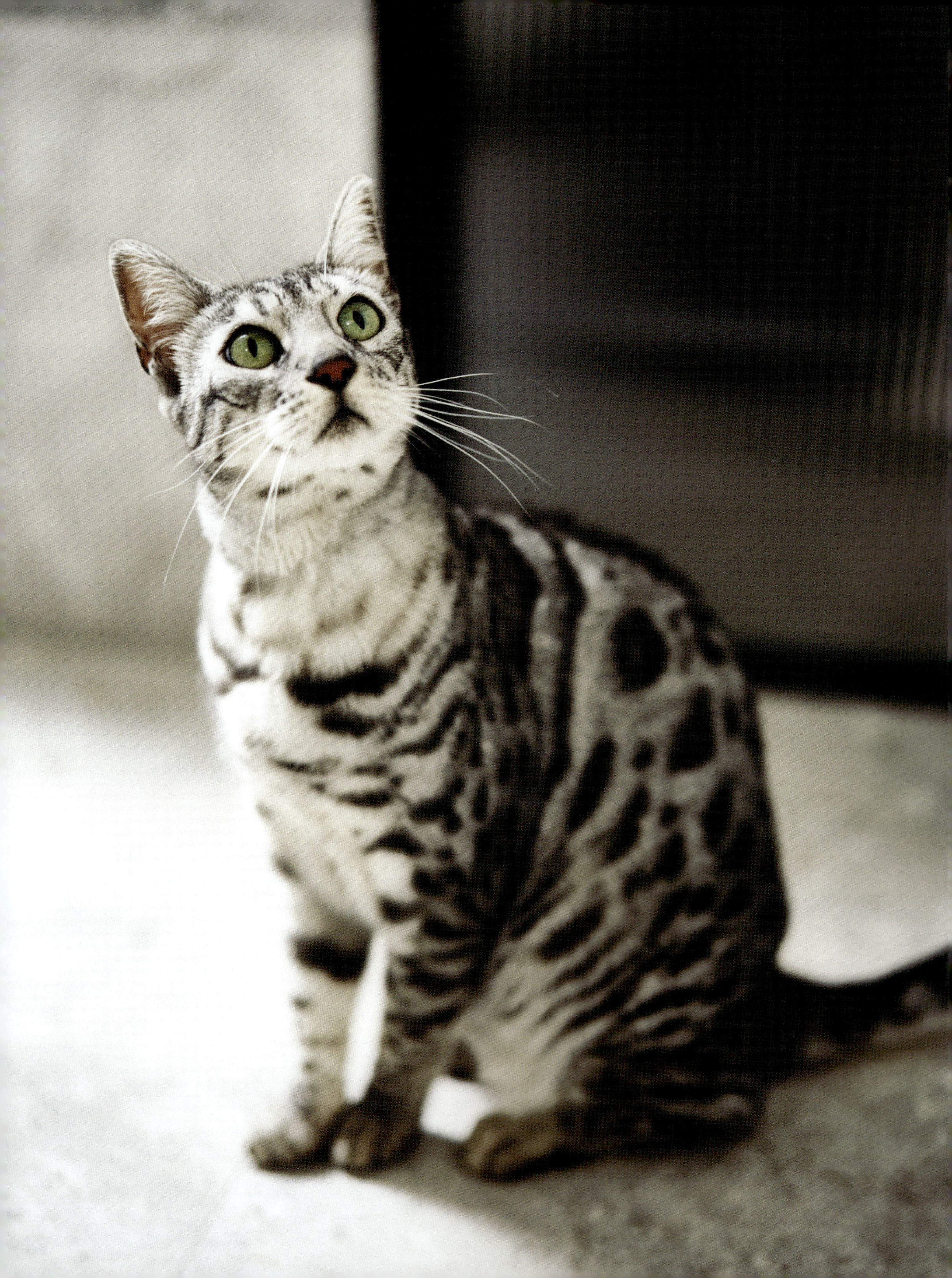

Q&A

DIVA OR DEVOTED FRIEND?

Devoted friend to her few favourites – not interested in others.

EXTROVERT OR INTROVERT?

Introverted jumpy jitterbug.

LAP CAT OR NOT?

Occasionally, yes. As long as the host doesn't touch her.

OLD SOUL OR KITTEN AT HEART?

Kitten at heart.

EXPLORER OR HOMEBODY?

Explorer.

LAZY OR ACTIVE?

Active.

DOGS – FRIEND OR FOE?

Foe. She turns into a bushy question mark whenever she sees a dog.

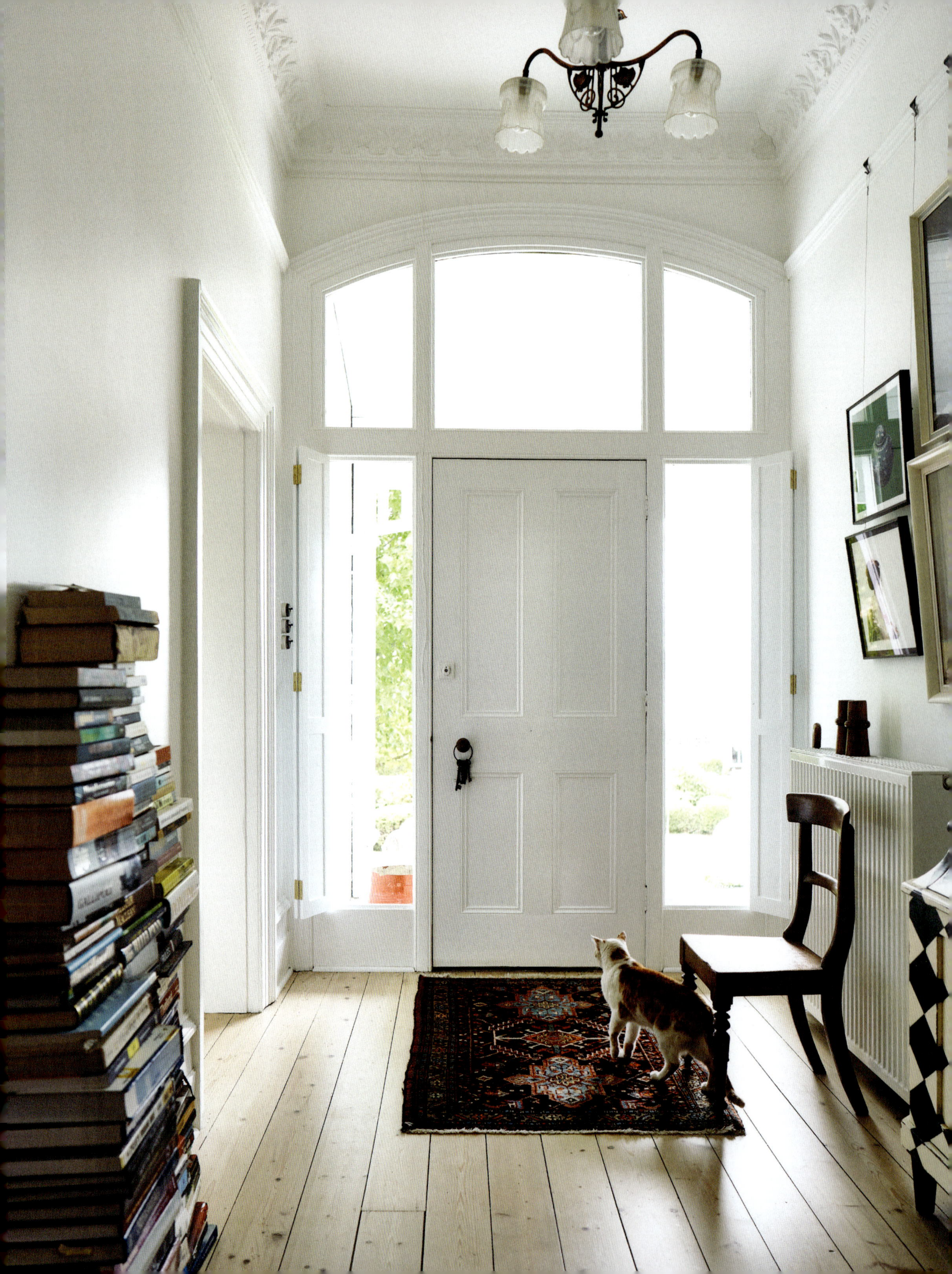

RED

ARCHITECT: PIPPA JENSEN / CUMULUS STUDIO WITH SIMONE PENN

Red is a self-reliant and headstrong mixed-breed cat who likes to be wild and free. His family lives in a beautifully renovated Federation home in Launceston, Tasmania, but Red generally prefers to be out in the garden, on his own, hiding in the grass. Adopted from a rescue shelter at eight months old, Red never really adapted to domestic life. It is only his attachment to the family's daughter that has kept him coming home for meals. After twelve years, he is slowly adjusting to the idea of spending short periods of time indoors, but he will usually run outside at the first available opportunity.

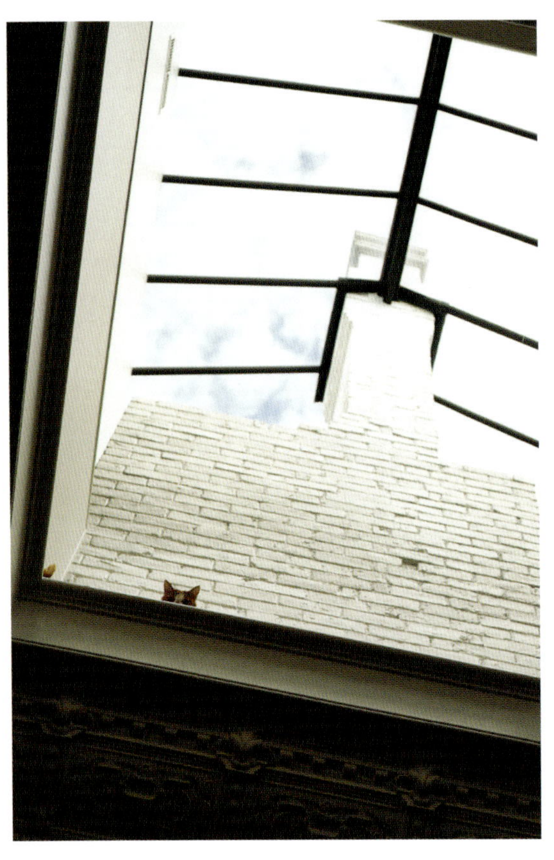

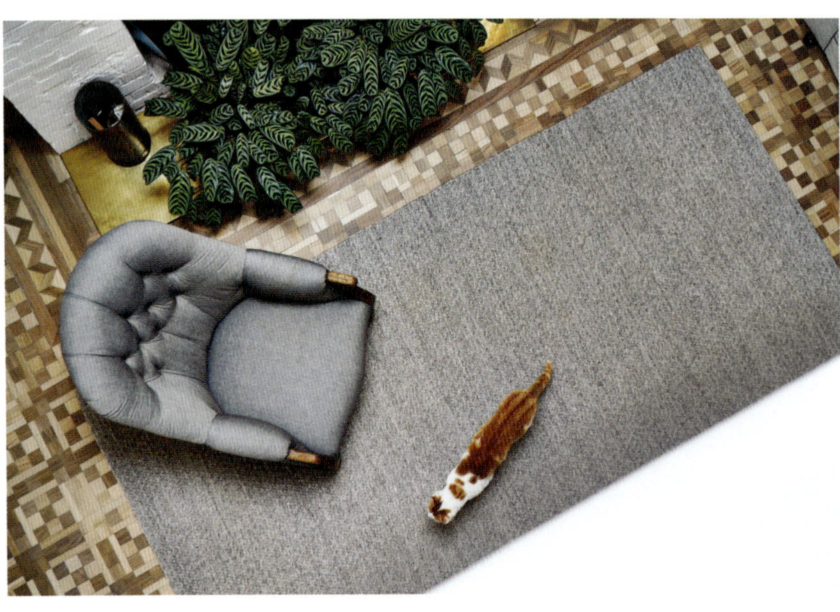

Architect: Pippa Jensen / Cumulus Studio with Simone Penn

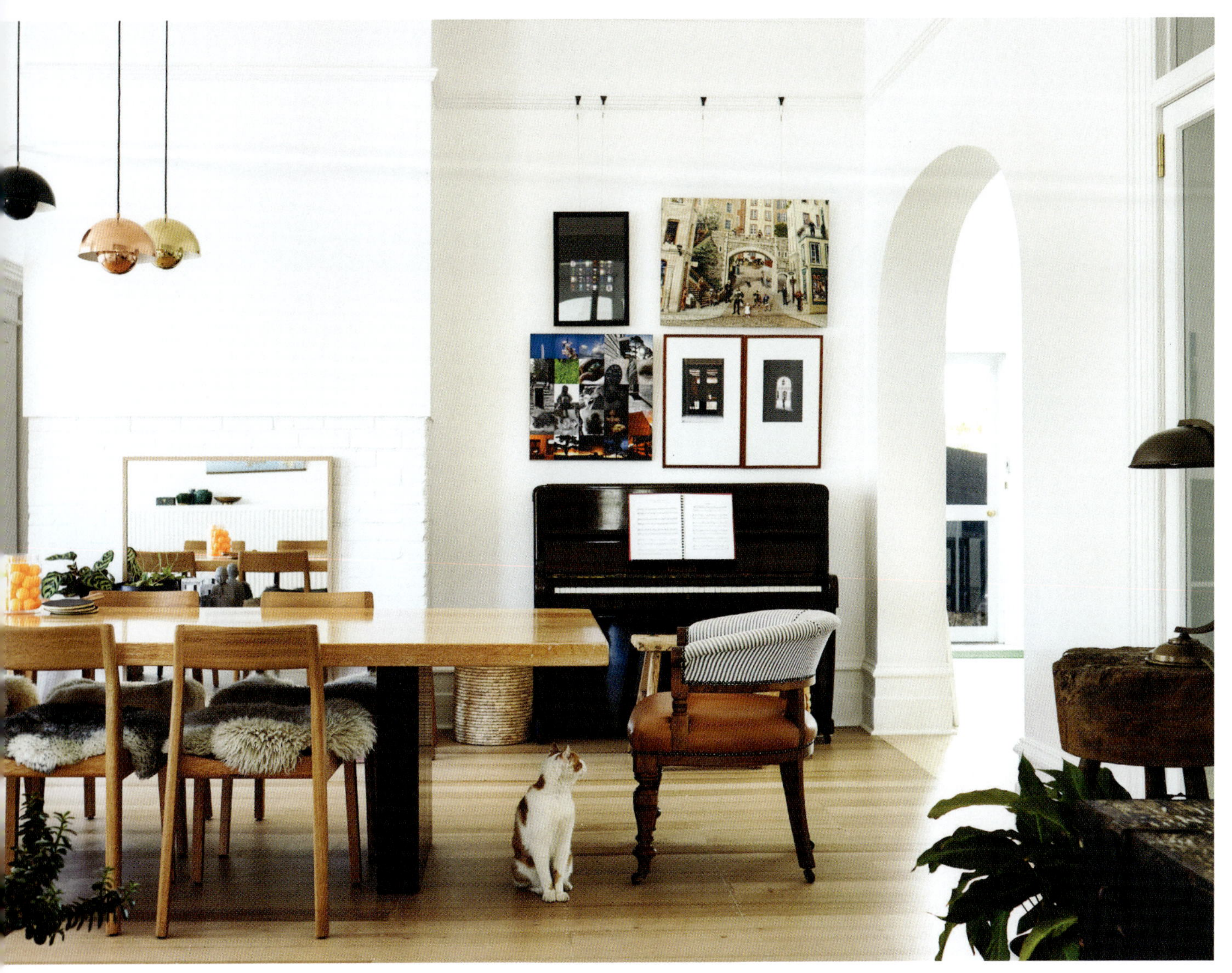

Red's owners worked closely with the architect to renovate this 112-year-old home, gently pulling back layers to celebrate old and new.

Reoriented spaces and internal voids allow light through, creating a bright open-plan home that will accommodate the family for years to come.

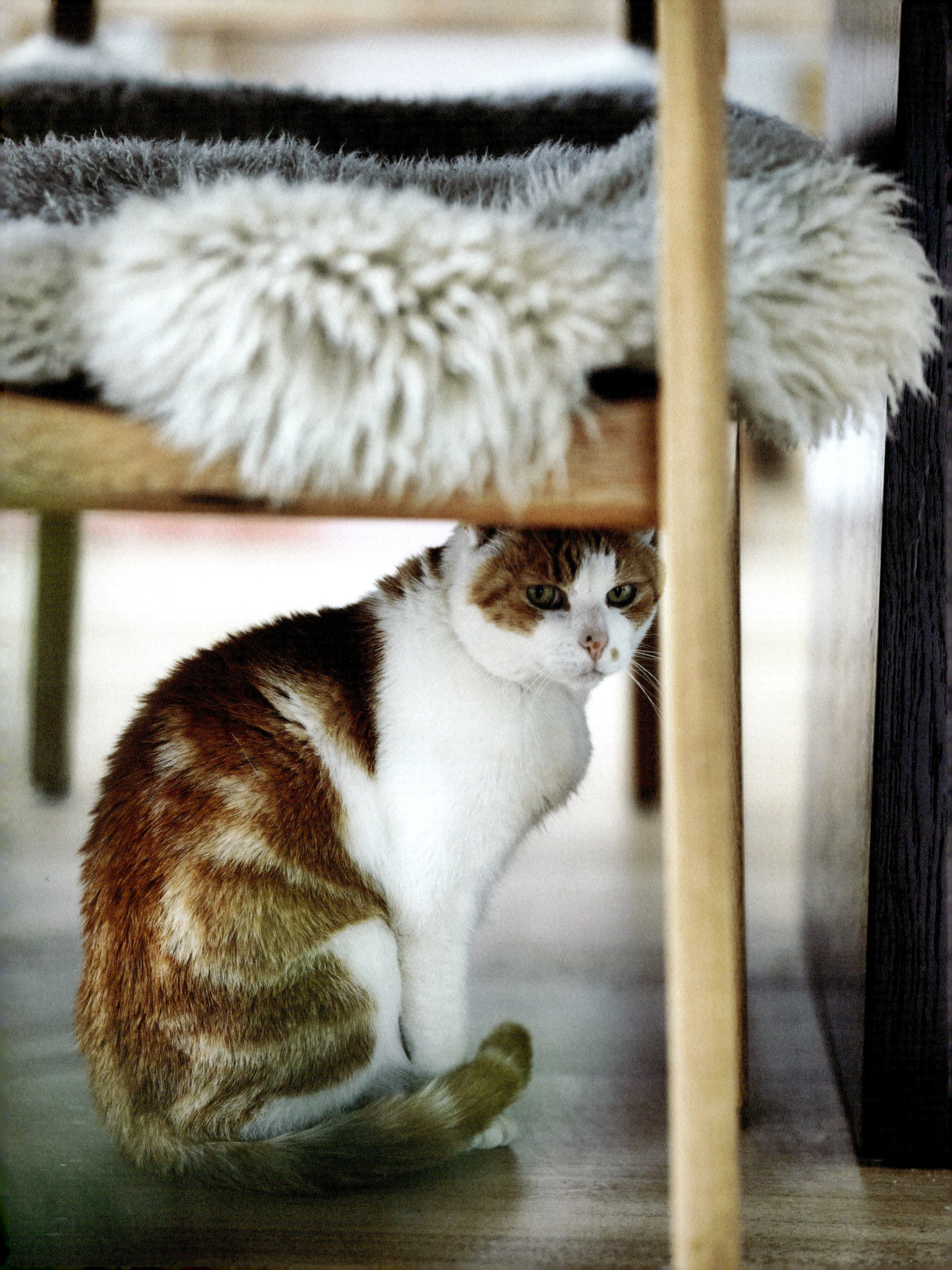

Q&A

DIVA OR DEVOTED FRIEND?

He is in love with his eighteen-year-old human sister.

EXTROVERT OR INTROVERT?

A loner.

LAP CAT OR NOT?

He will do anything for the family's daughter – but no one else.

OLD SOUL OR KITTEN AT HEART?

A hunter.

EXPLORER OR HOMEBODY?

Explorer.

LAZY OR ACTIVE?

Lazy. He's old now.

DOGS – FRIEND OR FOE?

He loves to antagonise the family's dogs.

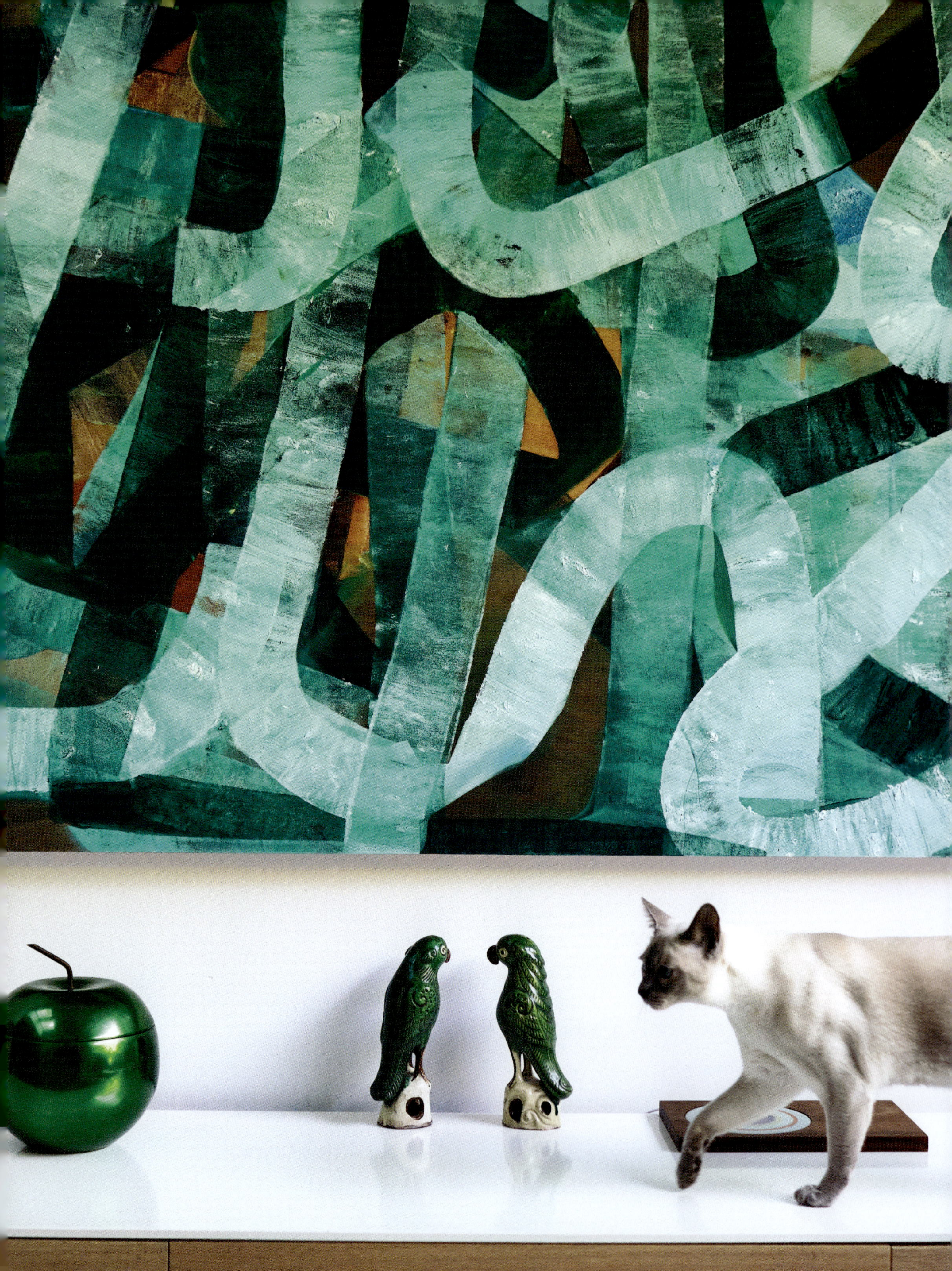

FRANK SCHNUPTON

STYLIST: LOUISE UPTON

Frank Schnupton runs the show in his household and the family's lifestyle has come to revolve around him. For example, his owners like a neatly made bed, but Frank does not – he prefers the covers to be messy, so he can burrow into them and sleep during the day. Frank is a two-year-old platinum colour-point Tonkinese, which is a cross between Siamese and Burmese. He is engaging and playful, yet not overactive. Frank was found through an online ad. Among the kittens in the photographs, he was the smallest and dazzlingly white. How could they resist?

Frank's three-storey terrace house is located on an old street with industrial heritage in the inner-Sydney suburb of Redfern. The home was already renovated when the family bought it, but they have made it their own with Scandi-inspired furnishings and a collection of modern art along the walls.

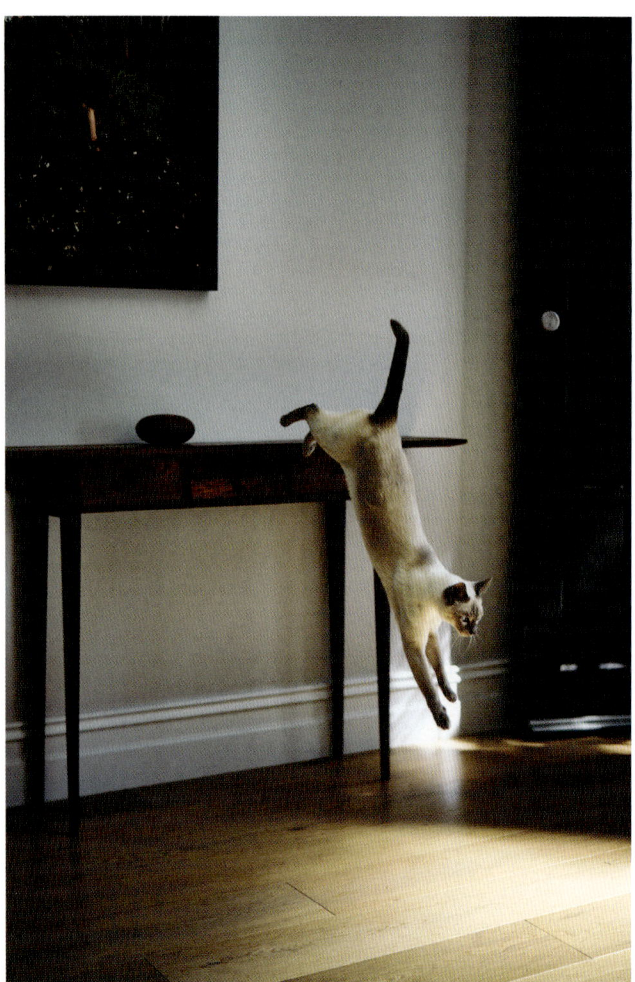

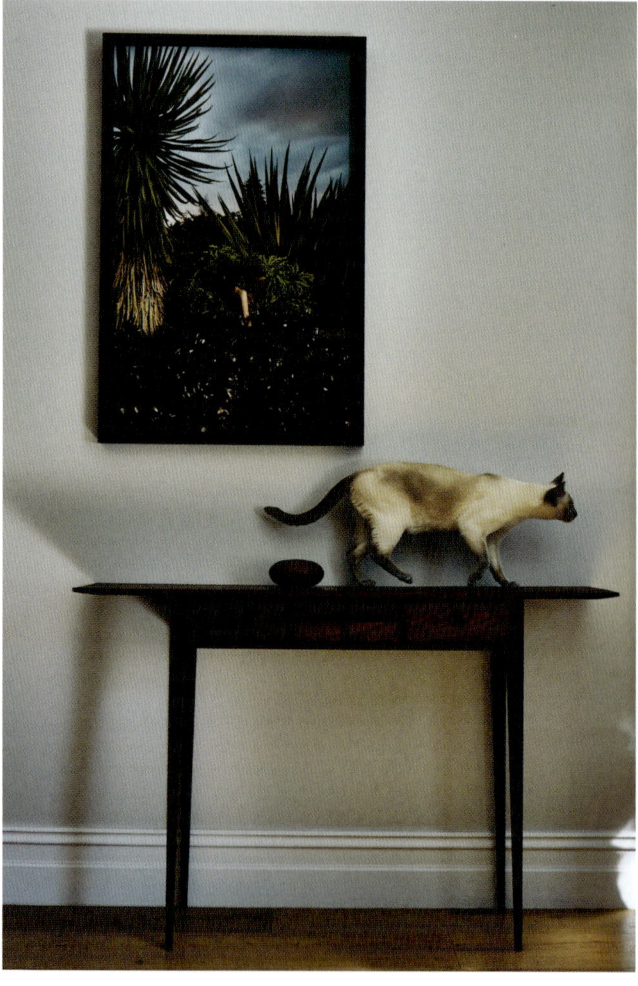

The family especially enjoys the courtyard, which brings the outside in. The folding glass doors maximise the light in the kitchen and living areas, while the use of furnishings and flooring made from organic materials like wood ensure the indoor–outdoor areas join seamlessly.

Stylist: Louise Upton

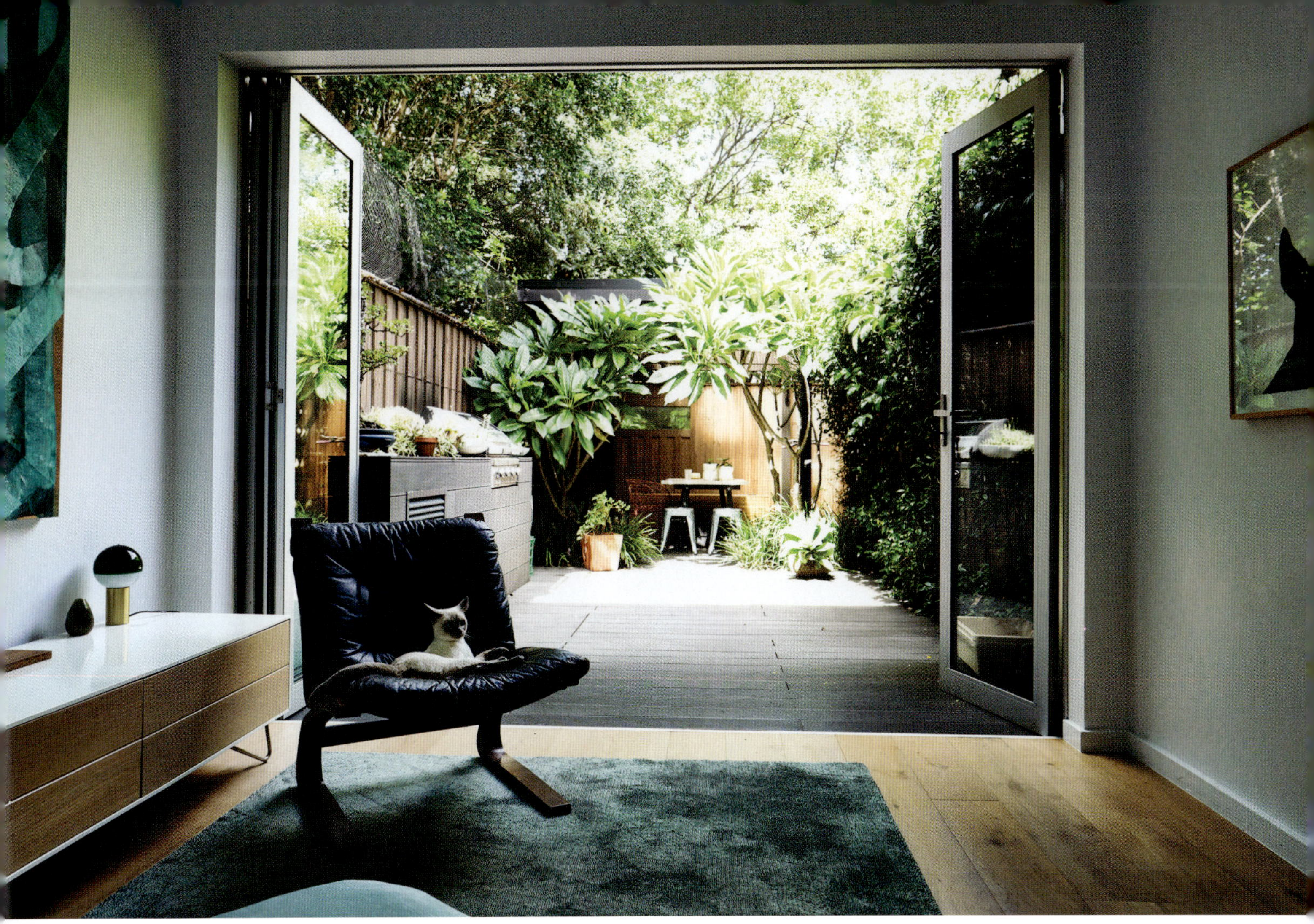

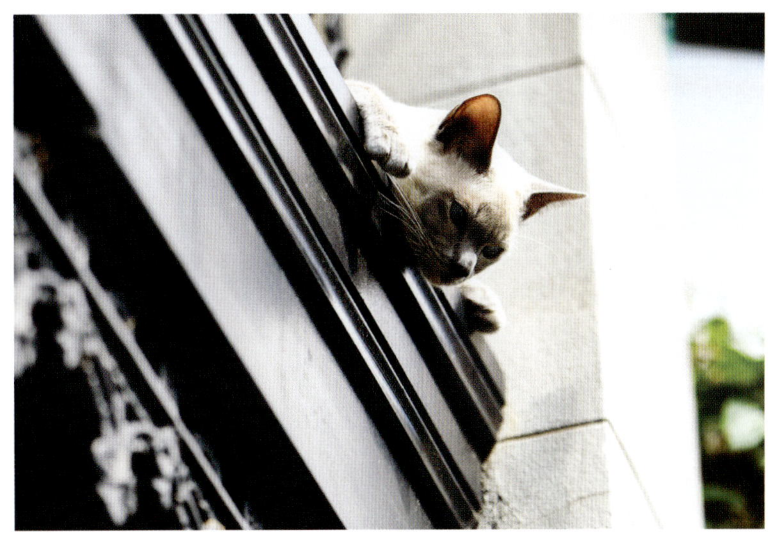

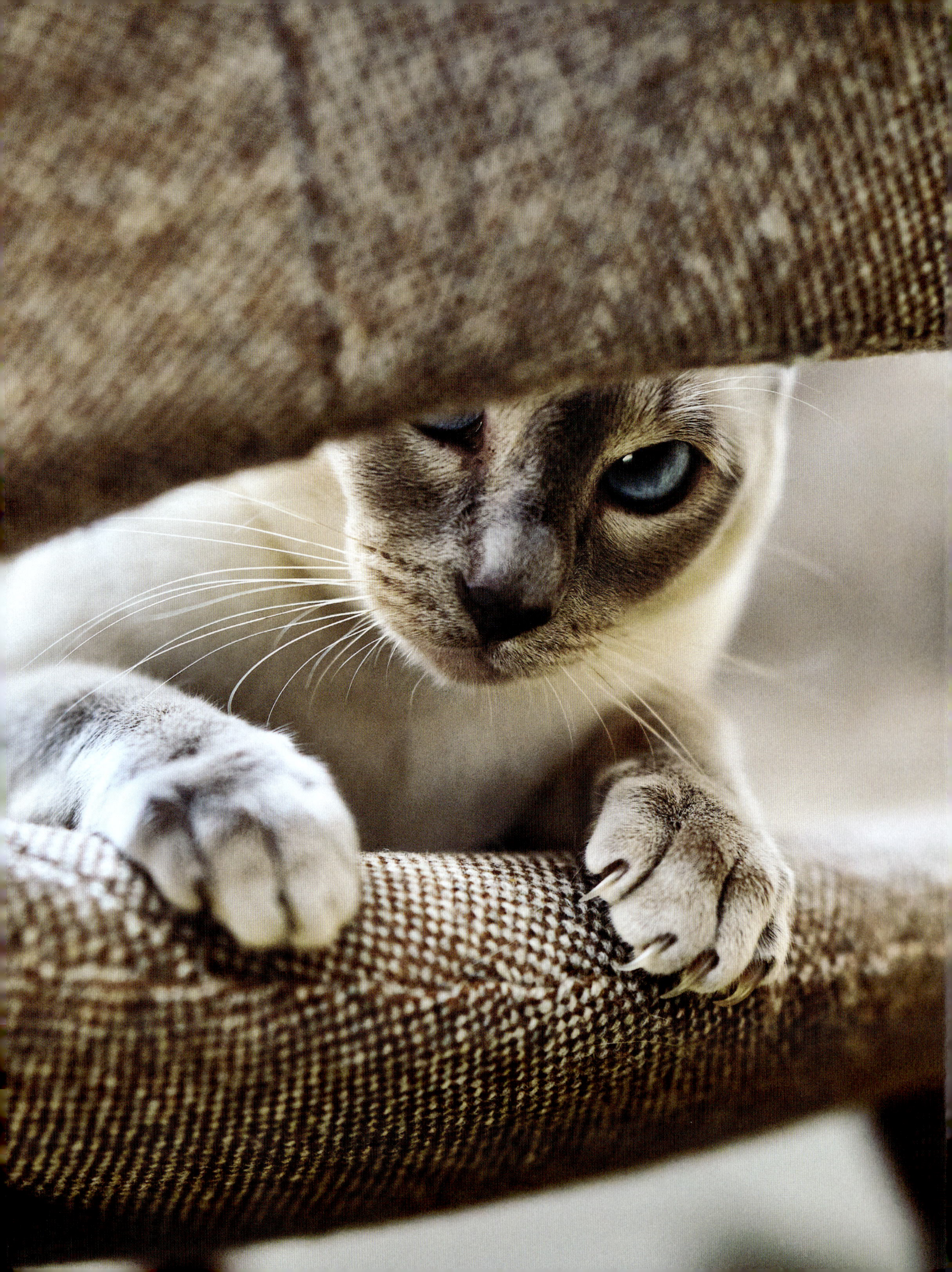

Q&A

DIVA OR DEVOTED FRIEND?

Both. If his owners feel sad or a bit down, Frank seems to know and will invariably do something sweet and endearing. But if cutlery or pots are being put away, his diva comes out. He hates the jangle of metal and, though usually non-vocal, will scream until the person either stops or lets him out into the courtyard. Neither does he take kindly to his owners being on the phone for too long. He will headbutt their arms to get their attention and try to knock the offending device from their hands – and he is surprisingly strong.

EXTROVERT OR INTROVERT?

Extrovert.

LAP CAT OR NOT?

Not.

OLD SOUL OR KITTEN AT HEART?

Kitten at heart.

EXPLORER OR HOMEBODY?

Explorer.

LAZY OR ACTIVE?

Active. Unless it is sleep time, Frank is always on the move.

DOGS – FRIEND OR FOE?

He has no experience of dogs really, but he's curious about them.

ARTIST CREDITS

ELLIE

6 / Sarah Shinners

10–11 / Bottom left image, from left: Jessalyn Brooks (colour print on side table), Sarah Shinners (artworks on wall); top right image, from left: Sarah Shinners, Van Tho

PUD

14 / From left: Mike Parr (work on paper), early 19th-century portrait (artist unknown)

17 / David Noonan

DIEGO

22, 27 / Maurice Golotta

25 / Top to bottom, left to right: Francesca Golotta, Bill Henson, Francesca Golotta, Magnus Gjoen, Magnus Gjoen

PANTHER

34 / Rosslynd Piggott

35 / Clockwise from bottom left: Emma Davies (yellow vessels), Kyoko Nagashima, Rose Nolan, Brook Andrew, Shigeru Moroizumi (centre)

HUMPHREY

40 / Right image, from left: Maria Svarbova, Leila Jeffreys

MALCOLM, AKA MOOGI

46 / From left: Adam Lee, Helen Johnson

48–9 / Top right image, from left: Tai Snaith and Simon Knott (ice cream lamp), Yuria Okamura (beside fire), Nathan Gray (top), Sarah CrowEST (bottom)

50 / From left: Katherine Hattam (in bookcase), Cherry Hood (on wall)

51 / Tai Snaith (ceramics)

KOBE AND KUMI

54, 56, 58 / Ted May

57 / Left image, from left: Kenya Peterson, Celine Wright; right image: Ted May

59 / Bottom right image: Patrick Francis

REUBEN

65 / Joseph Marr

66 / Holly Coulis

67 / James Turrell

WINSTON FLUFFYBUM

75 / Matthew Johnson

WOLFGANG, MINNIE AND ZAZA

78, 85 / Claudia Damichi

80 / Nick Pike

82 / Renita Stanley

HARVEY CRAFTI

98 / Robyn Beeche

CAROL AND LUTHER

106 / Frank Bauer

108 / Justin Trendall

109 / Telly Theodore

110 / Svetlana Bailey

112–13 / From left: Svetlana Bailey, Daniel Templeman

ESMERALDA

118 / From left: Marion Borgelt, John Firth-Smith

120–1 / From left: Emily Floyd (sculpture), Mike Parr

122–3 / Top left image, from left: John Firth-Smith, Justine Khamara (sculpture behind sofa), Charles Blackman; right image: Mike Parr

RAPHAEL AND FELLINI

136 / Christiane Spangsberg

MOLLY

144 / Michelle Ussher (in hallway)

148–9 / Valerie Sparks

150 / Jahnne Pasco-White

PRUDENCE GINGER, AKA PRU PRU

164, 165 / Kylie Thomas KT

GUS AND FREDDIE

168 / Kathryn Dolby

172–3 / Hannah Nowlan

175 / Mark Tweedie

PIPPI AND TED

178 / From left: Tony Martin, Meredith Littlejohn

181 / Meredith Littlejohn

MEW

196 / Anne Cleary and Denis Connolly

BILLIE AND TUCKER

207 / Hannan Munro

GUSTOV

213 / Caleb Shea (sculpture)

BUDDY

220 / Left image: Lance Ross

FRANK SCHNUPTON

232 / Ildiko Kovacs

234 / Tamara Dean

235 / Top right image, from left: Ildiko Kovacs, Deborah Williams

ACKNOWLEDGEMENTS

This book is dedicated to our baby boy, Santo, who arrived just two months before we began shooting for this project.

We're very grateful to the team at Thames & Hudson – especially Paulina de Laveaux and Elise Hassett for their support and guidance – and to Jessica Redman and Evi O. After the trials of 2020, where photo shoots and simply having face-to-face encounters had to be put on hold, this book was the perfect project to hit the ground running with once we were able to resume a new normal of travel and interaction.

Like all things in life, we build on top of the generosity and help of others. Finding stunning homes that had a cat (or two or three) in residence was not an easy task. These pages would be empty without Daniel Barbera, who opened his Rolodex and introduced us to the amazing interior designers and architects he works with. It was wonderful to see his incredible furniture in many of these homes – we joked that the book could serve as a catalogue of his work!

Thank you also to these wonderful contributors who put us in touch with the cats and their humans: Davina Shinewell, Pandarosa, Georgie Bean, Phoebe Whitman, Karen McCartney, Nicci Green, Georgie Cleary and Pino Demaio, Max Soans-Burne, Melany Wimpee, Dan Robertshaw, Dhiren Das and Adele Winteridge.

Thanks to Titus Cliff for retouching the cats' homes to look their very best.

Finally, to our dear Tati. She is our first love, and we couldn't have asked for a better feline companion.

First published in Australia in 2021
by Thames & Hudson Australia Pty Ltd
11 Central Boulevard, Portside Business Park
Port Melbourne, Victoria 3207
ABN: 72 004 751 964

First published in the United States of America in 2022
by Thames & Hudson Inc.
500 Fifth Avenue
New York, New York 10110

24 23 22 21 5 4 3 2 1

Thames & Hudson Australia wishes to acknowledge that Aboriginal and Torres Strait Islander people are the first storytellers of this nation and the traditional custodians of the land on which we live and work. We acknowledge their continuing culture and pay respect to Elders past, present and future.

ISBN 978-1-760-76184-4
ISBN 978-1-760-76228-5 (U.S. edition)

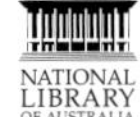

A catalogue record for this book is available from the National Library of Australia

Library of Congress Control Number 2021936900

Every effort has been made to trace accurate ownership of copyrighted text and visual materials used in this book. Errors or omissions will be corrected in subsequent editions, provided notification is sent to the publisher.

Front cover:
Ted May
Eagle, 2009
Oil on canvas, 167.5 x 198 cm

Design: Evi-O.Studio | Evi O & Nicole Ho
Editing: Jess Redman
Printed and bound in China by 1010 Printing International Limited

FSC® is dedicated to the promotion of responsible forest management worldwide. This book is made of material from FSC®-certified forests and other controlled sources.

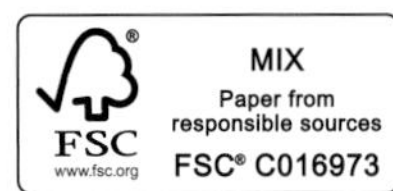

Be the first to know about our new releases,
exclusive content and author events by visiting

thamesandhudson.com.au
thamesandhudsonusa.com
thamesandhudson.com